EL CAMINO REAL
DE CALIFORNIA

QUERENCIAS SERIES
*Miguel A. Gandert and
Enrique R. Lamadrid, Series Editors*

Querencia is a popular term in the Spanish-speaking world that is used to express a deeply rooted love of place and people. This series promotes a transnational, humanistic, and creative vision of the US-Mexico borderlands based on all aspects of expressive culture, both material and intangible.

ALSO AVAILABLE IN THE QUERENCIAS SERIES:

Imagine a City That Remembers: The Albuquerque Rephotography Project by Anthony Anella and Mark C. Childs

The Latino Christ in Art, Literature, and Liberation Theology by Michael R. Candelaria

Sisters in Blue/Hermanas de azul: Sor María de Ágreda Comes to New Mexico/Sor María de Ágreda viene a Nuevo México by Enrique R. Lamadrid and Anna M. Nogar

Aztlán: Essays on the Chicano Homeland, Revised and Expanded Edition edited by Francisco A. Lomelí, Rudolfo Anaya, and Enrique R. Lamadrid

Río: A Photographic Journey down the Old Río Grande edited by Melissa Savage

Coyota in the Kitchen: A Memoir of New and Old Mexico by Anita Rodríguez

Chasing Dichos through Chimayó by Don J. Usner

Enduring Acequias: Wisdom of the Land, Knowledge of the Water by Juan Estevan Arellano

Hotel Mariachi: Urban Space and Cultural Heritage in Los Angeles by Catherine L. Kurland and Enrique R. Lamadrid

Sagrado: A Photopoetics Across the Chicano Homeland by Spencer R. Herrera and Levi Romero

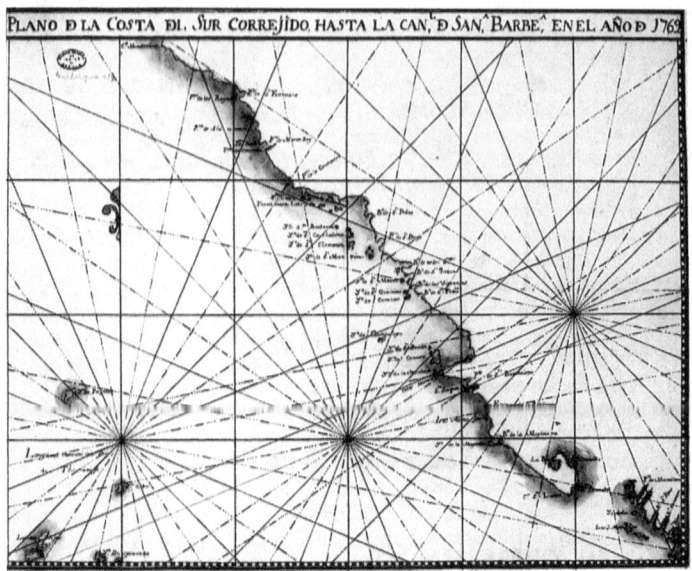

FRONTISPIECE   California coast from Cape Mendocino to Santa Bárbara, San Diego Bay and Baja California Peninsula, 1769. The map shows Cabo Mendocino, Punto de los Reyes, Punto del Año Nuevo, Punto de Pinos, Punto de Carmel, Isla de Catalina, Isla de San Clemente, Bahía de San Pedro, Puerto de San Diego, and other points south, including Isla de Guadalupe and Cabo San Lucas. San Francisco Bay had not yet been discovered. National Park Service–Spanish Colonial Research Center Map Collection, Center for Southwest Research, Zimmerman Library, University of New Mexico.

El Camino Real de California

❈ ❈ ❈ ❈ ❈

FROM

ANCIENT

PATHWAYS

TO

MODERN

BYWAYS

❈ ❈ ❈ ❈ ❈

Joseph P. Sánchez

University of New Mexico Press   Albuquerque

© 2019 by the University of New Mexico Press
All rights reserved. Published 2019
Printed in the United States of America

First paperback printing, 2022
Paperback ISBN 978-0-8263-6443-2

Names: Sánchez, Joseph P., author.

Title: El Camino Real de California: from ancient pathways to modern byways / Joseph Sánchez.

Description: Albuquerque: University of New Mexico Press, 2019. | Series: Querencias series | Includes bibliographical references and index.

Identifiers:
LCCN 2019020525 (print)
LCCN 2019981186 (e-book)
ISBN 9780826361028 (printed case : alk. paper)
ISBN 9780826361035 (e-book)

Subjects:
LCSH: Roads—California—History.
Portolá's Expedition, Calif., 1769–1770.
El Camino Real (Calif.)—History.
California—Discovery and exploration—Spanish.
California—History—To 1846.

Classification:
LCC F864. S225 2019 (print)
LCC F864 (e-book) | DDC 979.4—dc23

LC record available at https://lccn.loc.gov/2019020525

LC e-book record available at https://lccn.loc.gov/2019981186

COVER ILLUSTRATION tyndyra | istockphoto.com
COVER AND TEXT DESIGN Mindy Basinger Hill
COMPOSED IN Adobe Garamond Premier Pro

For all *Californians*

�; �; �; �; ✳

ESPECIALLY

Lee Layport

Larry West

Lee Ramírez

Guillermo Suero

Joseph M. Sánchez

Paul A. Sánchez

Donald C. Cutter
(1922–2014)

W. Michael Mathes
(1936–2012)

Donie Nelson

Richard Griswold del Castillo

Rita Sánchez

Iris H. Wilson Engstrand

Julianne Burton Carvajal

Jerry Jackman

CONTENTS

✽ ✽ ✽ ✽ ✽

xi PREFACE

1 CHAPTER ONE   "Doing the King's Business" on El Camino Real de California: An Introduction

12 CHAPTER TWO   Early Spanish Maritime Views of the California Coast

27 CHAPTER THREE   The Origins of the Camino Real: The Maritime and Land Expeditions of 1769 from Baja California Sur to Alta California

53 CHAPTER FOUR   Portolá's Expedition and the Establishment of Alta California, Part I: From San Diego Bay to the Santa Bárbara Channel and the Santa Inéz River, July to August 1769

74 CHAPTER FIVE   Portolá's Expedition and the Establishment of Alta California, Part II: The Search for Monterey Bay—From the Sierra de Santa Lucía to San Francisco Bay, September to November 1769

108 CHAPTER SIX   Portolá's Expedition and the Establishment of Alta California, Part III: The Expedition Returns to San Diego—November 1769 to January 1770

140 CHAPTER SEVEN   Missions and Ranchos in Spanish Colonial and Mexican Territorial Alta California

152 EPILOGUE

157 APPENDIX A   Identification of Presidios and Royal Presidio Ranchos

161 APPENDIX B   The Missions of Alta California

168 APPENDIX C The Missions of Baja California and the Early Camino Real de California

170 APPENDIX D "The King's Highway as Serra Knew It": Father Geiger and California's Camino Real de las Misiones

176 APPENDIX E Selected and Edited List of Land Grants in California, 1784–1848, Potentially Related to the Camino Real de California

195 APPENDIX F Examples of Maritime Lanes Used to Alta California

198 APPENDIX G The Camino Real de las Californias: The Land Route from Baja California to San Diego in 1769

201 APPENDIX H Summary of Fray Juan de Crespí's Diary Entry Locations by Date, and Notations by H. E. Bolton

221 NOTES

257 BIBLIOGRAPHY

265 INDEX

PREFACE

✺ ✺ ✺ ✺ ✺

> Along Highway 101 between Los Angeles
> and the Bay Area, cast metal bells spaced one or two miles
> apart mark what is supposedly a historic route through California:
> El Camino Real. Variously translated as "the royal road," or, more freely,
> "the king's highway," El Camino Real was indeed among the state's
> first long-distance, paved highways. But the road's claim to a more
> ancient distinction is less certain. The message implied by the presence
> of the mission bells—that motorists' tires trace the same path as the
> missionaries' sandals—is largely a myth imagined by regional
> boosters and early automotive tourists.
> NATHAN MASTERS | *Lost LA*[1]

THE ANNALS OF ALTA CALIFORNIA are filled with stories and legends about the *Camino Real* that runs from San Diego to San Francisco. The historiography of this legendary road abounds with references to place-names, fortifications, ports, missions, towns, and ranches that have lined the landscape of the west coast for hundreds of miles and hundreds of years. Much is known about the Camino Real in terms of its chronology, genealogical associations, historical personages, and history. But, save for certain locations, little is known about its exact route on the ground or its corridor formed by a braided trail that marked the way to forts, ports, missions, *ranchos*, and towns. Today's Camino Real is located by following directional signs along California streets, byways, highways, and freeways. The actual on-the-ground Camino Real is virtually unknown and largely forgotten except for signposted points along touristic pathways and sites that form a concrete or paved corridor between them.

Much-needed authentication through historical research and archaeological surveys would prove the significance and integrity of the Camino Real de California and ensure its preservation and place as a part of our national story, which is shared with Spain, Mexico, and regional Native American tribes. The historical and archaeological literature and the documentation from Spanish and Mexican archives utilized herein are, indeed, a starting point. It is the aim of this study to point the way toward renewing efforts to locate and effectively mark on the ground the braided corridor of the Camino Real de California, which has made California the great state that it is.

The idea for this study originated on May 6–7, 2012, when the Santa Barbara Trust for Historic Preservation sponsored a meeting to discuss the significance of the Camino Real de California. I was the keynote speaker for the event and my talk, "Caminos Reales in Comparative Perspective," focused on the Royal Road's past and present and stressed the need to authenticate and preserve it for future generations. The presentation also mentioned the need to recognize the importance of the maritime lanes emanating from Baja California Sur and the associated Manila Galleon routes. As the meeting progressed, it became apparent that the ultimate goal would be to propose World Heritage Site designation for the Camino Real de California from the United Nations Education, Scientific and Cultural Organization (UNESCO).

The meeting was attended by historians and archaeologists who pondered on the integrity of the actual trail and its corridor. W. Michael Mathes (1936–2012), an expert on the history of Baja California, strongly advocated that the Mexican portion of the trail from La Paz to a point near Tijuana in Baja California, south of San Diego, should also be considered for study along with that of Alta California and included in the proposal as a binational effort. All agreed to work toward eventually submitting such a proposal to UNESCO,[2] but they also recognized the need for authentication of the Camino Real de California, for while it is, indeed, historically significant, and while its trajectory is well-known, its exact pathway has been buried by time.

Why is it important to authenticate the Camino Real de California? By analogy, why do we revere the Seven Wonders of the World? They are not only a part of the ancient world that, through historical processes,[3] made our world cultures what they are: they are a part of the march of humankind. Authenticity is about undisputed credibility and integrity; it is about the quality of originality and historical significance. Authenticity is about the "first" step taken by man that changed the course of humankind. Therefore, authentication of the Camino Real de California is about commemorating California's rich prehistoric and historic past as well as its present by locating the actual route on the ground of the trail and its corridor and proving, once and for all, its integrity before the world.

Authentication of the Camino Real de California is about unraveling a part of the historical process that led to the development of modern California. Its pathways marked each historical event in the creation of the Spanish *Provin-*

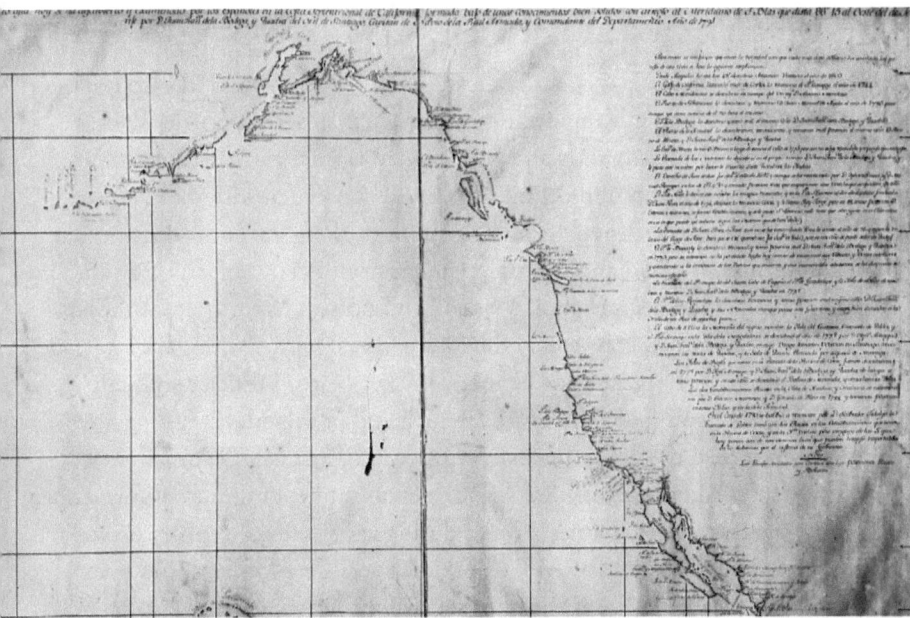

MAP 1   California-Alaska coastline, 1791. Ports, presidios, missions, ranchos, towns, and cities formed a braided corridor tied to maritime lanes along the California coast to Alaska. National Park Service–Spanish Colonial Research Center Map Collection, Center for Southwest Research, Zimmerman Library, University of New Mexico.

cia de California and its significance in shaping the future history of a people and its nation. Each step of the Camino Real de California is marked, but often invisible to the human eye, with hidden and scattered monuments of the past surrounded by modern developments. Ports, presidios, missions, ranchos, towns, and cities formed a braided corridor that tied to maritime lanes that supported the Camino Real de California by serving to transport people and things. (See Appendices.)

Significantly, authentication is also about the Native American presence and early native settlement and land usage patterns, as seen in early Spanish Colonial and Mexican Territorial documents as well as archaeological remains and the cultural underpinnings of Native American history, lore, traditions, and practices. Ancient Native American pathways aligned with and shaped the corridor of the Camino Real de California. In many ways, the activities of various tribes along the camino helped to prepare the way for California's future; the state, in turn, has played a role in world economies and affairs.

While this study, in a broader sense, aims to initiate and renew interest in new research and analyses focused on authenticating the actual on-the-ground

Camino Real de California, primarily north of the United States–Mexico border on the Pacific coast, it is important to reiterate that both countries share a common heritage and history. US and Mexican citizens are not often cognizant that the two land segments and the maritime lanes associated with the Camino Real de California run sequentially north and south along the entire coastlines of the Californias. By land and sea, the segment from Baja California Sur, inclusive of Loreto and La Paz as well as Cabo San Lucas, at its furthest southern point, to Baja California, connects at the international border with the US side stretching from San Diego to San Francisco. These early Mexican segments, established during and following 1769, are included in this study.

The Camino Real de California exists not only in Spanish Colonial documents, particularly in those that deal with the establishment of Alta California, but also in the many place-names created during the sixteenth-century explorations and Manila Galleon voyages, whose mariners were forever looking for *señas* (topographical signs) and the later settlements of the Spanish Colonial and Mexican Territorial periods. Today's Camino Real de California in both the United States and Mexico comprises a braided corridor that combines modern freeways, highways, byways, and city streets with the sixteenth-century routes (inclusive of maritime lanes) to Spanish colonial ports, presidios, towns, missions, and ranchos. Once Spain's colonies declared independence after 1821, all *caminos reales* throughout the empire were no longer "royal." The braided corridor of trails, nonetheless, continued to bear the name and survives into the modern day.

The State of California legislation establishing the Camino Real de California, which follows Assembly Bill 1707 of October 12, 2001, declares that

> State highway routes embracing portions of I-280, Route 82, Route 238, US 101, I-5, Route 72, Route 12, Route 37, Route 121, Route 87, Route 162, Route 185, Route 92, and Route 123 and connecting city streets and county roads thereto, and extending in a continuous route from Sonoma southerly to the international border and near the route historically known as El Camino Real shall be known and designated as "El Camino Real."

The pre-AB 1707 definition (established by Assembly Bill 1769, Chapter 1569, in 1959) was:

> State highway routes embracing portions of I-280, Route 82, US 101, I-5, and Route 72, and connecting city streets and county roads thereto,

and extending in a continuous route from San Francisco southerly to the international border and near the route historically known as El Camino Real are known and designated as "El Camino Real." Note that there are other routes that are part of El Camino Real, most significantly San Diego County Route s11.[4]

Although the legislation defines a corridor in which the route of the historic road may lie, it does not, however, preserve the historical integrity of the route on the ground. Authentication of the braided trail, as suggested herein, is required and can be accomplished through an interdisciplinary effort, especially with the combination of historical research and archaeological inquiry into past reports as well as surveys and test digs.

While some historical integrity of the actual trajectories is still discernible, there is a need to confirm, authenticate, and map the locations of the historic Camino Real de California and its corridor. As demonstrated in this study, authenticating the route that spanned geographically from points in Baja California Sur to San Francisco Bay will require further detailed examination and analysis of the historical documentation of early land explorations, particularly those of 1769 and 1770, and the maritime routes used by the Manila Galleons along the California coast, as well as the mission trails and the vias to presidios, ports, and ranchos.

Past, present, and future archaeological literature, surveys, and studies are important sources in the quest to reinforce the historical significance, authenticity, and integrity of the route. Ideally this would include historical and archaeological literature as well as archival sources from Spain, Mexico and depositories in the United States. This study aims to initiate and spark renewed interest in the preservation of one of California's bequeathed treasures.

It is important to note, that, especially in the case of *California's* Camino Real, while the land route has been the main topic of research to date, the braided corridor of the Camino Real de California also includes the maritime lanes. Indeed, much of the information to locate ports, places, and topographical features by land used particularly by Gov. Gaspar de Portolá, Lt. Pedro Fages, Captain Fernando Rivera y Moncada, and Fray Juan Crespí was based on information presented in the logs and navigational charts developed by early maritime explorers such as Juan Rodríguez Cabrillo and Sebastián Vizcaíno as well as other Manila Galleon mariners during a two-hundred-year period. The Laws of the Indies required the official diarists of Spanish expeditions to report on all discoveries made during their march or voyages. According to law and custom, diarists were required to read their entries daily to the commander of the expedition for agreement on details or resolution of discrepancies.[5] Along with locations and toponyms, the law required diarists and commanders to report on all people, settlements, provinces, rivers, ports, wooded areas, mountains, and resources seen on the expedition's route.

Between 1542 and 1603, in particular, place-names such as Cabo Mendocino, Punta de los Reyes, Punta de los Pinos, Punta de Concepción, Punta or Farallón de los Lobos, El Morro, Bahía de Monterey, Río del Carmelo, Sierra de Santa Lucía, Santa Catalina, and San Diego identified familiar topographical markers known to Manila Galleon mariners. Later, they served as markers for eighteenth-century land expeditions. Thus, the maritime lanes that transported people and things after 1769, based on knowledge of sea lanes and ports that connected presidios, ranches, towns, and missions by way of colonial roads, are a part of the braided corridor associated with the Camino Real de California.

The short-haul roads that ran from the ports to the main trunk trail have been overlooked in much of the previous research. These were, indeed, part of the concept of "*real*" that attaches to the Royal Road of California, for the transport of people and things was done in performance of the "king's business." Thus, authentication of the historical Camino Real de California and its corridor is paramount in preserving the rich heritage that resulted from the constant usage of the original route, which shaped the transportation infrastructure and place-names of present-day California.

Historically, the development of California owes much to the Camino Real de California, which shaped its settlement patterns, became a major part of its patrimony, and created the corridors through which the modern state emerged. As stated above, given ongoing development and urban expansion, it is important to identify the route and establish its authenticity so that it can be properly preserved and protected as part of our state, national, and world patrimony. For many years, interested groups in both Californias have discussed World Heritage Site designation by UNESCO for the Camino Real de California, or more appropriately, *Camino Real de las Californias* (inclusive of routes emanating from Baja California Sur and Baja California). Supporters include historians, archaeologists, concerned citizens, and preservation organizations such as the Santa Barbara Trust for Historic Preservation, Friends of El Camino Real de California, the California Missions Foundation, and groups and associations in Baja California and Baja California de Sur such as the Corredor Histórico CAREM, A. C. and the Instituto Nacional de Antropología e Historia (INAH).

Such a proposal has always been within the realm of a possibility, as is evident in the success enjoyed by other historic places in North America, including the Camino Real de Tierra Adentro in Mexico, which ran north from Mexico City through the interior to Santa Fe, New Mexico. Within the United States, a 404-mile stretch was designated a National Historic Trail by the US Congress in 2000. Later, in 2010, twelve hundred miles of the Mexican portion was designated a World Monument Site by UNESCO. Together, the two segments of the Camino Real de Tierra Adentro commemorate the common history of the United States, Spain, and Mexico, as well as that of local and regional tribes. Indeed, it is a common history that is a part of the world patrimony. The Camino Real de los Tejas National Historic Trail, which runs from Saltillo, Mexico to San Antonio, Texas serves as a similar reminder. It was designated a National Historic Trail by the US Congress in 2007. In 2015, UNESCO designated the San Antonio Missions in Texas as a World Heritage Site. Given the historical integrity of towns, ranches, presidios, and missions, California's Camino Real is worthy of a like designation. But first, the route's historical integrity must be defined and located.

The authentication of the Camino Real de California is aided by the documentation that historically recorded the development of towns, ports, presidios, missions, and ranchos along the braided corridor that evolved in the accomplishment of the "king's business." This work would not be possible without the assistance of archivists in record depositories in Spain, Mexico, and the United States. Special thanks to the staffs of the archives of Spain and Mexico, particularly the Museo Naval, Madrid; the Archivo Histórico Nacional, Madrid; the Biblioteca Nacional, Madrid; the Servicio Geográfico del Ejército, Madrid; the Archivo General de Indias, Seville; and the Archivo General de la Nación, Mexico City. A note of equal appreciation is extended to the staff at the Bancroft Library, University of California, Berkeley. A very special debt of gratitude for navigating this study toward its publication is due to Dr. Enrique Lamadrid, Distinguished Professor Emeritus, University of New Mexico, and W. Clark Whitehorn, Executive Editor, University of New Mexico Press. Similarly, special acknowledgment is owed to The UNM Center for Regional Studies, directed by Dr. A. Gabriel Meléndez, Distinguished UNM Professor, for funding the indexing portion of this important study. I also thank Katherine Harper, copy editor par excellence.

CHAPTER ONE

❈ ❈ ❈ ❈ ❈

"Doing the King's Business" on el Camino Real de California

AN INTRODUCTION

❈ ❈ ❈ ❈ ❈

> His Excellency [the viceroy] wanted the whole population forthwith to share the happiness which the information gave him, and therefore he ordered a general ringing of the bells of the cathedral and all the other churches, in order that everybody might realize the importance of the Port of Monterey to the Crown of our monarch, and also to give thanks for the happy success of the expedition; for by this means the domination of our king has been extended over more than three hundred leagues of land.
> FRAY JUAN CRESPÍ | 1770

THE DEFINITION of a *camino real* in accordance with Spanish Colonial law and practice is paramount in understanding the significance of the Camino Real de California and its origins. To be sure, the cultural heritage of the Camino Real is more than a mere line drawn on a map or a trajectory marked with signposts. The legacy of Spanish law that sprang from ancient traditions and practices lies at the base of the concept of *caminos reales* in Spain and the Spanish empire. From the rich cultural heritage that shaped western civilization sprang a body of laws that formed the legal practice and jurisprudence of Spanish America. Indeed, the entire enterprise of establishing California was based on concepts of sovereignty and legal precedents that originated within historical processes dating to Greco-Roman times. Thus, the history of the

Spanish colonial establishment of California is that of a people who touched the future by developing a given area, within the scope of the Laws of the Indies,[1] along with an infrastructure comprised of roads, towns, forts, ports, missions, ranches, and farms and their appurtenances. Beyond that, it is about a people who introduced governance into the region based on western civilization's traditions and practices, a new language, religion, folklore, institutions, and a myriad of cultural innovations inclusive of the technological advances of the times. Importantly, they introduced the power of the written word. The legal sources they followed were vested in established compilations of laws that pertained to establishment and development of places, trade, and immigration along the Camino Real de California.

Spanish laws and practices related to governance included the establishment of *cabildos*, or town councils, each presided over by an *alcalde mayor*. In provincial capitals along royal roads, the governor presided and the alcaldes mayores of the local towns reported to him. As in the English tradition that touts the concept of the town hall as the basic unit of democracy, the cabildos comprised elected and appointed officials. Predating by over a century the House of Burgesses established in Virginia (1619) and the New England town meeting halls (1620), cabildos had been established in many places, beginning at Santo Domingo (Dominican Republic, 1496), the oldest European town in the Americas. Other cabildos were created at Caparra (Puerto Rico, 1508), Mexico City (1525), San Agustín, Florida (1565), San Juan de los Caballeros (1598), San Gabriel (1599), and Santa Fe (1610), the latter three along New Mexico's Camino Real de Tierra Adentro.[2] Similar to the aforementioned towns in Spanish North America, the provincial capitals and cabildos in California, Arizona, and Texas were established along their respective caminos reales in the eighteenth century.

Spanish laws also pertained to roads that led to these residential areas. To be sure, all common or public colonial roads in the Spanish domain were protected, but the special distinction given to large trunk trails used for migration, trade, military uses, etc., that connected Spanish ports, presidios, villas, and capitals to each other qualified the specific designation of "camino real." The longest of these in North America is the Camino Real de Tierra Adentro (Royal Road of the Interior) from Mexico City to Santa Fe in New Mexico. That road was nearly 1,600 miles long. On the eastern frontier of Texas and Coahuila, the Camino Real de Tierra Afuera (Royal Road of the Exterior), which branched off the Camino Real de Tierra Adentro, ran eastward from Zacatecas to Cuencamé to Saltillo. From Zacatecas the trail swung eastward, then northeast for nearly one thousand miles over segmented trails such as the Camino del Río Grande, Camino de San Antonio, and finally, beyond the Río Guadalupe, the Camino de los Tejas[3] that terminated at Los Adaes, the first Texas capital, located near today's Robeline and Nachitoches in western Louisiana. Far to the west, a lone camino real dominated the Pacific coast. That road, combined with land and maritime routes, formed the Camino Real de California, which originated at La Paz on the east coast of Baja California Sur. The land route ran north from La Paz to Loreto and from there to Velicatá, in the interior of Baja California, and then, once on the Pacific coastline, due north to connect with the trail in Alta California that ran from San Diego to San Francisco. The land route from La Paz and Loreto to San Francisco ran nearly 1,400 miles.

The antiquity and dynamics of Spanish legal tradition and practice are found in the *Fuero Juzgo, Fuero Real,* and *Siete Partidas* compiled in medieval Spain. The laws of the Fuero Juzgo and others passed into the modern age through the *Nueva Recopilación,* the *Recopilación de Leyes de los Reynos de Indias*[4] and the *Novísima Recopilación de 1805.* It is clear from these laws that privileges were extended primarily to individual Spaniards or associations of Spaniards, primarily in the Peninsular and Creole social classes. Colonial minorities performing the business of the king benefited from certain privileges, especially when the latter were prescribed in contractual form and pertinent documentation attested to the former's merit. At the root of the term "camino real" was the all-important word *real,* which had a particular meaning depending on its connoted use.

A long history of juridical definitions and practices dating to the Roman Empire, along with Spanish legislation cited in the *Recopilación de las Leyes de Indias,* defined the variable purposes of a camino real as intended by Spain in the eighteenth century. As mentioned above, it is important to note that the maritime lanes along the California coast are a part of the Camino Real system, as are the ports and the roads from them that connected to the land route of the Camino Real itself.

What is a camino real? And how does the term apply to the Camino Real de California, particularly in Alta California where the road formed a braided historic corridor that evolved to transport people and things to Spanish forts, maritime ports, missions, ranches, and other places along the route? The term continued in use long after Mexican independence from Spain in 1821, when the road was no longer "royal," extending into the US territorial and statehood period. Pride in history and heritage have kept it alive wherever vestiges of a camino real survive. In modern times, the Camino Real de Tierra Adentro

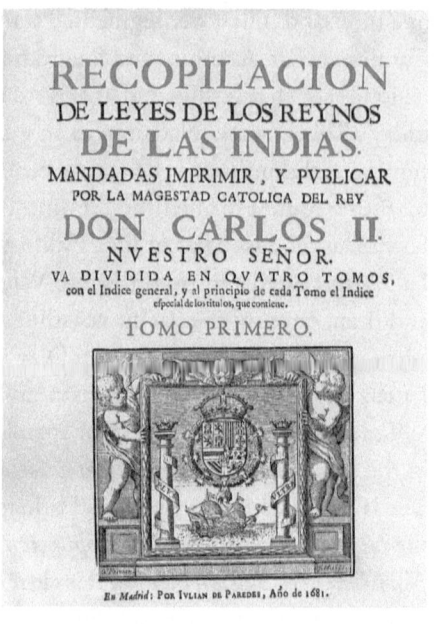

FIGURE 1 *Recopilación de Leyes de los Reynos de las Indias*, 1681. Cover.

National Historic Trail and the Camino Real de los Tejas National Historic Trail have been designated National Historic Trails, tying Spanish trade and immigration trails to our national story. California, through its state powers to preserve and protect its patronage, has done the same for the historic Camino Real de California as it applies to Alta California. Indeed, there is a strong linkage between the Camino Real de California and the Camino Real de las Misiones in Baja California, which ran its course from La Paz and Loreto to a point near Mexico's northern boundary.

Our national story is filled with histories of trails and corridors that explain European expansion in North America. The development of roads is, of necessity, a significant function of the historical process of nation-states. The historic roads of New Spain, present-day Mexico, are prehistoric in character and purpose. The development of Native American trails prior to European intrusions influenced the location of many colonial roads that were established between 1521 and 1821. Aside from Spanish military purposes, the colonial economic development of New Spain led to the continual development of roads throughout the period of the Viceroyalty of New Spain, 1535–1821.

During the colonial period, internal and external economic developments were tied intricately to indigenous routes that similarly had been used for trade and transportation of people and things as well as for war. Although pre-Columbian roads were not well developed beyond the central highlands, routes and corridors from the Central Valley of Mexico to places lying beyond the edges of the Aztec domain were well-defined for travel. Unlike the roads created by Europeans for wagons and beasts of burden, indigenous trails were relatively primitive and used for foot traffic.

By contrast, Spanish colonial roads combined primitive trails with ones newly constructed, some with bridges, to areas with economic potential. It is important to note that such roads were never static—that is, in one place—over time. As forts, towns, missions, or ranches were established, routes were often redirected to suit those needs. A widened corridor shifted over time to allow the original Native American footpaths to accommodate use by Spanish horses, mule trains, and oxen-pulled *carretas* and then modern automobiles and railroads. The corridors of caminos reales could vary by several miles from their original footpath to a route that would accommodate modern travel. More often than not, the route changed course to reach a new destination along the established trajectory. Still, the question is, what *is* a camino real?

The answer lies with the concept of sovereignty. As Spanish kingship evolved, especially under Ferdinand and Isabella, sovereignty—that is, the authorized power to rule—became a more legalistic and accepted practice. By 1492, the king had strengthened his control over jurisdictions, the privileges granted the nobility, clergy, and military orders in Castile and Aragon, and territorial acquisitions in the New World, Africa, and India. The Spanish word *real* not only grew in acceptance during the birth of the modern state, but its legality was reinforced by historical precedents dating to Greco-Roman traditions. The nobility, the church, and the towns themselves drew their authority from privileged positions acknowledged and approved by the crown. They, too, were unwilling to relinquish rights granted to them by the king. Thus, the crown, through tradition and practice, clearly defined its spheres of influence within the state.[5]

The king, as sovereign, wielded strong political power over the land, inclusive of all top- and subsoil property rights within his domain. Through contracts executed by the sovereign, his vassals received concessions for varied purposes. For example, he contracted out the right to explore under the name of Spain and the king. Christopher Columbus explored under contract, as did every legal, authorized expedition in the Spanish Empire.[6] Political titles, town charters, and land tenure considerations such as land grants were also done under contract. Santa Fe in New Mexico, San Antonio in Texas, Tucson in Arizona, and San Diego, Los Angeles, Santa Barbara, Monterey, and San Francisco in California were founded under royal instructions or orders or had contracts or charters issued to their founders in the name of the sovereign.

In Spain, the laws regarding town founding and the roads leading to them evolved slowly and were eventually applied throughout the Spanish empire. To that end, the sovereign sanctioned roads, caminos reales, and local roads. Most commonly, caminos reales in the Americas were created by authorized and traditional local usage that benefited the sovereign's purpose of empire. On the other hand, the sovereign placed great value in the military, political, and economic importance of caminos reales for the transportation of people and things. In later centuries, the construction and opening of roads, as in the case of the Camino Real de California, were often a military function as opposed to a political endeavor. Between law, tradition, and practice, many caminos reales evolved to do the king's business.

Spanish laws, tradition, and practice covered nearly every facet of life within the domain of the Spanish sovereign. Trade and trade routes, whether maritime or terrestrial, were subject to Spanish law. Routes to lands within Spanish control were subject to the Laws of the Indies. Even common or public roads were, in theory, protected roads. The legal sources regarding caminos reales are found in the many compilations or codes that follow Spanish tradition. From antiquity dating to the Roman occupation of Spain, an amalgamation of laws combined with Visigothic practices evolved that contributed to the customary practices and jurisprudence of Spanish law in Spain and the Spanish Empire.[7]

Between tradition, practice, and concordance with the law, the sovereign authoritatively and righteously approved the concessions of rights to the land and its resources. It is clear, for example, that the use of certain roads, mines, and roads by associations of cart drivers and by the Mesta,[8] a livestock association, for herding sheep, constituted a *regalía*, or privileges conceded by the king. The word regalía comes from the Latin *regalis* and equates to the Spanish *real*, royal prerogatives. The word is strongly related to the rights and powers of kings. Hence, the designation *real* was an exemption of a kind, one that could be approved only by the sovereign or his representative in the Americas, the viceroy. In many ways, the *real* was contractual. The term corresponds solely to the powers of a sovereign of a country and includes his or her right to tax, charge royal duties, grant land, establish governance of towns, and many other exclusive powers. Road repairs, especially near large towns or cities, were always an issue. The money for such repairs came from tolls, fees for areas occupied by grazing herds (*contribuciones de pisage*), and assessments made to towns along the routes; lack of funds often meant the repairs were not made. In Mexico, the *Tribunal del Consulado*, a royally constituted body, attended to the upkeep of royal roads.[9] For example, in 1798, Antonio de Basocs was the prior in charge of the tribunal. That year he oversaw the construction and repair of bridges on the Camino Real de Veracruz and the Camino Real de Tierra Adentro.

Roads held a preeminent position among resources in the realm because they were the arteries of the economy. Trade, mining, and *la transhumancia*, or movement of livestock along certain pathways, some of which crossed through the middle of towns, formed an important element of defining certain roads as caminos reales. Herders were often exempt from tolls, denial of pasturage, water, or campsites, or other local restrictions placed by townships because they were given right-of-way privileges by the king. Given that situation, all common or public roads were under the protection of the crown. Some roads, especially those that offered advantages to the sovereign, were favored through the regalías granted to the users. Still, towns benefited from the establishment of toll roads, which augmented the king's coffers and offered incentives to both the towns and the royal treasury.

Regalías could be granted for one or two lifetimes, or in perpetuity. Charters to towns were also given for indefinite periods of time. All privileges could be revoked or modified by the crown. Usually, economic benefits to Spain were the main consideration for the granting of privileges. Ever vigilant, the crown encouraged the search for mineral wealth by granting individuals certain privileges to do so under contract. Thus, throughout the realm, mines and the roads leading to them were referred to as reales, granted to mine operators for doing the king's business.

When applied to a camino real, the word *real* merely implied its status, defined by certain privileges as stated in a legal document. Broadly speaking, the designation was granted to an individual or a group or was attached to a place along the route by dint of the privileges or status conceded to it or its owners or proprietors by the sovereign. Often, that status was extended over time because of continued usage; in some cases, the privileges conceded to the original users remained in force through tradition and practice. For example, the Camino Real de Tierra Adentro began as a road to silver mines at Queretaro outside of Mexico City in the 1540s. As new veins were discovered along the route and beyond, the road became known as the *Camino de la Plata* (the Silver Road). By the end of the sixteenth century, the mining districts had expanded as far north as Santa Bárbara in present-day Chihuahua. The original regalías of the 1540s had given it its status, without renewal of the documentation, such that by 1598 the Camino Real de Tierra Adentro had reached as far north as San Juan de los Caballeros, the first capital of New Mexico.

When, in 1497, Queen Isabella established the *Cabaña Real de Carreteros*, the Royal Association of Cart Drivers, she reinforced and enlarged the concept of royal roads within Spain, setting the precedent for the Americas. The privileges granted the cart drivers included a right-of-way with free pasturage and access to pasture lands during the winter, off-the-road overnight camping with whatever needs attached to it, and use of the road without a toll or fee to a town it came near. The word *real* attached to the user, no matter what road the Royal Association of Cart Drivers used; as long as they were on it, it was temporarily a "royal road."

Such a precedent applied to other associations in the Americas. By the mid-seventeenth century, groups formed convoys for protection against attacks by marauders. Eventually, special militia forces were organized to further protect the convoys against them. The protective efforts were costly but necessary. Because towns still sought to curtail their privileges, the Cabaña Real, between 1734 and 1807, succeeded in codifying the applicable laws in Spanish law books, inclusive of the *Novísima Recopilación* (1804–1807). Thus, tradition gave way to practice, and practice became law.

Spain applied its laws to its new possessions throughout the colonial period. In 1537, the crown authorized the viceroy of New Spain to establish the Mesta, an association of drovers traditionally associated with the *transhumancia* in Spain. Regarding the term regalía, the crown reiterated that this *real* could be a one-time use or granted for a limited or indefinite period. The word could be used for a villa, a town, a road, a mine, an office, an army, a right-of-way, a campsite, or practically anything associated with the king's business. More often than not, a regalía was granted for a short period to permit the advancement of an undertaking that benefited the crown. To that end, just as laws pertaining to the Cabaña Real had been extended to Spanish America, others authorized that the Mesta be established throughout the empire. In theory, the privileges granted the Mesta, stemming from medieval traditions and the authority of the Cabaña Real, applied to all classes of drovers, and therefore to all Spanish users of roads or routes.

Travelers on caminos reales were protected not only from robbers or raiders on the trail (generally after the fact), but also from unscrupulous townspeople who sought to block their passage. Still, towns had their own privileges, and as roads passed through them, town officials enforced them over all comers by charging fees or tolls. Theoretically the "bearer" of a *real* was protected from such abuses. If nothing else, he had the right to redress the infringement against him. In 1734, for example, rancher José de Acevedo herded cattle from Tepic in Nayarit to Mexico City. He complained that he had suffered abuses at the hands of alcaldes mayores of certain towns who had charged him exorbitantly for use of their roads. The viceroy called for an investigation against the offending officials.[10]

In the seventeenth century, military expeditions throughout the northern frontier utilized the word "*real*" to designate their role in carrying out the king's business. To them, the usage was one of convention: that is, the king did not have to state the privileges; they were understood to be the approval of a military undertaking. The expeditions of Alonso de León in Texas in 1690 and Diego de Vargas in New Mexico in 1692 used the word in reference to the armies they led, the campsites they used, and the line of march they followed. The same was true of the California expedition led by Governor Gaspar de Portolá in 1769. In that case, the braided route, as it evolved, was identified by place-names and the establishment of presidios, missions, towns, and ranches along the much-used corridor. Continued use and occupation over time reinforced the status of "camino real" that had resulted from the traditional de jure Spanish origins.

In instances of exploration, the *real* was temporary while the army searched for any advantages for the crown that could be found in the area explored. Once the expedition had completed its mission and returned to its point of origin, the word was no longer applicable. Vargas in New Mexico did follow the Camino Real de Tierra Adentro, an established "royal" road. Yet, when he veered off of it, his pathway became "*real*," however temporary it turned out to be. The origin of California's Camino Real was not an exception to the general rule. There the use of "*real*" applied to a marching army performing the king's work of establishing an infrastructure in an occupied area claimed by the Spanish crown. Like the Camino Real de Tierra Adentro, which extended into New Mexico, the same basic route in California was used time and again following Portolá's expedition of 1769. In the following decades, the Spanish claim to California was reinforced by occupation of places along the established route. The road was also used as a trade and immigration route, as well as for a number of military purposes. All was done to carry out the king's business.

Missionary efforts fell into a larger grouping of privileges under the *Real Patronato*. The granting of privileges for mission programs was usually tied to the economy, for the crown felt that if an area could be pacified without military force, then it could be opened to investors—with privileges. Mission fields were tied to a larger picture in which Pope Alexander VI in the bull *Inter Caeterea*, issued on May 4, 1493, assigned the Spanish crown dominion over the Indies and exclusive authority to convert the natives. A second bull, *Eximiae Devotionis* (Nov. 16, 1501), granted Spanish kings control of the missions in the Americas. Within a decade, Pope Julius II, in the bull *Universalis Ecclesiae Regimini* (July 28, 1508), conceded the Spanish crown universal patronage within its territorial control. The king exercised the patronage of the Indies (*Real Patronato de Indias*) through the Council of the Indies and later, jointly, with the *Cámara de Indias*. Such concessions or empowerments did not mean that the pope, as the vicar of Christ on Earth, was not in charge of the church around the world, for the king of Spain was required to report to the papacy on all religious matters. The pope acknowledged that within the Spanish realm, no monastery, no church or chapel, oratory, or mission could be erected without the express approval of the king. The king was the sovereign of Spanish patrimony throughout the empire. In that regard, friars were obligated to spread and teach (*Sacra Congregatio de Propaganda Fide*) the faith, but on a more practical imperial level, he recognized that missionaries could serve to pacify an area, making it easier for investors to move into mining frontiers without the use of invading armies. In that way, the missionaries, dedicated to God's works on earth, were constantly, by dint of their presence, at work performing the king's business.

Missions, like towns, mines, and ranches, shared in the patrimony created by cooperative efforts throughout the empire. The *real* tied law, tradition, and practice to the participatory efforts of Spanish citizens. Land grants, from which ranchos and towns were created, were incentives for the widely dispersed Spanish populations in the Americas. Indeed, the same roads that tied ports, towns, and missions together connected the land-grant communities to the greater imperial effort.

Commonly, caminos reales in the Americas were created by authorized and traditional local usage that benefited the sovereign's purpose of empire. In some rare cases, roads were actually opened with ribbon-cutting ceremonies. In 1793, for instance, a new road between Yucatan and the Villa de Nuestra Señora de los Dolores in Guatemala was approved by the Tribunal del Consulado. Once the route was formalized with all the proper *cédulas*, it was opened to settlers along the seventy-four-league stretch of road. Many of the people in the area turned out for a celebration.[11] In general, while some roads in frontier areas were constructed and maintained by local settlers, in more developed and economically important cosmopolitan places, caminos reales such as those passing through Mexico City, Veracruz, and Guadalajara, particularly in the eighteenth century, were maintained by the Royal Corps of Engineers.

Thus, the *real* served as an initial legal step in Spanish exploration and settlement of the Americas. In the case of the military personnel and missionaries who established California in 1769, their purposes were sanctioned by Viceroy Marqués de Croix of Mexico, the king's representative. The instructions given to Governor Gaspar de Portolá and the permission granted to Fray Junípero Serra to initiate the establishment of settlements and missions in California clearly outlined the king's business.

CHAPTER TWO

❋ ❋ ❋ ❋ ❋

Early Spanish Maritime Views of the California Coast

❋ ❋ ❋ ❋ ❋

It was at the prayer hour when we came within a league of land, which appeared to be mountainous, heavily forested with many trees that could be identified. Among them were many pine trees growing very thickly near the sea and inland, which were made out as we went coasting along near the shore to see better where there might possibly be found opportunity and safe port in which to enter the ship. . . . Coasting along about half league from land a shoal was discovered which could be about a maritime league long, and that which was Cape Mendocino was seen.
SEBASTIÁN RODRÍGUEZ CERMEÑO | 1595

Travel from the Philippines became formalized by way of Cape Mendocino. A port to shelter the galleons in that area was required. One of the first questions Felipe III had was precisely on this problem; and, on September 27, 1599, he urgently ordered the viceroy, Conde de Monterey, to find other such places along the western coast of California.
IGNÁCIO RUBIO MAÑÉ | 1955

DESCRIPTIONS OF THE CALIFORNIA COAST from the sixteenth century to the end of the eighteenth are best examined from the accounts written by the early Spanish mariners and explorers who first ran the entire length from San Diego to San Francisco Bay. From their maritime and land expeditions emerges the origins and pioneering history of the Camino Real de California. Eyewitness accounts provide early descriptions of the land and its people. Place-names as well as cartographical and topographical features of the California coast documented in archaic Spanish colonial script can still be identified.

By the time that Spain implemented a plan to settle Alta California in 1769, the crown's interest in the area was nearly 230 years old. Indeed, the Spaniards who landed at San Diego in 1769 to establish coastal defenses against possible foreign intrusion and missions for the conversions of natives had specific information and maps of the coast. Geographic knowledge had been passed down to them by Manila Galleon mariners who had, since 1565, used California as a way station after zigzagging northeastward for nearly eight thousand miles from the Philippines across the immense Pacific Ocean. Once they made landfall, somewhere near or at Cape Mendocino, they sailed south, hugging the coast for another two thousand miles, to the port at Acapulco on the western coast of Mexico. Almost silently, the face of California, in small ways, began to change as Manila Galleon shipwreck survivors, some stranded for long periods of time or taken in by native tribes, fathered children. As they traveled north along the coast in 1769, Portalá and his men noted some fair-skinned, light eyed and fair haired Indian children along the coast. From time to time, vegetable gardens planted by Manila Galleon mariners provided food for other seafaring travelers. Slowly, their infrequent presence changed the future of California.

The importance of maritime lanes to the Camino Real de California should not go unnoticed. Significantly, much of the information used by explorers and missionaries between 1769 and 1776 to locate places and topographical features in California by land was based on data collected by Manila Galleon mariners for over two hundred years. After 1769, those routes continued to transport people and things by sea and connected to colonial roads leading from the California ports to presidios, ranches, towns, and missions. Thus, the broader history related to maritime lanes is a part of the corridor associated with the Camino Real de California.

It is a truism that the early maritime history of the California coast is tied to the exploration of the Philippines and the Manila Galleon trade that had evolved by the second half of the sixteenth century. Much earlier and far from California, an event of great historical importance took place that would bring California's Pacific coast into prominence. In 1519, Ferdinand Magellan, a Portuguese explorer sailing under the Spanish flag, claimed the Philippines for Spain. Magellan, however, had not always worked on Spain's behalf. Years earlier, while sailing for his homeland, he was among the Portuguese explorers who discovered many islands in the archipelagos within Indonesia, including

Malaysia. The Portuguese pioneered the way to the Indian Ocean by sailing south from the Iberian Peninsula along the western African coastline beyond the equator and around the Cape of Good Hope. About 1511, Francisco Serrão (sometimes Serrano), said to be a relative of Magellan, had reached as far as Malacca, where he heard about some "spice islands" to the east. Serrão wrote to Magellan about the Spice Islands or Moluccas, thus pointing the way eastward to other possible Portuguese discoveries beyond Malaysia.

Following Columbus's discovery of the New World, the Portuguese contested the Spanish claim to the territory. The outcome of this challenge was a compromise. The Treaty of Tordesillas (1494) divided the earth between Spain and Portugal by imposing the famous "Line of Demarcation" between them for colonizing purposes. Technically, beyond the far end of the Pacific Ocean, Portugal's claim to lands surrounding Malaysia and the Moluccas, which had been kept secret, ended there. Meanwhile, Spain continued to expand its claim to and possession of the New World in all directions. Early in the period of discovery, Spanish officials pushed explorers to reach as far west throughout the Americas as possible. Indeed, the nation still had dreams of reaching India. New hope emerged when, in 1513, Vasco Núñez de Balboa crossed the Isthmus of Panama and discovered and claimed all lands washed by the *Mar del Sur* (the South Sea, i.e., the Pacific Ocean) for Spain.

In 1517, having fallen out of favor with the Portuguese court, Magellan switched his allegiance from Portugal to Spain. He and his second-in-command, Juan Sebastián Elcano, convinced the Spanish crown that they could find a route to the Pacific Ocean from the Atlantic Ocean. Their hope was to establish a base for commercial purposes at or near India. Their first goal was to probe the southern Atlantic coastline of the Americas for a strait that could lead them toward India and the possible island world east of the Portuguese claim.

Once their plan was approved in 1519, Magellan and his men sailed south to the Canary Islands and beyond to Cape Verde before bearing across the Atlantic to Brazil. Sailing down the coast far beyond the equator, they found a strait that bore west, which historically came to be known as the "Strait of Magellan." There, they crossed into a large, calm sea they named "el mar pacífico" (the Pacific Ocean) and took advantage of its currents and the winds that swirled across its wide-open waters. Once beyond the strait, Magellan and his ships crossed the wide Pacific and discovered and claimed the island world of the Philippines for Spain. Twenty-five years later, in 1544, Ruy López de Villalobos bestowed on them the name "las islas Filipinas" after Prince Felipe.

In the Philippines, Magellan and his men engaged hostile natives in a series of battles. Their plan changed when Magellan was killed in a battle on the island of Mactan in 1521. With no other alternative than to leave, Elcano abandoned the original plan to establish a base for trade and departed the area by sailing past the Portuguese-claimed Indian Ocean toward Africa. Once on the Atlantic Ocean, they sailed northward beyond the equator to Spain. Finally, after sailing up the Río Guadalquivir, they arrived in Seville, their original point of departure. Of the 234 men who shipped on that voyage, only eighteen came home. Although they had not planned to do so, Sebastián Elcano and his men were the first to circumnavigate the earth in a single voyage.

Significantly, Magellan's discovery and claim of the Philippines for Spain further renewed interest in the quest to reach the Spice Islands. The claim also revived old issues between Spain and Portugal. In 1539, the Spanish and Portuguese kings met and signed the Treaty of Zaragosa, which recognized and granted Portugal's claim to the Moluccas as well as Spain's claim to the Philippines.

During the following quarter-century, Spanish officials revived interest in exploring a route from Mexico across the Pacific Ocean. Between 1525 and 1542, Spain continued to probe the possibility of returning to the Philippines and establishing a base of operations in that island world. In 1542, López de Villalobos left the Mexican coast bound for the islands. Two years later, he succeeded in establishing a short-lived settlement there, but hunger and hostile natives forced the people to seek refuge with the Portuguese, who imprisoned them for trespassing on the Portuguese claim. López de Villalobos died in one of their prisons.

Spanish attempts to reach the Philippines eventually involved the exploration of the California coast. The earliest such voyage was the Juan Rodríguez Cabrillo expedition of 1542–1543.[1] Cabrillo's exploration of the coast, which occurred fifty years after Columbus's first voyage of discovery in 1492 and twenty-three years after Magellan's Spanish claim to the Philippines in 1519, was part of a greater effort by Spain to connect the Philippines with the rest of its empire.

Cabrillo's voyage was rooted in the Spanish claim to the Philippines. Among those who turned his gaze toward the islands and their potential spice trade was Hernán Cortéz. After his conquest of Tenochtitlán (Mexico) in 1521, Cortéz and his lieutenants, in particular Pedro de Alvarado, planned to expand their enterprises across the Pacific Ocean and conquer the Philippines.[2] The planning alone took years, as ships were constructed on the Pacific side of Guatemala and Mexico and, later, men were recruited and supplies stockpiled.

One of Alvarado's trusted men was shipbuilder Juan Rodríguez Cabrillo, who had arrived in Mexico as part of Pánfilo de Narváez's army in 1520. When Cortéz overpowered Narváez in a fight, Cabrillo defected to Cortéz's army and took part in the conquest of Tenochtitlán.[3] Later, during the conquest of Guatemala, he served under Pedro de Alvarado. There, he was rewarded for his services with a land grant and became a *hacendado*. Cabrillo had helped construct ships for his commanders, one of them—requested by Alvarado, who planned to use it and others to conquer the Philippines—built at his own cost.[4] To Alvarado's dismay, some of his ships were diverted by the viceroy for use in the conquest of Peru by the Pizarro brothers.

While the planning was under way, Alvarado and Cortéz had a falling-out. The former asked the viceroy to deny a license to Cortéz for the venture and to give Alvarado, the conqueror of Guatemala, permission to sail to the Philippines.[5] But before the enterprise could get started, Alvarado led his army in the initial stages of the Mixton War (1540–1542) and was killed in battle with Indians at Nochistlán, Nueva Galicia, Mexico. At that point, the Philippine project nearly came to a halt. Soon afterward, Viceroy Mendoza authorized Juan Rodríguez Cabrillo to lead an expedition to the Philippines to find the Estrecho de Anian, sometimes referred to as the "Río de la Señora."[6] The viceroy's concern was that if his European rivals found the Strait of Anian or the Northwest Passage, they could sail across from the Atlantic Ocean to the Pacific and threaten the Spanish claim.

Although he is known as the explorer of the California coast, this part of his journey appeared to be a secondary objective. Cabrillo's plan called for sailing northward to Baja Point, the last known place on the California coast beyond Cedros Island, and find a route to China and the Philippines. While Viceroy Mendoza had hoped Cabrillo would find the elusive strait, his primary authorized mission was to find a route to the Philippines by following the coastline around the Pacific Ocean to Asia and the Chinese coast and down to the Philippines. Both Hernán Cortéz and Pedro de Alvarado had hoped to establish a more direct route to the Philippines by sailing north instead of following the route from Acapulco south to pick up the circular current leading westward across the Pacific Ocean. That fact was stated in several Spanish documents of that period. In 1929, Historian Henry R. Wagner wrote: "That [Viceroy] Mendoza really had expectations that Cabrillo would succeed in doing so [i.e., finding a large river or strait across the North American continent], is another matter. If we may credit the evidence submitted in 1560 in

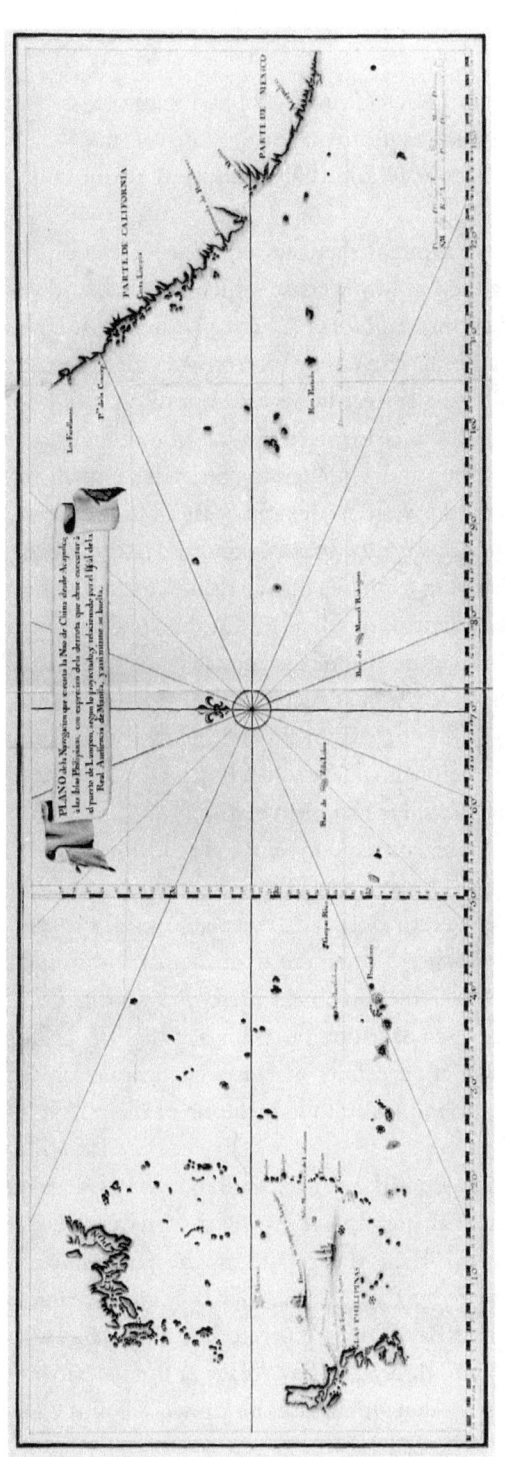

MAP 2   California coast and the Philippines with International Dateline as they appeared prior to the Juan Rodríguez Cabrillo expedition, 1542–1543. National Park Service–Spanish Colonial Research Center Map Collection, Center for Southwest Research, Zimmerman Library, University of New Mexico.

the *Información*, it was also hoped to reach China by following the coast. This was perhaps the case, as the idea was a favorite one during the century."[7] Still, some historians of California's history ignore that reaching the Philippines was the Spanish directive.

Cabrillo and his contemporaries thought that they could reach the Philippines by sailing northward along the California coast, which they believed was nearly continuously curved and connected North America with China. Based on explorations along the Baja California coast, they conjectured that the coastal lands curved to the west. Cabrillo was correct in his assumption, but did not have any knowledge about the vast distance involved in such an undertaking or the weather patterns during the late fall and winter along the Pacific Northwest.

Cabrillo set out from Navidad on the western Mexican coast on June 27, 1542, with three ships: the flagship *San Salvador*, *La Victoria*, and the lateen-rigged, twenty-six-oared *San Miguel*.[8] Moving to the Pacific coastline, the small fleet rounded Baja California and headed north. By August 1, Cabrillo had anchored within sight of Cedros Island. Before the end of the month, they had passed the last known point of Spanish exploration at the 30th degree north parallel reached by Juan de Ulloa in 1539. That day, Cabrillo and his men sailed into the unknown beyond Baja Point (then named "Cabo del Engaño") and entered "uncharted waters, where no Spanish ships had been before."[9]

Having sailed into the mysterious sea, on September 28, 1543, Cabrillo landed at a place he named "San Miguel,"[10] today's San Diego Bay, which would be settled 227 years later in 1769 by Governor Gaspar de Portolá. His ships continued sailing northward until they reached a small group of islands within sight of land. On October 7, the small fleet anchored near present-day Santa Catalina Island, which Cabrillo named "San Salvador," after his flagship.[11] Cabrillo's men rowed out to the island and met peacefully with a large group of armed warriors. They sighted other islands and Cabrillo named one of them "Victoria" after another of his ships.

Beyond the islands, Cabrillo sailed along the coast toward today's Los Angeles. On October 8, the small fleet passed an area apparently filled with campfires at Indian settlements, which they called "Bahía de los Fumos," the bay of smokes. They had reached present-day San Pedro Bay. The next day they anchored near what is now known as Santa Monica Bay. North of there, they met a tribe who told them about an uninhabited island, present-day Anacapa Island. Moving up the coast, they spotted a landmark that would later be known as Point Concepción, which they named "Cabo de Galera."[12]

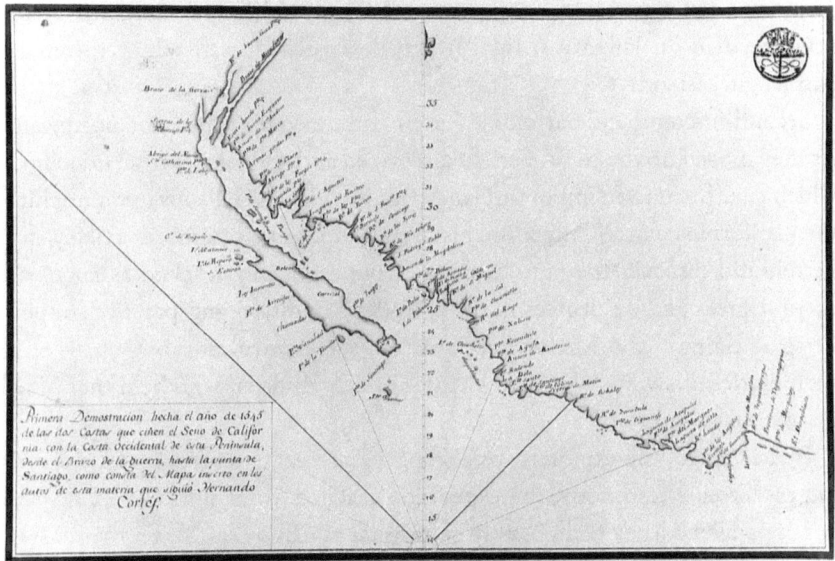

MAP 3   California coast as drawn in 1545 as far north as Baja California as it appeared prior to the Juan Rodríguez Cabrillo expedition, 1542–1543. National Park Service–Spanish Colonial Research Center Map Collection, Center for Southwest Research, Zimmerman Library, University of New Mexico.

Sailing for several weeks beyond the Santa Barbara Channel Islands, Cabrillo came within view of Point Reyes. In November, the expedition continued north, reaching as far as the present-day Russian River. Because of oncoming cold winter weather, Cabrillo turned around and headed back south along the coastline to repair his ships. Near Point Reyes, he noted a point filled with pines which he called "Bahía de los Pinos,"[13] but which later became known as "Punta de los Pinos" (Point Pinos). Moving southward, Cabrillo entered Monterey Bay.[14] Both Monterey Bay and Punta de los Pinos became well-known landmarks for later Manila Galleon mariners. Later, in 1769, both sites were sought by Portolá's land expedition as reference points in their exploration of Alta California.

Meanwhile, the continuing November winds had forced the expedition back to the Channel Islands. By November 23, 1542, the small fleet anchored off present-day Santa Catalina to winter and make repairs. The local tribes were not pleased and attacked the Spaniards. Cabrillo rowed out with some men to assist those on the island. When he stepped off his boat, he fell onto a jagged rock and broke his leg. Cabrillo's injury became infected and developed gangrene. The expedition returned to the Channel Islands where, historians note, he died on January 3, 1543. It is believed that his crew buried him on San Miguel Island.

Second-in-command Bartolomé Ferrelo continued the expedition northward. As they moved up the coast, Ferrelo discovered and named Cabo Mendocino,[15] which later became an important landmark for Manila Galleons upon reaching the California coast. While some historians[16] doubt this claim, it is likely that Ferrelo did discover the famous point, having possibly reached as far north as 40 degrees and 44 degrees north latitude.[17] Tradition and practice support Ferrelo's claim. Cabo Mendocino, after all, was named after one of his contemporaries, New Spain's Viceroy Antonio de Mendoza, who held that office between 1535 and 1550.[18]

By March 10, the explorers were faced with freezing temperatures. According to Ferrelo's testimony, the expedition reached as far north as 44 degrees north parallel.[19] They had possibly gone as far as Cabo Blanco, on the coast of present-day Oregon. At that point, threatening winter storms forced Ferrelo to turn around, bringing the expedition's objective to an end. In April 1543, the ships returned to their starting point at the port of Navidad, Mexico.[20] Without map or chart, Cabrillo, Ferrelo, and their men had sailed boldly more than 3,500 miles round trip from Navidad to Oregon's heretofore unknown southern coast. Both leaders had made important discoveries about the California coast and, importantly, had established a significant maritime lane with known topographical features and place-names.

Cabrillo's expedition (1542–1543), together with that of Francisco Vázquez de Coronado (1540–1542) and Hernando de Soto (1539–1543), had explored and claimed for Spain the entire southern tier of the present-day United States from the Atlantic coastline to the Pacific Ocean. All of the Spanish expeditions made first contacts with tribes along both coasts and the interior. On the California coast and nearby islands between San Diego and Santa Barbara, for example, Cabrillo identified the settlements of many Chumash and other tribes. Significantly, he and his pilots were the first to chart the maritime lane along the California coast and beyond. Places such as Cape Mendocino, Punta de los Pinos, and Monterey Bay would become important landmarks for voyagers along the coast. The explorers also passed and noted, sometimes under different names, Point Concepción, the Santa Lucía Mountains, and other known places. Later, Manila Galleon ships would sail southward along the coast, identifying and noting the latitude of some of the landmarks, inclusive of San Diego Bay, first seen through Spanish colonial eyes by Cabrillo and his men in 1542. That information gathered by sea over the centuries would be used by eighteenth-century land expeditions to fix their locations, cartographically and practically.

Cabrillo's expedition had resulted in the first European view of the California coast and its people as far north as southern Oregon. Historians retell the history of his expedition in terms of this exploration. Yet Cabrillo's objective was to reach China by sailing north along the California coast to a point where it would curve westward toward the Orient. In theory, Cabrillo's reasoning would have been correct except for the dearth of knowledge about the immensity of the North Pacific and the circular ocean currents that ran clockwise toward the coast. Still, the information gathered by Cabrillo, especially that about the landmarks at Cape Mendocino, Cabo de los Pinos, and Monterey Bay, would later help Manila Galleon ships find their way back to Acapulco. Spain, however, did not give up hope of reaching the Philippines.

In the end, although Cabrillo's goal to reach China did not succeed, his expedition did result in the acquisition of knowledge about the California coast and the Pacific Ocean as far north as Oregon. The place-names he gave to certain topographic features and notices about Cabrillo's landing at San Diego Bay and his death and burial at San Miguel Island in today's Channel Islands National Park would be referenced in the historical founding and settlement expeditions to California in 1769.

Interest in establishing a trade route from Mexico to the Philippines prevailed for another two decades. Seventeen years after Cabrillo's voyage, in 1559, King Philip II ordered Viceroy Luis de Velasco to occupy the islands. He wanted to take the spice trade away from the Portuguese. Five years later, in 1564, a fleet of five ships with over four hundred men sailed from Navidad, Mexico, to the Philippines. On their way, the expedition observed, actually discovered, and confirmed that the Pacific Ocean currents ran clockwise. Perhaps they were strong enough to carry ships back to the Western Hemisphere.

Augustinian friar Andrés de Urdaneta y Ceraín, an accomplished navigator, decided to put that hypothesis to the test. In June 1565, he left the Philippines bound for Acapulco and arrived there in October after four rigorous months of sailing. Urdaneta verified that the currents could indeed be picked up from the Philippines and, with the wind, ships could coast on them to the Californias. In that age of sail, his "discovery" of the "westerlies" that blew straight to the California coast was, along with the circular ocean currents, a significant find that would make the Manila Galleon trade possible.[21]

Actually, Urdaneta's claim was upstaged. Just before the friar set sail, one of his mariners, Alonso de Arrellano,[22] his pilot, Lope Martín, and a crew departed abruptly aboard the *San Lucas*. Arrellano reached the coast of Jalisco some time in August 1565. Thus, the route was tested twice that year, proving that the Manila Galleons could reasonably expect to make the long trip "safely" across the Pacific to the California coast. On the other hand, Urdaneta's probing of the ocean currents would revolutionize west-to-east travel across the Pacific Ocean in the age of sail.

Renewed interest in the exploration of the California coast occurred as a result of a sixteenth-century Manila Galleon shipwreck off the coast at present-day Point Reyes. In 1595, Sebastián Rodríguez Cermeño and a crew of over eighty men and passengers left the Philippines bound for New Spain on the nao *San Agustín*, alias *Philipinas*.[23] Rodríguez Cermeño was instructed to explore the California coast as he sailed southward.

The San Agustín reached Cape Mendocino in northern California in early November 1595 after a four-month voyage. The stormy weather and rough seas experienced on crossing the Pacific Ocean were factors in the deterioration of the ship, which was eventually lost off Point Reyes, north of San Francisco Bay. Nearly forgotten in official correspondence, two hundred years later Spanish maps of the California coast continued to record that the San Agustín wrecked off Point Reyes. The note on several of the maps read: "Aquí se perdió la nao Philpinas nombrada San Agustín en 1595." ["Here is where the Nao Philipinas, also known as San Agustín, was lost in 1595."]

The story of the last voyage of the San Agustín is told in the log and account of the voyage written by Sebastián Rodríguez Cermeño after his return to Mexico City during the viceregal maritime inquiry regarding the loss of his ship.[24] Having read through his account, Spanish officials investigating the causes of the catastrophe got their first real glimpse of the arduous journey from the Philippines to the California coast. Indeed, Rodríguez Cermeño recounted the treacherous voyage across the vast Pacific faced by all of the Manila Galleons, some of which were forever lost at sea.

Sailing out of Cavite in the port of Manila in Luzon on July 5, 1595, Rodríguez Cermeño plotted a course through the island waterways to the Pacific Ocean. Navigating his ships southward to round the shoals of Tuley, he then sailed through the Verde Island Passage. This sixty-two-mile gateway to the Pacific Ocean, which begins between Luzon and Mindoro, would lead him eastward past the interior island chain to the San Bernardino Strait that opened to the Philippine Sea, where the Manila Galleons would turn north toward Japan.

Once out of Cavite, however, the *San Agustín* encountered a headwind from the southwest and was forced back to Mariveles in the middle of the entrance to Manila Bay. After three days of fighting the wind, Rodríguez Cermeño made his way to Mindoro, the first large island to the south, which he reached three days later on July 8. There, he discovered that the *San Agustín* was taking in too much water. Rodríguez Cermeño unloaded the cargo and the passengers while his crew repaired the ship. Although most of the cargo was put back on board, it appears that most, if not all the passengers were left to wait for another ship to take them eastward to the Americas. Having made repairs and adjustments several times before he left the Philippine Islands, Rodríguez Cermeño, twenty-two days out of Cavite on July 27, finally headed out to sea through the San Bernardino Strait toward Japan.

South of Japan, the *San Agustín* angled northeastward, picking up the Japanese Black Current that would take them to the California coast somewhere along 42 degrees north parallel. The crew suffered contrary winds, storms, and ocean currents that carried them backward for days while their ship creaked and groaned from the strains of jostling and tossing in the sea. Rodríguez Cermeño noted that they finally sighted land on November 4, 1595. He expressed relief

> when the land and coast of New Spain appeared. The land which appeared was between two capes about twenty leagues from one coast to the other which from the west side, runs north, a quarter northeast. . . . we came within a league of the land, which appeared to be mountainous, heavily forested with many trees that could be identified. Among them were many pine trees growing very thickly near the sea and inland. . . . in preparing the boat with which to proceed with our exploration, they saw many campfires in the night on the seacoast and inland."[25]

Pursuant to instructions given to him by the viceroy of New Spain, Don Luis de Velasco, Rodríguez Cermeño sailed down the coast, explored the already-named Cape Mendocino,[26] and mapped the coast for newly discovered harbors and ports. Before anchoring at Point Reyes, he reconnoitered such places as present-day Bodega Head and Bodega Bay, as well as what is now called Drake's Bay, then named "Bahía de San Francisco" (also known as "la Bahía Grande"). Moving down the coast, Rodríguez Cermeño reported on the natives he observed living near the water's edge. To that end, he and his men met with many Indian tribes and described them in general terms.

The expedition had problems from the very beginning, even before leaving the Philippines, but none compared to the wreck of the *San Agustín* off Point Reyes and its aftermath. Later it was noted that the viceroy's instructions to explore the coast added more stress to the already debilitated ship. Although the date is not known, Rodríguez Cermeño lost his ship sometime around the end of the first week in November. Almost immediately after the shipwreck, his men were hard at work constructing a second boat, one they named the *San Buenaventura*.[27] Interestingly, while on the beach constructing the launch, Rodríguez Cermeño's men testified that in their first visit to the interior they saw smoke coming from a settlement and went to investigate it. There, they confronted Indians who had taken wood from the *San Agustín* to use as firewood. Rodríguez Cermeño, Juan de Morgana, Don García de Paredes, and nine others[28] approached them to take the wood, whereupon the Indians, defending themselves, shot at them with arrows. In the melee, they wounded at least one Spaniard. The confrontation ended when the Indians fled,[29] and Rodríguez Cermeño retrieved whatever wood he could salvage.

One of the mariners, Alonso Gomes, later testified that before leaving the Point Reyes area on November 7, Rodríguez Cermeño performed an act of possession in which he claimed the bay for Spain. Father Francisco de la Concepción offered the name "San Francisco," his namesake. Thus "Bahía de San Francisco" became an important place-name to mariners and was later associated with Drake's Bay within the vicinity of Point Reyes.[30] Regarding Bahía de San Francisco and other places on the coast, Rodríguez Cermeño wrote that

> This bay is at thirty-eight and two-thirds degrees [north parallel] and the islands which are in the mouth are at thirty-eight and a half degrees. From one point of the bay to the other is a distance of twenty-five leagues. I passed near the said islands, being about a league more or less from the land. . . . Running in the said direction, which is southeast, I came to a point, where I discovered a large inlet at the northwest point of a small island; and running along in the said inlet near the land to see if there was anything notable, there were observed on the shore of the sea many people on top of some bluffs where they had made their settlements. As it was late, I anchored in front of these settlement, and I saw how the Indians had on shore many rafts made like canoes, and with these they go fishing.[31]

The Spaniards communicated with these natives and asked them for food. They brought them "some bitter acorns and atole made of the same acorns in some vessels made of straw-like large jugs."[32]

By the third week in December, the expedition had gone past discernible places such as Monterey Bay, Punta de los Pinos, the Santa Lucía Mountains, the Santa Barbara Channel Islands, the Los Angeles area, and San Diego Bay. Once beyond the Alta California coast, Rodríguez Cermeño and his men made their way to Cedros Island and from there to the coast near Compostela, where a rancher fed the sick and starving survivors of the wreck. While some of his men remained on land, Rodríguez Cermeño and other members of his crew departed on the *San Buenaventura* bound for Acapulco. At the port of Navidad, Rodríguez Cermeño and some of his men left the vessel and went overland to Mexico City. The rest of his men sailed to the harbor at Acapulco, arriving there on January 31, 1596.

Rodríguez Cermeño's voyage, which began in the Philippines and ended in the shipwreck at Punta de los Reyes, demonstrated the route across the wide and wild Pacific and down the California coast to Acapulco. Following the shipwreck, he and his men took careful note of some of the places along the coast and reinforced the importance of the maritime lanes, knowledge of topography, and navigation skills. They also reaffirmed place-names given to bays, capes, and islands along the coast during the period of discovery. In 1769, information from this and several other records would prove invaluable when the first land expedition proceeded north from San Diego Bay. The maritime lanes and the land routes would throughout California's Spanish colonial and Mexican territorial periods form an important transportation corridor.

The upshot of Rodríguez Cermeño's shipwreck was a follow-up expedition led by Sebastián Vizcaíno that added more information to the accumulated knowledge. According to the account made by Fray Antonio de la Ascención,[33] a trained navigator who was on the 1602 expedition Vizcaíno mapped the place-names associated with the Alta California coast and recorded them in his diary: Cabo Mendocino, Punta de los Reyes, Puerto de San Francisco (Drake's Bay), Punta del Año Nuevo, Punta de los Pinos, Puerto de Monterey, Río del Carmelo, Sierra de Santa Lucía, Punta de la Concepción, Farellon de Lobos, Canal de Santa Bárbara, Punta de Conversión, Isla de Santa Bárbara, Isla de Santa Catalina, Isla de San Clemente, Ensenada de San Pedro, and Puerto de San Diego. Ascención noted that their expedition reached as far north as 42 degrees latitude. From there Vizcaíno continued mapping place-names along the Baja California coast until they reached Acapulco. Although his mission was to explore the coast, he had also been ordered to investigate the loss of the *San Agustín* and determine the location of the shipwreck at Punta de los Reyes. Today, the National Park Service protects Rodríguez Cermeño's shipwreck site at Point Reyes National Seashore as a part of our national story.

One of Vizcaíno's ships, commanded by Martín de Aguilar, separated from the fleet and may have reached as far north as Cabo Blanco on the Oregon coast. Fray Ascención, noting the latitude for each site, reported that Punta del Año Nuevo, Punta de los Pinos, Bahía de Monterey, Punta Concepción, and San Diego were between 34 degrees and 37 degrees north latitude.[34] All of those points would, when the first expedition to settle California landed at San Diego Bay in 1769, be the descriptive topographic features sought by Governor Portolá. The place-names and the latitudes known to Spanish mariners before and since Vizcaíno's 1602 expedition would be verified and found to be fairly exact. By this time, Spanish official interest in California was nearly 230 years old.

While explorers performed acts of sovereignty claiming territories for Spain throughout the Americas, Spanish officials recognized that effective claim to an area required occupation. Yet plans for the settlement did not emerge until the eighteenth century. While Cabrillo's epic expedition north along the California coast had resulted in much geographical knowledge, the attention focused on his plan to get to the Philippines, which, in essence, failed. For the next half-century, little thought, if any, was given to the possible settlement of California. Then Rodríguez Cermeño's shipwreck stirred up new interest. His instructions were to explore the coast, which he did in his efforts to save his crew. Despite his travails, he wrote descriptions of the California coast and about the land and its people and suggested its possibilities in terms of ports and what resources he could see from the sea. Afterward, officials decided that the stressed Manila Galleon ships that had crossed the Pacific Ocean were no longer to be used for exploration. The follow-up expedition by Vizcaíno in 1602 added much more in-depth cartographical information and descriptions about the coast, its people, and its possible resources, all of which encouraged interest in California. Yet more than a century and a half would pass before Spanish officials seriously contemplated settlement there.

CHAPTER THREE

✵ ✵ ✵ ✵ ✵

The Origins of the Camino Real

THE MARITIME AND LAND EXPEDITIONS OF 1769 FROM BAJA CALIFORNIA SUR TO ALTA CALIFORNIA

✵ ✵ ✵ ✵ ✵

> Until today, from the Port of Monterrey to that of Acapulco which, in truth is very well known, have been discovered from the Philippines, more than two thousand of Your Majesties vassals, soldiers, mariners, and passengers have died. Only when the Port of Monterrey is settled will the danger cease.
> SEBASTIÁN DE VIZCAÍNO | 1603

> The port of La Paz, which is the best in [Baja] California [Sur], is in twenty-five degrees north latitude . . . In this port of La Paz the Most Holy Cross of Our Salvation was planted.
> NICOLÁS DE CARDONA | 1632

EIGHTEENTH-CENTURY SPANISH OFFICIALS READ and reread the accounts of the Cabrillo-Ferrelo expedition of 1542–1543, which attempted to reach China and the Philippines by sailing up the California coast and around an unknown coastline. In their compendiums[1] of Spanish claims, they noted that the expedition had reached beyond Cape Mendocino as far north as present-day southern Oregon before it turned around, worn out by weather and the great extent of the northern Pacific coastline. Urdaneta, Vizcaíno, and others had left behind similar accounts describing the California coastline. Official documents noted that the northernmost reach of the Spanish claim to the Americas at that time had taken place in 1575. The fragmented documentation associated with the compendiums demonstrated that Juan de Fuca had sailed up the coast as far north as present-day Washington State. Indeed, the place-name "el Estrecho de Juan de Fuca" (the Strait of Juan de Fuca) still bears his name.

The officially sanctioned exploration of the California coast led by Sebastián Rodríguez Cermeño created renewed interest in the northern coastline. His 1595 shipwreck off Point Reyes clearly demonstrated that the Manila Galleons aimed to reach land as far north as Cape Mendocino. As a result of an inquiry, Spanish officials ordered follow-up expeditions, such as that led by Sebastián Vizcaíno in 1602 to find Cermeño's lost ship. Vizcaíno reconnoitered the California coast line and charted possible sea lanes and named important places along the way.

Sebastián Vizcaíno was no stranger to exploration of the northwestern coast of Mexico, particularly along the Sea of Cortéz on the east side of Baja California. In 1599, for example, while exploring this area, he discovered a bay that later became an important colonial port. He named it La Paz.[2] In his report to Spanish officials, he said that he had so named it because of the peaceful nature of the Indians they met.[3] Later, while exploring the coastal wilderness of Alta California along the Pacific Ocean, he discovered the location of another famous port, which he named San Diego. Both places, La Paz and San Diego, would become critical geographical points for the land and sea explorations of the California coast in 1769. Thus, while maritime lanes had long preceded the land trails, they had pointed the way north. To Spanish officials planning the settlement of Alta California, knowledge of their routes and potential hazards was essential to achieving their goals.

Whatever reasons these officials gave for establishing California, fear of losing territory to foreign powers figured into their thinking. Since the days of Francis Drake in the late sixteenth century, Spain feared that sooner or later Englishmen or their counterparts would discover the Northwest Passage or the Strait of Anian that the Spanish themselves sought. Both mythical passages were believed to run a course across North America and connect the Atlantic Ocean with the Pacific. Fear of Russian encroachment also plagued the minds of Spanish strategists. One thing was sure: eventually, the aforementioned powers would vie for the Pacific Northwest. The clash was coming.

The Bourbon reforms of the early eighteenth century renewed interest in California. Calling for "Defense of Empire" as a goal for military preparedness,[4] and assuming that the threat to Spanish interests would be external, Spain sought to buffer its defenses along coastal areas. In the end, the Spanish Empire fell to internal forces. Meanwhile, one of the immediate factors leading to the settlement of California was a military buildup in Sonora. Over 1,100 men were deployed to fight in the Sonora War in the late 1760s and early 1770s. The Sonora expedition of 1767 introduced Spanish political leaders, who pushed military expansion beyond Sonora to California. Visitador General José de Gálvez, who had planned the campaign against enemy Indians in Sonora, also took an interest in expanding toward Baja California. Defense of empire was behind his justification to push even beyond that and establish a base of operations in Alta California. His plan took stride in Sonora. The military force was large enough to spare at least one or two units to digress and move up along the coastlines of the Californias.

Gálvez laid out a two-pronged land and sea plan for settling San Diego Bay. It seemed simple enough, but its execution in this historical period would prove difficult. In 1768, Gálvez ordered Lieutenant Pedro Fages and twenty-five Catalonian Volunteers[5] to San Blas, where they would first guard a ship called the *San Carlos*, alias *Toisón de Oro* (The Golden Fleece).[6] From San Blas, the *San Carlos*, with the Catalonian Volunteers aboard, sailed to La Paz,[7] where they rendezvoused with another ship, the *San Antonio*, alias *El Príncipe* under captains Vicente Vila and Juan Pérez, respectively. Gálvez planned two land expeditionary forces, one led by the governor of Baja California, Gaspar de Portolá; the other by Captain Fernando Javier de Rivera y Moncada. Meeting with them, he laid out his plan. Once the two expeditions—that is, the maritime and the land forces—reunited at San Diego, Governor Portolá would lead a combined expedition to explore the coastline and establish an outpost at Monterey Bay.

Gálvez instructed the expeditions to keep a daily record of their march northward. Indeed, in all phases of the expedition, maritime or terrestrial, the participants left detailed entries of nearly every step of the way. They focused on time of day, leagues per day, and directions taken as they wended their way north. They noted native groups, their foods, their dress, their numbers, their perceived culture and traditions, the location of their settlements, and the constructions of their homes. In some cases, they described Indian burial grounds. On the land, they noted flora and fauna, rivers, arroyos, lakes, escarpments, proximity to the sea, and the fertility, aridity, or sterility of the land. Most importantly, when they could, they catalogued the latitudinal readings of their locations, climate, weather events, and even earthquakes and the zones in which

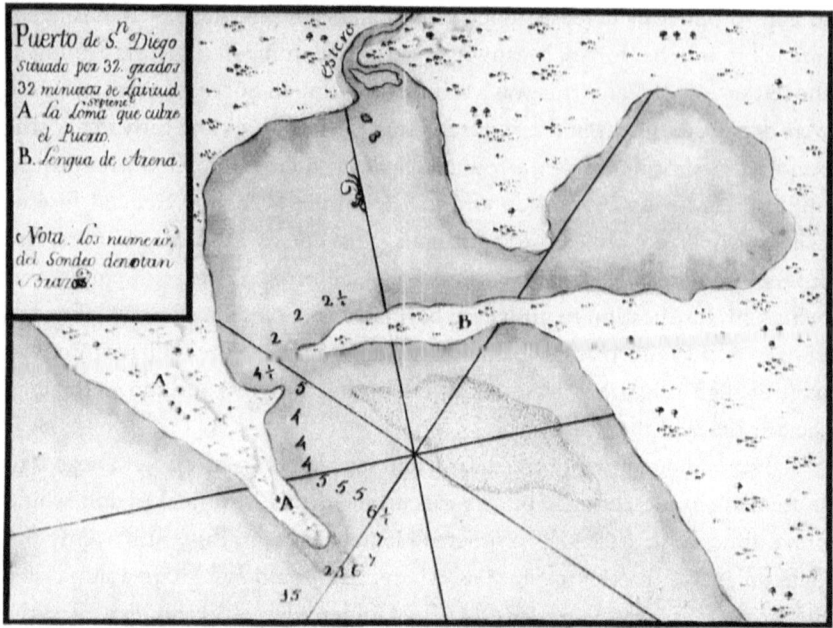

MAP 4   *Puerto de San Diego*, 1772. Compiled by Fray Juan Crespí. National Park Service–Spanish Colonial Research Center Map Collection, Center for Southwest Research, Zimmerman Library, University of New Mexico.

they occurred. The data they observed, collected, and recorded are clues for locating the Camino Real de California on the ground today.

On January 9, 1769, the *San Carlos* departed La Paz bound for San Diego.[8] On board were sixty-two men. Aside from crew members and soldiers, they included surgeon Pedro Prat, royal engineer Miguel Costansó, and a young Catalonian Volunteer soldier, Antonio Yorba, who would establish one of the early land grants in Alta California. The sea voyage was horrendous. After two weeks, the ship had made little headway. After suffering contrary winds, then periods of doldrums, the ship finally made it to Cedros Island.[9] There, on March 26, Fages and his men were relieved to find potable water, as many of the casks aboard had leaked excessively. Finally, after one hundred and ten days at sea, the *San Carlos* reached San Diego.[10]

Tragically, many of the men were ill with scurvy; some had died or were on their deathbeds. On April 30, Captain Pérez sailed the *San Antonio* into the bay.[11] His men were also plagued with the same disorder. Not a single person on board had been spared. The weather seemed threatening, as the sickly mariners had seen snow-capped mountains in the distance. Meanwhile, the expeditionary leaders established a hospital on the beach and tried to relieve the stricken men. Fages and Costansó, who were themselves ill, took any able man with them to look for potable water, as all they found on the beach was brackish. Meanwhile, Fages kept in mind the orders given to him by Gálvez: to make contact with the natives and keep relations on good terms so that they would be receptive to missionaries later.[12]

Having found water after a day of searching, Fages and his men encountered a group of native Californians. One of them thrust one end of his bow into the ground. Holding the other end, he danced around it.[13] When the Spaniards approached them, the group retreated. Finally, one of Fages's men, expressing an attitude of peace, thrust one end of his musket into the ground and danced around it. At that point, the natives, convinced of their peaceful intentions, approached them. Fages quickly brought out gifts for them. In return, the natives told them where they could find drinkable water. Pointing to the northwest of where they stood, the natives took them to a river. Costansó recorded his first descriptions of the area. He wrote that the landscape was arbored and filled with fragrant plants including sage, rosemary, and roses. He hoped the herbs might help the ailing men on the beach.[14] The men also noted some of the wildlife in the area and remarked about the fertility of the land and a faraway mountain. Quickly, Fages and his men returned with the much-needed water to the hospital camp on the beach.

Meanwhile, far to the south, the two-part land expedition, one section commanded by Governor Portolá and the second by Captain Rivera y Moncada, had commenced their east-to-west march across Baja California Sur so that they could follow the Pacific coast north to San Diego. To get to the Pacific coast, they first had to cross and wend their way through the Sierra de La Giganta, west of Loreto, and a series of other mountain ranges that extend nine hundred and thirty miles along the interior of the peninsula from Baja California Sur and Baja California to present-day Southern California. From Loreto, the expedition moved up the mountainous terrain to an Indian settlement called Velicatá, practically at the center of Baja California.

Portalá's visit to Velicatá was by no means the first time that Spanish explorers had penetrated the interior of Baja California. The historical unfolding of the exploration of the interior of the peninsula, then called Antigua California, is a part of the story of the Camino Real de las Californias (which included both segments of the Baja California and Alta California trail corridors) along its west coast. Spanish colonial efforts to connect the east and west coasts of the Baja California peninsula evolved slowly. By 1699, the land crossing from the east side at Loreto to *la contracosta* (the Pacific coast) had been accomplished. The protagonists of that venture were Antonio García de Mendoza, captain of the Loreto presidio, and the Jesuit Francisco María Piccolo. They had planned to run a trail southwest from Loreto to the mission at Viggé and from there across the mountainous and rocky peninsula to the opposite coast.

After reaching a Cochimí settlement inland, Piccolo and García de Mendoza stopped to assist in the construction of mission structures and a church. From there, they continued their quest to reach the coast. Guided by Cochimí warriors, they traveled slowly beyond the mountainous terrain to the Pacific Ocean. Their secondary objective was to explore the southern portion of the Baja California Pacific coastline and locate a good harbor for the Manila Galleons[15] that would connect overland with Loreto and La Paz. Failing in that, they returned to Viggé and Loreto. Their pioneering efforts showed the possibility of crossing the peninsula to establish an intercoastal route.[16] In time, the Baja California Pacific coastline would host an extended camino real that would connect the eastern and interior missions of Baja California Sur and Baja California to those along the Pacific coast. Seventy years later, in 1769, Loreto again served as the jumping-off point to cross the peninsula[17] to the contracosta as Governor Portolá and his second-in-command, Captain Fernando Rivera y Moncada, led the land expeditions to establish a coastal pathway northward to San Diego Bay.

Rivera y Moncada was selected to help lead the land expedition because he had firsthand knowledge of the interior of the peninsula. Earlier, in 1766, when the Jesuit father Wenceslao Linck explored the area and discovered Velicatá, Rivera y Moncada and two other soldiers served as his escort. Along on that expedition were two Germans who had escaped the English in the Philippines and crossed on one of the Manila Galleons.[18] Apparently they had been dropped off at the southern tip of the Baja California peninsula and made their way north. The expedition reached as far north as La Cieneguilla at the southern base of the Sierra San Pedro Mártir. Later, in 1769, Portolá's expedition passed through the area.

Among the members of Portolá's group was the newly appointed Commissary of the Holy Office of the Inquisition and Father President of the California Missions, Fray Junípero Serra. An experienced missionary accustomed to the rigors of frontier life, Serra had previously served for eleven years at the

Cerro Gordo missions between northern Querétaro and northwestern Veracruz. Until 1768, he had worked at other nearby missions in the region, when he and other Franciscans were summoned to Tepic, Nayarit, on Mexico's west coast. Their duty was to replace the Jesuits who were being expelled from the Spanish Empire because it was believed they were traitorous. (It was thought that the Jesuits planned a theocracy, a religious state within the temporal or secular state of the empire.) From there, he and several others were assigned to the Baja California missions. As part of Portolá's land expedition from Loreto, Serra moved inland to Velicatá. There, on March 22, 1769, at an Indian settlement, he established the mission of San Fernando de Velicatá, which still bears that name.[19]

By then, much of Portolá's two-part land expeditionary party had rendezvoused at that place. Their first objective was to cross over the mountainous and desert terrain of Baja California to the west coast and then to follow it north to San Diego Bay. At Velicatá, they were more than halfway to the coast. Captain Rivera y Moncada's command comprised twenty-five *soldados de cuera* (leatherjacket soldiers), three muleteers, and José Cañizares, a maritime navigator assigned to record the geographic and topographic places along the expedition's route. On that day, he observed the latitude at Velicatá to be at 30 degrees and 36 minutes north latitude.[20]

About forty-two Christian Indians from the missions of lower Baja California accompanied the expedition. Some of them were ill and caused concern among the priests: Fray Juan Crespí commented that "many . . . did not come, but fled, and of those that have arrived, some are ill; I very much feel sorry for these poor woeful souls considering how they will fare up ahead."[21]

On March 24, at about four o'clock in the afternoon, the group took its first steps toward San Diego Bay. The expeditionary force undertaking the king's business, was fully authorized and bore the privilege of a *real*. About one and a half leagues from Mission San Fernando de Velicatá, they came to Arroyo Seco, where they camped.[22] The route taken established the pathway north from Velicatá to San Diego for many years and rightfully bore the title "camino real." But first, the expedition had to find a way across the Baja California peninsula from Loreto via Velicatá to the Pacific coastline. (See appendix E for points along the 1769 Baja California route to the Pacific coast.)

The next day at about 7:30 in the morning, after the priests had prayed the Holy Mass celebrating the *Pascua de Resurrección* (Feast Day of the Resurrection of Christ), the expedition broke camp and veered north-northeast, passing through a plain and the Arroyo San Juan de Dios, named earlier by Father

Linck. That day, they marched twenty-four leagues in five hours.[23] Nearby was an Indian settlement, which they visited. When the natives saw the Spaniards, they ran away, but the Christian Indians went after them and brought back a naked boy with many tattoos (*muy rayado*) on his body. One of the soldiers gave him a lit *chiguarro* (cigar) and the boy smoked it.[24] Apparently, nothing more came of their meeting at the settlement, and the expedition moved on. That night, they stopped at the Arroyo de San Juan de Dios. One of the Christian Indians, named Rafael, became very ill. Crespí administered the last rites. That night Rafael died; the group buried him early the next morning.[25] The place-name San Juan de Dios is still so today.[26]

On Sunday, March 26, the group broke camp at about 2:30 in the afternoon, continuing in the same direction for three leagues. They passed along dry arroyos. The winding streambeds constantly forced the expedition to change directions as they looked for signs of the "contracosta": that is, the west coast of Baja California.[27] That day they stopped the *real* at the Arroyo de los Mártires. In contrast to the Arroyo Seco, this arroyo had water and pasturage for the animals. Its name is still shown on maps.[28]

The march on Monday, March 27 was delayed to allow the animals to pasture before the group broke camp at about 3:00 p.m. Dark clouds loomed over the land. After two leagues of marching through rain showers, the men were soaking wet. They soon learned that the fast-flowing Arroyo de los Mártires was a long, winding stream. Weaving their way alongside it, the expedition first traveled north-northeast, then northeast, and finally twisted west-southwest as the stream cut between some high mountains and along a maze of hills covered with very spiny *ocotillos* and *chollas*.[29] Still on the Arroyo de los Mártires after two hours, they had traveled only two leagues before they stopped to camp for the night. It continued raining the next day as Father Crespí celebrated the Holy Mass in Captain Rivera y Moncada's large tent. The weather forced the expedition to remain at their camp, where seven Christian Indians became very ill and were given the last rites. At dawn, one of them, a man named Luis from Mission San Ignacio, died.

Luis' funeral took place early on March 29. Before the expedition left, they placed a cross on his grave. Meanwhile, Captain Rivera y Moncada decided to send the Indians who were too ill to continue back to their missions. By 10:45 a.m., the expedition headed west-northwest along hills and arroyos for three leagues until they reached the Arroyo de las Palmas.[30] Today, the site is located at El Potrero near Rancho San Antonio.[31] The route they had followed was dry and unpopulated, and the trail meandered so much that, after several hours, they had only gone three leagues. About half a league from Arroyo de las Palmas, their scouts found water with good pasturage. They named the place "Santiago." That night, five of the Indians Rivera y Moncada had sent back rejoined them. They explained that on their way to the mission, they had been confronted by armed warriors. Fearing for their safety, they decided to rejoin the expedition.[32] That night, however, nine Christian Indians deserted the group.

The expedition spent the last two days of March moving directly north across arid terrain. They passed a place they called "Arroyo de la Beata Ángela de Foligno," which they described as arid and sterile. Today it is known as Cañada los Álamos.[33] From there they went north-northeast. Crespí noticed, by looking at the different types of trees and plants, that they had entered a new zone. After four hours of marching, they had progressed only three and a half leagues. Coming down a hill, they saw a native settlement of ten houses with people grilling *mescales*. When the natives saw them, they ran. The soldiers chased them and brought some of them back. The Spaniards gave them gifts to show that they had come in peace. In return, the natives shared their mescales with them. Eventually, others of the tribe called Axajui came into the Spanish camp. Meanwhile, the Christian Indians brought in a bound warrior who had resisted capture. They fed him, and he told him that other warriors were planning to ambush the expedition and kill them and the priests. The ambush did not take place, but the next day the warriors could be seen standing aligned along the ridges of hills watching the expedition leave their land.[34]

After passing Parage de Corpus Christi and Alamillo de la Tinaja, the group reached the Arroyo de los Álamos, where they camped for the night. Today it is called El Salto.[35] Along the way, they were met by nine warriors, who invited the Spaniards to their settlement where they traded for bread made from mescal flour. The expedition moved on following the same route north-northwest established by Wenceslao Linck in 1766. On April 1, 1769, they reached a place Linck called "La Cieneguilla,"[36] which was at the foot of a high mountain called the Sierra de San Pablo Mártir. On the east side of the mountain was the path running east to the coast of the Gulf of California. To the west of La Cieneguilla, the expedition crossed through the heart of the Baja California peninsula and headed toward the west coast. At that point, Crespí acknowledged that they were following the same "road" blazed by Linck in 1766. At least two of the soldiers under Rivera y Moncada had accompanied the priest on that venture and pointed out that the route veered away in the opposite direction

36 CHAPTER THREE

into the interior; they recommended to their leader that they leave it in order to get to the west coast.[37]

The Parage de la Cieneguilla[38] was at the foot of a high sierra and had very little water, "barely enough" for the people on the expedition and none for the animals. Of that situation, Crespí wrote that they "*abrieron batequi*,"[39] that is, dug for water. The pasturage at this place proved to be an amenity, for the moment. Still, some members of the expedition were suffering from exhaustion or other health-related issues. One of the soldiers, Guillermo Carrillo, became quite ill, and along with one of the Indians, had to be carried on makeshift litters.[40] That night, heavy clouds filled the sky and brought a cold wind from the northeast that seemed unbearable.

As the expeditionary party led by Captain Rivera y Moncada traveled lighter, they moved ahead of the main force to explore and establish a camp on the route before them. The second part, led by Governor Portolá and Father Serra, arrived late that night to rejoin the expedition. They spent the next day, Sunday, April 2, resting at La Cieneguilla.[41] Monday, April 3 seemed to come too soon. Packing the animals and breaking camp, the expeditionary force attended the Holy Mass prayed by the priests. By 9:30 that morning, they had departed the Parage de la Cieneguilla, bound by the topography on a north-northeast direction before veering northwestward. Two local natives who had been given handsome gifts guided them through the land. The march was slow going as the expedition carried the ailing Carrillo and, now, two natives on litters. About an hour and a half later, and after almost a quarter of a league of travel, they stopped along some well-pastured land near today's city of San José.[42] In the distance they could see some verdant hills, which the mission Indians with Father Serra said had plenty of water. Serra named the place "Santa Humiliana."[43]

To get there, they passed through very arid and sterile land. The trail was difficult, but had been fairly trampled by the natives, who used it as a pathway to some *rancherías* that had been abandoned. Beyond it, they reached an arroyo with running water and good pasturage. The land between Santa Humiliana and their new camp had a mix of pine and date trees. Later, scouts returned to tell the expedition that from a nearby high hill, they could see the sea, still very far away. That day the group had traveled long and hard, making three leagues in four and a quarter hours. They named the place "Arroyo de San Ricardo."[44]

They could feel the weather changing. On April 4, they left Arroyo de San Ricardo after passing the night with temperatures so low that Crespí wrote "*que ya nos moriamos del frio*" (we were about to freeze to death).[45] They were near present-day San Pablo.⁴⁶ To get to their next camp, they passed along rocky terrain, following the trees they had seen the day before and bypassing abandoned Indian settlements. After four hours and forty-five minutes, they came to a very pleasant plain at the foot of a high mountain, with good pasturage and an arroyo with running water. The panoramic vista impressed them.

There, they visited a friendly Indian settlement and traded for food. One of the items traded was a quantity of the ready-made delicious herbs called in Spanish *quelites*. "The delicacy is still made from wild spinach," wrote Crespí, "that grows in arroyos. The natives cooked them with many seeds. The usual pinole and bread likely made from mescal was also traded for beads and ribbons. They called the place "Paraje de San Isidoro."⁴⁷ The men camped along the arroyo there, near present-day San Isidoro.⁴⁸ That night, one of their Christian Indians, Gerónimo, died; the next day, they buried him and placed a cross over his grave. They spent Wednesday, April 5 resting in camp while their scouts reconnoitered the area ahead for the best route with water.⁴⁹

By 8:30 the next morning, April 6, the expedition had left the Paraje y Arroyo de San Isidro, bearing northeast along another arroyo that wound around some hills. Moving over the hills, they came to another arroyo covered with trees, but very rocky, through which they entered a canyon with grass and running water. They assumed that somewhere behind them it joined the Arroyo San Isidro. After three hours of marching and three leagues, they stopped to feed and water their animals in a canyon they called "Paraje y Cañada de San Vicente Ferrer." Father Serra, however, called it "La Cañada de Santa Petronila."⁵⁰ (Today, it is known as Cañón San Antonio; it is located near Rancho San Antonio.⁵¹) There, friendly natives came out to give them food and tobacco. The expedition spent two days resting from the arduous trail they had been following.

Breaking camp on Saturday, April 8, they headed on the route recommended by their scouts. Moving north-northwest, they followed an arroyo with a canopy of trees and so much water that they thought it to be a river. Near there, the scouts had seen nine very large wolves.⁵² The winding stream had to be crossed nine times in order to follow a certain line of march. While it ran east–southeast from the high sierra, it then turned and went southwest. The march that day took four hours and fifteen minutes, in which time they covered barely three leagues. After seeing that the stream had a deep bed and that it ran high and fast through the wild woods of a mountain, they named it "El Río de San Dionisio."⁵³ Today it is known as the Arroyo of San Antonio, near San Antonio.⁵⁴ Crespí wrote, as he did often throughout his diary, that at this point, "*Paramos el real*" (we stopped the expedition) along the banks of the river, where they watered their animals and let them feed on the grassy terrain. The group spent Sunday, April 9 there, resting. Meanwhile, the scouts went out again to explore along the lower river for a passageway out.

After Holy Mass on Monday, April 10, the priests administered the last rites to the soldier Guillermo Carrillo, who had, for the previous ten days, been carried on a litter. His condition had worsened and he seemed on the brink of dying. Yet he hung on. At about nine that morning, the expedition left the area, following the river for nearly a league. They spent time crossing and recrossing the Río San Dionosio looking for an exit from the mountains. Finally, they came to an *abra*, a narrow pass that opened into a plain, through which ran the river.

To cross the plain, they had to ascend three high, steep ridges, with the soldiers carving out a pathway for the mules. Once on the last ridge, they could see, in the distance, the Pacific Ocean and its coastline. To get to it, the expedition, all the while heading northwest, had to cross over hills and a deep canyon.

After three hours of hard climbing, the expedition made it to the banks of an arroyo with running water and good pasturage for their animals. They stopped in a small forest, where Crespí noted that the vegetation had changed as they entered a region comprised of junipers, oaks. small pine trees, and Rosas de Castillo as well as *romerillo*,[55] a weedy ground cover with medicinal properties. He also noticed that he had not seen any mescal for some distance, although the natives may have acquired it by way of trade. They named the place the "Arroyo de San León." There. they encountered a woman with three small girls and a baby boy. They were dressed poorly and Gov. Portolá made sure that they were fed. The Franciscan priests noted that this area would be a good place for a mission.[56] By the end of the day, the group had gone only two leagues. Nearby there was a place they named the "Paraje de San Andrés de Agua." Others on the expedition called it "Hispelo." Crespí reported sadly that night that one of his Christian Indians, Manuel Valladares, whom he highly respected, and who had served as an interpreter, had died. "I felt his death with all my heart," wrote Crespí, noting that he had placed a cross on his grave.[57] Present-day Valladares,[58] near the Arroyo de San León, may have been named after this man.

At about 1:00 p.m. on April 11, the expedition left the camp at San León, heading northwest. The route was hilly and the canyons kept them moving in a west-southwest direction. About four hours later, they climbed another high hill with little water. The ground was covered with romerillo, and the Christian Indians identified another plant called *yerba tabardillo*, which they used medicinally. Crespí noted that the area had an abundance of firewood. The Spaniards called the place "Loma Alta" and spent the night there.

Breaking camp at about 6:00 the next morning, Wednesday, April 12, the expedition headed southwest. Moving along a mesa through the hilly countryside proved arduous: there was no water and little or no pasturage. Although they saw tracks indicating a large number of Indians, they encountered no one. Meanwhile, their scouts moved ahead looking for water. Portolá and Rivera y Moncada were concerned that their animals had been entirely without water since leaving San León.

The expedition moved slowly, finding small pockets of water. Two hours later, they came to a place where they set up camp at a place they called the "Paraje de San Ángel a Cavasio." (Father Serra preferred the name "San Pacífico.") Soon, the scouts returned and proclaimed joyously that they were very close to the Pacific coast. From a ridge, they could make out a blurry view of the ocean. They were still some distance from it and the hilly and arroyo-scarred terrain slowed their progress.[59]

At three o'clock on the afternoon of April 13, the group left San Ángel. Following the configuration of the land, they turned north-northwest. The arid, sterile land still presented problems as, with little exception, it provided negligible pasturage and water for the animals. About halfway into the day's march, they came into an area filled with mescal, whose spiny needles did not affect the animals that fed on it. While the plant provided a juicy substance that sufficed for the thirsty men, they still lacked sufficient water for the animals. Finally, the scouts returned to say that to the west of that place, they had found water. They named the place where they camped "Principio del Llano de San Telmo." That day, the expedition went four leagues.[60]

The group rested for part of the next day, April 14. At four o'clock in the afternoon, they saddled up and left San Telmo, covering another four leagues, part of it through a large valley that stretched from east to west and was probably about a league long. Crespí thought that the plain itself could be about five or six leagues long. He noted that the soil was dry and the area apparently received very little rainfall, though the soldiers felt that with irrigation, this could be good farming land. They noted many native footpaths through the area. They were impressed with the large antelope and deer herds in the area, along with many coyotes.

Looking for water, the men traveled into the night, arriving at about nine o'clock in the evening at a campsite with a large waterhole filled with abundant reeds and turtles. They figured the waterhole was many *estados* deep and about a hundred and fifty *varas* long and twenty varas wide (an estado being seven feet and a vara about 32.5 inches). The place was a virtual paradise compared to the desert lands they had crossed before getting to the "Pozo de San Telmo," as they called it. (Father Serra, ever contradictory, called it "Santos Mártires Gorgomienses.") This oasis was likely located five kilometers from today's city of San Telmo.[61]

To the west was another "blessed" valley. From one of the heights in the area, they could plainly see the ocean. They reckoned it was four leagues away,[62] roughly ten miles. They were close, but still had to deal with the winding terrain to get there. They spent the next day, April 15, resting and enjoying the campsite. Guillermo Carrillo, the ailing soldier, was still alive and on the litter. That night, another four Christian Indians abandoned the expedition.

After Sunday morning Mass on April 16, the expedition departed San Telmo at about 8:30, heading north. The terrain they followed twisted and they found themselves moving away from the ocean in a north-northeast direction. Finally, the land turned again and they were moving northward. After approximately three leagues, they found an Indian pathway and followed it to a lush valley, surrounded by hills with excellent pasturage. The valley was a league long and four leagues wide. The *real* stopped in a spot with many trees and water. Later that day, the two parts of the expedition reunited. To the north-northeast was a mountain with a small valley through which a stream of water ran from a small spring. Although Crespí named it "El Valle de San Rafael Arcángel," Father Serra called it "Santa Margarita."[63] It is near the area today called San Rafael.[64]

On Monday morning, April 17, just as the party was ready to leave, an armed warrior approached the camp. Crespí admitted fearing him because he was tattooed and appeared threatening. One soldier tried to give him food, but he refused it. He communicated that they should leave the food on the ground because he was a *bailador* (dancer) and could not eat until he had performed a ritual dance. He did say that the place the Spaniards called San Rafael was known by his people as "Matyropi." Then he began a chant and his dance. Oddly, after this he left suddenly for the hills "como un venado" (like a deer), without taking any of the food. Likely, the warrior prayed to ward off any evil spirits among those in the expedition. By this time, it was too late for the group to make any progress traveling, so the expedition delayed leaving until the next day.[65]

At eight o'clock the next morning, Tuesday, April 18, the two-part expedition left El Valle de San Rafael, headed north. Again, the terrain forced them to turn north-northwest. They marched for five and a half hours and five leagues, crossing through rough terrain covered with *salitre* (saltpeter) and over high hills until coming to another valley with a wide and verdant plain. The land ran north to southeast. They noted a large waterhole and abundant pasturage in the valley. Some of the men thought the land would be suitable for ranching. They called the place "San Toribio." Serra, on the other hand, called it "San Bernabe."[66] It was near present-day El Salado.[67]

On April 19, at eight o'clock in the morning, the expedition began the day's march in a north-northwest direction. After a league, they turned northwest and came to a settlement of two houses, one of them occupied by an elderly man who told them, through signs, where to find water. They fed him and he guided them to water and pasturage. From there, they moved along a water-filled arroyo that ran northeast by southwest through fertile lands. After four leagues of travel, they stopped to camp near some mescal at a place near present-day San Vicente that they called "Ciénega de Santa Isabel Reina de Hungría" and Father Serra called "San Guido."[68]

The next morning, April 20, the men headed northwest and veered westward after a short distance. That day, they traveled for five and a half hours through hilly country and some canyons. They entered a mountainous area filled with oak and junipers, but the land was barren of grasslands. Following Indian pathways, they surmised that the land was well-used for transit and that there were likely several settlements in the area. After five leagues, they came upon an arroyo near today's Cañón Santa Cruz near Santa Cruz.[69] It had no water for the animals but was surrounded by grasslands, scrub bushes, and trees. Crespí named it "Arroyo Seco de los Alisos," and Father Serra, "San Nazario de los Alisos."[70]

On April 20, they left the dry arroyo at 7:30 in the morning, moving in a northwesterly direction. After traveling over small hills, they descended into a canyon that had grass and some water. They camped on a mesa, where the soldiers dug for additional water for their animals. They called their campsite the "Arroyo o Cañada del beato Jacobo Ilírico, de nuestra Orden." As it was the feast day of San Antonio, Serra called the spot "San Antonio de los Trabajos."[71] There is a spring nearby which today is known as Agua Grande.[72]

While exploring a short distance away, a scouting party came to a small canyon with running water, where they stopped to rest. After an hour of hard travel, they had gone only two leagues. Yet they were heartened when they climbed a small hill and could see that they were only a quarter of a league from the sea.

All they had to do was ascend to the beach. However, the steep escarpments blocked their path.

The last thing Crespí did before leaving on April 21 was to place a cross on the grave of a Christian Indian named Enrique, or Merico as some called him. Enrique had died of the unidentified illness that had plagued the other Christian Indians and some members of the expedition. That day, the expedition pushed north along an arroyo that took them to an area with trees and good pasturage. In three hours, they managed to travel three leagues. They stopped along another arroyo running north-northwest to south-southeast with a spring of water; beyond it, the soldiers found a water hole. Crespí called the place "El Arroyo de los Alisos y Ojo de Agua de San Anselmo." Serra called it the "Paraje San Basilio."[73] Today it bears the name Cañón el Chocolate.[74]

By eight o'clock on the morning of April 22, the expedition had departed the Arroyo de San Anselmo, heading north-northeast. After a while, they turned due north through some canyons and along sides of hills on land that seemed easy going, at least in contrast to some of the trails they had followed. They found a way to descend into a large valley, but the escarpment seemed a bit steep. The animals had a hard time descending along that route.

Crespí looked back and thought they had taken a chance on something that could have gone wrong. Yet they had made it down and stood in a large valley with many trees at one end. The valley had pools of water with reeds growing in them. The scouts had told them that further down, there was a large stream, like a river, that ran into the sea. To them, it had the appearance of a port. They guessed that the bay could be the port of Todos Santos.[75]

They stopped to camp on the edge of a stream that ran down from a cave to a waterhole. Nearby was a second waterhole; both had fresh potable water.[76] They named the place "San Francisco Solano" (today's Valle Santo Tomás)[77] and hoped that a mission would one day be founded there.[78] They were now four leagues from the sea. Just north of San Francisco Solano, the expedition would be able to follow the coast northward to a point just south of present-day Tijuana, where they would move inland for a pathway leading to San Diego.

While exploring this area, Father Serra and Sergeant José Francisco de Ortega encountered a number of natives. Most of these were women and children, so the pair were not alarmed—until they noticed that behind them were several well-armed warriors. One of the latter began speaking in a loud voice, as if animating them to some action. Quickly, Ortega put on his leather armored jacket and pulled back to avoid a confrontation.[79] Fortunately, nothing happened and the explorers were allowed to continue on their way. They discovered a place with many *Rosas de Castilla* and other plants with tasty seeds that the natives used for food. Serra called this place "San Antonio de Padua."[80]

The next day, Sunday, April 23, the expedition left San Francisco Solano at about eight o'clock in the morning. Marching due north through the plain, the explorers ascended a ridge and a pass, which were very stony. After two hours and ascending and descending hills through a grove of oak trees, they arrived at a wide valley. They found water—actually a hot spring—and named the place "Valle y Ciénega de San Jorge." Father Serra called it "San Atenógenes" after a bishop and martyr of the church. Today, modern maps show it as Cañón la Grulla, Uruápan.[81] The water was too hot to carry, but the men found that if they let it sit in the containers for half an hour, it cooled off and was drinkable. That day, they covered a league and a half.[82] They also came across two other springs with running potable water.

Later that afternoon, Captain Rivera y Moncada and eight soldiers explored the land ahead. They climbed a ridge not far from their campsite and looked out to the sea, which they estimated was three leagues away. They said they could see the ocean as it hit the rocks and skirts of the coastal terrain, which appeared to open into the wide bay they believed was Todos Santos. Three islands were also visible. However, Moncada y Rivera reported, the high mountain before them blocked the way to the sea. He figured that the party would have to go further north because the mountain lined the coast with a long escarpment that the expedition's beasts of burden could not readily descend. He recommended that the expedition remain where it was for another day, while he and his men explored for a way to the sea.[83]

The next day, the scouts went out to look for more water and a feasible route. They returned in the afternoon with good news about what lay ahead. Meanwhile, the weather had worsened. A big storm hit the area and it rained into the night and for the next two days, April 24 and 25. All the while, the expedition was at a standstill.

By Wednesday, April 26, the sky had cleared. Everything the travelers had was soaked through. They left the Valle y Ciénega de San Jorge at about ten-thirty in the morning. The route found by the scouts led them north-northeast, then veered northeast, and then finally due north. By three-thirty, the expedition had stretched out like an accordion and the men in the lead stopped to wait for the others to catch up. Although they did not see a single native warrior, they found plenty of tracks in the area. Deep in the mountainous terrain filled with bushes and forests of scrub oak and other unknown trees, they stopped at an arroyo with running water and grass. They named the place "Arroyo de los Santos Mártires San Cleto y Marcelino." Father Serra noted in his diary the name of "San Gervasio."[84] The area is near present-day Cañón San Francisquito.[85]

The group spent the next day, Thursday, April 27, ascending and descending hills and the winding sierra proved. This proved fatiguing to both men and animals. The scouts reported that water was becoming scarce. The travel was slow as the group stopped to fill canteens and several barrels of water when they could and loaded them on the mules. Constantly moving ahead of the expedition, the scouts searched not only for water, but also a better way to the sea. To their dismay, there was not a drop of water to be found on that arid, flat segment of the trail. When they stopped to refresh the animals with the water from the barrels, Crespí dubbed the place "Bajial sin Agua" (waterless plain or flat).[86]

Friday, April 28 found the expedition in a quandary. They needed water and to find a better way out of the mountain range. To that end, they sent out six scouts under the command of pilot José Cañizares. His orders were to determine where they could descend to the shore near the large bay that they had seen from the heights at San Jorge. On the scouts' return, Cañizares reported that they were still far from the bay and they had not found any water except for a small waterhole half a league away.[87]

Fine weather blessed them on April 29 as they left Bajial and headed the half league to the small waterhole reported by the scouts. They traced it to an arroyo and found more water than they had expected and a good area with grass to pasture their herds. The soldiers dug to expand the spring and water spouted forth for both man and beast. They camped there for the rest of the day and named the place "Ojito de agua del arroyo de San Pedro Mártir." That afternoon, Captain Rivera y Moncada decided to take ten soldiers and go directly to the shore where they had seen the bay and backtrack from there to find a route. The rest of the expedition spent the next day resting. As it was Sunday, the priests celebrated the Holy Mass and asked for God's help. Later in the afternoon, the captain and his men returned to say that they found water but no direct route to the bay from their camp. They were still caught in the mountainous and hilly maze.

Monday, May 1, 1769, began with the priests saying the Holy Mass. Soon after, the expedition left along the route of the scouts had followed the day before.[88] Moving west-southwest, carrying two barrels of water and some canteens, they traveled for five hours. The steep up-and-down march on rocky hillsides took them to vistas of the ocean between the steep sides of the mountains. As they reached the last flat that would lead them to the shore a league away, they saw a large feathery cloud of dust kicked up by a large number of natives moving away from the expedition. The warriors had been following them at a distance since the day before. Wary of a potential attack, the expedition went another three leagues and stopped to camp at a place Crespí called "Bajial de los Santos Apóstoles," near present-day Cañón San Carlos, Valle el Maneadero.[89] The place lacked water, but had sufficient grass for their animals. They reckoned that they were a league from the bay.[90]

Up early the next day, the expedition packed their gear and readied their animals, as usual, and marched out of the Bajial de los Santos Apóstoles. Their first steps were toward the north-northwest through a flat plain. A league later, they descended with elation onto the beach of the large bay. Shortly, they passed along a small canyon and reached a *rinconada*,[91] a topographic corner shaped by land formations. (In this case, Crespí said, it was formed by the first small curving side of the bay.) The expedition had reached the great bay known by mariners as the Ensenada de Todos Santos.

Once on the beach, they established their camp about two hundred varas from the edge of the bay, near some waterholes on a rise above the shoreline near some low-lying hills. They named it "La Santísima Cruz de las Pozas de la Ensenada de Todos Santos." Today it is known as Ensenada.[92] The place had many amenities: water, grasslands, potential for irrigation, humidity, and plenty of elbow room. The party thought it would one day be the site of a great harbor city where mariners could stop and rest. The priests thought it would be a wonderful place for a mission.[93]

So that their animals could feed and water, the expedition rested there on May 2 and 3. Meanwhile, the scouts were sent out ahead to look for a route with water. While they were gone, they noticed an Indian settlement nearby. They approached it, but the natives ran away and, some distance away, stood their ground. All the while, their armed warriors yelled at the newcomers to go away. Governor Portolá attempted to persuade them to return, indicating that the Spaniards had come in peace, but the natives wanted no part of them.[94]

On May 4, the priests celebrated the Holy Mass and the expedition left on a north-northwest course following the hills along the coast. After three hours, they had traveled three leagues. Then a large hill that ran into the sea forced them to change direction. Still, they found a good waterhole, where they stopped the *real* and set up camp.[95] From there, the scouts went out to explore the area and found numerous rancherías, some of them unprotected and abandoned. By the time the second part of the expedition caught up, some natives had come to the camp with fish and clams. They also put on a dance. At first, they were afraid of the mules. However, the soldiers reassured them by teaching them to call out to them: "*mula, mula!*" These men were armed and painted. They wore headdresses and otter skins. They wore their hair short and, in some cases, shaved. Crespí called the place "Paraje las Pozas de Santa Mónica." Father Serra called it "La Ranchería de San Juan." Today it is known as El Sauzal.[96]

The explorers noted that the bay had two islands in the middle and conformed to descriptions by Manila Galleon mariners, especially that of Joseph González Cabrera Bueno in his diary.[97] Cabrera Bueno's *Navegación Especulativa y Practica* was published in Manila in 1734 and dealt with, among other topics, maritime lanes used by the Manila Galleons across the Pacific Ocean. His book was therefore among the most recent reports used by the Portolá expedition. It is believed that they brought along at least two copies. A native of Tenerife in the Canary Islands, Cabrero Bueno began his naval career in the Philippines in 1701 and made several crossings from Manila to Acapulco. Eventually, he rose to the rank of admiral. Chapter four of his book describes the route between Cape Mendocino and Acapulco via the entire California coastline.[98] Portolá and his men consistently referred to this work as they marched north.

The group spent May 5 and 6 resting, while the scouts went out to explore the route and seek water as well as a way out of the bay area.[99] At about 6:30 on Sunday morning after Mass, the expedition left the bay behind as they headed inland toward the north. The scouts had found a large waterhole about four leagues ahead that would serve as their destination for the day.[100] To get there, they followed an arroyo at present-day Cañón Arce,[101] which was filled with stones. They climbed a hill, which they descended within sight of the shoreline. They crossed an arroyo with scrub plants and oak trees, but did not find water on that part of their march. Finally, after four leagues, they arrived at a large valley near present-day Valle Guadalupe[102] with excellent pasturage, trees, and a good arroyo with much water. The *real* halted under a canopy formed by a grove of oak trees. They named the place "El Valle de San Estanislao."[103]

All along the route that day, warriors backed by other villagers lined the ridges of hills and mountainous terrain, yelling in an uproar for the explorers to leave. The warriors were heavily armed but did not make a move against them. Some continued to follow them for some distance. Governor Portolá instructed his men not to yell back at them, because they were not sure what was being said. Finally, Captain Rivera y Moncada stepped forward to find out if they could understand that the expeditions came in peace and to invite them to the Spanish camp. Just before sunset, the warriors gave one more warning yell and disappeared.

On this leg of the journey, the men were able to see the ocean at a distance, including some islands different from those seen at the Ensenada de Todos Santos. Early the next morning, about 6:30, they left the Valle de San Estanislao and roamed west-northwest. Along the way, they could hear the taunting voices of the warriors, probably with the same number of people as the day before. The warriors darted in and out of the hills and ran up along the ridges as they watched the expedition go by.

The expedition crossed warily over hills and ascended toward a pass. There, after a half-league of travel, Captain Rivera y Moncada ordered his men to put on their leather jackets and mount their horses in case of an ambush. The armed warriors, probably twenty-nine in number, split up into two groups: one on a ridge, the other on the side of a hill. Their bows were at the ready; all they needed to do was let their arrows fly. The standoff lasted half an hour, with one of the warriors signaling the Spaniards with his hands and yelling something at them as a group of Indians went around some bushes toward the horse herd. Portolá took four armed soldiers to head them off.

Both sides were just beyond arrow and musket range. The warriors' arrows did not reach the expedition, not even by a few paces. The Spaniards fired their *escopetas* to frighten their attackers. The warriors made one last uproar and retreated behind the hills, ending the confrontation. However, the soldiers held their position until they were certain that the natives had fled.

The expedition had been stalled for two hours by the confrontation. Soon after, the group moved forward.[104] About a league and a half from the confrontation site, they came within view of a small valley, very green with abundant water. However, they needed to find a safe way down to it. Once on the flat land of the valley, they camped and named the place the "Mesa de Paraje de San Juan Bautista."[105] Today it is known as Boquilla de Santa Rosa near Mission San Miguel.[106] They looked behind them at a ridge, and there saw the twenty-nine armed warriors watching them as the sun set. Doubtless the Spaniards posted a guard that night to watch the camp and the herds. The night was spent without incident.

The next morning, April 9, the expeditionary force followed a west-northwest bearing to a long ridge. From there, they could see that the valley where they had spent the night was extremely large. From the ridge on the opposite side, they began a dangerous descent down a steep incline. The men feared that their animals could easily slide down its side and forced them to move slowly. Below them was a ranchería. Upon seeing the expedition descending, the people began yelling and fleeing in fright. The Spaniards tried to calm them, but they continued running to the hills for safety. The expeditionary force decided it would be best to keep moving toward the second part of the plain not far from the ranchería before setting up camp. The priests thought that this place with water, woods, and pasturage, along with a native population, would be a fine place for a future mission. There they pastured their animals and the large waterhole was enough for both man and beast. The entire day had been slow-moving and the expedition traveled barely one league. North of their camp was a canyon that would lead them out of the valley. Crespí wrote that of all the places they had seen with good amenities, "this is the king of all of them."[107] Rivera y Moncada recommended that the place be called the "Valle de San Juan Bautista." Father Serra, on the other hand, called it "San Juan Capistrano."[108]

The Spanish camp was close to the Indian settlement. When they went there, the natives again fled to the hills; they would not come down, but stood and sat, just watching the Spaniards. Finally, Rivera y Moncada made some friendly overtures to them, and, with one soldier, walked over to them. Some met him without fear. Rivera y Moncada gave them ribbons, beads, necklaces, and whatever else he had brought with him to give. Still the others would not come down. Rivera y Moncada was walking back to the Spanish camp when one warrior yelled out to him. He put down a fish net he carried in his waist band and some arrows and motioned for the captain to come back and get them as objects of trade. Then he retreated. Rivera y Moncada retrieved them. Later, three warriors came down to the camp to trade with the soldiers. Rivera y Moncada gave them some presents, and soon many of the women and children visited them as well. Just when things appeared calm, everyone turned to hear a commotion on a nearby ridge. The twenty-nine armed warriors had watched it all and again began to make their demonstrations. This time, they discouraged the friendly Indians, who left the Spanish camp and disappeared over a ridge. The Spaniards were surprised that the warriors had persisted in following them for two days.[109]

The next day, early in the morning, the expedition departed to the north-northwest, turning northwest through the canyon they had seen the day before. Marching through a small forested area, they ascended a high ridge and afterward followed some mesa tops, where they found good grasslands along with patches of wild beans, some of which the Christian Indians quickly gathered. Soon after, they continued onto higher ground. When they looked back, they found that six natives from the Valle de San Juan Bautista had followed them. Three others were seen accompanying the soldiers who were herding the horses. After five hours and four leagues, nine natives stayed to guide them through the rest of the valley and mesa lands. Once again, they were within sight of the sea.[110] Somewhere along that route they came to an area with several waterholes, where they stopped to water their animals. While Crespí noted that they named the place "Pozas del Valle de San Antonino," Father Serra called it "San Francisco Solano."[111] Soon they came to another area with several large rancherías. Luckily, these natives were friendly and they stopped to trade with them before setting up camp for the night.

On May 11, they expedition went north-northwest, followed by a large number of friendly natives from the rancherías in the area who showed them the way north where they would find water. Soon afterward, they descended to the sea. They followed the shoreline along flat terrain that was broken up with small canyons and loose soil that had been washed down from the nearby escarpments. They followed the coast to another green valley, which also followed the shoreline. But the water in the area was not drinkable, for it had mixed with sea water. Moving upland, they could see the possibilities of well-irrigated farmlands, but for now were concerned with moving the expedition forward. Again, they were in a transition zone, with the flora changing between the coastal lowlands and the uplands toward the mountainous terrain. As soon as they departed from the coast, the natives left them. The group had traveled four leagues in five hours. They moved inland a very short distance from the sea to a small valley with an arroyo with trees and running water. They named the place the "Vallecito de San Pío." Father Serra called it "San Benvenuto."[112]

There, natives came to visit them, offering clams and other foodstuffs in return for Spanish trinkets. Some wore jewelry dangling from their noses. Surprisingly, they had pieces of European-style clothing that they said they had gotten from some ships that went by.[113] Were these possibly the *San Carlos* and the *San Antonio*, which had previously headed north toward San Diego Bay? If so, that would be the only reference the land expedition had of the maritime part of the expedition headed north to establish a Spanish outpost at San Diego. On the other hand, the natives could have been referring to a Manila Galleon.

After their visitors had gone away, the soldiers noticed that some things were missing, such as a pair of spurs and some clothing. The soldiers knew which man had done it and named him Barrabás. One native had taken the *campanilla*, the small bell to announce the beginning of the Holy Mass, but Barrabás took Father Serra's reading glasses! The bell was found buried in the sand and recovered.[114] It appears that Father Serra had to trade back for his glasses.

Doubtless, the expedition was glad to leave El Vallecito de San Pío on May 12, quickly heading north, then turning north-northwest in the vicinity of present-day El Rosarito.[115] Guided by some natives for a short distance, the expedition traveled three leagues through terrain that made for easy walking. Soon they passed through some small canyons. After three leagues, they encountered another ranchería of friendly natives on top of a mesa that, to the Spaniards, resembled an island. Although the inhabitants directed them to pass along one side of the mesa through their settlement, the expedition instead moved westward along the mesa on the edge of the beach. They knew that the settlement had its own waterhole, but, according to Crespí, the Spaniards did not want to pollute the water with their animals. So they moved their herds around the mesa to set up their camp near a small waterhole. That evening, the natives visited the camp. They seemed to know about the ships and said that they were not far away. Crespí noted four islands called Los Cuatro Coronados near the camp. He named their campsite the "Pocita de la Ranchería de Santos Mártires Nereo y sus Compañeros." Father Serra called it "La Cárcel de San Pedro."[116]

The next day, May 13, the expedition departed, accompanied by six natives who guided them to the north. They moved from the shoreline and descended a long, steep hillside; then they found the beach they were on blocked by a high escarpment and had to ascend to a high pass. About a league beyond, they saw a point of land that jutted out to the sea and moved up toward a long grassy plain from which they could see the ocean. Indeed, they could see the poles of the ships in the distance. The men realized that they must be very close to the Port of San Diego. After three hours' march, they came to a heavily populated ranchería with a long arroyo with running water. They were greeted by the natives, but could not stop as they had traveled only two leagues toward San Diego. They eventually stopped to camp as heavy rainfall began to fall, soaking them and their baggage. They named the place "La Ranchería y Arroyo de Sancti Spiritus," as it was the feast day of the Holy Spirit.[117] It was near present-day Tijuana at the US-Mexico International Border.[118]

Although the expedition was eager to get moving on Sunday, May 14, the rain fell hard and delayed them for an hour and a half. Crespí wanted to say Mass while they waited, but Captain Rivera y Moncada advised against it because there were too many armed natives in the area. He urged the expedition to move forward. About ten o'clock that morning, they began marching due north toward San Diego. After six hours, they could see, from a distance, the *San Carlos* and the *San Antonio*. They approached the port and the *real* or camp set up by the mariners and the Catalonian Volunteers. Little did they know that all of their former comrades were scurvy-ridden: some had died, while others lay dying on the beach.

As they approached the camp, Captain Rivera y Moncada and the advance group fired volleys from their muskets to announce their coming.[119] The first person they saw was Father Juan Vizcaíno. Behind him were Father Francisco Gómez, who had been on the *San Antonio*, and Father Fernando Parrón, who had arrived on the *San Carlos*. Much later, on June 29, Governor Portolá and the second part of the expedition arrived with the rest of the baggage, which had slowed them down.

The deadly scurvy had promised a slow death for some of the men who had arrived on the *San Antonio* and *San Carlos*. Crespí explained that "only three are well, all the rest being sick, many dying, the majority with cramps in the legs or all over the body."[120] A number of them had succumbed, while others still suffered from their symptoms. Father Juan Crespí noted in his diary that by the last week in June, twenty-nine mariners and two Catalonian Volunteers had died. The casualty rate among the Catalonian Volunteers was high. Of the twenty-five in the unit, only ten survived the ordeal. On July 3, 1769, Father Serra wrote that three of these soldiers had died and, of those remaining, a "great number had little to live."[121] Two more died eleven days later, on July 14.[122] When Pedro Fages returned from Portolá's expedition months later, he learned that eight more had succumbed. Fages and six of his own men had suffered the effects of scurvy, but had somehow managed to survive its ravages.

On July 16, two days after the expedition's departure, Serra founded California's first mission and named it "San Diego de Alcalá." Its construction would be slow in coming. The high casualty rate among the land and maritime expeditions was unexpected. For those who survived, the suffering would seem endless, for provisions and medical supplies were a long time in reaching San Diego Bay. Overall, of the Catalonian Volunteers who had remained at the death-infested hospital there, only four survived the ordeal. While the expedition was away, the patients had been left under the charge of Father Serra.

They had been expected, upon recovery, to assist in the construction of the newly established mission.[123]

Despite this tragic turn of events, Governor Portolá still hoped to carry out his instructions and meet his objectives. The packet boat *San Joseph* had been scheduled to leave La Paz with supplies three months after the *San Carlos* departed for California.[124] Little did anyone know that the *San Joseph* had been lost at sea.[125] Such was the cost of establishing a base of operations at San Diego.

CHAPTER FOUR

❈ ❈ ❈ ❈ ❈

Portolá's Expedition and the Establishment of Alta California, Part I

FROM SAN DIEGO BAY
TO THE SANTA BÁRBARA CHANNEL
AND THE SANTA INÉZ RIVER,
JULY TO AUGUST 1769

❈ ❈ ❈ ❈ ❈

> When we left this port of San Diego for Monterey we always kept close to the shore . . . until, about a month after setting out from here. . . . We entered the first regular town of the Channel of Santa Bárbara. . . . This place has a pretty river, land and numerous peaceful and friendly Indians. . . . This channel of Santa Bárbara is very well settled. . . . with a very great number of peaceable and friendly Indians.
> FRAY JUAN CRESPÍ | 1770

FROM THE DIARIES, CORRESPONDENCE, AND REPORTS made by members of the expedition, the daily account of the expedition's route, presently known landmarks, and locations of place-names used at the time can be ascertained. A credible description of the Camino Real de California's location at certain points can be confidently rendered using such sources. The documentation produced by Portolá's expedition is the first step toward identifying and authenticating the royal road's origins. The documentary narrative of the Camino Real began at San Diego Bay.

As he stood on the beach pondering his objectives, Portolá, despite being afflicted by scurvy, decided to lead an expeditionary force north to Monterey Bay by land while the summer weather cooperated. Assembling those who could still stand and walk, Portolá ordered them to gather enough supplies and be ready to leave as soon as possible. The men's condition would ebb and flow as they marched north from and back to San Diego during the next six months. Unlike those who remained on the beach, they would recover. Ailing from scurvy and its attendant inflammation, they suffered from swollen and bleeding gums, leg and body cramps, and fever, along with the effects of near-starvation and poor diets and diarrhea caused by the consumption of foodstuffs from the wilderness. The hard work of trailblazing included slashing their way with machetes through thick undergrowth, breaking through rock, reconstructing level pathways with pick and shovel, and constructing makeshift bridges from poles and dirt for the mule train to cross over.

It was July 14, 1769 when the expeditionary force loaded their mules with supplies to carry out their primary objective: to find Monterey Bay by land. Among those performing the king's business with the *real* were Portolá, Rivera y Moncada, twenty-seven *soldados de cuera* (leather-jacket soldiers), Miguel Costansó, and Pedro Fages, plus a few friendly Indians carrying shovels, axes, crowbars, hoes, and other tools essential for military operations. With five of the Catalonian Volunteers dead and fourteen seriously ill left at San Diego Bay, Fages's effective command on the expedition totaled just six Catalan soldiers.[1] Unsung but important to the expedition, dogs, used to guard the campsites and for hunting, ran alongside the mules and horses.[2] From this small, humble beginning, the expedition blazed a route from which would evolve the Camino Real de California with all of its manifestations.

Father Juan Crespí served as diarist, chaplain, and missionary of the expedition. He wrote in almost surrealistic fashion that they crossed over verdant hills populated by rabbits and hares in abundance. The beauty of the land must have appeared incongruous to the men, given their feverish condition. Traveling along the wild coastline and keeping the mountains to their right, they reached an Indian settlement at a place that formed a rinconada "which is made by this second bay."[3] Nearby were some waterholes with fresh water. They called the place "ranchería de los ojitos de agua de la rinconada de San Diego."[4] Men, women, and children from the settlement came out to greet them in friendship. From there, they left the beaches of the bay, and two and a half leagues later, entered a canyon between some hills that also held potable water, pasture, and woods.⁵ There, at a place they called "pocitos de la cañada de San Diego" (Pools of the Valley of San Diego),⁶ Crespí wrote that "we stopped the *real* [i.e., the expeditionary force] near the referenced waterholes."⁷ In some places, these were caved-in or too shallow to draw enough water. The soldiers used their shovels to dig them wider.⁸ Their campsite was the first point beyond San Diego that would form the route and corridor of the later Camino Real de California. For Portolá and his men, it would be the first of many *reales*, or campsites, along the California coast for the next five hundred miles. That night, local natives brought them sardines, for which the Spaniards traded with glass beads and clothing.

The next day, July 15, they traveled another two and a half leagues. Portolá sent scouts ahead of the main force, sometimes for days at a time. That day, they passed through a small valley they named "el valle de Santa Isabel, reina de Portugal."⁹ They named the *real* "San Jácome de la Marca." Crespí noted that eighteen men, women and children lived in the settlement and wrote that they were "affable and not so aggressive as those in San Diego."¹⁰

On Sunday, July 16, after Crespí and Fray Francisco Gómez had celebrated the Holy Mass, the men loaded their mules, but did not leave until after 2:30 in the afternoon. By the end of the day, they had traveled six leagues (nearly sixteen miles) from San Diego. Still heading north, they crossed over some hills. After two and a half leagues, they saw another settlement. The natives came running to greet them. Crespí noted that they named the place "la cañada del Triunfo de la Santíssima Cruz." Nearby, they found a small waterhole, which they named "el ojito de agua de la cañadita de los Encinos." That evening they stopped the *real* near an Indian settlement and named their camping place "la lomita de la cañada de San Alejo." Today it is known as Batequitos Lagoon. At that point, Crespí wrote "I observed our latitude and it proved to be thirty-three degrees, exactly."¹¹ For the next six days, July 16 to 22, the expedition marched north through the Soledad Valley, San Dieguito Canyon (near current-day Del Mar), Buena Vista Creek (near Carlsbad), the future site of San Luis Rey Mission, Las Pulgas Canyon, and Cristianitos Canyon (north of San Onofre).¹² They kept careful notes of the people, flora, and fauna they saw along the way. At a place they called "beato Simón de Lípnica," they entered a valley close to the beach but out of sight of the sea. It seemed to them by the look of the terrain that perhaps there could be a saline flat nearby.¹³

Beyond San Alejo, on Tuesday, July 18, they came across two large Indian villages with more than forty people. Although Crespí named the place San

Juan Capistrano, the first mission established near there several years later was called Mission San Luis Rey. The party noted the possibility of saltpeter in the area, for Crespí wrote that "*aunque algo parece que pinta en salitroso en algunas partes.*"[14] The next day, Crespí located the site at 33 degrees and 6 minutes.

By, July 20, this early phase of the expedition had traveled thirteen and a half leagues (about thirty-five miles) from San Diego, to near present-day Carlsbad. Crespí observed the latitude where they camped to be 33 degrees, 8 minutes.[15] The next day, they reached present-day Las Pulgas Canyon. Probing northward, they came to a place they called "Santa María Magdalena," today's San Juan Capistrano. Near there, natives from a village approached them and told Crespí and his fellow missionary of two very sick and dying children. With the mothers' permission, Crespí and Gómez baptized the children as María Magdalena and Margarita—and in so doing, Christianized them. The place, north of San Onofre, is now known as Cristianitos Canyon.[16] Although deathly ill, the little girls were still alive when the expedition departed.

On Sunday, July 23, the group camped at the "arroyo de la cañada de Santa María Magdalena." They noticed that the local Indians had dogs with black-and-white markings.[17] There they took a reading of the altitude at 33 degrees and 14 minutes.[18] They were now twenty-five leagues (65 miles) from their starting point. The first week's travel established Portolá's line of march from San Diego toward present-day San Onofre and continued initiating a trail that marked a corridor of travel for the next two centuries, through which California's modern highways would run.

The following week, beginning on July 24, they continued their march from the area of the ranchería at Santa María Magdalena,[19] which would become the site of Mission San Juan Capistrano. The *real* stopped to rest nearby on a long mesa with dark loamy soil on its east side.[20] That night, they camped at a place they called "Señor San Francisco Solano."[21] Their march had taken them to the foothills of the Santa Ana Valley, near El Toro, where they traded with friendly Indians, whom Crespí hoped someday to introduce to Christianity.

The scouts rejoined the main force at this point and reported that they had seen six islands off the coast about a day's ride from a hill where they stood.[22] Quickly consulting the maritime maps and documents Portolá had with him, they identified them as the San Clemente Islands,[23] which had been known under various names since Cabrillo's time in the early 1540s. In 1602, Sebastián Vizcaíno renamed them "San Clemente" in honor of the saint's feast day. Portolá's next targeted place would be San Pedro, as shown on the coastal maps at his disposal. At Señor San Francisco Solano on July 25, they took another reading and located the place where they stood at latitude 33 degrees and 18 minutes.[24]

At sundown, the men stopped to camp and were approached by more friendly natives, with whom they exchanged beads and ribbons for quantities of edible seeds, which the Spaniards called "chia." In areas between San Diego and north of Los Angeles, Costansó noted, the natives gathered these seeds, placed them in large bowls carved from wood, and threw heated pebbles in with them to toast the chia without burning the bowls. Once toasted, the seeds were ground with a pestle. That done, they probably added water to make a paste for porridge or tamales.[25] Once in that zone along the California coast, Crespí noted that the members of the expeditionary force appeared to be recovering from scurvy. At other times, especially when they were not eating the Indian foods, they would relapse. This must have been mystifying in a time before the discovery of vitamins and the conditions caused by diets deficient in substances such as vitamin C. It certainly explains why the men on the expedition fared much better than those left behind on the beach at San Diego. Crespí also noted that once they had moved up the coast toward Santa Bárbara, where little or no chia was traded, the men seemed to suffer relapses.

Anthropologist Jan Timbrook addresses the topic in her article "Chia and the Chumash: A Reconsideration of Sage Seeds in Southern California."[26] She writes,

> The most detailed information is found in Crespí's journals of the summer of 1769 and spring of 1770. These indicate that the food offered by the natives changed from one region to another. Chia was prominent all through the interior valleys from the Juaneño-San Gabrielino border to the Thousand Oaks vicinity of Eastern Chumash territory; from there to the Santa Bárbara Channel, roasted yucca heads were common; and along the channel the gifts were all in fish. According to Crespí's diary, for example, the explorers were presented with bowls or baskets of "chia de refrescar" or "chia para refrescar," which seems to be refreshing drink prepared from chia seeds. The published version [of Crespí's Diary] refers to "baskets of sage and other seeds."[27]

Timbrook's article supports the benefits of chia to members of the Portolá expedition, which may account for his men's recovery or temporary relief compared to those who remained at San Diego. While Portalá did not lose a single man to the effects of scurvy, many on the beach who did not have the benefit of native foods died.

While at Señor San Francisco Solano on July 24, the party could hear coyotes and wolves howling nearby in the night. Sitting around a campfire with the Spaniards, the natives told them about other Spaniards they had met who had come there from the interior lands to the east. Crespí wrote, "They led us to believe that in the interior there are people like us, they dress the same as the soldiers, that they carry swords, sombreros, and have mules, pointing to the mule train we had; who knows what it can be?"[28] Portolá's men could only ponder about the identity of these people. Could they, as Crespí wondered, have been New Mexican traders? During the seventeenth and eighteenth centuries, New Mexicans had been, contrary to Spanish policy, trading clandestinely with Utes in present-day southern Colorado and Utah as far west as the Great Salt Lake and the Great Basin.[29]

On July 26, after spending the day prior resting, they left the *real* at about three o'clock in the afternoon. They moved northeast and through a small canyon in search of the waterholes of which their scouts had told them. Near a dry lake that they had passed earlier, they found and camped at a spot with two, which they named "Los Dos Ojitos de Agua de San Pantaleón."[30]

By July 27, they had traveled thirty-three and a half leagues (about eighty-seven miles) from San Diego. The expedition passed by Santiago Creek, in the hills northeast of Orange, where they camped. Having traveled since six that morning, they were in the vicinity of the Santiago Hills east of Tustin. They took water from a small creek they named "Señor Santiago Apóstol,"[31] after Spain's patron saint, Santiago, which still bears that name today. Spotting a nearby Indian settlement, they traded beads for food with them. They observed the latitude as 33 degrees and 36 minutes.[32]

Not far from there on Friday, July 28, at about four o'clock in the afternoon,[33] the men and their animals were shaken by a violent earthquake. Portolá's diarists were the first Europeans to record a California quake and the three aftershocks that followed it. Crespí noted that although he named the place "Dulcísimo Nombre de Jesús de los Temblores,"[34] the soldiers simply called it the "Río Santa Ana," by which the Santa Ana River is known today. That night they camped near Olive, east of present-day Anaheim.[35] Fifty-two natives[36] came to their camp and the expedition traded beads and a silk handkerchief for seeds and some meat from antelope and hare. The natives showed them nine belt knives without handles (*belduques sin cabo*), five awl tips without the eye, and a long, thick metal rod measuring about 16 inches. The Indians also showed them some white-colored rocks that appeared to be fine crystal.[37]

Again, the Indians told them about other Spanish traders who had entered the area. They insisted that these men had had priests with them and that they came from the north. Crespí speculated, "We do not know if it could be that they [the Indians] communicate with New Mexico, or with the Apaches, or that there is some other nation that has intruded through the interior land from the north, to where they [the Indians] have pointed."[38] However, it seemed probable that the mysterious "New Mexican" traders from the east had left these items. After all, the Indians said the traders looked just like Crespí and his comrades.

The next day, July 29, Portolá's men reached a place they called "Ranchería de la pocita y valle de Santa Marta," north of present-day Fullerton.[39] Soon after, they moved over some hills and found water, where they camped. Nearby was an Indian village whose inhabitants had been celebrating with a feast and a dance.

By Sunday, July 30, after another week of toil, they were forty leagues (approximately 104 miles) from San Diego. By then, the expedition had passed present-day Fullerton and reached the area of La Habra near the Puente Hills. Crespí wrote that the arroyo was terribly muddy. Worried about getting stuck in it, the soldiers constructed a bridge.[40] That day, Crespí observed the latitude to be at 33 degrees and 24 minutes. They called the valley "San Miguel Arcángel,"[41] today known as the San Gabriel River Valley. They set up camp near present-day Bassett. On the afternoon of July 31, they felt another earthquake.[42] Crespí reckoned that they had experienced seven or eight since they had left Jesús de los Temblores.[43] By then, they had covered forty-two and a half leagues (110 miles) from San Diego to El Monte, south of present-day Mission San Gabriel.

The expedition spent Tuesday, August 1 resting in camp while scouts surveyed the pathway ahead. Crespí noted that a tremor that hit about 10:00 a.m. Several others shook the ground throughout the afternoon. That day, he observed the latitude at 34 degrees and 10 minutes.[44] Costansó, whose readings were always higher than those taken by Crespí, recorded their position at 34 degrees, 30 minutes.[45]

The first week in August found the Spanish expedition along the Los Angeles River about three leagues from San Miguel Arcángel. On August 2, they named the valley and the river (near where tremors had plagued them as they moved along the Elsinore fault line into the San Fernando Valley) "Nuestra Señora de los Angeles de la Porciúncula."[46] Crespí wrote that they had felt fourteen tremors since Jesús de los Temblores.[47] They continued to visit native settlements and meet their chiefs, and engaged briefly in a lively trade for native foods with Spanish glass beads.

By August 3, they had reached the Alisos de San Estévan at Ballena Creek west of La Cienega. Nearby they noted "springs of pitch," or tar pits. Historian Herbert E. Bolton later surmised that they were at La Brea.[48] There, they traded tobacco and beads for baskets of pinole made from sage and other grasses. The chief also gave them strings of shells.

By Friday, August 4, the men had crossed present-day Ciénega, heading in the direction of Santa Mónica and Sepúlveda Canyon. Not far from there, one of the Catalonian Volunteers reported that while hunting for antelope and wild goat in what today would be Greater Los Angeles, he had seen still more tar pits,[49] the Spanish name for which, "La Brea," readily gave the area its modern toponym. Crespí wrote that scouts, in crossing the basin, reported having seen tar issuing from the ground like springs, which boiled up molten with water running to one side and tar to the other. The scouts reported that they had seen as many as forty pools as well as large marshes filled with molten tar, enough "to caulk many ships."[50] Although Crespí wanted to go see them, Portolá discouraged it because they were out of the way. Crespí said they were named "Los Volcanes de Brea" (the Tar Volcanoes.)[51] Costansó observed the latitude to be at 34 degrees and 22 minutes.[52] Another area place-name was the "Antelope Springs," or literally the Springs of "El Berrendo,"[53] probably present-day Serra Springs (California Historical Landmark #522). Soon, the expeditionary scouts hunting deer and antelope reported they had explored beyond El Berrendo, probably to a point near present-day Santa Monica.

On August 5, Portolá's men camped in a place they called "Santa Catalina de Bononia de los Encinos," near present-day Encino, in the San Fernando Valley.[54] Their camp was just northwest of today's Mission San Gabriel. Crespí took the latitude there at 34 degrees and 37 minutes.[55] North of El Berrendo, the explorers marched along a beach with steep mountains that did not allow easy passage. There, they turned northwest and saw a pass in the mountains. Bolton believes that the expedition had been on the beach west of Santa Monica and that the pass was Sepúlveda Canyon.[56]

The next day, Sunday, August 6, while still in their Santa Catalina camp, some natives approached the party and said that, in the past, they had seen Spanish ships along the coast. One warrior knelt down and drew the channel on the ground to show where the ships had passed. The natives said that they had made contact with some Spaniards who had come ashore. That piqued the curiosity of the expedition's members, along with their observation, specifically made by Crespí, that some of the children had blond or brown hair.[57]

Then the warriors said something that astonished them. Santa Catalina de Bononia de los Encinos was the third settlement where the California Indians told them about "bearded men" from the east. The first time was on July 24 at San Francisco de Solano, the second on July 28 at Dulcísimo Nombre de Jesús de los Temblores. And now, on August 6, many of the Indian informants spoke up, wrote Crespí, to say "that in about ten or fourteen journeys [days], pointing to the northeast, that there are people like us, pointing at the soldiers with their swords, arms, and horses; who have houses and who also had three priests with them, pointing at us. In that referenced faraway place there was a sea and many buffalo, and that those people had come by horse to their land and returned." While the natives added much to what they said, Crespí wrote of their mentioning that they had sent three or four warriors with them as guides for the beginning part of their return.[58]

Did Hispanic New Mexican traders who had been trading with the Utes, possibly as far west as the Great Basin, reach California from the interior, probably reaching points of Los Angeles, before 1769? When the natives described a place with a large body of water, which the Spaniards translated as *mar* or "sea," could they have been referring to the Great Salt Lake in the land of the "Yutas"? After all, since sometime after the 1650s, New Mexicans had known about a place called Teguayo, later Timpanogos, on the shores of a great salt lake.[59] Or could the Spaniards mentioned by the California tribes have been part of an unknown expedition from Sonora? The Jesuits of that period, who had explored as far north as Baja California and the mouth of the Colorado River, would certainly have written about such an intrusion.

Astonishingly, there was yet a fourth mention of Spanish traders from the east. At one of the rancherías along this stretch of the trek northward, Costansó mentioned that he noticed pieces of a sword and fragments of worked silver, which appeared to be of low quality. Using signs, he asked the natives how they got these items. Their response was that the pieces came from the interior to the east. Even though New Mexico was far away, Costansó conjectured that through trade and over time, these items could have reached there.[60] Yet, as referenced above, New Mexicans had been traveling to the Utah country for trade since the middle-to-late 1600s. When the first of these reached the salt lakes is unknown, as is the date they might have crossed into California. If the

California natives were correct about their presence, the unauthorized New Mexican *entradas* must have occurred prior to 1769 at the latest.

The week from August 7 to August 15 found the expedition moving northward at a very slow pace. Almost everywhere they went, they stopped at Indian settlements and traded glass beads for food. At nearly each place, Crespí wrote in his diary "paramos el real," meaning that the expeditionary force stopped either to rest or to camp for the night. Having departed the *real* where they had camped on August 6, the expedition spent August 7 moving through an area they called the Valle y Poza de Santa Catarina de Bononia.[61] Having departed late that day, about at 3:00 p.m., they headed north and stopped in a canyon for the night at the foot of a mountain. The canyon had oak trees, cottonwoods, and laurels. This was good farming land, was lush, and had water. Wheat could be grown there, the men remarked. At that point, they had traveled fifty-seven and a half leagues (about 150 miles) from San Diego. Historian Bolton wrote that the party was in the San Fernando Valley, northwest of present-day Mission San Fernando.[62]

The next day, August 8,[63] they continued for three hours and three leagues of marching through the canyon they had entered at the end of the previous day. Again they remarked on its excellent potential farming soil. They reached the mountain and ascended to a high pass. Bolton surmised that the expedition crossed over San Fernando Pass near Newhall.[64] Upon descending, they entered a small valley. A warrior who had accompanied them from their camp at Santa Catarina de Bononia was still with them. Somewhere along the way, another native had joined him. As the expedition progressed, natives from the settlements came out to meet them and traded with them for food. One place they visited was called "Ranchería del Corral" by the soldiers because it was nothing more than an enclosure for protection against wild animals. Bolton wrote that this was on the Santa Clara River near present-day Castac in Los Angeles County[65] They named another of these rancherías the "Pueblo Santa Rosa de Viterbo." The natives there wanted them to stay: they were so accommodating that they even brought firewood to their camp.

All that day, they had followed the valley along an arroyo in which they said began the long canyon they had called "La Cañada de la Señora de Santa Clara."[66] They remained there through August 9, recuperating from the previous day's trek and sending out scouts. That day, Crespí observed the latitude near Santa Rosa de Viterbo to be 34 degrees 47 minutes. At that point, they had traveled sixty-one and a half leagues (about 160 miles) from San Diego.[67]

The next day, August 10, the expedition continued west-northwest through the twisting canyon before turning west-southwest.[68] The scouts told them that they had another day in the canyon. They traveled for three hours and three leagues. At the end of the day, they estimated that they were sixty-four and a half leagues (about 168 miles) from San Diego. Marching west-southwest along a river bank, they walked along a sandy path. They stopped to camp for the night near present-day Camulos Rancho[69] at Piru, California. Crespí noted that the terrain that formed the canyon had high mountains on either side, with a very steep summit.[70] They were still in the long canyon on August 11 and followed an arroyo for some distance.[71] By the end of the day, Crespí wrote, "*Paramos el real cerca de este arroyo*," where they camped for the night.

Near their camp was an Indian settlement with subterranean houses. These were round and large, with thatched roofs. The excavations were deep and the residents used ladders to come out through the roof tops.[72] That afternoon, seven chiefs visited the expedition's camp with a number of warriors carrying their bow-strings loose, as a sign of peace. They brought seeds: acorns, walnuts, and piñon. When they learned that Portolá was the commander, they offered him and his officers necklaces made from white, black, red stones, similar to coral. Crespí estimated that Portolá gave glass beads to more than five hundred natives in return.[73] Crespí took the latitude there as 34 degrees 30 minutes.[74] That day, they estimated that they were sixty-seven and a half leagues (about 175 miles) from San Diego.

By August 12, the expedition had marched another two leagues and remarked that they were now sixty-nine and a half leagues (approximately 180 miles) from their starting point. That day they reached a place near the canyon they called the "Ranchería de San Pedro Moliano del Pueblo de Santa Clara."[75] Bolton noted that this settlement was near present-day Fillmore.[76] The canyon they followed continued to twist to the southwest as it seemed to narrow.

The next day, Sunday, August 13, after Mass, the men broke camp about 3:00 p.m. Still plagued by earth tremors north of Fillmore, they followed the canyon bearing southwest.[77] Judging from the terrain, they concluded after one league of marching that they were getting near the end of the winding canyon. After two hours, they had marched two leagues and arrived at the abra, or narrow pass made by the mountain.[78] They stopped at a place they called the "Ranchería de los Santos Mártires San Hipólito y Casiano."[79] This settlement was along an arroyo with much water "which we would call at this point a river."[80] Bolton noted that this was near today's Santa Paula. The part was now seventy-one and a half leagues (about 186 miles) from San Diego.⁸¹ The atmosphere was misty: in the distance they could see something that was either a grove of trees or a bay. After they set up camp, Crespí and Father Gómez went down to see the river, which was a good distance away.

On August 14, the group continued down the Cañada de Santa Clara at 7:00 a.m. At this point, they sought a landmark from their maps, "la punta de la Concepción."⁸² Diligently, they traveled along a long curve on the land. At a certain spot, they could see a high mountain point along the coast which they thought might be their goal. They also noted that the land curved and formed a cove in the shape of a half moon.⁸³ They met many natives along the way. They named a nearby place "Asunción de María Santísima de los Cielos" because the two priests hoped that they could return someday and set up a mission there that they would call "misión de la Asumpta."⁸⁴

After two and a half hours, they had traveled two leagues and a half along the coastline and arrived at a very large settlement. The wife of the chief greeted them, saying that her husband was out fishing. After sunset, the chief with many people visited the Spanish camp and brought pinole and different kinds of fish.⁸⁵ Portolá, in return, gave them ribbons and beads. In the afterglow of that day, Spaniard and Indian sat communicating amicably with each other into the evening. The Indians told Portolá that the river forked downstream from their current location. The explorers noted that the stream did not carry a lot of water on the fork that they followed, for it reached only to the knees of the horses.⁸⁶ According to the natives, the other fork downstream carried more water. Near this place, on August 14, they observed the latitude to be 34 degrees 36 minutes.⁸⁷ Bolton notes that the expedition had reached the site of present-day Ventura.⁸⁸ On Monday, August 14, they camped near an Indian settlement they called "La Asunción de Nuestra Señora," near the future site of the Mission San Buenaventura.

Surviving place-names and latitudinal readings related to the Spanish "*reales*" or campsites can generally be identified in relation to the nearby Indian settlements. Although Miguel Costansó's and Father Crespí's readings differed, they, along with the later establishment of a mission in that area, support identification of the location where they stopped. Somewhere near the Santa Bárbara Channel, for example, Costansó read that they were at 34 degrees and 13 minutes, while Crespí argued that when he observed the latitude at ten o'clock in the morning, they were at latitude 34 degrees and 36 minutes.⁸⁹ Costansó, using his instruments, took the following data:

The height of the lower limb [of the sun] . . . 69°42'

Semidiameter of the sun to be added . . . 16'

In consequence of the observer's eye being six to seven feet above sea level, subtract . . . 3'13"

Meridian altitude of the center of the sun . . . 69°55'

Zenith-distance . . . 20°5'

Declination of the sun for the meridian of this place, 106° to 107° west of the Isla del Fierro . . . 14°8'

Latitude of the town . . . 34°13'[90]

At that place, they encountered natives who had come from the Santa Bárbara Channel, who told them that other islanders were on their way to see them. Later, after Portolá and his men had set up their campsite, a group of Indians brought them food and visited with them.

Travel was slow at times as the men marched through difficult but unavoidable places. Continuing their march west along the beach on the edge of the sea, on August 15, 1769 they crossed the river, which cost them time and work because it was stony, with high water that reached to Crespí's stirrups.[91] Other places presented other problems for the fatigued explorers. Moving westward, they came to another ranchería, where they stopped. Crespí credited the soldiers as having named present-day Pitas (Whistle) Point, north of Ventura. Warily passing the night, sentinels observed natives dance to music made from flutes or whistles. Some of the soldiers, trying to sleep, complained that the noise from the whistles kept them awake all night. In the margin of his diary, Crespí annotated the day's entry that "*Hoy en esta ranchería empezaron a pitar de noche.*"[92] They named the village "Santa Cunegundis, del Pueblo de la Asumpta."[93]

Departing the area at 6:30 a.m. on August 16, the expedition continued to the west as they had the day prior. They were accompanied by fourteen warriors who led them to the next ranchería, where they said there was abundant water. The expedition traveled about two hours and two and a half leagues.[94] The ranchería was on the edge of the sea and had about seventy houses, all round with thatched roofs. Apparently, this was a successful settlement, for the Spaniards saw six or seven canoes with men out fishing. These large craft were eight varas long (roughly seven feet) and at each end, or prow, there were two or three men with paddles, which allowed them to maneuver and speed up through the water. The explorers named the ranchería "Santa Clara de Montefalco" and observed the latitude as 34 degrees and 40 minutes. By then, they were over seventy-eight leagues (about two hundred miles) from San Diego.[95] One of the most colorful place-names on the expedition's route was a place the soldiers called the town of "El Bailarín," owing to the chieftain, an exceptional dancer, who apparently performed for them. The dance took place on August 16, near Rincón Point, on Rincón Creek.[96]

Once past El Bailarín, the rest of August saw the expedition meandering its way north past Sepúlveda Canyon. Continuing west on August 17, they crossed over hills and came down a steep incline to the beach. The point made a bay. After marching another half a league, they came to a large settlement with thirty-eight houses, again round with thatched roofs. They entered the village and traded with the natives. Not far from there, they camped on a long plain that ran about a league from north to south. The soil was rich and covered with grass. From east to west, the plain was four leagues long. The mountains were to the north of the plain. Near one of the rancherías, they mentioned finding some small pools of tar.[97] They named the area San Roque, as a place that the priests would one day like to return and set up a mission.[98] The soldiers said that they saw Indians making canoes at a place they said reminded them of a dock. The woodworking natives inspired the place-name still known today as "La Carpintería."[99] Within sight was an island off the coast, which they had missed because of the fog. About five or six leagues to the west of their camp, the mountain stretched into a long point, which they "conjectured would be Point Concepción."[100]

The next day, August 18, the Spanish departed La Carpintería and proceeded past the ruins of a village. The natives told them that "not too long ago . . . about three months," Indians from the sierra had come down and killed all the men, women, and children living in two large settlements.[101] Two leagues beyond there, they came across the second destroyed village. Four leagues and four hours later, they arrived at a place near a large lagoon that they called "Laguna de la Concepción,"[102] present-day Santa Barbara. There, they found traces of bears along the beach. Again, they could see the long, low point they thought to be "la punta de la Concepción." Nearby was another Indian settlement that they called the "Ranchería de San Joaquín de la Laguna de la Punta de la Concepción."[103] Although they could see the islands from where they stood, Crespí could not take the latitude because it was too cloudy.[104] They camped, as Crespí wrote, "two musket shots from the ranchería."[105] Surprisingly, many people from the islands came to see the Spaniards and asked them to accompany them there.[106] Naturally, the expedition could not divert from its planned mission: to get to Monterey Bay.

The next day, August 19, the expedition withdrew from the beach, largely because there were too many people in that area. Crespí noted that they were now eighty-three leagues (about 215 miles) from San Diego. Moving westward, they ascended some steep and high hills and crossed over mesas. The met other warriors who told them that the tribe that had destroyed the two settlements they had seen the day before had tried to do the same to the one they last saw, but the defenders drove them back.[107] On Sunday, August 20, they traveled in a westerly direction on level ground between mountains and hills along the coast. They encountered at least five rancherías that day. Within three leagues of marching, they saw a long point of land bordered on the west by a large estuary. From their campsite, the explorers could see one large, tall island. Later, they could see three or four more with a *farallón* (outcrop) near them.[108] Still unsure that they had reached Point Concepción, they named the place "Santa Margarita de Cortona" with the hope that a large mission would one day be founded there.[109] In the bay was an island[110] that was covered with trees. On the island they reported seeing a large Indian settlement of more than a hundred houses. Beyond were four other prosperous towns.[111] The soldiers named the habitations collectively as "Mescaltitlán," today's Mescal Island;[112] otherwise, some of the men called them merely "la Isla" or "towns of the island."[113]

Crespí's description of the culture of these particular settlements is ethnographically invaluable.[114] Since leaving Santa Catarina de Bononia, the priest had observed that the people of the settlements near Point Concepción along the Santa Bárbara Channel had similar cultural traits. He took note of their activities and, writing through Spanish colonial eyes, commented that in this area almost all of the populations of the rancherías they encountered "lived in well-organized settlements, in well-built houses made of grass, rounded in shape of a half circle. Some of the houses in the center of the settlement were so large that without a problem they could house seventy or more people. It appears that they sleep above ground, because inside they have tapestles or platforms that are two varas high, long and wide."[115] Crespí noted that the tribes were governed by "two, three, or four chieftains," one of whom was the principal chief. He wrote that these *capitanes* had two women, while other tribesmen had only one. He also noted the wooden flute and whistle music played in their

68 CHAPTER FOUR

dances. There, he wrote, they wore "large headdresses of feathers. The rest of their body is painted with many colors which appears to be a grand costume. All of the people are nude and they have splendorous colors adorning their heads." Of their cultural customs and traditions, the burial practices and sites intrigued him:

> They bury their dead and they do have cemeteries: one for men and the other for women. All are enclosed by tall pointed poles, painted with various colors, and some standing wooden slabs painted in the same style which encircle or enclose the cemetery which have very large spirit protecting whale bones. In all of the cemeteries there are one or two circular piles of rocks very delicately carved, which could very well serve as fonts for holy water, and even for baptismal fonts. They have another section very clean with many standing rocks all around with much plumage fixed in the middle, which we conjecture are for their prayers. They also have another place, very clean, a stopping place in the middle of which is nailed a very large whale bone. Thus, when they die, they take the dead to this last place to watch over them, as in a wake. They place the head of the deceased to rest on a whale bone. If it is one of their own men, they bury him in the men's cemetery. They hang a long lock of the hair of the deceased on one of the many poles. If it is a women, they do the same. They take the deceased woman to the cemetery. There they hang on one of the poles a painted wooden wash pan or stone utensil belonging to her. Thus, one sees many of these items in the two, men and women's cemeteries.[116]

Before departing the campsite on August 21, Crespí observed the latitude to be 34 degrees, 43 minutes.[117]

On Monday, August 21, they set out from Santa Margarita de Cortona at 2:00 p.m. Heading west in the direction of the coastline, they traveled two leagues over high hills, within sight of the Pacific Ocean. Their march was blocked by large arroyos flooded by rain in the mountains, which they kept to their right. At some places, the mountains came close to the shore, while at others they retreated, leaving level ground between them and the sea, sometimes as much as a league wide.[118] The men marched for three hours before stopping, in which they went two and a half leagues. They set up the *real* near two large rancherías, where they estimated that they were now eighty-seven and a half leagues (nearly 228 miles) from San Diego. They called the place

"San Luís Obispo." Crespí said the latitude was 34 degrees and 45 minutes.[119] There, they spent Tuesday, August 22 resting as the scouts went out and returned saying that within four leagues there were at least three or four waterholes that did not flow to the sea. They also said that there were some steep canyons along the way and that while on the way out along the shoreline, when they returned the tide had risen along their same path.[120]

On Wednesday, August 23, the group left early, at 6:30 a.m., and crossed an arroyo with water running to the sea. As the sea had risen, they had to go over the hills, some of which were cut off from the sea. Passing over ravines and gullies, they crossed other arroyos. Having marched for four hours, they traveled four leagues through areas with live oaks before reaching two rancherías, one of which had forty-two houses and the other thirty-seven.[121] Continuing west, they stopped to camp and trade as Portolá sent out his scouts. They named the place "San Guido de Cortona." From there, they could see "two islands, a small one to the south and a large one to the southeast."[122] Crespí continued that these appeared "to be the Farallón de los Lobos which Cabrera Bueno asserts falls in front of a low long point of land which juts out to the sea and it is conjectured that it is the *punta de la Concepción*."[123] Referring to the last point that they had earlier thought to be Point Concepción, they agreed that the current one was actually the point they sought.[124] Portolá and his men noted that the Indian settlement of the area was extensive. They reported that the Indians there had fifteen canoes and that there were other villages in the Santa Bárbara Channel.

On Thursday, August 23, Crespí commented on a peculiarity that he had noticed elsewhere in their travels. He wrote that

> We have observed in all of these *rancherías* along the coast line, that in all the larger settlements there are two or three or four men who arrange their buckskin clothing the same as all other natives, and, moreover, adorning their ears, necks and heads like the women; we could not tell if they could be men dressed as women. We see that they are well respected. Because we do not understand what each other is saying, we can do no more than stab at the air with our finger as if figuring out the date on a calendar to determine whether they are one or the other.[125]

August 24 was the feast day of San Bartolomé. After Mass, the expedition moved westward along the beach until they were blocked by the sea and terrain and had to climb up a steep mesa. Moving up and down across arroyos, they found water for themselves and their animals. After three hours of marching, they had traveled two and a half leagues and reached a large settlement near the edge of the sea with a small creek running into it.[126] Along the way, they found other Indian villages and camped in a valley which led to the salt-water estuary. There they saw a village with fifty-two houses and about three hundred people.[127] They named the place "San Luis Rey de Francia."[128] That day, however, the soldiers killed a seagull and renamed the place "La Gaviota," as it is still known today, near present-day Santa Barbara. At that settlement, they met an Indian they called "El Loco," who accompanied them as a guide for many days, not only on parts of their explorations when they were traveling north but also when they returned south months later.[129] On August 25, before breaking camp, Crespí observed the latitude to be 34 degrees and 47 minutes. From a certain point along the coast near the Santa Bárbara Channel, they estimated that they were now ninety-four leagues (about 245 miles) from San Diego.[130] From there they could see "the last three islands of the channel of Santa Bárbara. They are," wrote Crespí, "San Bernardo, the most western; Santa Cruz, which follows to the east; and Santa Bárbara, the most eastern."[131]

By that afternoon at 2:30, the expedition was heading west, as it had on previous days. They passed the ranchería and continued along the coast to a point where they climbed a small mesa along the steep sides of the mountain. All day, they were up and down mesas and at other times marching along the beach. After three hours, they had made only two leagues. The going was tough through rough terrain. The fourteen Indian guides who led them told them that the route they had taken was the best of all alternatives.

That day they did not see a single tree, nor fuel for their fire, only bare land and grasslands. Finally they came down to the edge of the sea. They came to a ranchería with fifty houses and possibly two hundred inhabitants.[132] From there they saw the last two islands in the Santa Bárbara Channel. They were confident that in front of them was Point Concepción. They arrived at a settlement that they called the "Ranchería de San Zeferino Mártir." Their scouts told them that ahead were mountains with pine trees.[133] A cold wind blew in from the north. Crespí began to worry about what the temperature might be in the winter months if it was that cold in August.[134] Miguel Costansó took a reading and observed the latitude to be 34 degrees and 30 minutes,[135] which appeared to be at variance with Crespí's observation of the day before. Costansó's remarks were as follows:

The horizontal altitude of the lower limb of the sun, observed with the English octant, facing the sun, was found, at noon, to be . . . 65°47'

Semidiameter of the sun to be added . . . 16' Inclination of the visual [horizon] in consequence of the observer's eye being six to seven feet above sea level, subtract 3'13"

Horizontal altitude of the center of the sun . . . 66°00'

Its zenith-distance was found to be . . . 24°00'

Its declination at that hour was . . . 10°30'

Latitude of the town . . . 34°30'[136]

The next day, August 26, the group came to a settlement they called the Ranchería de Santa Ana.[137] Moving along the beach, they ascended a mesa and traveled over it for nearly three hours, crossing ravines that contained flood water from the mountains. In the distance, about a league from a visible ranchería, they could see another point of land jutting out into the sea. Talking among each other, they reckoned that it must be Point Concepción. Near there they noted another settlement. They called the area of the two settlements the Rancherías de Santa Teresa. Crespí took a reading of the latitude and noted that it was 34 degrees, 51 and a half minutes.[138] At the second settlement, the soldiers met a chief who walked with a notable limp. It was little wonder, Crespí said, that they dubbed the place "Ranchería del Cojo." The present-day Cañada del Cojo has retained that name.[139] Interestingly, Crespí noted that they had left a lame mule[140] at that place, which they would recover later on the return trip.[141]

Breaking camp at 2:15 p.m. on Sunday, August 27, they continued going west over low-lying mesas for two and a half leagues. Shortly, they arrived at a low-lying, barren point of land which they again hoped would be Point Concepción, as it jutted far into the sea. The descriptions they had seemed right. This should be the spot, wrote Crespí, because "according to Cabrera [Bueno] the sea and the land twist toward the northeast."[142] Verily, the explorers stood where the Santa Bárbara Channel meets the Pacific Ocean and forms a corner between the east-to-west-trending portion of the coast as it bends northward along the coast near Santa Barbara. Today, it marks the natural division between Southern and Central California. Oddly there were no rancherías in that area.[143] As they had been moving westward throughout the day, Crespí again took a reading of the latitude and observed that they were still at 34 degrees and 51 and a half minutes.[144]

That day, an unexpected new place-name appeared on California's map. It occurred when a careless soldier, Corporal Ochoa,[145] had his sword stolen as he, lost in the moment, watched a group of natives fishing in a canoe. Before he realized it, a quick-moving warrior had slid his sword from its scabbard and fled with it. Not realizing that he had been robbed, he walked away. But other honest warriors chased the thief into the water, took the sword, and returned it to the soldier. The expedition rewarded the warriors for their honesty with a gift of beads and named the Indian settlement Ranchería de la Espada. The village's water source took its name from the incident and is today known as Espada Creek.[146]

On Monday, August 28, the group traveled northwest over a hill; half a league later, they went through a small pass with good grasslands that ran to the sea. Some time later they found a water source and stopped to camp. They calculated that they were now 103 leagues (about 268 miles) from San Diego.[147] They visited a nearby village of ten dwellings in which lived about seventy people. The soldiers traded with the Indians for flints. The group named this place "La Ranchería de los Pedernales de San Juan de la Punta de la Concepción,"[148] today's Rocky Point. Father Crespí preferred to call the village San Juan Bautista, because August 28 was the saint's feast day.[149]

From their camp, the could see another point of land, about a musket shot away.[150] They reasoned that between that and Point Concepción there had to be a good bay. They called this second point "Punta de San Juan Bautista de los Pedernales"; it would later also be known as Point Arguello. Of the two points, Crespí wrote that "from Concepción Point to the other point of San Juan Bautista de los Pedernales, are two islets in a large bay which is formed by these two points that form the end of the Santa Bárbara Channel." Crespí noted that the larger one was closer to Point Conception and that the Farallón de los Lobos was a part of the formation.[151] Near it was a smaller point. From there, the coastline ran northwest.[152]

Passing the second point at about 1:15 p.m. on Tuesday, August 29, the group left the settlement heading northwest. Guided by four or five natives, they marched on level ground along the beach. Spotting the second point[153] and one other beyond it, they confirmed that there was a large bay between them. Next, they crossed an arroyo that carried fresh water toward the sea. Soon after that, they encountered a large sand dune, which they crossed with difficulty. It was nearing 4:30 and they had made but little headway, roughly two and a half leagues. Luckily, the expedition had brought enough water in large bags for its horses, as the place was arid and had barely enough water "with which to make tortillas."[154] Noting that the sun was setting, Portolá stopped to camp. They named the place "La Cañada Seca" (Dry Canyon), but Crespí called it "Santa Rosalía."[155] The campsite was near present-day Surf, California.[156]

After friars Crespí and Gómez celebrated Mass on Wednesday, August 30 in honor of Santa Rosa de Lima on her feast day, the expedition set out following a northwest line of march. Guided by local natives, they crossed a long stretch of dunes until they came to a large river with fresh water. Crespí said it was "more than a hundred varas wide and ran to the sea."[157] It was the Santa Inés River, the widest river they had seen thus far. They named the area "Santo Mártires San Bernardo y Sus Compañeros."[158] Crespí, on the other hand, wrote that "because we arrived on this day [meaning a feast day] we called it the Río Santa Rosa."[159] A reading of the latitude was made by Costansó and Crespí at 34 degrees and 55 minutes.[160]

The next day, August 31, they headed north over sand dunes and scattered shells before reaching some hills. Contradicting his account, Crespí wrote, "we left this camp and the large and deep running Río del Señor San Bernardo." After three hours, they stopped to rest near a large pond of fresh water "eighty varas across."[161] Ahead of the expedition, the scouts reported, there was a very large waterhole. Crespí wrote that it was seventy or eighty varas long.[162] Just past the Santa Inéz River, they stopped to camp near present-day San Antonio Creek.[163] Natives from a nearby village entertained them that night with dancing. It was the "first place we saw the women dance,"[164] wrote Crespí, "for which reason this lagoon is known by the name of El Baile de las Indias."[165] (The soldiers called it "La Graciosa.") The place was "in a hollow, surrounded by hills, not very high. The water comes from a spring, at whose source there is a good watercress, tender and savory. We named the settlement near the body of water ranchería de la Poza de San Raimundo *Nonato*, as it was his saint's day."[166] Bolton concluded that it was San Antonio Creek.[167]

CHAPTER FIVE

✻ ✻ ✻ ✻ ✻

Portolá's Expedition and the Establishment of Alta California, Part II

THE SEARCH FOR MONTEREY BAY—
FROM THE SIERRA DE SANTA LUCÍA
TO SAN FRANCISCO BAY, SEPTEMBER
TO NOVEMBER 1769[1]

✻ ✻ ✻ ✻ ✻

The time that we spent going and coming was six months and eight days. We did not find Monterrey in all the distance that we passed over; and I do not know whether it exists or not. We did find the Sierra de Santa Lucía, which is a high, white, rough mountain, very steep at the sea. . . . we found a point of pines at about six or eight leagues distance, and . . . we explored the mountain twice with the greatest care possible.
FRAY JUAN CRESPÍ | 1770

AS THE PORTOLÁ EXPEDITION moved slowly forward, they sought landmarks that had been located and named by earlier explorers and ship commanders. Portolá and his officers and diarists matched latitudinal readings used by Manila Galleon pilots with their own and found that they matched closely. As they moved north past Santa Bárbara, their interest and focus on their main objective to reach Monterey Bay sharpened. Nearing the Santa Lucía Mountains, they found their way north blocked by a large escarpment that jutted out into the sea. Their alternative was to go around it by crossing the mountain range. About fifteen miles north of present-day San Simeon, they turned inland over the rugged terrain looking for a route that would bring them back to the coast. Their passage through the mountains in search of the Río del Carmelo, an important landmark leading to Monterey Bay, was blinded as they lost sight of important topographic features and the visual continuity of the coastline. Until then, they had verified what they saw with the maps and documents they carried. Now, their trust in what they saw would be tested from their vantage points on land by comparing it with the information they carried in the form of reports and logs of places seen from passing ships.

September brought cooler weather as the expedition continued northward. Breaking camp at about six o'clock on a foggy Friday morning, the first day of the month, the expedition headed north from the Poza de San Raimundo.[2] Crossing through sandy areas, they came to a verdant pasture with water, sprouting tules (bulrushes), and many ducks. Beyond it, they continued trudging over sand dunes for nearly a league. Moving toward a wooded area, they descended to a valley after traveling a league and a half. Having marched for four hours over difficult terrain, they reached another valley three leagues wide and more than seven leagues long. In the middle was a large lake, which their scouts had reported on a day earlier.[3] Crespí reckoned it must have been five hundred varas long and "of unknown length, for we could not see the end."[4] Portolá halted the *real* to camp near a ranchería located on the bank of the lake.[5] There were two villages, one small, the other larger. The people there met them with gifts, mainly baskets and pinole. Crespí called it the "Laguna Grande de los santos mártires San Daniel y sus compañeros."[6] Bolton surmised that the expedition had described present-day Guadalupe Lake. The natives told them that the large lake reached the beach along the coast and that it flowed into an arroyo that entered the sea.[7] They also said that in about six days the expedition would reach the last of four mountains. There, they would see a river with many trees, some of which bore edible fruit. They conjectured that it was the Río del Carmelo. Portolá and his men understood from the natives that possibly there was a bay after they passed the river and the trees.[8] Crespí observed the latitude to be 35 degrees and 13 minutes.[9]

The next day, Saturday, September 2, at about 8:15 a.m., they left the lake. Marching north, they crossed the valley and approached a small mountain. After four hours and a quarter, during which they went about three leagues, they reached a lake about a hundred varas long and forty-five varas wide. Not far from there, the scouts said, was another laguna that was longer. Nearby were two rancherías. Six warriors came out to meet with the group. The encounter was friendly and Portolá learned that they were not far from the sea.

Throughout the wilderness, the soldiers saw many tracks left by bears, which they hunted that afternoon.[10] The one they killed measured "fourteen spans from the soles of its feet to its head." The paws were one span long, and the bear probably weighed less than four hundred pounds. They named the lake "Holy Martyrs, San Juan de Perucia and San Pedro de Saxoferrato."[11] Meanwhile, at the camp, some of the soldiers complained of pain and soreness in their legs.[12] They stayed there the next day, September 3, to recuperate. Sergeant Francisco de Ortega had been suffering greatly from fatigue and had a stomachache throughout the night. Herbal suppositories were applied to him for relief. The soldiers called the camp "Real de las Víboras" for the many snakes in the area. Others called it the "Paraje del Oso Flaco."[13] Historian Bolton explained that it is still called Oso Flaco Lake, or Lake of the Lean Bear.[14] While there, they noticed that the mountain chain they could see in the distance was probably a part of the *cordilleras* to their right, which they had been following from as far away as San Diego.[15]

Early the next morning, Monday, September 4, at about 6:30 a.m. the men left the laguna heading northwest. Going over some large dunes, they descended toward the sea about half a league away. Bounded by the laguna, they could go only in that direction.[16] Walking along the beach for a while, they turned north-northwest and, again encountering some dunes, headed toward another small mountain.

Turning farther inland, they veered somewhat eastward. Again, they crossed some sand dunes and finally found solid land through which they could pass between two bodies of water. Crespí wrote, "At the right we had a lagoon of fresh water which was bordered by the dunes and prevented it from emptying into the sea; on the left we had an estuary which penetrated into the plain. We rounded it by turning to the northwest; then we took the road to the north and entered the mountains through a valley grown with live oaks, alders, willows, and other trees."[17] There, they stopped to camp near an arroyo of running water. The natives came out to visit them, bringing fish and seeds, for which the Spaniards gave them some glass beads. Crespí wrote that their chief had a large goiter "which hangs from his neck. On account of this the soldiers named him El Buchón"[18] (from *bocio*: goiter), a name also retained for the village. Crespí called it "San Ladislao." That day they had covered four leagues and met with Indians in a very small settlement without houses, who greeted and fed them.

Bolton determined that the men were in Price Canyon, north of Pismo. Crespí took the latitude at 35 and 28 minutes.[19] That day, they estimated that they were 118 miles from San Diego.[20]

On Tuesday, September 5, they broke camp at 6:30 a.m. and marched over rough country within sight of the beach. They stopped at a narrow valley surrounded by high hills. The friar called the camp "Cañada de Santa Elena," the soldiers "Cañada Angosta," or narrow canyon. Crespí said it was at latitude 35 degrees and 3 minutes."[21] Bolton wrote that this was today's San Luis Canyon. At the end of this day's entry, Crespí wrote a special note: "Each one of the two arroyos of this ranchería has its own canyon. The scouts learned that the one that runs from the north-northeast along the upper canyon expands wider, and has much more flat land and runs a good way with much grass. This canyon has many and large waterholes of good, potable water."[22]

The next day they began traveling at sunrise. They followed one arroyo that ran northeast as it twisted in its course. After a league, the canyon ended and they ascended the mountain for about a half league. Then they descended into another canyon that opened into a valley with many pools of fresh water.[23] Until this point, they had not seen any natives or settlements. After three hours of marching, they camped near an arroyo with fresh water, which they called "El Arroyo de Santa Elena."[24] Bolton identified the place as another area of San Luis Canyon.[25] The expedition members believed that they were not far from the Río del Carmelo. While the scouts went out to look for water for the next day's march, Crespí observed the latitude as 35 degrees, 33 minutes.[26]

Portolá and his men spent the next day, September 6, resting, largely because the mules were fatigued and Captain Rivera y Moncada and his scouts did not return until early in the morning. They had found it necessary to repair the pathway for the mule train along points where they would be passing on their next march. On September 7, the band headed northwest but, upon entering a winding canyon, soon found themselves turning in several directions. They entered a valley full of ferocious bears that had dug many holes looking for some savory roots. It was said that the natives in the area lived off the roots as well—however, there were no settlements in the area owing to the large bear population. The scouts had warned the expedition about the bears, some of which they hunted and killed with much difficulty because of their size. After marching four more hours, the men camped along what was officially Chorro Creek[27] but the soldiers called "Los Osos." Crespí disagreed as usual: he wrote that because "we arrived [during] the vigil of the Nativity of Holy Mary, we named the place la Natividad de María Santísima." Bolton said the spot is still called Cañada de los Osos and is located a few miles west of San Luis Obispo.[28]

On Friday, September 8, the feast day of the Nativity of Holy Mary, the churchmen celebrated Mass before the group broke camp, heading westward toward the sea. Deep gulches blocked their path and the soldiers had to prepare the road so that the pack train could pass through them. Of the six arroyos, the soldiers repaired three of them for a safer and easier passage.[29] Crossing through the hilly, treeless terrain, they came upon a valley that they named "El Vallecito de la Ranchería de San Adriano de la Natividad de María Santísima."

Finally, they had come within sight of the sea, and stopped alongside an arroyo to gather fresh watercress. Near there was a very small settlement whose residents seemed to be nomadic, for they did not have houses. About sixty people came out to see the Spaniards and presented them with porridge made of roasted seeds that "tasted like almonds."[30] The governor, as usual, returned their favor with gifts. From their camp, they could see the estuary with a "great rock in the form of a round morro, which, at high tide, is isolated and separated from the coast by a little less than a gunshot."[31] Because of the foggy and cloudy day, they were unable to observe the latitude. The place, wrote Bolton, was Morro Creek: the estuary is now called Morro Bay and the rock in front of their camp, Morro Rock.[32]

Saturday, September 9 found the expedition heading northwest over treeless mesas. They were now 128 and a half leagues from San Diego.[33] After four hours, they had traveled three leagues, moving along the beach when they could, but largely through rough terrain. Along this route, they crossed seven arroyos with water running from the mountains to the sea. At the eighth arroyo, they made camp.[34] Crespí found the latitude to be "exactly 36 degrees," but wrote that Costansó said it was 35 degrees and 27 minutes.[35] They named the place "El Arroyo y Estero de la Cañada de la Señora Santa Serafina."[36] That night, the scouts returned, saying that they had found an arroyo that followed a wooded but hilly terrain. They were uncertain if they were approaching the Río del Carmelo.[37] Costansó's observations with his instruments were as follows:

The horizontal altitude of the lower limb of the sun, observed with the English octant, facing the sun, was found, at noon, to be . . . 59°21'

Semidiameter of the sun to be added . . . 16'

Inclination of the visual [horizon] in consequence of the observer's eye being six to seven feet above sea level, subtract . . . 3'13"

Horizontal altitude of the center of the sun . . . 59°34'

Its zenith-distance was found to be . . . 30°26'

Its declination at that hour was . . . 5°1'

Latitude of the place . . . 35°27'[38]

After Holy Mass on Sunday, September 10, the party followed a valley toward the northwest for two leagues, which took them two and a half hours to cross.[39] They had been following the large arroyo through the valley mentioned by the scouts, which indeed had an abundance of pine trees. As the valley turned north, they left it and bore northwest. From there, they could see a mountain range covered with pines and a very deep valley with cottonwoods and other trees. Marching along the arroyo, they came to a large waterhole. They stopped there, near a settlement. Soon, about sixty men came to greet them with baskets. The Spaniards gave them beads in return. The Indians presented them with a little bear that they had reared, but the Spaniards did not accept it. They did, however, name the place "El Osito," Little Bear. The good priests preferred to call it "El Arroyo del Pinal de San Benvenuto," which they thought to be a good name for a future mission. Crespí observed that latitude to be 36 degrees and 2 minutes.[40]

The next day, Monday, September 11, they traveled on the seashore toward the northwest. It turned out to be a typical cloudy day along the California coast. Moving forward, they found water at a place the soldiers called "El Cantil." Costansó, wrote Crespí, read the latitude as 35 degrees and 35 minutes,[41] a variance with Crespí's reading the previous day. Bolton placed El Cantil at Little Pico Creek, near San Simeon Bay, east of San Simeon Point.[42] On this leg of the journey, the men crossed over mesas and low hills along the beach. Following a straight line, about a hundred paces from the pine tree line and two hundred paces from the sea, they walked about a league and arrived at another arroyo that formed a large water hole near the beach. Along that route, they did not see any Indian settlements. However, six Indians visited them and showed them other watering places. Again, the soldiers had to repair the road so that the mule train could ascend below the pine tree line.[43] From there they went another league over low-lying mesas, where they came to two arroyos with running water. After two more leagues, they stopped on a mesa that had been burned. It was close to a third waterhole formed by the arroyo. They named it the "Arroyo de San Nicolás." Beyond it was a larger waterhole. They did not assign names to the waterholes,[44] basically so that they could be a part of nearby San Benvenuto later when a mission could be established. Crespí noted that almost all the rancherías in the area had dogs of all colors and some even had tamed coyotes.[45]

Herbert Bolton wrote that Tuesday, September 12, the expedition party ascended the Arroyo Laguna and followed it to Arroyo de la Cruz.[46] It was another cloudy day when they broke camp at 6: 30. They walked along low-lying mesas and hills close to the beach as they headed northwest. They moved toward the mountains, went through a pass, and came out heading northwest. They walked about three and a half hours, making about three leagues. It was slow moving because they were ascending and descending hills along the way and had to cross about six arroyos. Crespí wrote that "the land was very rough and much broken; on the road, there were many arroyos and gullies full of water, and they gave a great deal of trouble fixing the bad spots that we found."[47] Shortly, they came to what seemed to be a forest of laurels; Crespí said they were not laurels, but two or three similar species. They were about two and a half leagues from San Benvenuto when they passed an area that looked good for a future mission. Crespí called it "San Juan de Dukla." There, along the seventh arroyo, which was large and deep, they stopped the *real*. They named the arroyo "El Arroyo Grande de San Vicente."[48] Their camp was at the edge of a deep valley. Near there, at the foot of the sierra with a long pine tree line on top, was a settlement, from which six men came out to talk to them. They were now 135 leagues (about 350 miles) from San Diego. Crespí observed the latitude to be "north of 36 degrees and 10 minutes."[49]

At daybreak on Wednesday, September 13, the expedition headed northwest. Marching along a high mesa at the foot of the sierra, they descended along an arroyo that did not reach the sea. Throughout, the expedition experienced particularly rough terrain. They marched northwesterly for two leagues, partly through the valley and partly along the referenced high mesa with a steep incline to the sea. They followed the escarpment for most of the day.

They stopped at midday between two arroyos. Indians at a nearby settlement of five houses came by to greet them, with baskets filled with pinole and fresh fish. The Spaniards gave them gifts in return. Looking at the rugged mountain range in front of them, Crespí wrote that it was the "Sierra de Pinos or Santa Lucía."[50] The men set out after their rest but the rough terrain soon proved too much for them. (Bolton noted that they were near Ragged Point "on San Carpoforo Creek. Here, the coast becomes impassible."[51]) Portolá ordered the expedition to stop for a few days while Captain Rivera y Moncada and his scouts "went ahead to explore this arroyo and sierra to see what kind of passage it could have or to assess what kind of work the trail would need."[52] It appeared that the coastline was blocked by the high mountain. Crespí, with hopes that one day a mission would be established there, at the foot of the Sierra Santa Lucía, about a half league from the mountain, named the place with three waterholes "Santa Humiliana de la Playa."[53]

The next day, September 14, Captain Rivera y Moncada and his scouts returned and reported to Portolá that they had found a pass, but that the road needed to be repaired by "pick and bar."[54] Thus, the expedition was stalled at the camp from September 13 to the morning of September 16, while the soldiers worked on the road ahead. By the night of September 15, enough work had been done to lead the expedition into the first part of the pass.[55] The entire time, according to Crespí, the sun had not shone.

On September 16, the men set out northeastward, away from the sea, and entered the valley that led to the pass that they believed, based on their documents, to be the beginning of the Sierra de Santa Lucía. Also, they understood from the natives that "on the other side of the mountain was the Río Carmelo with its port and that of Monterrey."[56] Bolton's analysis placed the expedition moving up San Carpoforo Creek to its junction with Chris Flood Creek.[57] The trail was only as good as the reconstructions made by Portolá's men. Indeed, as Crespí wrote, the mountain valley was very narrow, perilously steep, and "inaccessible, not only for men, but also for goats and deer."[58] Laboring to move forward, the expedition crossed and recrossed a large arroyo that ran through the middle of the valley before they reached a good place to rest and eat. This impediment, which they identified as "El Arroyo Grande y Hondo de la Sierra de Santa Lucía," ran between two mountains, one higher than the other, "which is the one we need to follow."[59] About a league beyond, they passed through a large forest with many species of trees, some of which they could not identify. Somewhere in that large canyon, they stopped to camp.

Looking ahead, they knew they had to construct the trail because their line of march was hampered by the steep slope of the pathway they were taking to get out of the area. At the bottom of the slope, the arroyo forked "where the two arroyos meet to form one with a fast current to the sea. One runs northeast, the other north-northwest, which is the course of the one we need to follow through the mountain."[60] Afterward, the soldiers went back to open the trail over steep, rough, and stony terrain, some of which they had to ascend in order to move forward. Fog set, in blocking the sun and making it impossible for Crespí to take a reading of the latitude. They were now 138 leagues (nearly 360 miles) from San Diego.[61] They named the stretch of the trail where they camped the "Pié de la Sierra de Santa Lucía" (Foot of the Sierra de Santa Lucía).[62]

Sunday, September 17 was no better. Their direction would be northwest for most of the day. Even though it was the feast day of St. Francis, the patron saint of his order, Crespí acknowledged that there was no place to celebrate the Holy Mass and decided to forgo the Sunday prayers in lieu of the main objective: to find a way out of the mountains. Besides, it was not going to be an easy day. After two hours, they had traveled only one league. Everyone was tired, for it had taken everyone in the camp to work to construct a passable trail. That day, they began to ascend the high slope of the mountain so that they could go over its crest. Breathing heavily and "with a prayer in our mouths,"[63] they made the climb, followed the ridges that formed the valley below, and continued moving northward.

Once over the top, Crespí noted that going down was easier. They could see an arroyo below, probably the arm that they had been following the day before, and discerned that it was the one they needed to follow northeast from the foot of the slope so that they would exit the mountains. They trekked up and down, through canyons and over long and steep skirts, until they finally halted in a hollow that had water, firewood, and pasture.[64] Nearby, they saw a ranchería of sixty to eighty natives, who approached the Spaniards and asked them to accompany them back to their settlement, which they said was on the way to where they wanted to go. Crespí called the place both the "Paraje de Santa Lucía de Salerno" and "La Hoya de la Sierra de Santa Lucía" and named, as patron saints for the natives there, San Francisco and Blucía de Sulermo. Crespí hoped someday to establish a mission there called Monte Alverne. He observed the latitude to be 36 degrees, 18 and a half minutes.[65]

Monday morning, September 18, came too soon. Up early, the soldiers were hard at work for the next two days preparing the trail for the next part of the march. They finished their work the following day.[66] By Wednesday, September 20, they were up at dawn and ready to ascend a long, steep skirt of the mountain. Leveling out the march, they went along the slope of the valley, narrow and deep as it was, for it carried water. Crossing winding arroyos, sometimes two or three times in a row, they finally found a broad stretch of terrain and were able to climb to the top of the mountain. Worn out, the men, pulling and herding their jaded animals, were disappointed at what they saw: more mountains without surcease. Through steep hills, woods, sand dunes, swamps, and stony ground, the soldiers had worked hard all day clearing and repairing the trail for better footing. A cold snap set in and the soldiers, some of them still afflicted by scurvy, were barely able to move forward. Somehow they managed to travel for five hours, covering two leagues. Somewhere in that wilderness, they stopped to camp in a small, very narrow valley. They stayed there to rest for a day and a half (September 17, 18, and 19), and to finish with the construction of the trail.[67] Oddly, they encountered natives, where they thought there was no one around. They were picking pine nuts. Their settlement was not far from the camp. They named the place the Camp of Piñones, now known to be near Burros Creek, west of the Nacimiento River. That day, September 20, they traded beads for pine nuts.[68]

Meanwhile, on September 19, Captain Rivera y Moncada and his scouts returned to say that there was a better camping place not too far away. Before they could move there, however, they again had to repair the trail to get the mule train through.[69] The next day, September 20, at about 6:30 a.m., they broke camp and headed north, following the course of the arroyo along the skirt of the mountain. They passed four smaller arroyos, all with running water. Beyond them, they began to climb the mountain over a sharp ridge which cost them much time and labor. After five hours, they camped by another arroyo.[70] All the while, they had marched only two leagues.[71]

That evening, they met with other natives from three to five settlements and again traded beads for pine nuts. They estimated that there were six hundred kind souls in the area.[72] Some of the Indians were from the coast, others lived on the mountain, and a third group said that they lived along a river near a bay on the other side of the mountain. With great hope, the explorers conjectured that the river must be the Río del Carmelo.[73] They stayed at that camp for two days so that both man and beast could recover from the hardships they had suffered.

After Holy Mass on September 21, the soldiers went out to work on the trail. By 1:00 p.m., the workers came back to say the trail was ready to cross. An hour later, the expedition moved out due north, crossing through the mountain for about two hours in which they traveled only one league. They came to a stream that they thought was a river. It ran west to east and wound around in many places. Somewhere in that wilderness, they stopped to rest and learned that there was a settlement nearby. Beyond that was another bay.

The next day, September 22, Captain Rivera y Moncada and his scouts went out again to explore what lay ahead. This time, they explored far ahead of the expeditionary party. They returned late the following evening and said that they had gone as far as twelve or fourteen leagues, to a valley covered with fog and pine trees. On this trek, they believed they had reached the Río del Carmelo and, in the distance, they thought they could see its bay.[74] That would mean that they had reached land close to the ocean. But they were wrong. Their camp, as they noted, was near the headwaters of the Río San Elzeario.[75] Herbert Bolton surmised that they were along the Salinas River.[76]

To the men's dismay, they were still far from their destination, Monterey. In the meantime, they still had to contend with their present-day reality deep in the mountainous valleys with only a ray of hope that they would soon be out of that forbidding terrain. Crespí observed the latitude to be 36 degrees 28 minutes. They had remained at that camp for three days.[77]

On Sunday, September 24, they set out again at 7:30 a.m., after celebrating the Holy Mass. Leaving their camp along the Río San Elzeario, they went north over low-lying hills. Ascending over higher hills within the Sierra de Santa Lucía, they followed some small canyons through a forest of pine and different kinds of oak trees. After two leagues, they came to a large arroyo that ran through a canyon. Both ran northwest to southeast. They named the area "El Grande Arroyo y Cañada de las Llagas de Nuestro Señor Padre San Francisco."[78] In the next day's diary entry (September 25), Crespí wrote regarding the place-name, "I dedicated this arroyo to the impression of his stigmata, reserving that saint's name for the famous town, as his Excellency the visitor-general [José de Gálvez] said to our father president [Father Serra] at the camp of Santa Ana before taking leave of him."[79] It appears that the name San Francisco was reserved and would only be applied to a place deemed to be particularly special by Governor Portolá and/or Father Serra. Because Crespí had used it only for an arroyo and a canyon, Gálvez's instruction was not violated. Within the area was an Indian settlement. Crespí hoped a mission could be established there.

The scouts went ahead to see if the expedition should continue to the end of the canyon, which they hoped would lead them to the Río del Carmelo.[80] Following a large stream of water (which Bolton figured was the San Antonio River, near Jolón),[81] they descended a slope going eastward, then wending north and twisting to the east until they stopped to camp. The terrain through which they passed had an extensive forest of large white and live oaks. The area where they camped had plenty of water and pasturage.[82] Nearby was an Indian settlement. The natives told them that the stream flowed into a river, which the Spaniards figured was the Río de las Truchas.[83] They also learned that in the winter it was very cold, with heavy snows as deep as eight to twenty-four inches. Crespí estimated that they were at latitude 36 degrees 30 minutes,[84] not much different from his previous reading.

Monday, September 25 found the expedition moving north through a series of eight contiguous round limestone hills. They had left their camp at about 2:00 p.m. and had completed only one league of travel the entire afternoon. Wending their way north and northwest, they noted that the hills were covered with oaks. Much of the grass had been burned by the natives, so there was no pasturage for their animals along the route. They came to a small waterhole where they filled two barrels of water. Their guides led them to a canyon that had enough grass for their beasts. Crespí noted that they were 145 leagues (about 377 miles) from San Diego.[85]

On Tuesday, September 26, the group broke camp at 6:30 a.m. and crossed the valley along stony ground to the northeast. Following the tree line of oaks along the lime-covered hills, they passed through a canyon for about a league and a half. There they found a village of nearly two hundred people, whom Portolá actually counted. The natives did not have houses, but they did share the seeds and piñon they had. The Spaniards, in return, gave them beads. It seems that a few days before, the scouts had passed by the settlement and left a fatigued mule, which the people of the settlement fed and watered. The Indians had helped the animal recover and now returned him to the soldiers.[86] The scouts went ahead hoping to find the Río del Carmelo. Meanwhile, the expedition paused to rest at the village and then moved on to the next canyon. Leaving the hills and the tree line they had been following, they came to a wide forested canyon, in the middle of which ran a large river. Bolton surmised that they had descended Kent Canyon and reached the Salinas River,[87] the one which the scouts a few days earlier thought was the Río del Carmelo. The expedition stopped there after having traveled for four hours and covered four leagues.[88]

The next day, September 27, they broke camp at 6:00 a.m. and followed the river valley to the northwest. Crossing the river at their first opportunity, they followed it as it flowed northwest, where it narrowed, forcing the expedition to move up into the hills.[89] That day, they marched four leagues in five hours and camped near some cottonwoods at a place they called the "Real del Alamo." Crespí observed the latitude to be 36 degrees and 38 minutes.[90]

On Thursday, September 28, the expedition traveled northwest along the canyon over burnt land without pasturage for their horses and mules. Along the way, they found a well-worn pathway made by the natives, although they had not seen any settlements. They observed many herds of antelope of varied colors. After five hours, they had walked four leagues. They stopped along the banks of the same river that they had been following through the canyon.[91] Bolton figured that their camp at Real del Alamo was near today's Metz, a day's march from their next camping place, the "Real Blanco," near Camphora.[92]

On Friday morning, September 29, the feast day of St. Michael the Archangel, the party celebrated the Holy Mass and departed Real Blanco about eight o'clock. Moving northwest along the river through the wooded canyon, they walked for four hours, making three and a half leagues. There they stopped for the night. They were now about 160 and a half leagues (about 417 miles) from San Diego. As they settled down, the men were suddenly disturbed when a bear came dangerously close to the *real* and killed some of their dogs.[93] Later, from their camp along the river, they heard a great deal of shouting and followed the sounds. It turned out that the local warriors were hunting, but when they saw the Spaniards they stopped, for they were surprised and had not seen them until that moment. They began to blow on a pipe and throw dirt into the air. The Spaniards backed off, realizing that they had interrupted some sort of activity. They did not know where the Indians came from, for they never saw a settlement in the area.[94] They named the place "Real de los Cazadores" (Camp of the Hunters), which Bolton believed to be near Chualar.[95]

The next day, Saturday, September 30, they traveled northwest and west-northwest along the twisting course of the river, seeking a way out of the mountains. The path they followed was treacherous and the mules hesitated and struggled to keep their balance.[96] They noticed that little by little, the hills were getting lower and the valley was beginning to widen. Again Crespí noted that even though they had walked along a beaten path made by natives, they did not see a single ranchería.[97] That night they camped where the soil was "whitish and short of pasture on account of the fires set"[98] by the Natives. The Spanish camp was not far from the river.

From their location, they could hear the pounding and the roar of the sea in the still, quiet air, but they were still too far away to see it.[99] At that point, they were two and a half leagues from the coast. (Bolton thought the camp was below Old Hill Town.[100]) From their camp, they could see two mountains that formed two points, which they conjectured were close to the beach. The point of the mountain to the west had a river running along it. It was not far from the camp along a west-northwest alignment. The other mountain, to the north of them, was far away, but not too tall. Discussing what they saw, they conjectured that that the river was the Río del Carmelo, near what they guessed was the Punta de los Pinos (Point of the Pines). This raised their hopes that they would soon finally be out of the mountain and that they were not too far from Monterey Bay.

That afternoon, the scouts returned to confirm that two leagues and a half from where they stood was a beach with a large bay, from which could be seen two points at the far end, with many tall trees at the point that lay to the south.[101] For now, they held fast to the description written by Cabrera Bueno.[102] At first, Portolá and his men thought that, because of the mountain that took days to cross, they had missed Monterey and it was somewhere south of them. The Punta de los Pinos was a clue to finding Monterey. But according to the scouts, this lay to the south. What to do? Portolá's documentary sources based on notes by mariner Joseph González Cabrera Bueno indicated that Monterey Bay was situated "between the Point of the Pines and Point Año Nuevo."[103] They must have scratched their heads as they read his description:

> From this Point [Año Nuevo] the coast runs more to the east, making a large bay until it comes out from a point of low land, very heavily forested to the very sea, to which was given the name of Punta de los Pinos, and is in 37° of latitude. . . . It is heavily grown with pine forest, as I have said, and forms near the southern point a maze of barrancas, which is a sign by which to recognize it. . . . On the northeast the Punta de [los] Pinos forms a famous harbor, and by steering straight one may enter it and run close to the land in six fathoms. . . . it is a good port in which to succor the China ships, because the land is the first they see when they come to New Spain. Following the coast from the Point of the Pines toward the south-southwest there is another fine harbor running from north to south. It is sheltered from all winds and has a river of very good water and of slight depth, whose banks are well grown with black poplars very high and smooth, and other trees native of Spain. It comes down from very high, white mountains, and is called Río de Carmelo, because the friars of this Order discovered it.[104]

To add to the discussion, Crespí had observed that their party was quite far north and that they were at "thirty-six and a half degrees," not thirty-seven. For that reason, once on the beach, Portolá decided to backtrack and make sure.[105] Costansó recorded that they were at 36 degrees and 30 minutes.[106]

Somehow, reaching and confirming the location of Monterey Bay proved to be an elusive task. The problem is that these explorers were looking for an enclosed bay or port. The one they saw was wide open to the sea. They simply could not believe that Cabrera Bueno would recommend a bay open to the sea, where storms could wreak havoc on anchored ships. So they thought that the geographic space between the start and end of the large mountain they had crossed—that is, the Sierra de Santa Lucía—held the secret to the Monterey Bay. They had envisioned and hoped to find a safe harbor defined by two points jutting out to the sea. Perplexed, they were determined to solve the riddle. To do so, they would need to explore northward for nearly 120 miles to identify the next known points on their agenda between Punta de los Pinos and places south of Point Reyes.

It was Sunday, October 1, 1769. After Mass, the expedition broke camp and followed the river to the beach a league from their old camp.[107] They set up a base camp near today's Blanco, California.[108] Crespí wrote that their camp was named the "Paraje y Río de Santa Delfina."[109] They would remain there until October 7.[110] Portolá, Costansó, Crespí, Rivera, and four or five others climbed a hill and looked down at the great bay. They conjectured about what they saw. It seemed to fit the description given from the sea by Cabrera Bueno. Portolá sent a detachment under Captain Rivera y Moncada to explore the Punta de los Pinos, which they figured was seven or eight leagues away. They also calculated that the distance from point to point, that is from Punta de los Pinos to Punta del Año Nuevo, was ten or twelve leagues.[111] Doubts, however, lingered, even after they saw the two points jutting out to sea.

The next day, Monday, October 2, Crespí observed the latitude at the camp as 36 degrees and 53 minutes, while Costansó, using the gnomon method, read it at 36 degrees and 44 minutes. Modern-day latitudinal readings may shed some light on Cabrera Bueno's calculations depending on his location, on or near Monterey Bay, when he made his observation.[112] Early that morning, Captain Rivera y Moncada and his scouts left the camp bound for Punta de los Pinos to ascertain whether they were in the vicinity of Monterey Bay or not. They needed to know if, in their detour through the mountain, they had passed the bay somewhere to the south of them.[113] On October 3, they returned at midday and Rivera y Moncada reported that they had not seen a harbor either to the north or south of where they supposed the bay to be. They did, however, see a point covered with pines and after passing it, a small bay beyond that and another one further south with an arroyo that came down from the mountains and emptied into the estuary. Bolton noted that they had reached the Río del

Carmelo and its bay.¹¹⁴ They continued southward and came to the impassable cliff that they figured was the one that had forced the expedition to go inland and over the mountain.¹¹⁵

Upon hearing Rivera y Moncada's report, Portolá called all of his officers together to compare notes on the location of Monterey Bay. Scouting parties had reported a discouraging description. They simply could not believe what they were seeing. Portolá had recent maritime maps dated to 1734 that showed the location of Monterey by sea. Lieutenant Pedro Fages explained,

> We knew not if the place where we were was that of our destination; still after having carefully examined it and compared it with the accounts of the ancient voyagers, we resolved to continue our march; for having taken the latitude, we found that we were in 36°44' while, according to the reports of the pilot, Cabrera Bueno, Monterey should be in 37°, and so serious an error was not supposable on the part of a man of well-known skill. The configuration of the coast did not agree either with the accounts which served us as a guide.¹¹⁶

Between what they were looking at, what they perceived, the documents, and the disparity between the topographical features in front of them and the ones described in writing, Fages had summarized their perplexities on the issue.

Portolá reconsidered the group's options and, on Wednesday, October 4, called a meeting to discuss the dire situation. First, they had a problem with the latitudinal observations by Crespí and Costansó with that of 37 degrees given by Cabrera Bueno. Second, they were not sure if they had passed Monterey Bay or it still lay ahead. Third, the two points appeared correct, but were they? Portolá called for a vote by his officers to decide whether they should continue northward along the coast. But first, the two friars, Crespí and Gómez, would celebrate Holy Mass and pray for guidance.¹¹⁷

Their situation, as Portolá saw it, was not good, as the men were ailing, the animals were fatigued, and their supplies were almost depleted. Many of Rivera y Moncada's men were still suffering from scurvy. Some had many sores; eight of the eleven soldiers could barely walk and could not work; some were paralyzed; others were crippled by their ailments.¹¹⁸ Given their health, most of the men could not be used to open the trails if needed, or to perform other chores such as guard duty or tending to the animals, especially at night. In addition, he was constantly having to send out available men to scout the terrain.¹¹⁹ To add to Portolá's woes, they believed that had not found Monterey Bay by land.

90 CHAPTER FIVE

Too, the weather was changing at this far northern latitude and no one knew what to expect as autumn turned to winter.[120]

The weather had not been merciful as cold snaps and fog made the men's lives all the more miserable. Hunger followed them with every painful step they took. Crespí noted that they had not, since the Ranchería y Cañón de San Elzeario, seen a single Indian settlement.[121] In many ways, even though they had hoped that Spanish ships would supply them by now, trading with the natives for seeds, acorns, and other foodstuffs with glass beads had kept the expedition going.

They were now 168 and a half leagues (about 437 miles) from San Diego, with no relief in sight. The vote was to keep exploring northward despite their travails beyond Cabrera Buenos's notation of 37 degrees north latitude to make sure the old records were not in error.[122] In regard to measuring the distance from San Diego, the expedition now began to measure the distance forward from Cabrera Bueno's Monterey Bay. Portolá and his men, by all reason, thought that they were where Monterey Bay should be, but they doubted it based on the difference between the latitude given by the mariner and what they were now recording. Either they had passed Monterey Bay because of the detour through the mountain, or it was ahead. They probed in both directions, marked the place where they believed Monterey should be according to Cabrera Bueno, but were still perplexed. Therefore, they hesitatingly accepted that where they now stood had to be Cabrera Bueno's Monterey Bay—which it was in actuality, and which fact they acknowledged weeks later in hindsight. For now, doubt filled their minds. Nonetheless, they now tracked their traveling distance with the base camp as their starting point. At that time, on October 3, they figured that they were three leagues from Monterey.[123]

On October 5, six or seven scouts commanded by Sergeant José Francisco de Ortega were sent out to explore the second point, Point Año Nuevo, that made up the large bay.[124] At the foot of a high mountain, eight leagues from the camp, they encountered several Indian settlements with many people along the banks of a river covered by a large canopy of trees. Ortega and his men believed that they had reached the Río del Carmelo because, from there on, they could see many pine trees and what they believed was a port.[125] Bolton deduced that they had instead reached the Pájaro River near Watsonville.[126]

Ortega and his men returned to camp on the afternoon of October 6 with what, at first, appeared to be good news. They said that earlier that day, they had moved north through the pines and found "tracks of large animals with cloven hoofs, which they judged to be buffalo."[127] Ortega and his men continued forward when, by accident, they stumbled close to an Indian settlement and sent all the natives scrambling in confusion at seeing them approach. The Indians did not permit them to come closer; they made "signs to him to stop, and instantly they all took up their arrows and thrust them into the ground, points down. They did the same with some small daggers and feather headdresses which they immediately brought from their houses. Then they retired and the sergeant, understanding that they had done these things as a sign of peace, approached and took some of the arrows and other things they had planted there."[128] To that, the Indians realized that Ortega and his men had come in peace and accepted them. Having gained their trust, Ortega traded beads for food. Just as importantly, he reported that he had learned "that the river they had seen was the Carmelo, and that, therefore, near that Point of the Pines (Point Pinos), which they said they had seen, must be the desired port of Monterey."[129] Strong-willed Portolá, given that they had camped for five and a half days in that area, decided to proceed a little further north to verify if they were indeed in the correct harbor or if there was another that better fit what they were hoping to find. The next day, he ordered the expedition to resume the march northward.

On this segment of the march, the Spaniards noted that the Indians who had greeted them had soon afterward made themselves scarce. Some had recently abandoned their homes along the path that the expedition had passed.

Wary of their situation, the explorers continued north after breaking camp at Santa Delfina on Sunday, October 7. Heading north-northwest, they entered a canyon that lay between low hills and passed by four lagoons. They walked two leagues in three hours and stopped in a canyon near a waterhole and an abandoned Indian settlement.[130] Travel was slow because many of the men's conditions had worsened. Scurvy had taken its toll. Some of the men seemed on the verge of dying. Crespí and his fellow priest confessed some of them and administered the holy *viaticum* (last rites) to at least two men. These were carried on litters as the expedition made its way, stopping to explore each bay and lagoon that had caused so many detours to their projected route. The men who were crippled by disease hobbled every step of the way. At that point, they had marched from the "supposed" Monterey Bay near Punta de los Pinos to a place the soldiers called "Laguna de las Grullas," a place Bolton ascertained to be near Del Monte Junction. He wrote that "the laguna was perhaps Espinosa Lake."[131] Near there, the Spaniards noted that the Indians had recently abandoned their settlement. At that point, they marked that they were five and a half leagues from the "supposed" Monterey.

Before breaking camp on Sunday, October 8, Crespí celebrated the Holy Mass. Afterward he and Father Gómez administered the viaticum to two of Captain Rivera's soldiers. The day was cloudy as they broke camp at about 8:00 a.m. Moving north through hills and canyons and ascending to a higher level of land, they found travel to be slow as they carried the two sickly men and had to go around a multitude of small lakes. Their path twisted to the northeast with many turns along the terrain. After five hours, they had made four leagues. Along a river, which they believed to be the Río del Carmelo,[132] they saw the settlement that Ortega had earlier surprised with his presence. It had been abandoned and burnt to the ground. Just beyond that point, they stopped to camp. To their surprise, they found a large dead black bird hanging from a pole and stuffed with straw by natives, and so they named the stream nearby the "Río del Pájaro." Bolton said it is still called the Pájaro River.[133]

The scouts went out again, probably on October 9, to explore downriver to see if it led to the beach, if the river flowed a bay, or if a port was evident.[134] The scouts were to ascertain whether there was more to the Sierra de Santa Lucía or if they had left Monterey behind them to the south. Crespí noted that the river was not very deep. He named the place the "Río y Llano de la Señora Santa Ana."[135] The scouts returned from as far away as the point that everyone believed was a tree line of pines. In fact, they reported, these were not pine trees at all. The trees they saw were very tall and thick, with different leaves. The color of the bark on the trunks was red. They were unlike any other tree they had hitherto seen.[136] When the members of the expedition passed by them the next day, Crespí wrote that the trees were "very tall of red color, not known to us. They have very different leaves from cedars, and although the wood resembles cedar somewhat in color, it is very different, and has not the same odor; moreover, the wood of the trees that we have found is very brittle. In this region, there is a great abundance of these trees and because none of the expedition recognizes them, they are named redwood from their color."[137] The expedition left behind a lame mule, suffering from malnutrition, which they recovered later, on their way back to San Diego, from the natives who had nursed it back to health.[138]

Moving northwest for the next two days, their marches became shorter each day as the sick either relapsed or worsened. On October 10, they went northwest and reached the redwood forest. After two leagues of marching, they stopped to camp at a place that Bolton said was at modern "College Lake or Pinto Lake, evidently."[139] The forest was filled with wildlife: stags, deer that looked like mules which were "long-eared and have short, flat tails."[140] The lagoons were inhabited by cranes, and many chestnut trees were in abundance. At their camp, Holy Mass was celebrated and the viaticum administered to three more soldiers. The men reckoned that they were now eleven and a half leagues (almost thirty miles) north of the place they had supposed to be Monterey Bay.[141]

Meanwhile, still doubting that they had actually reached the correct location, a scouting group had been sent ahead to see if the actual bay could be found. They followed the river downstream to the shore to see if it flowed into the sea.[142] They returned to say that, given the terrain and the description—that is, by such signs—they believed that the port of Monterey was near. As if in prayer, Crespí wrote, "It has been decided to send out scouts to explore some days ahead, to see if Our Lord would favor us in that we run into the port at Monterey, because our supplies and medicines are low and getting less and less, and because we have ventured very little from here without knowing when we will be at the port of Monterey."[143] The scouts reported that the entire area contained hazelnut trees. Some of them still bearing nuts had been burned by the natives. The scouts gave some to Crespí, which, to him and the starving members of the expedition, was a godsend. Still, they had no real proof that they were at Monterey Bay.

By October 11, it was evident that more of the men were ill. Some were unable to continue. Three more men were given the viaticum. The expedition stopped to rest for the next few days. Eight scouts under Ortega were sent forward to learn all they could about what lay ahead. They each took three mules for a relay as the animals too were becoming weaker by the day. Crespí observed the latitude on Thursday, October 12: they were at 36 degrees and 57 minutes.[144] When he did so again the next day, a perplexed Crespí wrote that he read it at 37 degrees and 35 minutes. Later, on October 25, he read it at 37 degrees and 30 minutes.[145] Ortega returned two days after leaving camp and said he had gone twelve leagues without seeing any signs of another harbor. He said his party had reached "the foot of a high white mountain range."[146]

The next day, October 15, after Sunday Mass, they moved north again, crossing from one canyon to the next without seeing a single Indian settlement. Finally, after a league and a half, they came to a canyon with water, where they stopped to rest at a place they called "La Laguna y Cañada de Santa Teresa."[147] Bolton surmised that they had reached present-day Corralitos Creek and paused at what is now called Pleasant Valley.[148] Leaving Santa Teresa on October 16, the men marched northwest and shortly turned west-northwest. It was a foggy day as they walked along the same canyon as the day before. Crespí noted that the natives, while around the area, did not show their faces. After three and a half hours and two leagues, they reached a place they called "El Riachuelo del

Beato Serafín de Asculdón" at present-day Soquel Creek.[149] The next day, they headed west-northwest along some mesas from which they could see the sea. They traveled two leagues in three hours, passing three arroyos, one of them large, and many trees along the way. The expedition turned west, not far from the sea, and arrived at a fast-running river. The scouts had reported that the beach formed an estuary with a good bay. They named the river the "Río de San Lorenzo," which still bears that name today.[150] They camped at the river's edge among the redwoods. Oddly, they did not meet any natives. They figured that they were now seventeen leagues (forty-two miles) north of the "supposed" Monterey.

The next day, Wednesday, October 18, they left the river at 8:00 a.m. and headed west-northwest. About 1,500 paces from there, they came to a fast-running arroyo that passed through a series of high hills. Shortly they crossed over a mesa they reached a stream at a place they called Santa Cruz, which still bears that name. Indeed, they named it "El Arroyo de Santa Cruz del Paraje de San Lorenzo."[151] Traveling for three hours and a half, they covered two leagues, crossing arroyos and moving over mesa tops. That day, they looked back and saw that they had left the redwoods behind them. At "the fourth arroyo, which ends in an estuary,"[152] they stopped and named it "Arroyo de San Lucas," today's Coja Creek, where the soldiers constructed a makeshift bridge "with poles and earth before it could be crossed."[153]

On Thursday, October 19, at about 8:00 a.m., they were on their way, still heading west-northwest. The terrain was rough as they crossed along and through many gulches. Crespí wrote that they had crossed at least seven of them. The pathways were filled with obstacles. The soldiers had to work hard to make them passable. The work was dangerous, as the sides of the gulches were very steep.[154] On the last one, a mule loaded with a large cooking pot fell. For that, the soldiers called it the "Barranca de la Olla." After four or five hours, they had traveled only two leagues. They reached the coast, which turned northwest and portended precipitous grades and ravines. From one of them, the men could see "some bare white hills"[155] near where they stopped "in sight of the white mountains." Two streams ran from the hill near their campsite, one to the right of them, the other to the left.[156] Crespí wrote that "the large arroyo ran north-northwest to the shore and forms a large estuary in the same canyon through which water from the sea enters it for about 600 paces."[157] Although they did not meet the residents of the village that they passed near, they did note that the village had been "deserted shortly before."[158] The priests called the place "San Pedro de Alcántara" and the soldiers, "El Alto del Jamón." They were at today's Scott Creek.[159] They estimated that they were twenty-one leagues (nearly fifty-five miles) from the place they had supposed was Monterey.[160]

Getting out of the area along the arroyos and canyon on Friday, October 20 proved to be as treacherous an undertaking as some of the other places they had seen. They had to ascend a long ridge after crossing an arroyo that ran along the foot of the hill going north. The uneven terrain made it necessary to open the trail "by force of a pick."[161] It took at least two hours, nearly all morning, and so they had a late start.[162] The rough terrain of broken hills had them marching along a ridge that dropped to the sea. It led them back to the arroyo they had followed as it ran to the sea. They had managed to go a league and a half. While the rocky coastline ran northwest by north, the valley stretched to the northeast. Crespí named one feature the "Arroyo de San Luis Beltrán" or "de la Salud."[163] Today it is called Waddell Creek.[164] Crespí pointed out that this was "one league before Point Año Nuevo; thus, from Monterey to the Point Año Nuevo is twenty-three and a half leagues."[165] As they were still within sight of the point called Año Nuevo, which was a league from their camp along the beach, the party admitted, "we still found ourselves on the great bay which we supposed to be the port of Monterey."[166]

On Saturday, October 21, Crespí, who had faced one foggy day after another, was finally able to observe the latitude at 37 degrees and 22 minutes. Costansó reported a reading of 37 degrees and 3 minutes.[167] Using his instruments, Costansó recorded the following readings:

> Observed with the English octant, facing the sun, the meridian altitude of the lower limb of the sun was found to be . . . 41°41'30"
>
> Astronomical refraction to be subtracted . . . 1'
>
> Inclination of the visual [horizon] in consequence of the observer's eye being three to four feet above sea level, subtract . . . 2'
>
> Semidiameter of the sun to be added . . . 16'13"
>
> Altitude of the center of the sun . . . 41°54'30"
>
> Zenith-distance . . . 48°5'30"
>
> Its declination at that hour was . . . 11°2'3"
>
> Latitude of the place . . . 37°3'[168]

It rained for the next two days. The men camped for the sole purpose of resting. The sick made but little improvement. The fog hampered any visibility, and the heavy rains made their day that much more miserable. They passed a windy night in a storm that blew in from the sea.[169] Sunday, October 22 was no better. Everyone had spent a wet night and was fatigued from lack of sleep. Some of the men slept out in the open, for there were not enough tents to go around. Portolá, realizing that he could not push his men further, declared another day of rest to dry out. Surprisingly, the sick seemed to have responded positively to the weather and appeared to be recovering. Crespí had thought that the bad weather would make things worse, but he could only praise the Lord for their good fortune. He named the valley "La Salud."[170]

Monday, October 23 seemed to be a better day. They left La Salud, also called "La Playa de San Luis Beltrán," around 8:30 a.m. Following the beach, their only obstacle, which they avoided, seemed to be the precipitous Sierra Blanca. They made their way across some low land and climbed a mesa of level land that turned northwest by north. Traveling two leagues in three hours, they stopped in a little valley between some hills near an Indian settlement. The Indians were expecting them and welcomed the Spaniards with friendship, food, and water. The Spaniards repaid their kindness with much-coveted beads. Crespí described the settlement: "In the middle of the village there was an immense house of spherical form, large enough to hold all the people of the town, and around it there were some little houses of pyramidal form, very small, constructed of stakes of pine."[171] Crespí wrote that the Indians there had tobacco. One old man, in fact, smoked a *"chacuaco* of hard rock, very large, and very well made."[172] The soldiers called this place the "Village of the Casa Grande." It was near Gazos Creek.[173] Crespí called it "La Ranchería de San Juan Nepomuceno."[174]

The next day, October 24, the explorers left the village about 8:45 a.m. following two native guides who took them in a northerly direction, within sight of the sea, across some broad, forested hills.[175] Intermittently between the hills, they could see the Sierra Blanca. Crossing arroyos, canyons, and valleys, they passed by a lagoon,[176] which caused Crespí to think that this spot would be a good place for a mission. He named the place "San Pedro Regalado."[177] The entire area, however, was filled with thorny shrubs, which made walking through the thickets difficult. Crespí wrote, "It is horrible to see the area filled with so much *zarza* [bramble] that is everywhere in this terrain, which impedes much of our way."[178] That day, they traveled seven hours and managed to move two leagues before they camped. Near their camp was a friendly village. They met the natives and described them as "fair, well formed, and some of them are bearded."[179] Crespí thought the place would make a good mission site and named it "Nuestro Padre Santo Domingo." Bolton noted that it was at San Gregorio Creek, near the coast.[180]

The expedition spent Wednesday, October 25 at the camp, resting. The pack animals were greatly fatigued and so Portolá extended the rest another day. Crespí observed the latitude to be 37 degrees and 30 minutes.[181] Meanwhile, the scouts were sent out with the guides to explore the area. Extremely low on foodstuffs, they traded glass beads with the Natives of the ranchería for food. They spent the rest of that day and the next at that campsite.

It seemed that scurvy still afflicted the expedition. Some of the men, including Captain Rivera y Moncada, had fallen ill with diarrhea. Crespí wrote that it appeared some of the men were recovering; however, Rivera y Moncada's condition caused the expedition to rest another day. Even the men who had received the viaticum, Crespí wrote, "about whom we felt great anxiety before, continue to improve, thank God."[182] Costansó opined that after a bout with diarrhea the maladies from scurvy were alleviated. "Little by little the swelling and aches began to disappear," he wrote. He was amazed that this could happen without medication.[183]

The next day, Friday, October 27, Rivera y Moncada and others felt better, and so the expedition moved on, ever northward. After three hours or two leagues of marching and crossing three arroyos that emptied into the ocean, they halted at the third, where they camped. Crespí called it the "Arroyo de San Ivo."[184] Nearby, they found an abandoned village. Their guides told them that the people had moved to the mountains.[185] Inspecting some of the structures, the soldiers noticed the houses were infested with fleas, so they called the village "Las Pulgas." They spent the rest of the day working on the trail so that the animals could pass over it.[186] For two days, they moved steadily to the north. From one of their vantage points, they could see a very long point of land jutting out to the sea, and discerned that "at this distance appear to be *farallones*" (islets), which seemed to stretch away from the land to the west. Their guides told them that there was a settlement in that area. Although the natives who met them hoped they would go back with them to their settlement, Portolá's men, noting that it was late and they were too tired to move forward, declined. However, they camped near the settlement.[187] The soldiers called the place "Los Ansares" because of the many wild geese in the area. Bolton noted that they were at "Pilarcitos Creek, just north of the town of Half Moon Bay (or possibly Frenchman Creek). The point of land is Pillar Point."[188]

On Saturday, October 28, Fathers Crespí and Gómez celebrated Holy Mass on the feast day of San Simón and San Judas. The expedition departed at about 10:00 a.m. along the mesas of the beach. They walked north-northwest[189] about two and a half hours, covering about two leagues, when they came to a large arroyo near the beach. At that point, they reckoned that they were thirty-three and a half leagues from Monterey. Four Indian guides took them to a settlement near the point, which they named "El Paraje de San Simón y San Judas."[190]

Doubtful that they had found Monterey Bay, Portolá and his men, with wavering resolution, wondered where they were in relation to Cabrera Bueno's descriptions. Crespí observed the latitude to be "37 degrees and a half without being able to say whether we were distant from or near to the port of Monterey."[191] He admitted that the point they were viewing lay on a north-northwest axis, with high rocks that looked like "thick farallones of an irregular and pointed shape. On seeing these we did not know what to think."[192]

The rainfall pestered them all day. The group was very low on food, which they saved for the sick. The rations were five tortillas a day per man. Even though they could have killed the weaker mules for food, the men refused to do so. Portolá himself was ill, as was Rivera y Moncada. Many of the others were afflicted with recurring bouts of diarrhea. The weather added to their misery. Crespí, however, credited the cool northwest winds, rains, and other land breezes with purifying the air. He noted that the swelling in the legs of the men had been reduced. The pains in their limbs "which kept them constantly groaning" had ceased, and the swelling of their gums diminished. They hoped for a continuing recovery.[193]

The rains continued throughout the weekend. Sunday morning, October 29, emerged dark because of the heavy cloud cover from the rains that persisted throughout the night. After Mass, the expedition waited for the first appearance of light to begin their day. However, as Governor Portolá continued feeling ill, they remained in the camp for another day. Meanwhile, except for a few items, their food supply was depleted.[194] Luckily, the people of the settlement came by with tamales and *atole* (gruel) made of black seeds, which the scouts quickly took as they moved out to do their reconnaissance.[195]

On October 30, the expedition broke camp at about 9:00 a.m. and proceeded in a northwesterly direction. The weather had cleared. The ailing and sick felt better. Keeping the mesas and low-lying hills to their right, they crossed four or five arroyos with fresh water. In some cases, the soldiers had to build bridges for the pack train to cross. As they approached the point, they noticed a small bay with pasture but, unfortunately, nary a twig to build a fire. However, the soldiers had thought to pack some firewood from their previous camp.

The beach came to an end at some hills that blocked their way. The hills formed a small valley with fresh water running through it where, at about 12:30 in the afternoon, they stopped to camp after marching three and a half hours.[196] Meanwhile, the soldiers went on to construct bridges across two deep arroyos.[197] The leaders named the point "Ángel Custodio," but the soldiers called it "Punta de las Almejas" because of the many mussels they found on the beach. Bolton surmised that they were in the vicinity of San Pedro Point.[198] From there, they could see in the sea to the west of them, three or four submerged rocks and two points with very narrow tips and thick, rounded bottoms.[199]

On Tuesday, October 31, the group broke camp about 9:00 a.m. After traveling about a league, they figured that they were now thirty-six and a half leagues (nearly ninety-five miles) from Cabrera Bueno's Monterey Bay. Still probing for the elusive harbor, they ascended and descended high treeless hills that had prevented their passage along the beach a day before on a trail newly repaired by Sergeant Ortega and his men.

The expedition next moved northwest, up and down some high hills with steep slopes. From there, they could see, far from the land, six or seven white farallones. Because of those sightings, they expected to see the port of Monterey soon.[200] The islets appeared to lie southwest of a large bay. From the side that they were on, the bay seemed to round; in the distance, they could see a large point of land that appeared to extend to the west, one-quarter northwest.[201] They reasoned that the latter conformed with the signs and descriptions given by Cabrera Bueno.[202] Reasonably, they concluded that what they saw could be none other than the port of San Francisco (Drakes Bay) and Point Reyes. From their vantage point, both—probably because of the large estuary (present-day Drakes Estero)—appeared like large islands; but it was all terra firma. Still, they were perplexed about the location of Monterey Bay. After sighting Drakes Bay, it seemed to them that Monterey Bay must be south of them, where they had originally suspected it to be. Yet, what they saw, what they read, and what they thought seemed to defy all reason. Thus, they were still not totally convinced. Yet, a bigger surprise was in store for them.

Later that morning, Portolá led the expeditionary force over a high hill. As soon as they reached the top, they witnessed a most astonishing sight.[203] Once at the summit, Crespí wrote, "we descried a great bay formed by a point of land which runs far out into the open sea and looks like an island."[204] He continued, "This port is huge, having a three or four league span and its curved configuration is very large in which can fit all of all of Spain's armadas."[205] From where they stood, Crespí's first impression was that the port's entrance was from south to north. He also noted three white cliffs in the distance. Regarding the winds in the bay, he thought they were fairly spread out. Nearby was an Indian settlement, whose people came to greet them with food. The expedition soon learned that there were many other settlements around the bay.

They descended the treeless hill and pitched camp in the middle of a small valley, which measured six hundred varas long and about a hundred wide with fresh water from two small arroyos that united before they entered the sea. Soon after, they were visited by local natives who brought them tamales made from black seeds. The Spaniards figured that the population surrounding the bay was large because they had seen many fires on the beach from the settlements in the area.[206]

Seeing the great bay astonished the explorers and they began to rethink what they knew about the location of Monterey Bay. From the beach, they could clearly see that the farallones lay west by southwest. The point they saw had to be Point Reyes. Of the situation, Crespí wrote,

> All the signs that we find here we read in the itinerary of the pilot Cabrera Bueno, from which we conclude that this is the port of San Francisco [Drakes Bay],[207] and we are confirmed in this by the latitude in which we find ourselves, which is a full thirty-seven and a half degrees: for although that author [Cabrera Bueno] places it in thirty-eight and a half, that does not disturb me, considering that we have observed that this happens in all his reckonings whenever he describes this coast and its latitudes. For example, he puts the harbor of San Diego in thirty-four degrees, while in the observations repeatedly made there it came out a little more than thirty-two degrees and a half. Point Concepción, we found in thirty-four and one-half degrees while he puts it in thirty-five and a half. And so, it would not be surprising if this harbor which is in full thirty-seven and a half degrees should turn out to be that of our father San Francisco, since we find all the other signs that the author gives for the port referred to.[208]

Still, because of the latitude readings, doubt persisted. Some members of the expedition argued that they had not left Monterey Bay to the south. Others doubted that they had reached San Francisco Bay. To that end, Portolá ordered Sergeant Ortega and his men to spend three days exploring the area to see if they could clear up the confusion regarding where they were. After all, as Crespí wrote, "Some of our party do not yet believe that we have left the port of Monterey behind or that we are on that of my father San Francisco."[209] Meanwhile, Crespí took a reading of the latitude at 37 degrees and 49 minutes, while Costansó had it at 37 degrees and 24 minutes.[210] The next day, he wrote that "In the middle of the port it can be 38 degrees."[211]

Those soldiers who had remained in the camp were granted permission on November 2 to hunt for deer. Crespí wrote that

> some of them went quite a distance from the camp and climbed the hills, so that it was already night when they returned. They said that toward the north they had seen an immense arm of the sea, or an estuary, which penetrated into the land as far as the eye could reach, extending to the southeast; that they had seen some beautiful plains well adorned with trees, and that the smokes which they saw in all directions left no doubt that the country was thickly populated. . . . This report confirmed us still more in the opinion that we were on the port of Our Father San Francisco, and that the arm of the sea which they told us about was certainly the estuary of which the pilot Cabrera Bueno spoke, the mouth of which we had not seen because we went down to the harbor through a ravine.[212]

Even before the scouts had returned, Portolá had assessed the information gained from his hunters in addition to the astonishing sight of the great bay. In his mind, the farallones fixed the cartographic position of the Port of San Francisco and Point Reyes. That could mean only that Monterey lay to the south of them as they had earlier concluded, albeit with diffidence.

The one point on which Portolá harped, even after Ortega and his scouts had returned, was that Cabrera Bueno had stated, "Through the opening in the center enters an estuary of salt water without any breaking of the waves at all, and by going in, one will find friendly Indians and can easily take on water and wood."[213] Still, Portalá could not deny that the six or seven farallones that they saw could only be in the one place described by Cabrera Bueno. Crespí wrote that "We rejoiced much" over Ortega's report, "although in the middle of this we are very much apprehensive and careful regarding the point that Monterey was behind us and in addition to this, having seen the six or seven farallones, that nowhere else are they placed in the Histories other than at the port of San

Francisco. Too, we find ourselves at the aforementioned latitude that I have observed . . . and that of Miguel Costansó by means of his instruments read it at 37 degrees 24 minutes."[214]

Ortega and his men returned after nightfall on Friday, November 3, and talked about the marvelous things they had seen. After two days of marching some distance from the camp, the scouts had climbed a hill. They recounted that they had looked out "toward the north and hand seen an immense arm of the sea, or an estuary, which penetrated into the land as far as the eye could reach, extending to the southeast that they had seen some beautiful forested plains"[215] They explained that they had gone out along the arm of the sea and at the end of it saw many large birds such as cranes, geese, and ducks, as well as numerous large oak trees. Near there, they encountered seven Indian settlements. The Indians had told them that there were two ports close together and that at the second port there was a ship.[216] The scouts listened incredulously as the warriors told them "that two days' march from the place which they had reached, which was the end or head of the estuary, there was a harbor and a ship in it."[217] The Indians offered to take them there. They did not go.[218] Was the ship the *San Joseph* or the *San Carlos* with supplies for the expedition? In retrospect, it turned out to be wishful thinking because they would have expected the ship to have waited for them at Monterey Bay. Again, they questioned whether they had misidentified their location.[219] The intelligence gathered by their scouts, however, was inconclusive.

From their report, Portalá realized that Ortega and his explorers "could not have crossed to the opposite shore which was seen to the north, and consequently would not succeed in exploring the point which we judge to be that of Los Reyes [Point Reyes], for it would be impossible in the three days that they were to be gone to make the detour that they would unavoidably have to make to round the estuary, which they said was very great."[220] The misinformation caused Portolá to again rethink his position. Subsequently, he determined that the expedition would continue north to see if there were other possibilities that they had missed Monterey Bay.

The next day, Saturday, November 4, at about one o'clock in the afternoon, they set out again following the beach northward. They entered hilly terrain where the grass had been scorched. After bearing northeast along some canyons, they climbed to a higher altitude and "beheld the great estuary or arm of the sea, which must have a width of four or five leagues, and extends to the southeast and south-southeast."[221] From there, a league and a half or two away, they could see some sierras "which appear to make the harbor, and through there the arm of the sea should originate."[222] Moving in the opposite direction from the bay, the expedition entered a valley that ran south and southwest. Of the change in direction, Crespí wrote, "Keeping it always on the left hand, and turning our backs to the bay, we took a valley open to the south and southwest."[223] After three hours and two leagues of marching, they stopped in a canyon at the foot of a mountain range covered with very green scrub. Crespí noted that "between this arm of the sea and this mountain, are some very grassy high hills."[224]

The next morning, November 5, after Sunday Mass, the party began following the edge of the estuary at about nine o'clock. The day was dreary and very cloudy. Trudging along a southern line of march, they kept the mountain to their right and the high hills to their left basically between themselves and the aforesaid arm of the sea.[225] They traveled for over four and a half hours, making their way for about three and a half leagues, where they stopped near a lake.[226] This area was well endowed with fresh water, abundant pasturage, many *madroños* with edible fruit, numberless geese, and much large game (undoubtedly bear and deer and possibly buffalo). The explorers seemed to be in a good place. Three warriors, acting as envoys from various villages, came to meet the party and invited them to camp with them. They brought black seed tamales and a plumlike fruit.[227] The groups exchanged gifts and spent the night at the camp.

The next day, November 6, they broke camp at about nine o'clock in the morning and, exiting the canyon, headed south, keeping the mountain to their right and the high hills to their left as on the day before.[228] Approaching the foot of the mountain, they met three warriors with bows and arrows, who came out to greet them. Through signs, they communicated that their ranchería was on the mountain and they had come to invite the visitors to partake of their hospitality.[229] The expedition followed the warriors to their villages, crossing through forests of redwoods, live oaks, and oaks loaded with acorns. Arrived at the settlement, the explorers noted that there were many villages in the area. The native fed them with acorn porridge, black tamales, and pinole. Even though their hosts wanted them to stay longer, after trading and gift-giving Portolá communicated to them that they had to move on.[230]

That afternoon, the Spaniards left the villages and, picking up their trail, continued on their march northward, keeping the estuary at their left. After going up and down hills, they came to a plain that stretched five or six leagues, all of it forested with oak and other trees. From a hill, they could see the arm of the sea about a league away.[231] They walked for four and a quarter hours, covering a distance of three leagues, and stopped the *real* in an oak forest near an arroyo with water that emptied into an estuary along the arm of the sea.[232]

They spent the next day, Tuesday, November 7, at the same camp while eight scouts under Captain Rivera y Moncada went out for four days[233] to ascertain if, indeed, there was a ship in the port waiting for them. They left that afternoon guided by natives of the area. The men spent November 8 resting and tending to the sick, as some of the men had experienced a fever and indigestion issues. While waiting for the scouts to return, Crespí on November 9 observed the latitude to be 37 degrees and 46 minutes.[234] He said that this was 3 degrees less than when he had taken it on the side of the port on November 1, given the distance they had covered in three days' southward travel.

On Friday, November 10, the scouts returned at night, disappointed that they had found no signs of Monterey Bay. Rivera y Moncada reported that they had moved along the arm of the sea within the port and found nothing. Their doubts had given rise to the hope that perhaps they should move forward. Rivera y Moncada wrote that on seeing "not a single sign made by Cabrera [Bueno] regarding the Port of Monterey to be found," he decided to return to camp.[235]

Crespí wrote, "They said that all the territory which they examined to the northeast and north was impassable because of the scarcity of pasture and especially because of ferocity and ill-temper" of natives who angrily blocked their passage.[236] The scouts reported that they had seen another estuary of "equal magnitude and extent with the one we had in sight and with which it communicated, but in order to go round it one would have to travel many leagues."[237] About five leagues from the camp, they had come to a fast-moving river with a large canopy of trees. They said it was virtually unpassable.[238] They saw no evidence of the proximity where the port terminated and the mountains were too rough to pass through. Likely, Pedro Fages was aware that Ortega had, in 1769, seen the present-day inner San Pablo Bay from a distance. Beyond San Pablo Bay, Carquinez Strait blocked their way to Point Reyes.[239]

On Saturday, November 11, Portolá called a second meeting to determine the opinion of his officers regarding farther exploration in regard to confirming the location of Monterey Bay. They agreed unanimously, by posting their votes in writing, that given all the signs of the terrain, "it was necessary to turn back, for they saw that the harbor of Monterey must have been left behind, and [they] considered it foolhardy to go on after having seen in the coast all the marks of the harbor of San Francisco, according to the descriptions and signs given by the pilot Cabrera Bueno in his itinerary."[240] They agreed to return to the Punta de los Pinos and from there backtrack along the entire coastline to where the Sierra de Santa Lucía began to see whether their exploration had missed Monterey Bay.

That afternoon, Portolá ordered the retreat to San Diego and the continued search for Monterey Bay. To that, Crespí wrote, "May God let us find it, so that it would not be the great failure of the entire expedition."[241] Indeed, despite their beliefs, they had already succeeded in finding Monterey Bay, but the disparity between Cabrera Bueno's written word as seen from the sea and the optical perspective of the topography as seen from the land, not to mention the configuration of the bay, did not meet their expectations. The disparity between what they saw and what they read continued to create tremendous doubt among the members of the expedition. At the place Costansó called the "Rincón de las Almejas," near the port of San Francisco, on November 14, he used his instruments to observe the following readings:

At this place we succeeded without difficulty in observing the meridian altitude of the lower limb of the sun, with the English octant, facing it . . . 33°50'

As [the observation] was made on a cliff about forty feet above sea level, the inclination of the visual horizon was six minutes, subtract . . . 6'

Astronomical refraction, subtract . . . 1'

Semidiameter of the sun to be added . . . 16'9"

Altitude of the center of the sun . . . 33°59'

Zenith-distance . . . 56°1'

Its declination resulting from the equations . . . 18°30'

Latitude of the place, north . . . 37°31'

The southern shore or beach of the port of San Francisco is about four marine miles north of this place.

Its latitude, then, would be about 37°35'.[242]

On November 26, the group would be back at their old camp along the Río de la Señora Santa Delfina, to try again to unravel the mystery of the location of Monterey Bay which they had hoped to do from their camp on October 1.[243]

In retrospect, part of the dilemma in trying to unravel the bay's location lay with the context in which Portolá and his explorers were working. As they proceeded northward, they were using Manila Galleon descriptions that were gathered as the ships sailed southward. There was also a large gap of coastline that the mariners did not see between Point Reyes and the Santa Lucía Mountains off the coast north of Santa Barbara. Historian William Lytle Schurz explained,

> Cabrera Bueno gives the point of demarcation, which are practically in reverse order of Vizcaino's *derrotero* of 1602. Turning SE by E from off Cape Mendocino, the next prominent landmark was Point Reyes outside the sheltered harbor of Drakes Bay. The galleons were directed not to follow the bend of the coast at this point, but to stand out a little to the sea, in order to keep clear of the Farallones which lie somewhat to the east of south. Some thirty leagues south from Point Reyes the Galleons sailed well out from the broad sweep of Monterey Bay, sighting the familiar Point Pinos. Thence the course lay down barren coast by Point Concepcion, through the Santa Barbara Channel, to the lower California coast.[244]

Schurz's explanation may add another factor in the failure of Manila Galleon mariners to sight San Francisco Bay. Thus, after Point Reyes and the Farallones, the next major landmark to be seen would have been the northern end of the Santa Lucía Mountains and the wide-open bay at Monterey.

As it turned out, Portolá's expedition to find Monterey Bay resulted in the accidental but significant discovery of San Francisco Bay. This was neither Monterey Bay nor Drakes Bay. It was a perfect and greater bay that they had discovered. They named it San Francisco based on Visitor-General José de Gálvez's mandate that the saint's name be reserved for an important location for a town, presidio, or port. To that end, Crespí remembered that it would be applied "as his Excellency the visitor-general said to our father president at the camp of Santa Ana"[245] months earlier, as the land expedition had prepared to depart Baja California.

Portolá and his men had discovered a land route that stretched hundreds of miles between San Diego and Monterey. They had verified many of the coastal place-names applied by Manila Galleon mariners by retracing the documentation they carried with them and applying a land-to-sea perspective to sites originally seen from the sea. Equally important, they had made contact with countless Indian settlements and had, according to Crespí, designated places

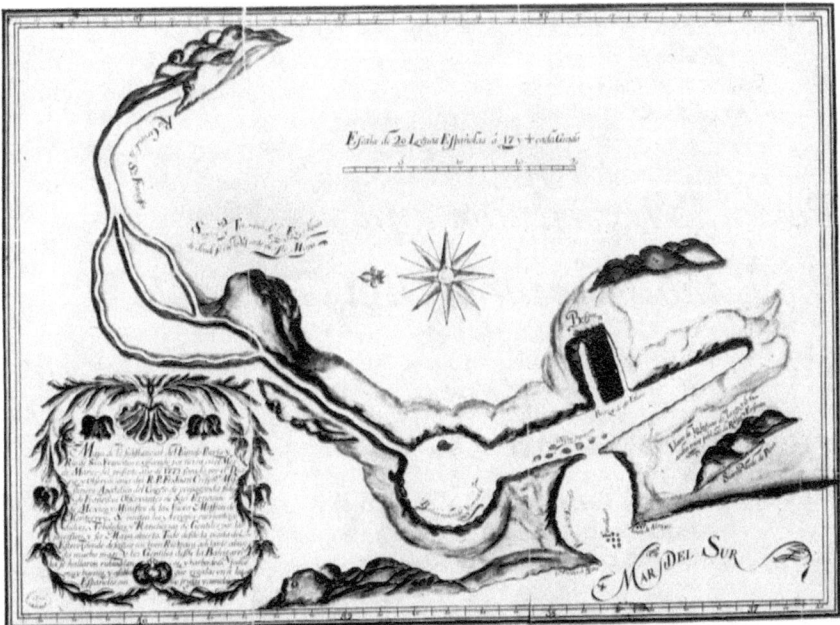

MAP 5 *Plano del Puerto de San Francisco*, 1772. The first map of San Francisco Bay, drawn by Fray Juan Crespí. National Park Service–Spanish Colonial Research Center Map Collection, Center for Southwest Research, Zimmerman Library, University of New Mexico.

that could eventually become mission sites. Above all, the land expedition accomplished a significant, long-lasting objective while doing the king's business: they opened a land route from one end of Alta California, at San Diego, to the other, at San Francisco, which would serve a movement of people who would establish forts, towns, missions, and ranches that created the modern California. In many ways, some of the routes along the corridor that became known as the Camino Real de California emanated not so much from the expedition's newly blazed route and its later constant use, but also from the ancient indigenous pathways. In many cases, various Indian tribes either guided the Spaniards through the land or they told them which way to travel as they wended their way north along the California coast in 1769. Indeed, the Camino Real de California celebrates a shared history and heritage with Spain, Mexico, and Native American tribes along the California coast.

CHAPTER SIX

✿ ✿ ✿ ✿ ✿

Portolá's Expedition and the Establishment of Alta California, Part III

THE EXPEDITION RETURNS TO SAN DIEGO—NOVEMBER 1769 TO JANUARY 1770[1]

✿ ✿ ✿ ✿ ✿

We were now approaching the port of San Diego, and this whole day was passed in conjecturing what state we would find it in, whether settled by the few people whom we left there and the packets in the harbor, or whether it might have been entirely deserted in the six months since we left it. . . . In addition, there was much to be feared from . . . the Diegueño Indians . . . and we were fearful that they might have attempted some offense against the mission and its small guard.
FRAY JUAN CRESPÍ | JANUARY 24, 1770

HAVING MADE A GREAT DISCOVERY, San Francisco Bay, the expedition began its return to San Diego. The accounts of the return trip reinforced their knowledge of the place-names and descriptions of the land and people they had noted on their northward trek. They also adjusted portions of their original route, named new places, and saw, from virtually a reverse angle, the lay of the land as they reviewed it going south to San Diego Bay. The origin of the Camino Real de California was thus documented twice by the Portolá expedition of 1769.

After four days exploring the great harbor, the expedition began its return to San Diego from its camp in the valley near San Francisco Bay.[2] Before they left, the Indians brought them foodstuffs for which the Spaniards repaid them with trade items. Heading south on Saturday afternoon, November 11, the expedition retraced its steps for two leagues, wending slightly northward before veering to the southeast on November 13 to where they had camped earlier on November 4 and 5.[3] On their return to San Diego, the expedition continued to adjust the route based on new information about the land and the discovery of new and easier passages through mountains, ridges, valleys, and other topographic concerns. As was their practice, on the return trip they calculated the distance traveled by day from a point in the bay. Thus, on the first day of travel, they went two leagues. That night, November 11, they stopped to camp in the same canyon that had previously led them to the great harbor.[4]

Following Holy Mass on Sunday morning, November 12, they continued through the same canyon. After four and a half leagues, they camped toward the end of the canyon along an arroyo with a wooded area and good pasturage for their animals. That day, they marked that they were six and a half leagues from San Francisco Bay.[5] The next day, November 13, they left early in the morning along the arroyo and reached a canyon with two arroyos. At one side of this place, they were at the end of the great bay, from which they could see the six or seven farallones "of this port of San Francisco. It was where they had been on October 31 and the latitude was at 37 degrees and 49 minutes." Along this route, they did not see a single ranchería.[6] That night, they camped "near the shore of the harbor of San Francisco."[7]

Following the valley of San Francisco on November 14, they ascended some high hills and traveled through heavy bramble. Descending an arroyo, they traveled one league. From there they could see the six or seven farallones appearing parallel to them. About a league from there, toward the south, the land formed a low point extending out to the sea. To the west of it, they saw three or four large submerged rocks that could be seen better at low tide. Quite visibly, another two rocks stuck out from the sea—the ones they had noted earlier that had pointed tops. They named that distant place "La Punta de los Ángeles Custodios."[8] On this leg of the return trip, they retraced their path to the valley of Las Almejas "in the same spot where we had been before, about a league distant from the point of Angel Custodio. Costansó took the latitude at thirty-seven degrees and thirty-one minutes."[9] That Wednesday, November 15, they rested at their camp and gathered a supply of mussels for their march.[10]

The next day, Thursday, November 16, they resumed their travel, moving

MAP 6 *Plano del Puerto de San Francisco*, 1777. National Park Service–Spanish Colonial Research Center Map Collection, Center for Southwest Research, Zimmerman Library, University of New Mexico.

south-southeast.[11] About a league from there, they passed near La Punta de los Angeles Custodios, and from there they began to follow the sandy beach. Crossing arroyos that ran toward the point slowed their travel. The expedition passed four or five other arroyos that emptied into the sea. At two of them, they constructed pole bridges to get the mule train across. After moving two more leagues all day, they arrived at the Arroyo of the Santos Apóstoles San Simón y San Judas Tadeo in the plain of Los Ansares, the wild geese. There, they stopped to camp while the soldiers hunted for geese, killing twenty-two for much-needed food.[12] Their camp was near a ranchería they had seen on their way north, where they again traded beads for food. They were now eleven leagues south of San Francisco Bay.[13]

On November 17, the party left early in the morning. Backtracking on their old route, they came to the valley of San Ivo after two leagues of marching. There, found the village where they had traded with the natives on October 27. It was deserted. The expedition marched on for three leagues in the rain and finally halted on the banks of a deep arroyo, where they camped for the night. They were now fourteen leagues from San Francisco Bay.[14]

Early the next morning, November 18, they broke camp and, within a league, came to another arroyo that they had named Nuestro Padre Santo Domingo when they passed it on October 28. They were now seventeen leagues south of San Francisco Bay.[15]

On Sunday, November 19, after Holy Mass, they headed south. After two leagues, they entered a small valley with an arroyo that ran from San Juan Nepomuceno, alias La Casa Grande. They recalled that they had been there on October 23 and had traded with the inhabitants. That cold day in November, however, they found the settlement deserted.[16] Moving on, they came to a cliff where they stopped to camp. It was near the point which they believed was the Punta del Año Nuevo.[17]

On Monday, November 20, the expedition descended the cliff, which turned toward the north as far as the port of San Francisco. From there, wrote Crespí, it formed "a very large bay as far as the Punta de los Pinos."[18] The expedition continued backtracking and reaching old familiar campsites from the month previous. Finally, after two leagues and a half of marching, they arrived at San Pedro de Alcántara or, as the soldiers had called it, El Alto del Jamón, where they had camped on October 19.[19] The next day, November 21, after two leagues of meandering first east-southeast and then west-northwest, they stopped at Arroyo de las Puentes de San Lucas, where they had camped on October 18.

They recalled how the travel had been slow as the soldiers had to fix the trail.[20] Breaking camp on November 22, they forded the Río San Lorenzo and continued until they reached El Rosario de San Serefino, where they had stopped on October 16. They were now twenty-nine leagues from San Francisco Bay.[21] Traveling three and a half leagues on Thursday, November 23, they halted at Los Avellanos de Nuestra Señora, where they had stopped on October 11. Moving as quickly as they could "without stopping in order to hasten on as fast as possible," the men of the expedition felt as if time was running out on their supplies and health. As there were so few men healthy enough to pull guard duty for the night, they built a small corral on the edge of one of the lakes for the mules and horses. Their camp, which they named "El Paraje del Corral," was thirty-two and a half leagues south from San Francisco Bay.[22] They realized that they were not far from Nuestra Señora del Pilar, where they had camped on October 12. In reflection, Crespí added a note stating: "I now find myself in this port of Monterey . . . I say that this camp of Nuestra Señora del Pilar is twelve leagues from the port of Monterey . . . the explorers . . . encountered this port which is where his Divine Majesty placed it at the creation of the world."[23] On November 24, the group reached a river they called the "Río de Santa Ana" after traveling two leagues and a half from north to south. Earlier that day, the scouts had left to explore that section of the coast. They followed a straight road that ran inland and passed the village of Santa Ana, which the soldiers had called El Pájaro (Bolton's Watsonville), and halted near a lagoon they called El Macho. The next day, November 25, the expedition remained at that camp. The scouting party returned that night without any new information. They had gone as far south as Santa Delfina, which, as Crespí wrote, "is the camp from which we departed for San Francisco"[24] earlier. (Actually, they had camped at Santa Delfina on their way north on October 6.[25]) After Mass on Sunday, November 26, the expedition traveled five leagues and reached the river and valley of Santa Delfina. This time, the village they had visited was deserted.[26]

On November 26, they broke camp and went three and a half leagues to a waterhole where they had camped on the way north. There was a ranchería in the area, but that day it was abandoned. Not far away, they came upon another settlement with 1,500 people, made up of villagers they had met at El Pájaro and Santa Ana. Indeed, some of the soldiers recognized individuals as people they had met before; they had merely moved and constructed a new settlement.[27] Crespí confirmed that they had arrived in the area the first time around

October 1 and had searched for the Río del Carmelo and the port of Monterey. La Punta de los Pinos could be seen from there looking east-southeast. That day the group had meandered five and a half leagues in a north-northwest and south-southeast direction. In sum, they were now forty and a half leagues from San Francisco Bay.[28] Crespí could now confirm that they had found Monterey Bay. "I find myself," he proclaimed, "situated in this port of Monterey and I say that the great plain and the good river of Santa Delfina is about four leagues from the port of Monterey."[29]

Breaking camp at Santa Delfina on November 27, they looked for a ford to get across. They backtracked north for a league, where they crossed the river.[30] Once on the other side, they went south until they came near the beach with large sand dunes. They veered southwest, they followed the coast until they reached the Point of the Pines[31] they had seen in late September and early October.

The next day, Tuesday, November 28, they entered a large pine forest before ascending a ridge from which they could see a medium-sized bay sheltered from the north-northwest winds. On its south side, the point protected it from south and southwest winds. They did not comment on the depth of the water for lack of a canoe to test it.[32] The estuary had many amenities, including a freshwater river that emptied into it. The bay had little beach other than what was on the east side. After four leagues, one league spent backtracking and three forward, they stopped to camp[33] and spent the next day, November 29, recuperating and scouting around the area, hopeful of defining the exact location of Monterey Bay.[34] They remained in the area while Captain Rivera y Moncada and twelve soldiers once again set out to explore and reached the Sierra de Santa Lucía, which had blocked their way on September 13. Although they knew that Cabrera Bueno's explanation left no doubt that from the Sierra de Santa Lucía to Monterey Bay was six miles, they felt that the area was so nondescript that they could not define it as described by the old mariners.[35]

On Thursday, November 30, the expedition continued to rest from the intense cold weather that had afflicted the area. Meanwhile, the men hunted gulls and pelicans. Costansó took a reading of the latitude which he noted as 36 degrees and 36 minutes—the same, he said, as in the bay of Cadíz in Spain.[36] Using his instruments, he recorded the following:

> Today, the meridian altitude of the sun was observed with the English octant, facing the sun, and the altitude of its lower limb was found to be . . . 31°23'

Semidiameter to be added . . . 16'

Correction in consequence of the elevation of the observer's eye above sea level, subtract . . . 3'

Astronomical refraction, subtract . . . 2'11"

Altitude of the center of the sun . . . 31°34'

Zenith-distance . . . 58°26'

Its declination . . . 21°50'

Latitude of the Ensenada de Pinos . . . 36°36'[37]

That afternoon, they were visited by twelve local warriors who told them of their village in the valley along the river that emptied into the estuary. They brought pinole and seeds to trade for Spanish glass beads.

Herbert Bolton summarized the expedition's travel in November and December by citing the various modern-day location points as follows:

> on the return journey to Monterey bay, the expedition camped on the 11th near Woodside; on the 12th at San Andreas Lake, or possibly at Pilarcitos Lake; on the 13th on San Pedro Creek; on the 14th at San Vicente Creek; on the 15th at Half Moon Bay; on the 17th at Tunitas Creek; on the 18th at Pescadero Creek; on the 19th at Año Nuevo Creek; on the 20th at Scott Creek; on the 21st at Coja Creek; on the 22d at Soquel Creek; on the 23d in Corralitos Valley; on the 24th near Elk Slough; on the 26th on the Salinas River southeastward of Blanco. On the 27th they crossed the Salinas and went to camp on the site of Monterey. On the 28th they halted beyond Carmel River, near Point Lobos, where they remained in camp until December 10. It was from this camp that the exploration of Santa Lucía Range was made, and it was here that the council was held December 7.[38]

All the while, on the return from San Francisco, Portolá had to be sure that they had not again bypassed Monterey Bay. Still seeking confirmation, he kept his scouts under Captain Rivera y Moncada busy exploring along the way in the hope of verifying its location. At this point, the expedition was in dire straits regarding its basic foods: the original supplies that they had brought with them from San Diego had dwindled to a few morsels. Almost all of the flour for tortillas and lentils were gone. Were it not for the occasional deer and fish, they were on the point of starving to death. Of the remaining food from the original supply, Crespí noted that Portolá reported that in "actuality, there is very little" food left.[39]

For a few days, the men remained in the area, exploring and hunting. During that time, about fifty warriors armed with bows and arrows came down from high hill. Portolá, through signs, signaled them that they could approach in peace. Some of the soldiers went out to receive them. Ten or twelve warriors approached; the rest remained at the side of the hill. They told them that their ranchería was near the Río del Carmelo, about a half league away. They communicated to Portolá that they had come only to give them some pinole. Portolá gave them glass beads in return. The warriors stayed a while and left. Crespí also mentioned that there were many wild geese in the area, which they hunted for much-needed food.[40]

The men spent Friday, December 1, exploring the mountains and the next few days fixing the trail for the mule train. Six Indians worked with them clearing and opening the path, taking enough tortillas for several days. A mule was killed for food, but Rivera y Moncada's men refused to eat it. The Catalonian Volunteers and the Indians who had been with them did.[41] The next day, two mulatto muleteers asked permission to go hunting, but did not return. Portolá speculated that some harm came to them, or they got lost, or they simply deserted.[42] Sunday came and went as rain drenched the area. By nightfall on Monday, December 4,

> the captain arrived with his soldiers, tired from the rough nature of the mountains. They told us they had to go on foot most of the way as far as their exploration reached. From it they drew the complete certainty that those mountains are the Santa Lucía Range, because for the signs which were found to conform to those given in the itinerary of the pilot Cabrera Bueno, such as a high white cliff extending along the coast, which can be seen for many leagues out at sea, and a rock shaped like a large top which resembles a farallón and is about six leagues from the Point of the Pines.[43]

By December 5, the *Día de San Nicolás*, the expedition, flustered by their attempts to confirm or conclusively find Monterey Bay determined, as expressed by Crespí, that since we have not found in this vicinity the very celebrated harbor of Monterey, which was enthusiastically described in their time by men of character, skill, and intelligence, experienced navigators who came expressly to explore these coasts by order of the king, who was then governing in the Spains; we have to say that it is not to be found, after the most exacting efforts made at the cost of much sweat and fatigue. Or perhaps it may be said that it has been hidden or destroyed by the passage of time, although we have not seen indications to support this view.[44]

At that moment, Costansó, likely corroborating with Crespí, weighed in on the issue and drew the same conclusion. He wrote: "The accounts of General Sebastián Vizcaíno, and his contemporary historians, give the port of Monterey as being in 37° north latitude. We not only saw no signs of it, but not even the possibility that such a port had ever existed in that altitude, for there the coast is bordered by a range of very high hills terminating in the ocean, as the navigators may see."[45]

Costansó posited that the expedition's instruments to measure latitude had failed them. By the same token, it could have been that the instruments used by the earlier navigators caused the error. For that matter, measuring the latitude and describing Monterey Bay from the sea would be a different perspective than viewing it from land.[46] He wrote, "On some coasts . . . which do not give an opportunity for observing the northern horizon (as is the case on these coasts of which we speak), the altitude of the sun, or other heavenly body, whose declination is less than the latitude of the place in which the observer is, can be taken in no other way than by facing it."[47] That being the case, Costansó would not have been surprised if Monterey lay at a greater or lesser latitude than those reported by the mariners. That reasoning left Costansó with one possible conclusion. He wrote:

Now, then, we will say positively that the port of Monterey does not exist in the latitude (37°) indicated in the old sailing-directions; nor between 37° as far north as 37°44', in which, as we believe, lies the Punta de los Reyes. It happened that we found the port of San Francisco [Drakes Bay] first, according to the signs, which, without the slightest variation (as far as we were able to see and judge) agreed with those given by the pilot Cabrera Bueno. And as this port of San Francisco, according to the pilot mentioned, and the others who have examined these coasts, lies to the north of Monterey, what hopes remain now that this port may be found farther north? Neither is this port south of the parallel of 37°, either in the Sierra de Santa Lucía, or out of it; for, having examined the whole coast, step by step, we have not the least fear that it may have escaped our diligence and search.[48]

Yet later they came to realize that they had made a better discovery in the bay and great harbor at San Francisco. Despite their inability to match or believe the description made by Cabrera Bueno and what they were looking at from the land, they had succeeded in their quest. Months later, Fages and Crespí returned to the area and concluded that they had, indeed, found the elusive Monterey Bay.[49]

As commander of the expedition, Portolá had to decide whether, despite the men's condition and their lack of supplies, it was worth staying in the area to determine convincingly the location of Monterey Bay or return to San Diego. In the context of the times, the decision was not an easy one, as he was charged with, as Crespí noted, "his service to our catholic King."[50] Had he fulfilled his mission and duty?

On December 5, after Holy Mass, the group decided to return to San Diego. But first, they had to recross the difficult terrain posed by the Sierra de Santa Lucía, this time from the north. To that end, Portolá mulled over what the next plan of action should be. At first, he thought to divide his force, with some men remaining at that place to await one of the ships (the *San Joseph*) that was sent to supply them in May and should have been there by now. The rest of the expedition would return to San Diego. Time seems to have stood still; for the next few days, the expedition was stalled at their camp on the Carmel River. Portolá then decided that the entire expedition would retreat together to San Diego.[51] It was then decided that two large crosses should be set at Point Año Nuevo and another at the Punta de los Pinos on its northeast side. Very cold weather with rain set in and the expedition remained in camp for the next few days.

On December 9, still camped at Point of the Pines, the priests celebrated Mass. Oddly, that day, the Indians who were with the expedition found a very large and heavy worn-out iron hoop on the beach. The explorers figured it was from a ship's mast that must have been blown off in a high wind, probably falling into the sea. Possibly it had drifted onto land with other debris from an old Manila Galleon that had shipwrecked off the coast.

The men awoke on Sunday, December 10 to find snow in the mountains. After Mass and just before departing the area, Portolá ordered that a large wooden cross be erected with the words "Dig at the foot and you will find a letter."[52] It was hoped that a packet boat sailing within sight of the cross would stop and find the communication there, buried in a bottle. In brief, the letter outlined the itinerary of the expedition since it left San Diego by land on July 14, 1769. It noted that by early August, the expedition had passed by the Santa Bárbara Channel and that by the end of August it had sighted Point Concepción. Blocked by an escarpment, it had, by September 13, arrived at the foot of the Sierra de Santa Lucía. The letter mentioned that the men had reached the mountain on September 17 and gone around it by October 1. That day, the letter noted, they had observed the Point of the Pines and had determined that the description did not fit the details regarding Monterey Bay presented by Cabrera Bueno. Therefore, the expedition had moved on to within sight of Point Reyes and the farallones near Cabrera Bueno's Port of San Francisco (Drakes Bay). Unable to reach Point Reyes because of the immense estuary, they attempted a long detour. Lack of provisions forced the expedition to abandoned plans to go further north. They still believed that they had missed the harbor of Monterey. On November 11, the expedition left San Francisco and arrived at Point Año Nuevo on November 19 and the Point of the Pines on November 27. They stayed there until December 9, hoping to find the harbor of Monterey within the area described by Cabrera Bueno.[53]

On the other side of the bay across from Point of the Pines, at the second point called Año Nuevo, they set up another large cross, upon which they carved with a knife the words "The land expedition is returning to San Diego for lack of provisions today, December 9, 1769."[54] They wrote another letter with a list of latitude observations made by Engineer Miguel Costansó, which included the readings made from several places on the coast, such as the following:

San Diego, in the camp occupied by the land expedition, 32 degrees and 42 minutes.

The most eastern town . . . on the channel of Santa Bárbara, 34 degrees and 13 minutes.

Point Concepción, 34 degrees and 30 minutes.

The beginning of Sierra de Santa Lucía, 35 degrees and 45 minutes.

The end of the range at this bay of the Point of the Pines, 36 degrees and 36 minutes.

On land near the harbor of San Francisco having the farallones west by north, 37 degrees and 35 minutes.

The point of Los Reyes, which was seen to the west-northwest from the same place, 37 degrees and 44 minutes.[55]

They ended with a prayer to the reader that should their letter be found, the finder make every effort to contact them, as they were in a bad situation. A copy was placed at both points in spots that they hoped would be visible from the sea. If nothing else, it offered its reader notification of the group's whereabouts.

That day, December 10, the expedition set out again at about two o'clock in the afternoon "from this *arroyito* a half league south of the Río Carmelo" and traveled eastward two and a half leagues, where they stopped "on the other side of Point of the Pines." It was near their old camp where they had stopped on their trek northward. This was near a lake one league to the south of Monterey Bay. They were about forty-eight and a half leagues from San Francisco Bay.[56]

The men spent the next day, December 11, walking over a plain toward the northeast, where they forded a river at the same place where they had camped on September 30. Crespí noted that after three leagues, they stopped in a canyon along the Río de la Señora Santa Delfina. They crossed the river and camped along the edge as on the earlier trip.[57] There, they hunted for geese.

Leaving Santa Delfina on December 12 at about 2:00 p.m., they traveled four and a half leagues along the canyon following the Río San Elzeario, where they stopped in the same area as in their earlier march north. Crespí noted that they were "followed" by thousands of geese such as those seen along the Río del Carmelo.[58] Traveling southeast along the same canyon and river, they came to a campsite where they had stayed on September 29.[59] The next day, December 13, they awoke to another freezing morning with a wind out of the northeast. Still within sight of the large flocks of geese, they traveled three and a half leagues to an old campsite, Real Blanco, where they had stayed on September 28. They were now fifty-nine and a half leagues south of San Francisco Bay.[60] December 14 dawned cold and windy, but they continued in a southeast direction through the canyon and along the river. After four leagues, the stopped to camp along the same canyon and river near a native settlement located along the riparian forest. They called the place Los Álamos.[61] When they came upon the settlement, the Indians were dancing, but they stopped when they saw the expedition. Many of the villagers came to their camp and gave them food, fish from the river, and an acorn porridge. The Spaniards communicated that they had gone days without salt. One of the chiefs motioned to his people to give them some with a yellowish color. The Indians visited for a while, then returned to their settlement and continued their dance.[62]

Just as they had for the past few very cold days, the men headed south along the Río San Elzeario and canyon. Their route twisted and turned as they wended their way southward for about four leagues. Finally, they arrived at the place where they had camped on September 26, which the soldiers had called the Real de Chocolate. This time, the ranchería that they had visited was no longer there. They were now sixty-seven and a half leagues from San Francisco Bay.[63]

On Saturday, December 16, they left the canyon and river and crossed into a valley "which the explorers found, more convenient and with a better road by which to enter Sierra de Santa Lucía, which runs from northwest to southeast."[64] After two leagues, they stopped to drink water at a village they called "Palo Caido." Nearby, they found a mule they had left behind on September 26 because it was exhausted. The natives had nursed it back to full recovery by giving it water and feeding it grass.[65]

Sunday, December 17, was one of the coldest days they had suffered through. Now at the foot of the Sierra de Santa Lucía, the priests had a difficult time praying the Mass. When a cold wind blew through the area, Crespí suffered a severe chill, and it was with difficulty that he spoke the final words. The soldiers, warming their hands over coals, tried to warm him. Soon after, they left the waterhole at the Cañada de los Robles de las Llagas de Nuestro Padre and went southwest, following an arroyo with fresh water. After two leagues of march, they wrote that they stopped on the mountain on the bank of a river they called Las Truchas de San Elceareo where they had stopped on September 21.[66] (Actually, the camp was at the headwaters of the Río San Elzeario.[67]) The next day, December 18, they left the *nacimiento* of the river and, after a league heading south, stopped to camp at Los Piñones, where they had stayed on September 20.[68] They found fresh water in an arroyo, which they thought was from the melting snow on the mountain. They noted that it had snowed a great deal throughout the range during the month. Luckily, they had already passed through the sierra on their way north. Now, on the return trip, they could see how perilous it could have been for them.

On Tuesday, December 19, the cold persisted early in the morning. The men left the canyon, moving southward, and ascended and descended through the terrain of the sierra for the next two leagues. After the first league, they arrived at an arroyo they had called Santa Lucía de Salerno, which they said was the first stopping place on the mountain. Ascending another league, they stopped at a campsite close to an Indian settlement they had visited on the outbound march. Some of the natives were still there. The expedition was now seventy-five and a half leagues from San Francisco Bay.[69] As they passed through the rough terrain, they began to recognize landmarks. With picks, hoes, and shovels, they carved out a trail along their path from September 20.[70] There, they met friendly natives who treated them well, as was customary with them.

The pack train lagged behind the main force as they moved slowly across the mountain. By Wednesday, they were reunited. The entire expedition stopped to rest for an entire day. The group was again facing starvation: some of its members desperately ate flour for their own survival. Portolá, seeing the injustice of their theft, ordered that the sacks of flour be divided among all the men in order for each to have his own to guard. Sadly, that was all the flour left. Was it enough to get them back to San Diego? Portolá had his doubts. Every third day, they killed a mule for food.[71]

On December 21, after praying the Holy Mass on the feast day of Santo Tomás, the expedition left their camp at Santa Lucía and about a league later, descended a steep slope toward an arroyo. Shortly, they walked along the Arroyos de Santa Humiliana where they had been on September 13. That morning, they had crossed over the trail they had constructed on the way north.[72] Soon after that, they exited the Sierra de Santa Lucía and descended to the beach, which they followed for four and a half leagues until they came to a native settlement. Some mountain natives had preceded them to that place and announced that the Spaniards were coming. When they got there, the natives traded them foodstuffs for beads. They told Portolá that they had housed one of his men, who had been there for three days. Portolá immediately ordered a guard to bring him to their camp. It turned out to be one of two men who were thought to have deserted the expedition before it left San Francisco Bay. Portolá had him interrogated. The man, a mulatto named Badiola,[73] explained that he and the other man, along with two California Indians, had not deserted. Instead, while they were out hunting geese in the bay area, they decided that they would cross the mountains along the coast and be the first ones back to San Diego "to be the first to discover the harbor of Monterey and win the reward by returning to the camp with the news."[74] Later, fearing that they would be punished for being absent without permission, they decided to keep going, make the announcement, and be forgiven for their fault and besides, receive the reward. They had followed the coast to the Sierra de Santa Lucía, and crossed it with great labor and fatigue, "sometimes rolling down the declivities."[75] For that reason, one of the two men, suffering much from his march through the mountain, had decided that he could not go on and begged the two Indians to allow him to remain in their company with some fishermen until he could recover. Fearing punishment and afraid to cross the mountain, he decided to stay with the natives.[76] The expedition remained at that camp for two days.

Finally the men were out of the mountain range. They spent a rainy December 22 resting. At their camp, they were surprised by several warriors who approached them with a mule that had run away from the expedition the month previous. The Spaniards were impressed with their honesty. That day, they had traveled two leagues in a south-by-southeast direction.[77] On Saturday, December 23, they left Santa Humiliana and set out once again in the midst of threatening weather. After three and a half leagues, they marched along the San Juan de Dukla arroyo they had last seen on September 12. They stopped along an arroyo at another familiar place called El Laurel. Just as they got there, it began raining heavily. The rain continued well into the night. A group of natives came to visit the party, and they traded beads for seeds and pinole.[78]

Christmas Eve began with a Mass said by the priests. Departing the Arroyo de San Juan de Dukla, they resumed the "same road by which we came." The rains had washed away a part of the trail they had constructed through a pass when they went north; this now had to be reworked. In addition, the area was full of brush, which the men cleared with machetes. After three leagues, they reached "the same spot as on the 10th of September, which was in the valley of El Osito de San Buenaventura, also known as El Paraje y pinal de San Benevenuto."[79]

Christmas Day, Monday, December 25, opened with the celebration of a Mass in honor of the "Nativity of the Lord" in the cold valley air. The expedition packed up and left in a southeasterly direction at about two o'clock in the afternoon. After traveling three and a half leagues, they stopped at the estuary called Santa Serafina, near an Indian fishing village. They traded beads to the villagers for fish and celebrated with native foods of pinole, atole, and fish.[80]

The next day, December 26, the group traveled four leagues along muddy terrain caused by heavy rains and stopped at their old camp in the valley of San Adrián, or Los Osos.[81] Crespí wrote that they "departed from this ranchería and seventh arroyo for the cove at el Morro. This arroyo is the seventh in the trek from el vallecito de San Adriano to the camp at Santa Serafina, which we left one league behind us to the north and six arroyos of running water at the ranchería de San Adriano."[82] When they got there, the ranchería they had seen in September was abandoned. Another league beyond, they stopped at an arroyo and set up the *real* at Nativitas B. Mariae. On this leg of the journey, they did not see a single settlement. However, Crespí noted that the entire route from the time they left El Pinal de San Benevuto was heavily populated by bears. They were now ninety-two leagues from San Francisco Bay.[83]

By Wednesday, December 27, the weather seemed to have cleared, at least for the moment. After Mass, the men packed the mules. However, just as they started to leave, a cold, heavy rain hit the area and followed them throughout the day and into the night.[84] They entered a large plain with many bears near La Ranchería de San Ladislao, o del Buchón, where they had stopped on September 4.[85] The men wanted to explore the area, but time ran out as the rains continued to pelt them. Portolá, refusing to bend to the weather and knowing that they were almost out of supplies, pushed the men to march three full leagues in the drenching rain. They finally pitched camp and tried to sleep in the mud, wet, and cold. They next morning, they were unable to move forward because of the mud. They spent the day waiting for the ground to dry out as much as possible. Some native fishermen came by and offered them two or three octupuses. Other people from the Santa Bárbara Channel also came to see them. One of them was very affable and talked incessantly. They recalled having met him before on their way north and had named the place El Loco because of him. This man had accompanied them for a few days when they went north. He now offered to accompany them southward to the ranchería at San Luis Rey. Seeing that the expedition was famished, he went back and alerted the ranchería to help the travelers with food, which they provided. The expedition stayed at the settlement of "San Luis Rey de la Canal," as they called it, through December 28, because they needed to dry out their soaked clothing and baggage.[86]

On Friday, December 29, the group left the edge of the bear-filled plain and approached a lake filled with hundreds of wild geese. The hunters were not very lucky, but managed to kill a few of them. Their guide suddenly left them overnight. The men did not know it at the time, but he was their guardian angel. Still, the expedition meandered its way south by southeast for three leagues, crossing arroyos and passing through the Cañada de San Ladislao.

With great difficulty, they marched over a "spur of the mountains which extend to the sea." Avoiding the spur as much as possible, they descended into a valley, which offered them a more direct route to a place where they could camp.[87] By late afternoon, they stopped to rest. Suddenly they beheld a great number of Indians from the Santa Bárbara Channel and their great chief, El Buchón, the warrior with a large goiter whom they had met in September, approaching the camp with pinoles, atole, fish, deer meat, and other foodstuffs. The Spaniards paid them with glass beads. They thanked El Loco for his friendship, for it was he who went to El Buchón to ask him to help the Spaniards.[88] It was a godsend for Portolá and his starving men. Chief Buchón even showed them a ford where they could cross and avoid "the inevitable detours of the road inland, which is a labyrinth of lagoons and estuaries."[89] They were now ninety-five leagues from San Francisco.

Before the expedition broke camp on December 30, the natives, again led by Chief Buchón, came out to offer food and trade for glass beads. But the kind chieftain, realizing that the Spaniards were in a bad way, sent back to his village for even more food, which was divided among all the men. After walking along the beach for a league, they moved inland for two leagues and reached two lakes between some sand dunes.[90] On September 3, they had named the lakes San Juan de Perusio and San Pedro de Saxferrato. It was also the place that the soldiers had earlier called Paraje de las Víboras and Paraje del Oso Flaco.[91]

Daybreak on Sunday, December 31 gave them more reasons to say a Mass of thanksgiving. The natives in the area came out with pinole, atole, and tamales, for which the Spaniards gave them beads. After a march of three leagues, they spent New Year's Eve at a camp along a long lake, where they again traded beads for food from the local natives. They recalled how they had spent the night there four months before on September 1, 1769. They had named the camp Los Santos Mártires San Daniel y Sus Compañeros. They were now 104 leagues from San Francisco Bay.[92]

Herbert Bolton summarized the locations of each camp of the return march throughout December 1769:

> at Monterey on the 10th; near Blanco on the 11th; near Chualar on the 12th; near Camphora on the 13th; above Metz on the 14th; near King City on the 15th; in Jolón Valley on the 16th; at Nacimiento River on the 17th; near Los Burros Creek on the 18th; in the Hollow at the forks of Campoforo Creek on the 19th; near Arroyo del Oso on the 21; near San Simeon Bay on the 23d; at Santa Rosa Creek on the 24th; east of Ellysby's Creek, at the north end of Estero Bay on the 25th; at Chorro

Creek on the 26th; near the site of San Luis Obispo on the 27th; north of Pismo, in San Luis Canyon, on the 29th; at Oso Flaco Lake on the 30th; at Guadalupe Lake on the 31st.[93]

Crespí continued to report on the group's progress. His account for the month of January 1770 identified the length of their daily marches and location of their camps, leaving behind invaluable information regarding their trail back to San Diego. The expedition spent New Year's Day marching from their camp at the long lake on the trail they had used earlier on their way north. Their pathway led them to a passage in the valley, which they descended. There, they visited the same ranchería they had on the outbound exploration to Monterey Bay.[94] The Indians came out to meet them with fistfuls of feathers and some food. Portolá gave the chiefs glass beads in return. They rested there a short time, then moved on.[95] They next came to a canyon, where the soldiers killed two bears, which fed them for the next three days. After three and a half leagues of march, they stopped to camp at San Raimundo Nonato or La Graciosa, where they had stayed on August 31, 1769. They believed there was a village nearby that they had seen on the way north, but that day, it "was not found here."[96]

The next day, Tuesday, January 2, they left the waterhole at San Raimundo Nonato and traveled southeast two and a half leagues to the Río de San Bernardo (which Crespí spelled "Berardo"), also called Santa Rosa, where they had passed three days on the outbound trip, August 29 through 31.[97] At that time, they had met Indians from a nearby settlement, but this time, the village was abandoned. Moving slowly, they found pasturage for their animals. About another league beyond the river, they stopped at an arroyo near the beach with running water. There, they supplied themselves with water because they remembered that further ahead, beyond the Punta de los Pedernales, at the Cañada Seca where they had been on August 29, there was none to be had.[98]

On the morning of Wednesday, January 3, they traveled south for a league beyond the Río de San Bernardo with their friend and guide "El Loco," who wore a headdress of feathers "like a crown" and carried a bow and quiver full of arrows.[99] Crespí noted that this man had accompanied and guided the expedition from the Santa Bárbara Channel, but from time to time would disappear then suddenly reappear. This time he returned to their resting place with a number of natives from nearby rancherías with food for the expedition, including atole and pinole for their breakfast.[100] The hungry Spaniards greatly appreciated him and his native friends for the helping hand. The natives asked for nothing in return, but the Spaniards gave them the cherished glass beads for their kindness.¹⁰¹

Marching from there for two leagues later that morning, the expedition reached the settlement they had on August 28, 1769 called San Juan Bautista de los Pedernales, from which they could see Point Concepción, the most western point of the Santa Bárbara Channel. A good-sized cove from Concepción to Pedernales was visible from the Ranchería de los Pedernales, the last formal Indian settlement of the Santa Bárbara Channel. The expeditionary force noted that beyond the ensenada to the north were the last two islands of the Santa Bárbara Channel and to the west, the Farallón de los Lobos and the last small island in the channel.¹⁰² Crespí said that the point was "eight degrees east of southwest."¹⁰³ From a different perspective, Costansó wrote:

> From the Punta de los Pedernales, the Punta de la Concepción—the most westerly point of the Canal de Santa Bárbara—can be seen to the southeast, 8° east; the most westerly point of the Isla de San Verardo, to the south, 33° east; the westerly point of the Isla de Santa Cruz, directly to the southeast.
>
> To the Punta de los Pedernales, 2 leagues. From the Ensenada de Pinos, 64 leagues.¹⁰⁴

The next day, January 4, the expedition left the Punta de San Juan Bautista de los Pedernales with their guide, "El Loco," at the head of the group. The people at the ranchería gave them some pinole, fish, and clams to take with them.¹⁰⁵ Crespí noted, "We set out early in the morning, and following the channel by the road over which we came, we passed by the town of La Espada, and continued the march for four and a half leagues."¹⁰⁶ About a league away, Pedro Fages encountered some Indians who traded an assortment of fish for glass beads. They passed a ranchería at the Arroyo de la Concepción and then came to two rancherías at Santa Teresa, one of which was the Ranchería del Cojo from their stay the previous August. There, Chief Cojo presented them with a fattened mule that they had left behind as skinny and ailing. His people gave the soldiers dried sardines and tuna in great abundance. Portolá assuredly gave the villagers the only thing the expedition had of value to them: glass beads. Along with that, the Indians wanted anything of metal, such as knives, nails, or spurs.¹⁰⁷

The lush green pasturage in the valley of El Oso helped to rejuvenate the expedition's animals.¹⁰⁸ Crespí noted that their camp that night was one league from the Punta de la Concepción.¹⁰⁹ Costansó's entry for that date read:

The weather, from the time we left the Cañada de los Osos, had been very clear. Only the nights were cold; the days were more like those of spring than of winter.

POSITIONS OF THE ISLANDS FROM THIS PLACE
San Bernardo: western point . . . S 12° SE
eastern point . . . S 17° SE
Santa Cruz: western point . . . S 30° SE
eastern point . . . S 41° SE
Santa Bárbara: western point . . . SE 8° E
eastern point . . . SE 22° E

The island of San Bernardo, in the language of the natives, is called Thoa; that of Santa Cruz is called Lotolic; that of Santa Bárbara, Anajup.

To the Pueblo del Cojo, 4 ½ leagues. From the Ensenada de Pinos, 68 ½ leagues.[110]

On January 5, the band left early in the morning and traveled two and a half leagues that day. About one league out, they came to the Punta de la Concepción; nearly two leagues later, meandering eastward along the coast, they passed the Ranchería de Santa Ana, twenty thatched houses on the edge of the beach.[111] Another half a league beyond Santa Ana, they arrived at the Ranchería de San Zeferino, which was also on the edge of the beach, with fifty thatched houses that housed about two hundred people. There, they traded glass beads for fish. A short way beyond that, they stopped to camp for the night.

On January 6, the feast day of the Epifanía del Señor, also known as Día de los Reyes (Three Kings Day), they broke camp following the Holy Mass. Making their way southward and then east, they crossed several arroyos and crossed land they found familiar in several places. After two leagues, for example, they came to San Luis Rey de Francia, also known to the soldiers as La Gaviota, where they had camped on their way north on August 24. There, "El Loco" left them. The Spaniards were sad to see him go, as he had been their friend and *bienhechor* (benefactor).[112] The ranchería in this place had about fifty-two houses and about three hundred residents. At that point, they were 122 and a half leagues from San Francisco Bay.[113]

While there, Costansó summarized the group's travel from January 5 to January 7 by writing that on January 5,

In the morning, we left the Pueblo del Cojo or Punta de la Concepción. We traveled for two leagues to the east, and halted near the town which was given the name of San Zeferino Papa.

There was enough fish in this village for all the men.

POSITIONS.
San Bernardo: western point ... S 5° SW
eastern point ... S 1° SW
Santa Cruz: western point ... S 5° SE
eastern point ... S 25° SE
Santa Bárbara: western point ... S 35° SE
eastern point ... SE 9° E
Falsa Vela: middle point ... SE 28° E

At sunset, with the same compass, the center of the sun was ascertained to be west, 36° southwest; its declination was 22°32' at that hour, with a slight difference. The altitude or latitude of the place, by observation made on August 25, is 34°30', and, consequently the western amplitude of the sun would be 27°42'; this being subtracted from the magnetic amplitude gives the variation of the compass on these coasts of 8°18'.

To San Zeferino, 2 leagues. From the Ensenada de Pinos, 70 ½ leagues.[114]

On January 6, while camped at San Luis Rey, the natives came and gave them more fish. Costansó noted:

From San Zeferino Papa it is two short leagues to San Luis Rey. We covered the distance before noon and halted at the same place as on the former occasion.

POSITIONS OF THE ISLANDS FROM THIS PLACE.
San Bernardo: western end ... S 23° SW
eastern end ... S 8° SW
Santa Cruz: western end ... S 3° SW
eastern end ... S 8° SE
Santa Bárbara: western end ... S 13° SE
eastern end ... SE 2° E
Punta de la Conversión ... SE 23° E
To San Luis, 2 leagues. From the Ensenada de Pinos, 72 ½ leagues.[115]

Finally, after Mass on Sunday, January 7, they marched two more leagues to San Guido, where they stopped to fish. Costansó wrote:

> From San Luis Rey we passed to the town of San Guido, a distance of two short leagues over a bad road; this was covered in the morning.
>
> POSITIONS.
> Punta de la Concepción to the . . . W 5° SW
> San Bernardo: western end . . . S 28° SW
> eastern end . . . S 22° SW
> Santa Cruz: western end . . . S 12° SW
> eastern end . . . S 10° SE
> Santa Bárbara: western end . . . S 21° SE
> eastern end to the . . . SE
> To San Guido, 2 leagues. From the Ensenada de Pinos, 76 leagues.[116]

By January 8, they had reached the Indian settlement they had called San Luís Obispo. Using his instruments, Costansó recorded their position and wrote:

> In the morning, we moved our camp from San Guido to San Luis Obispo, a distance of three short leagues from the former place.
>
> POSITIONS.
> Punta de la Concepción to the . . . W 1° SW
> San Bernardo: western end . . .
> eastern end . . .
> Santa Cruz: western end . . . S 25° SW
> eastern end . . . S 4° SW
> Santa Bárbara: western end . . . S 2° SE
> eastern end . . . S 42° SE
> Falsa Vela to the . . . SE 2° E
> Punta de la Conversión . . . E 26° SE
> To San Luis Obispo, 3 leagues. From the Ensenada de Pinos, 79 ½ leagues.[117]

They were now 129 leagues from San Francisco Bay.[118]

The next day, January 9, after traveling for two and a half leagues along the Arroyo de San Luis Obispo and over the rough and difficult terrain of coastal California, filled with live oaks, they arrived at a settlement they called La Isla.

On the outbound part of their journey, they were at the island ranchería of the "gran paraje del pueblo islado y estero de Santa Margarita de Cortona," which the soldiers had, on August 20, 1769, named Mescaltitlán.[119] Crespí wrote that the five or six settlements there housed between seven hundred and eight hundred people. The Spaniards bypassed the villages and pitched camp to the east. The place, wrote Crespí, had "no fish; I do not know whether it was because there was none at this season, or whether the Indians had not gone out for it."[120] He noted that the flocks of geese that had followed them by the thousands also had diminished in size. They figured that they were now 131 and a half leagues from San Francisco Bay.[121]

Lack of fish at La Isla bothered them because they had counted on it for sustenance. The same was true of the next place they stopped on January 10. From Santa Margarita de Cortona, they marched two leagues to a settlement they had called San Joaquín. From there, they continued four more leagues to their old familiar place at La Carpentería, also known as the Pueblo de San Roque.[122] Near San Joaquín, they stopped at the "same spot where we were on the 17th of August, the fish being absent here also."[123]

Meanwhile, Pedro Fages, Miguel Costansó, and friars Crespí and Gómez had gone ahead to see if any of the natives had dried fish for trade. When the expedition caught up with them, they found the entire village of four hundred to five hundred people wailing loudly. They quickly learned that this was a burial ritual for one of their dead. They had wrapped him in many rabbit pelts, sewn together as a large cape and tied to the body. Crespí wrote that warriors, probably chiefs, decorated the pelts. As part of the ritual, one of them went around the body smoking from a stone pipe and blowing smoke toward the sky. Then he approached the deceased, and slightly lifting his head, blew a large amount of smoke at it, and raising the leg and arm, blew more smoke at the body. Aware of the Spanish presence, the warriors asked them to leave. That day the expedition traveled eastward for six leagues and were now 137 and half leagues from San Francisco Bay.[124]

On Thursday, January 11, they headed eastward out of La Carpentería and moved along the beach in an easterly direction. About a half a league later, they reached the Ranchería de Sana Clara de Montefalco, which was on a hill along the edge of the beach. Another two and a half leagues of march brought them to the Ranchería de Santa Cunegundis before reaching a campsite at La Asumpta de María Santíssima en los Cielos. Crespí wrote that La Asumpta was the last and best of the settlements on the Santa Bárbara Channel.[125] They spent the day there. As they passed the settlement at El Bailarín, Crespí recalled that when they came through the area earlier, there were plenty of fish. Now, there were very few. Still, Fages was able to trade ribbons and glass beads with natives in the area for some dried fish and salt. That day, the men traveled five leagues. Costansó observed their bearings and pointed out:

> From this place the most westerly islands of the channel could no longer be seen. That of Santa Bárbara was the only one observed.
>
> Its western end was to the . . . SW 22° W
>
> Its eastern end was to the . . . S 35° W
>
> Falsa Vela to the . . . S 6° W
>
> Las Mesitas, three in number, to the . . . S 40° E
>
> A low point of sand, at a distance of three miles to the . . . S 33° E
>
> Note: Las Mesitas are small islands of moderate elevation above the sea, and level on top, to the west of La Falsa Vela, another islet of greater elevation, which, the first time we saw it, appeared to us to be a vessel.
>
> To La Asumpta, 5 leagues. From the Ensenada de Pinos, 91 ½ leagues.[126]

Early the next day, Friday, January 12, the men left La Asumpta and the Santa Bárbara Channel heading east. The expedition crossed the valley of Santa Clara "in a southwesterly direction in order to enter the Sierra de la Conversión, with the object of going to take the valley of Santa Catarina."[127] Moving over they mountain through a pass for two leagues, they crossed the San Hipólito River. A guide from a village near its banks led them near where they had camped the previous August 13. He took them southwest through a low range of hills that came out on a large plain, which ended on the west side at the sea. They climbed the opposite hill to the east and entered a valley, which they followed to the southeast. They stopped at a very poor settlement of sixty people and camped nearby. They named the place "San Higinio." That day, they had marched six leagues.[128]

The next two days, January 13 and 14, their guide took them southeastward through a long mountain pass. Following an arroyo, they came down a hill to a large spring, where they filled their water bags. Crespí named it "El Ojo de Agua de la Cañada de los Reyes." Ascending another hill, they came to a small valley, which took them to another ridge where they visited a small settlement they called the Ranchería de los Reyes. There, the natives traded them roasted mescales for glass beads.[129] Although the Indians wanted their visitors to stay, they continued on their way. After climbing a hill, they saw a very beautiful plain with another settlement, which they called "San Pedro Mártir." That day, they marched three leagues.[130]

The next day, Sunday, January 14, after praying the Holy Mass, the party traded for food with the natives. Resupplied, they headed northeast through a pass in the mountain that twisted eastward and finally southeast. After one league, they stopped to camp. They named their camp "El Triunfo de Dulcísimo Nombre de Jesús."[131] There, two local Indians offered to guide them through the mountains. They followed them through very rugged and winding terrain for a half a league and found the land, as Crespí noted, so rough that the mule pack train could not negotiate it. Apparently the guides were accustomed to foot trails for humans. Portolá decided to turn back to the village, where they "took better guides." Crossing some hills, they found level land to the east and traveled two "short" leagues. The halted near a settlement they called "El Triunfo del Nombre de Jesús," where the Indians guides urged them to camp for the night because the next watering place was some distance away.[132] Tired from marching back and forth, they spent the night near the Indian settlement.

Early on the morning of January 15, they followed two or three guides in a southeasterly direction. They entered a small canyon in the Sierra de la Conversión.[133] They traveled a league and a half to another village. There they left their original guides and took on another, who led them in a northeasterly direction, then east, until they climbed a long steep hill from which they could see a familiar large valley. After four leagues more, they entered the valley of Santa Catarina de Bonania, where they had been in early August. Marching another three leagues through it, they came to a hot spring "which this valley has to the south."[134] They traveled from northeast to southeast until, after sunset, they reached a place they called Los Robles. There, as they had on August 7, 1769, they set up their camp in the afterglow of day. That cool January day, they had marched seven leagues.[135]

The next day, January 16, they left their camp and traversed the valley to the east to get south to the Río de la Porciúncula. They knew that to the southeast was a plain that would take them through the mountain. They rounded the mountainous terrain to the east by the same path they had taken in 1769. On crossing the area to the southeast, they discovered a pass that led them to the plain of Los Alisos. Having covered three and a half leagues, they camped near an arroyo "which sinks into the sand near its source."[136] A little beyond there, they noted two more arroyos running through the canyon they called Los Santos Mártires San Cleto y San Marcelino. That day, Crespí noted that they had covered nearly four leagues.[137]

Upon entering a valley the next day, January 17, they could see not only a chain of mountains covered with snow, but also the Porciúncula River (also known as the Los Angeles River). They crossed the plain in a southeasterly direction and after two leagues reached the river and forded it. The land was filled with fallen trees and rubbish-filled pools of water and they realized that a great flood had hit the area. In the woods, they could see a ranchería. About five leagues east from the river, they could see the cordillera (range) that they had seen on their way north, which they recognized as the one that ran to the port at San Diego. That night, they camped in the valley of San Miguel where they had stopped outbound on the night of July 30, 1769.[138]

The next day, January 18, 1770, heading south, they passed through a gap in the valley of San Miguel and managed to march six leagues. They had traveled a long distance to the southeast on the edge of a stream in the gap, forded the river named for the valley, and traveled southeast to the river they had earlier named El Río de los Temblores, which they forded. They also noted that this river was carrying more water than the Río Porciúncula. The next day, Friday, January 19, the stopped at the springs of San Pantaleón (or Padre Gómez, as they also called it) and noted that they were on the same path they had taken on the outgoing part of the expedition the previous July. Moving three leagues beyond to the valley of San Francisco on January 20, they found the arroyo dry, even though it had run full from melted snow when they passed it the first time. They moved on another two leagues to the Valle Santa María Magdalena, also called La Quemada, whose arroyo was also dry. Some of the men fell sick with diarrhea, which was cause for concern as they camped for the night. They reckoned that they were 174 and a half leagues from San Francisco Bay.[139]

The next day, January 20, they headed southeast, the route they had taken the previous July. After two and a half leagues, they reached the Cañón y Arroyo de San Francisco Solano. As the arroyo was dry, they did not stop there. Moving forward, they arrived at their previous summer's camping area at Santa

María Magdalena. That day, they traveled five and a half leagues in a southeast and south-by-southeast direction.[140]

On January 21, the men marched until they came to a waterhole they had dubbed San Apolinario on July 20, which was in a canyon with an arroyo. It was now dry and the settlement there had been abandoned. It was in this place that the priests had baptized two dying children. They wondered if the little girls had lived or died.[141] That day, the expedition had covered five leagues.[142] They were now 184 and a half leagues from San Francisco Bay.[143] San Diego was not far from there, probably twenty-five leagues (about sixty-five miles). Crespí wrote that from San Apolinario, one could see the first island of the Santa Bárbara Channel, San Clemente.[144]

Herbert Bolton explained the trajectory of the route taken by the expedition between January 16 and January 22 as taking in territory from the San Fernando Valley to San Onofre Creek. He wrote:

> On January 16, Portolá left San Fernando Valley by Cahuenga Pass and camped near its mouth north of Hollywood; on the 17th he camped at the San Gabriel River near Bassett; on the 18th, instead of recrossing Puente Hills through La Habra, he followed the San Gabriel till near Whittier, then struck southeastward to his old camp on the Santa Ana near Olive. From there the northward route was retraced to San Diego, but as the homeward marches were so long, several of the old camps were passed without stopping. On January 21 camp was apparently on San Onofre Creek.[145]

Traveling through the valley of Santa Margarita without stopping, on Monday, January 22, the expedition went five or six leagues headed south-southeast.[146] That day, they crossed through the valley of San Juan Capistrano along a road of sloping hills. In the canyons, they noticed several lagoons which they had not seen in the outgoing stage of the expedition in July 1769. Their perspective, of course, was different as they headed south. The next day, January 23, they reached San Jácome de la Marca after "marching seven leagues and passing Santa Sinforosa, two leagues from San Alejo, and two or three more to San Jácome, which is the camping place."[147] Their march for that day totaled eight leagues and they now had turned directly south. They were now 203 and a half leagues from San Francisco Bay.[148]

On Wednesday, January 24, they marched six more leagues, marking 209 and a half leagues from San Francisco Bay.[149] They knew they were close to San

Diego. They could only guess about what the place looked like now. Was it even still there? Was everyone dead, or had some of the sick men survived? They also feared that the Indians from San Diego had wiped out the small colony and mission. They would soon know the answer to their grim predictions, one way or another. Approaching the area at about noon, the men "at last made out the fence of poles and the humble buildings that contained the mission. Immediately all the soldiers discharged their firearms, our first announcement to the inhabitants of the mission, who, in the greatest excitement, came out immediately to welcome as with open arms."[150] They, along with Fray Vizcaíno and Fray Fernando Parrón, quickly met Father Serra.[151] While some of their worst fears were realized, they found most of the men who had remained at San Diego alive. Father Junípero Serra and others were still convalescing from scurvy. One of their missionaries, Fray Vizcaíno, had been hit in the hand by an arrow in August. Some of the men had died, but the colony was still there.

The priests who had remained told about the attack by the Indians of San Diego. It occurred on the feast day of La Asunción de María Santíssima a los Cielos, August 15, 1769. Forty or more Indians, well-armed, attacked the new mission. After first entering in a friendly manner, they mixed with everyone, then suddenly, when everyone's guard was down, violently began their attack. They killed one man, a servant named José María, and wounded three others, although none seriously. It was then that Fray Vizcaíno was wounded in the hand. The attack was quickly put down when the soldiers fought back, but it left the small colony in shock.[152]

As they exchanged stories, the men must have realized that California's future had changed. Portolá's expedition had resulted in a significant event in establishing the route to San Francisco from San Diego. It had also established the trajectory for settlement, which, in proximity to the sea, would shape the location of the villages, forts, ports, missions, and ranches of early California. These would inevitably become the homes of millions of people inhabiting modern California, particularly around the coastal route. The route itself established the corridor for the Camino Real de California, which would connect towns, missions, ranches, and coastal fortifications along with maritime ports of entry at the many harbors along the coast. Thus, they had accomplished the first phase of accomplishing the "king's business."

There was, however, more to the story about the route. While the settlement of Alta California by Spain preordained the future of the region, one of the results was the creation of a line of communication, travel, and transportation

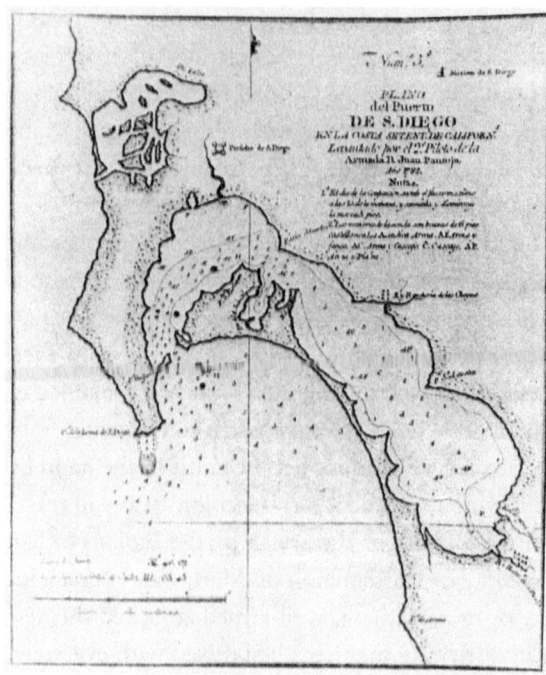

MAP 7 *Puerto de San Diego*, 1785. National Park Service–Spanish Colonial Research Center Map Collection, Center for Southwest Research, Zimmerman Library, University of New Mexico.

of people and things that came to be known as the Camino Real de California. The expedition commanded by Governor Gaspar de Portalá and accomplished under extreme hardship opened the first pathway. It confirmed known geographic and topographic place-names that had been established by Spanish explorers and Manila Galleon mariners after 1542 when Cabrillo's ships first ran the coast as far as southern Oregon. Portolá not only located known places along the California coast, but confirmed the latitudinal readings of each site as noted by mariners during the previous 240 years of maritime experiences, particularly from Point Reyes to San Diego. His religious cohort, Friar Juan Crespí, also sought possible mission sites, some of which became reality in the next two decades. Soon after the first expedition, Portolá commanded a second in an effort to confirm the location of Monterey Bay, which they knew to be at 37 degrees north latitude, but which eluded them because they were expecting to find an enclosed harbor and bay instead of the open unprotected bay that lay before them.

After Portalá's round-trip march from San Diego, Spanish explorers returned to the northern coastline beyond Monterey to the explore the area surrounding San Francisco Bay. On November 21, 1770, Pedro Fages, following Portolá's land route, left San Diego, accompanied by Fray Juan Crespí, six Catalonian Volunteers, six leather-jacket soldiers, a muleteer, and Crespí's Indian servant Paje. Their objective was to find a way by land to Point Reyes by traveling along the southern arm at the entrance to San Francisco Bay. They hoped that the arm would take them there directly. As they discovered, the two arms, which formed the entrance to San Francisco Bay from the sea, did not connect. In the twentieth century, a manmade connection was added with the construction of a suspension bridge, the Golden Gate Bridge. In the eighteenth century, the solution was not as simple.

Fages followed a route that veered northeast from Monterey and across the wide Salinas Valley, past the sites of present-day Hollister, Gilroy, Coyote, and San José. From there, the expedition turned toward the coast and, within five days of travel, reached the area of present-day Berkeley. Of that event, Fages wrote on November 28: "Four soldiers went out to explore the country, and at night they came back, saying that they had gone about seven leagues toward the north. The said that the land was very good, and level; and they had climbed to the top of a hill, but had not been able to discern the end of the inlet which lay before them and communicated with one which was at our right hand."[153] In all likelihood, they were looking across to the opening of the sea where the Golden Gate Bridge would later stand. From there, they could see the mouth of the estuary and two arms of San Francisco Bay. This was the second time that Spaniards had stood in the area, once led by Portolá in 1769 and now by Fages in 1770. Still, Fages and his men, twelve Catalonian Volunteers and seven *soldados de cuera* had been pathfinders, for they had traversed along the 1769 route and, from their new vantage point, proclaimed that they were looking at the "entrance through the bay of the port of San Francisco." Fages remarked that he had "made certain by having viewed it" for himself.[154] Indeed, they had discovered and verified the entrance to the bay from the sea. After fourteen days of marching, the expedition party returned to Monterey Bay.

Meanwhile, Fages and his men turned to establishing the Presidio de Monterey. On June 3, 1770, they had witnessed Fages perform an act of possession there. First, the Spanish standards were planted in the ground. Father Serra, who had arrived aboard the *San Antonio*, sang a High Mass. Next came the formal act of sovereignty, after which everyone present sang the *Te Deum Laudamus*. The soldiers then fired their muskets and artillery.[155] Fages confirmed that the formal act of possession had been taken. Of the event, Fages, referencing the earlier expedition led by Governor Portolá, later wrote:

As Lieutenant of the Free Company of Volunteers of Catalonia, assigned by Your Majesty to this New Kingdom of Spain, I certify that the commandant of this expedition, Don Gaspar de Portolá, has taken possession of the Port of Monterey and its environs the day cited in the name of Your Catholic Majesty, and with attention given the history of Californias of the voyage of Sebastián Vizcaíno, and by collection of sea charts of Cabrero Bueno, he [Portolá] found signs, similarly by sea as by land without any [signs] missing, and so that it be certified wherever necessary, I sign it today, June 11, 1770.[156]

Finding a land route to Point Reyes still challenged Fages. As they could not get to it across the entrance to San Francisco Bay, he decided on a second expedition, which took place in 1772. On March 10, at about 10:30 in the morning, Fages and his men departed Monterey.[157] Following the general routes of the 1769 and 1770 expeditions, they reached the Santa Clara Valley four days later. The Spaniards noted that this was a great plain with oak trees and named it the "Robles del Puerto de San Francisco." A few days later they reached San Salvador de Horta (San Lorenzo Creek).[158] Throughout the expedition, they met friendly natives who welcomed them to their land. By March 27, Fages, still seeking a way to Point Reyes, reached Oakland, skirting the bay, which he looked across toward the present-day Golden Gate Bridge and sighted five islands of which "three form a triangle."[159] The three islands are today known as Alcatraz, Yerba Buena, and Angel. On March 29, after climbing hills and crossing arroyos, the party came to a place formed by hills and a round estuary forming a large bay. They were at the inner San Pablo Bay[160] within San Francisco Bay. They concluded that San Pablo Bay was the end of the estuary they had been trying to circumvent. They hoped that all they needed to do was to follow it around to Point Reyes. A large channel of water, Carquinez Strait, stopped them and proved impassable.[161]

The next day, the expedition headed in a northeasterly direction, still following the channel. They encountered friendly natives and shortly came out at the entrance of a large plain. Fages described it as teeming with animal life. Ascending the pass to its highest point, the Spaniards observed the breathtaking panoramic view as far as the eye could see. Crespí wrote, "We saw that the land opened into a great plain as level as the palm of the hand, the valley opening about half the quadrant, sixteen quarters from northwest to southeast, all level land extending beyond the horizon. Below the pass, we beheld the estuary that we were following and saw that it was formed by two large rivers."[162] The two rivers were the Sacramento and the San Joaquín.[163] Standing on the edge of the Great Central Valley, they could foretell its great potential. Later, in 1775 and 1776, Fages wrote several reports extolling California's valuable resources, inclusive of flora and fauna.[164]

Fages concluded that it would be impossible to cross the Strait of Carquinez or the two rivers, neither of which could be circumvented without a boat at that time. He then divided his command to explore the land. One group followed the channel to the north; the other went south to find a better way back to Monterey.[165] By March 31, the disappointed explorers started back to their home base from a camp Fages called "the Camp of the Return," near present-day Pittsburg, California.[166] By April 5, the expedition was back at Monterey.

From the point of view of not finding a land route to Point Reyes, the expedition was unsuccessful. The explorers did, however, succeed in making three important discoveries: the entrance to San Francisco Bay, the inner San Pablo Bay, and the Great Central Valley of California. They were also successful in gathering valuable information for future settlers of San Francisco Bay. Significantly, in 1772 Fages and his men were the first non-native explorers to enter the Central Valley from the north.

The southern extent of the Great Central Valley was yet unexplored. Later that year, Fages and a detachment of soldiers left San Diego en route to San Luis Obispo, searching for deserters. Following the established route that passed through Mission San Gabriel, Fages veered westward through El Cajon Pass and traveled along the San Gabriel mountain range. Shortly, he entered the Mojave Desert via the Palmdale area to Antelope Valley. Passing through present-day Grapevine Valley to an Indian village near Buena Vista Hills, Fages and his men had entered the southern end of the San Joaquín Valley and were the first to realize the two valleys' north-to-south continuity.[167]

CHAPTER SEVEN

✤ ✤ ✤ ✤ ✤

Missions and Ranchos in Spanish Colonial and Mexican Territorial Alta California

✤ ✤ ✤ ✤ ✤

One league to the westward from the mission [San Gabriel] there are great forests of oak. . . . A great many Indians live there, hidden in their villages, which are found also on the seashore and on the plain. . . . The Rio de Porciúncula . . . contains water sufficient to use for irrigation, as does also another copious stream . . . to the west. Nor are there lacking in the vicinity of the forest . . . small streams from which water can be taken for the cultivation of the adjacent fields, so that the entire locality is most alluring, and offers facilities for the settlement of a few families of Spaniards. There might, without prejudice to the missions, have an assignment of fertile fields, with places adapted for all kinds of cattle. They would live in comfort, and with them we might begin to have hopes of very important settlement.
PEDRO FAGES | 1775

IN 1769, the first settlement expedition took place. This was sometimes referred to as the "Sacred Expedition" because part of the objective was to establish missions along the California coast. Its primary mission was a part of the Bourbon plan for the defense of empire. It was then that Spain aggressively occupied California by implementing its plan to establish presidios (forts), missions, ports, and settlements. Between 1769 and 1821, Spanish California touted four presidios with ranches, twenty-one mission sites with ranches, four

Pacific coast ports, four presidios, and numerous settlements between San Diego and San Francisco. Thus, the establishment of ports and presidios to defend against possible foreign intrusion by Spain's enemies called for effective occupation of California.

Within a few years of the tragedy-laden landing at San Diego Bay and the discovery of San Francisco Bay in 1769, California's new future lay in the hands of the Camino Real de California that connected the two distinct outposts. The exploration of California between 1769 and 1772 resulted in settlement over the next seventy years inclusive of missions, ports, ranches, and presidios, as well as the extension, development, and continued usage of the braided corridor of the Camino Real de California. To that end, California's early settlers had accomplished and continued doing the king's business as prescribed by the Laws of the Indies.

Once the Camino Real de California had been established by Portolá, ports, missions, and military outposts began to mark the map of California. In the wake of several settlement expeditions, the Juan Bautista de Anza expedition of 1775–1776 aimed to populate the San Francisco area. Anza ran his route from Horcasitas, Sonora, to San Francisco via the Tumacácori and Mission San Xavier del Bac in Santa Cruz Valley of Arizona at the confluence of the Gila and Colorado rivers. From there, the route crossed the Mojave Desert to a mountain pass near present-day Riverside, California. Once across the mountainous terrain, Anza and his people reached Mission San Gabriel in today's Los Angeles. After that, they basically followed the old Portolá route, which by then ran along newly established portions of the Camino Real northward to the new missions. Like Portolá, Anza led his expedition north from the Los Angeles area to Santa Barbara through the Santa Lucía Mountains, but along a more direct route than that taken by Portolá, past the Río del Carmelo and Monterey Bay to San Francisco Bay.[1]

Anza's route is today commemorated by the National Park Service as the Juan Bautista de Anza Historical Trail. Anza's expedition began its epic march from San Miguel de Horcasitas on September 21, 1775 and reached San Francisco Bay on June 27, 1776. The expedition included a mix of European, Native American, and African heritage groups. The colonists numbered over 240 (some histories estimate three hundred), of whom thirty soldiers took their wives, along with over one hundred children. Included were eight pregnant women. Moving the caravan forward were *vaqueros* (herders), muleteers, servants, and Native American guides. Aside from wagonloads of supplies, provisions, religious paraphernalia, and military accoutrements, the expedition included over one thousand head of livestock, largely cattle, horses, and mules.

The specific objectives of the Anza expedition were to reach San Francisco Bay and establish a presidio, a mission (Nuestra Señora de los Dolores) and a settlement in the surrounding area. It met all three. One other objective was to explore the area looking for the legendary Rio de San Francisco, basically beginning at Carqinez Strait, which was believed to be associated with the Strait of Anian or some waterway that reached the Atlantic Ocean. In the end, the expeditions determined that such a river did not exist. However, the search is part of the legacy, genealogical heritage, and history that shaped the Camino Real de California and led to the permanent establishment of San Francisco.

Throughout the history of Spanish America, missions developed a history of their own. In accordance with the Laws of the Indies and the Patronato Real, twenty-one missions were established in California from San Diego northward between 1769 and 1823. Almost immediately, as Portolá and his men were marching north along the California coast, Fray Junípero Serra and his missionaries established the first mission at San Diego. The last to be established was San Francisco Solano de Sonoma in 1823. Another important mission, San Francisco de Asís (Mission Dolores), was founded in 1776. (See appendix B, Parts I and II.) The mission trail of Alta California accounted for about five hundred miles of the Camino Real de California. An additional mission trail between Loreto in Baja California Sur and Rosarito Bay in Baja California is nearly seven hundred miles in length. (See appendix C.) Those missions were established between 1697 and 1833. Local histories recount that they were established about a day's horseback ride from each other, theoretically twenty-five to thirty miles apart. (For Alta California, see appendix D.) With the exception of a few founded inland—on the edge of the Salinas Valley, for example, or at Velicatá—most of the missions were closer to the coastline.

The history of missions in the New World predates the founding of California. By the end of the fifteenth century, the Middle Ages had come to a close as the modern world emerged. Yet the legacy of that time, with its attendant "Age of Faith," had left its mark on the future of religion in Europe and, after 1492, on the Americas. That year, Spain militarily defeated the Moors and initiated a period of expulsion for those who would not convert to Christianity. Following Columbus's first voyage, Spain had a new goal. Indeed, when cartographer Juan de la Cosa drew the first map of the Americas in 1500, he included a symbol of the medieval past that would lend significant application to the transmission of Christianity across the Atlantic Ocean. On the extreme left of his map, where he had placed the North American coastline, he depicted St. Christopher bearing the Christ Child across the sea. In his *Book of Prophecies* (1501), a collection of biblical texts presented to Spain's sovereigns, Christopher Columbus, who signed his name *Cristo Ferens*, or Christ Bearer, asserted that the first steps toward bearing Christianity across the Atlantic had been taken. Symbolically, just as Saint Christopher had carried the Christ Child across a raging river, Spain was poised to send missionaries across the Atlantic Ocean to Christianize the New World.

Once Spain embarked on the establishment of missions in this virgin territory, the mission churches that dotted the map across North America from Florida to California would across time become a part of our national story. As such, it is a shared history and heritage with Spain, Mexico, Latin America, and regional Native American tribes.[2]

Aside from spiritual conquest through religious conversion, Spain hoped to pacify areas that held extractable natural resources such as iron, tin, copper, salt, silver, gold, hardwoods, dyes, and tar, which could then be exploited by investors. Still, the missionaries hoped to create a utopian society in the wilderness. As an objective of the state, however, colonial areas could be pacified through missionization without the use of armies. Natives throughout the Americas did not agree with colonial philosophies or occupation of their land and sought remedies from warfare to coexistence strategies.

To assure that the missionaries would be able to sustain themselves, the king of Spain established the *Patronato Real de las Indias* (Royal Patronage of the Indies), which supported the Spanish Crown's absolute control over ecclesiastical matters within the empire. In that regard, the Spanish king and his council approved missionaries to go to the Americas, directed the geographic location of missions, and allocated funds for each projected enterprise. Under the Patronato Real, which also governed appointments of church officials to high office, some viceroys in Mexico and Peru were also archbishops, further cementing the church-state alliance in a common cause. The missions were, in effect, at once both agencies, charged with spreading the faith to natives, but also pacifying them for the state's aims. By intermingling religion, politics, and economics, the Patronato Real formed a large archival record of exploration, settlement, missionary activity, ethnographic data, and extraction of raw resources.

By definition, the "mission" was nothing more than a plan of conversion. Missionaries, usually working alone or with an *escolta* (military escort of one or two armed guards) would approach a group of natives and literally, with a portable altar to say the Mass, begin preaching through a translator. The construction of a church, a garth with a corridor, a garden, classrooms, housing for priests and neophytes, a refectory, corrals, and a defensive wall with a gate came later in time. Architecturally, the structures lent themselves to a variety of purposes in a completed mission site. Principally, the mission complex served as a religious center, as well as a vocational center and an economic center for trade and the production of crops, for it was also supported by noncontiguous lands for ranching and farming. Lastly, the mission served as a defensive center with heavy gates and doors, shuttered windows on high walls, and clerestories. Aside from the modern-day misconception that the church was the mission, the architectural splendor of these structures is a part of the romantic past tied to song, poetry, and history.

Deep in the wilds of North America, early missionary efforts commenced in places known as *La Florida* (following 1565 and along the eastern coastline to Chesapeake Bay by the early 1570s, and later in the Tallahassee area). Missionaries expanded into the Greater Southwest of the present-day United States in the sixteenth century. They founded missions in New Mexico (beginning in 1598), Texas (as far as San Angelo in the 1620s from New Mexico and along the Río Grande northward to East Texas and western Louisiana in the late 1690s and along the San Antonio River in the early 1700s), Pimería Alta, now southern Arizona and northern Sonora (1680s), and lastly California (1770s). Far from Spanish settlements, lone missionaries lived and worked among natives who were mostly hostile to them, at great peril. Generally avoiding Great Plains and mountain tribes with strong warrior castes, missionaries focused their efforts on sedentary farming tribes such as the Pueblos of New Mexico and semisedentary tribes along river valleys in Texas and Arizona. In California, missions were founded along the coast and interior lands. For the missionaries, it was truly an errand into the wilderness.

In most cases, Spanish arms were necessary for the mission program to succeed, especially in the hostile lands of northern New Spain, today's Greater Southwest and northern Mexico. In 1772, Friar Romualdo Cartagena, guardian of the College of Santa Cruz de Querétaro, one of the training centers for missionaries, wrote:

> What gives the missions their permanency is the aid which they receive from the Catholic arms. Without them, pueblos are frequently aban-

doned, and ministers are murdered. . . . It is seen every day that in missions where there are no soldiers there is no success. . . . Soldiers are necessary to defend the Indian from the enemy, and to keep an eye on the mission Indians, now to encourage them, now to carry news to the nearest presidio in case of trouble. For the spiritual and temporal progress of the missions two soldiers are needed . . . especially in new conversions.[3]

Thus, the role of the state was ever more present in the evolution of the missions throughout the Americas.

The mission fields were theoretically designed for a ten-year period, after which the missionaries were expected to move on to newly established areas. The scheduled plan of conversion did not work well due to Indian resistance to the rigors of the missions. In the long run, arguing that the natives were imperfectly converted because they reverted to their spiritual ways in secret, friars proposed that mission fields be extended another decade. Often such extensions lasted for several decades, if not a century longer than intended. By the end of the eighteenth century, and especially after Latin America's movement for independence from Spain, secularization would be the rule as mission lands were removed from church authority by newly established revolutionary governments. In most cases, emerging Western Hemispheric nations would either bestow citizenship on native groups, keep them as wards of the state, or treat them as social outcasts.

The significance of Spanish colonial missions in North America lies in their almost universal establishment. As such, their legacy is firmly a part of our national story and patrimony, and, equally so, it attaches to the common heritage that the United States shares with Spain, Mexico, and Latin America. Spain, it should be noted, was not alone in missionary enterprises throughout the New World, for French and Portuguese missionaries also made inroads in Canada, Brazil, and other parts of the Americas. In North America during the nineteenth century, the missionary zeal spread from east coast of the United States to the Great Plains, Utah, Idaho, and the Pacific Northwest. Thus, the mission served similar purposes inclusive of the spiritual conversion of natives: it was also a way to pacify and hold their precarious frontiers together for settlement and European economic exploitation and development. It would be a method employed by other nations in remote places such as India, the African continent, and Australia. The Spanish missions, like forts and towns, were frontier institutions that pioneered colonial claims and sovereignty to North America.

Much has been written about the missions and their legacy that ranges from the diffusion of Spanish culture, religion, governance, language, and the like to polemical dialogues condemning their role in altering native cultural practices, customs, and spiritual beliefs. There is no doubt that a cultural syncretism resulted from European and native contact, for Catholicism and other Christian denominational beliefs are still practiced among many of the tribes that participated in the evolving mission process.

Despite economic-based colonial regimentation that worked against native interests, the missions were devised to convert and "civilize." Still, colonial practices resulted in the exploitation of native groups. Although vestigial practices and perceptions about native groups persist into the present as a part of the European colonial legacy, the natives had their own notions about being exploited or having their cultural and spiritual domains threatened by the catastrophic colonial policies imposed on them. Their view, far from the utopian dreams of the missionaries, was often expressed as an unequivocal rejection of the mission process. Rightfully, native Americans viewed the mission programs throughout the Americas as destructive to their cultures. Their resentment toward the missions and overall colonial policies resulted in rebellions and open warfare that sometimes took years, if not decades, to resolve. Over time, the missions had made their mark on such tribes, for Indian spiritual customs had melded, at least in part, with Christianity.

The Spanish missions serve to remind us that the human experience is relative to the cultural values, people, traditions, and language of a different time. Beyond the splendor of their architecture, what we see today is the cumulative effect of a historic process triggered by Spain's efforts to govern and Christianize the New World, which culturally changed the land and people forever. Still, the tribes considered the mission process as destructive to their way of life; and. the intrusion of colonial populations and systems in their midst was unwanted. As First Peoples, Native Americans know and believe that their homelands were despoiled by the outside presence, whether Spanish, English, Portuguese, French, or Anglo-American. Perhaps Geronimo said it best in 1905, when he met President Theodore Roosevelt. In explaining why he fought to protect his homeland, Geronimo began with a traditional greeting and said these words: "Great Father. . . . Did I fear the Great White Chief? No. He was my enemy and the enemy of my people. His people desired the country of my people. My heart was strong against him. I said he should never have my country."[4] The vestigial dynamism of such a legacy continues across cultures and time, spilling into our present day.

Along California's Camino Real, mission churches, farms, and ranches were unilaterally established to sustain the missionary efforts and for trade. Typically, in California, the missions had one or two Franciscan friars, an escolta of two to eight soldiers, and a cadre of neophytes, or newly converted mission Indians. The escoltas were used to protect the priests from Indian retaliation, for recapturing runaway mission Indians, and to mete out the punishments ordered by the priests. The mission regimen was difficult for Indians for many reasons. They did much of the labor in the fields, although the soldiers also assisted. While the padres taught the natives to make adobe bricks and tiles for roofs, building mission structures, planting fields, constructing irrigation ditches, and herding cattle, sheep, goats, horses, and mules were a part of the acculturation and vocational training meant to help mission Indians learn to live in a Spanish society.

In California, as elsewhere, the mission, as a religious but imperial institution, had many roles, administered by the friars, who truly believed in their cause. First, it was a religious center for the conversion of natives. Second, it was a vocational training center, where natives were taught carpentry, masonry, and other skills. Third, it was a defensive center, whose architecture reflected defensive positions. And, fourth, it was an acculturation center, where the natives learned to speak Spanish and, once converted and acculturated, live within the Christian communities around it as citizens of Spain. The California missions reflected the missionary goals of church and state. Indeed, they were a center for conversion, with a customary lifespan of ten years, after which they would move from mission status to parish as a part of a new mission's congregation. Once the decade was reached, however, the friars realized that the conversion process was imperfect and, as stated above asked for another ten years. The decades passed. The Indians had by then largely adopted Christian ways, but continued to practice the beliefs of their ancestors. In reality, imperfect conversion was a way of life in the missions.

However, not all Indians in California were a part of the missionary effort. Many tribes refused to cooperate and stayed away from the missions except to attack and carry off herds and sometimes free other Indians. Indian rebellions at the Spanish missions were few: the first was at San Diego in 1769, the last the Chumash uprising of 1824. Antonio María Osio shed light on attitudes and issues that sparked the latter rebellion. He wrote:

> It is known and well proved that the Indians of Alta California, especially the adults, who were called Christians simply because they had been sprinkled with baptismal water were never true Catholics. They would leave their *ranchería* or their errant lifestyle and, out of fear, deceit, or self-interest, head for the mission that was beckoning them. They listened to the Fathers preaching the gospel, but they did not understand what was being said. . . . At Mission San José, administered by Reverend Father Narciso Durán, a number of Indians from the Cosumes tribe appeared and claimed that they wanted to become Christians. A few days later they received the baptismal water and the usual blanket and shirt. A custom had been established that a neophyte who had not appeared for work or who had committed some minor crime during the week would receive a dozen or more lashes at the church door after Sunday mass. Then, as a sign of submission, he would go and kiss the Father's hand. Among those to whom this happened was one of the Cosumes. . . . When he approached the Father, he took off his shirt and wrapped it up in the blanket. The he threw them both at the reverend's feet and said, "Father, take your Christianity. I don't want it anymore because I am returning to my land as a gentile." The Catholicism of those poor souls was more or less of this sort.[5]

The intrusion of the missions in their midst, the concern that Christianity would erode their culture, the disdain for Spanish colonial occupation, and the colonial system in general caused much resentment not only in California but elsewhere in the Spanish empire. This did not go away, although in a modern sense a sort of syncretism evolved, for the tribes, by dint of the historic process, learned to survive the onrush of Spanish colonialism, the Mexican national period, and the tumultuous arrival of Anglo-Americans during the Gold Rush, which proved to be disastrous for California tribes along the coast and in the interior.

During the Mexican Territorial period of California, 1821–1848, the missions throughout Mexico underwent a secularization process that had actually begun under Spanish rule in Texas in the 1790s. From the point of view of the Mexican national authorities, the missions were obsolete in regard to the needs of the new nation. In general, they had failed: the mission Indians were imperfectly converted Catholics, were not self-sufficient or proficient Spanish-speakers, and lacked the proper education required in that society at that time. The mission population, too, had declined severely, making the missions useless as a tool for government. In many ways the former mission Indians were left to fend for themselves. In order to survive, many of them Hispanicized and became hands or vaqueros on the many ranches throughout California.

In 1834, Mexico ordered the Catholic Church to give up much, if not all of its mission property and initiated a secularization process. The mission land, once part of the Spanish king's *Patronato Real*, or royal patronage based on sovereignty, now belonged to the Republic of Mexico. As such, it reverted to the sovereign as a part of the public domain. Soon after Mexican independence from Spain the process of secularizing the Franciscan missions in California was initiated. The first to undergo it was Mission San Juan Capistrano when, on August 9, 1834, Governor José Figueroa issued his "Decree of Confiscation." By 1835, sixteen missions had been secularized. The process continued until all mission lands were reverted to the state. The missions of San Buenaventura and San Francisco de Asís were the last to be secularized, in December 1836. Just ten years after Osio had written his opinion about the ineffectiveness of the missions, the end of an era was at hand.

The mission lands became, for the moment, part of the public domain and were sold off to bidders or granted to applicants. At that time, under Mexico, land grants, which included former mission lands, were given out to individuals willing to establish the ranchos of California (See appendix E). Earlier, during the Spanish Colonial period, in order to encourage settlement, California governors had granted nearly thirty land grants to loyal citizens and families to establish farms and ranches and eventually towns. In the late eighteenth century, Spanish jurists devised the Plan de Pitic of 1789. This revisited the legal usage of *propios* (public/community lands) in establishing of the town of Pitic, present-day Hermosillo, Sonora. Later, the Plan de Pitic was applied to establishing towns in New Spain's northern frontier.[6] In effect, it was a short, ready-to-use reference of those Laws of the Indies that related to land tenure. Because it was a restatement of a municipal ordinance and embodied the regulations used for town founding throughout the frontier provinces of New Spain, the plan is "a key document to be studied in understanding Spain's well-established rules for civilian settlement."[7] One of the California towns established under the Plan de Pitic was Branciforte near Santa Clara, California.

Changes were in the wind, as a new political vocabulary blew northward to California from Mexico City. Soon after Mexico had achieved independence from Spain, the Mexican National Congress established a series of land laws that applied throughout the nation. While the laws had the effect of breaking up the mission lands forever, they did codify the policies for establishing land grants. Colonization policies established under Spain set a precedent and greatly influenced legalists and officials during the early period of Mexican nation-building. As the transition took place, Mexican officials merged old practices and customs with new policies.

Late in the Spanish Colonial period, there occurred a change of mind when Spanish policy allowed outsiders into Spanish territory. The practice began in Texas, where Spanish officials allowed Anglo-Americans to settle—provided, of course, that they learn Spanish, convert to Catholicism, and attract a prescribed number of families to develop and protect the land. In 1798, Moses Austin had a small land grant in Spanish Louisiana. In 1821, his son, Spanish-speaking Stephen Austin, became an *empresario* under Mexico in Texas. Such policies would later have tremendous consequences for New Mexico, Arizona, and particularly California, as immigrants from the United States entered that area by both land and sea. The Oregon-California Trail, the Gila River Trail, and the Old Spanish Trail emanated from the east and became gateways to California. The traditional maritime lanes soon had immigrants entering California who had crossed Mexico and departed Mexican ports bound for San Diego, Santa Barbara, Monterey, and San Francisco.

The Colonization Act of 1824 outlined the procedure to be followed by officials who made grants within their territories. The language in the provisions specified the size of the grant, which had previously varied depending on the official. Article 12 stipulated, "It shall not be allowed that more than one square league of one hundred varas of irrigable land, four of temporal land, and six of range land, be united as a property in a single hand." This translated to a total number of square leagues per land grant to a single individual, which was established as eleven square leagues per person, roughly 48,800 acres of land.[8] In some instances, local Mexican authorities issued grants larger than this. Before long, New Mexico and, later, California began to see land grant activities under the new law. The provisions stipulated in the Colonization Act of 1824 were reinforced and clarified by the Regulations for Colonization issued in 1828. The Mexican National Congress ordered that the provisions of the act be observed by contractors and settlers of land grants.[9] Thus, the establishment of the ranchos, along with their juridical and legislative history, has a long and complicated history that awaits its historian.

The US-Mexico War of 1846 and the Treaty of Guadalupe Hidalgo of 1848 changed the course of California's history. Land grant issues proliferated throughout New Mexico and Arizona between 1848 and 1900. The West Coast ranchos, created from grants of land, took a different path when California became a state in 1850. Unlike the New Mexico and Arizona land grants, which, given their territorial status, were subject to Congressional action, those in California were adjudicated by state courts. Similarly, the establishment of ports and presidios was subject to laws, ordinances, policies, and other legal precedents dictated by both Spain and Mexico and, later, the United States. These ranchos, missions, ports, and presidios were the building blocks of the modern state. The ranchos formed yet another significant braid in the corridor of the Camino Real de California.

EPILOGUE

❋ ❋ ❋ ❋ ❋

The historical and cultural foundations of the Nation should be preserved as a living part of our community life and development in order to give a sense of orientation to the American people. Historic properties significant to the Nation's heritage are being lost or substantially altered, often inadvertently, with increasing frequency.
SECTION I OF THE NATIONAL HISTORIC PRESERVATION ACT, PUB. L. NO. 89–665, AS AMENDED BY PUB. L. NO. 96–515

GIVEN ITS HISTORY, HERITAGE, AND LEGACY, the California's Camino Real is more than a mere line drawn on a map. Locating its associated place-names and sites on the ground is paramount for the authentication of the route and its variants. History, on the other hand, is a living memory of places and events by the cultures that created them. Commemorating past cultures and peoples and their significance to the march of humankind requires an understanding of historical processes.[1] Native Americans played a large role in our national story, and one that needs to be commemorated.

The prehistory and history of California's Camino Real is of epic proportions in regard to the people who settled and developed the land, places, towns, and cities. To study solely the route for the route's sake is to deny the cultural dimensions of time, place, and the people who pioneered its founding, in this case, both Native American and Hispanic Californians. The word "culture" has many meanings, but one thing is sure: at its very least, culture is the way a group of people define their environment. This is done through language and practices that turn into customs, traditions, laws, and institutions. It is done by defining the homeland and its components, as well as how they are governed, protected, and preserved.

To that end, in 1966 the United States Congress, concerned with preserving and protecting our national heritage for future generations, enacted the National Historic Preservation Act.[2] This legislation rekindled the notion that historical significance is at the heart of the criteria for determining authenticity, and that wonderment, investigation, and analysis are its building blocks. The philosophic tenets of the act clearly apply to state and local justifications for authenticating California's Camino Real.[3]

The American national story runs deep, especially in California. The native tribes who met the Spaniards in 1769 had defined their environment and had learned to live in it. As the First Peoples they had, for centuries, lived their lives in a perilous territory, which in time had become even more dangerous as events that were not within their control unraveled before them. Despite being attacked by other tribes, sometimes with entire settlements being wiped out, they managed to recover and hold on to what mattered most to them. But in the long haul of history, the historical process of modern times proved unforgiving and harsh to them. While many of their languages have survived into the modern day, others have long since disappeared and, along with them, these peoples' conceptual worldview and traditions. While many tribes survived the Spanish Colonial period, the Gold Rush years proved to be the harshest of all tests that they would undergo. During the last half of the nineteenth century, their populations were decimated and displaced. In the process, many of their ways were destroyed and numerous cultural threads that held them together torn apart and lost forever.

To be sure, the missionization of native groups did not end with Spanish colonialism; it came west with Anglo-Americans who continued to attempt to convert Indians along their paths. In some cases, they went a step further and practiced policies of removal and waged wars of extermination. Later, under American rule, some native peoples were moved from their homelands to boarding schools, a practice aimed at religious conversion and acculturation. One can go further with a discussion about the disruption of Indian cultures, but the main point here is that their legacy in regard to the Camino Real de California would have been all but forgotten were it not for the earliest Spanish colonial documents that mention and describe them and their settlements, which in the modern world can be supported by archaeological findings and ethnographic studies. Modern-day tribes in California retained a memory of the past, but their role in forging the Camino Real de California can be reconstructed with an Indian perspective and included as a part of our national story. We owe the First Peoples the credit they deserve in defining the history of the United States, with both its positive and negative aspects. The history of California's Camino Real through the ages also ought to include their story.

The arrival of Spaniards under Governor Gaspar de Portolá in 1769 served as a defining moment for California's future. Members of his expedition described the local people and their cultures, albeit through European colonial eyes. Still, they left us a window through which to see the First Peoples of California along with what would become the Camino Real. Portolá and his men were the first to see and write about their settlements firsthand, eat their food, describe their distinct ways of doing things, and experience their personal kindness in sharing resources and knowledge, as well as appreciate their customary willingness to help strangers in distress. Members of Portolá's expedition described the native houses, their canoes, their styles of fishing and hunting, their weapons; they noted their languages and wrote down, phonetically, some of their words; they told about their cemeteries and noted their religious practices in their careful burial of their dead. The history of the Camino Real de California is not necessarily a romanticized story of a place, but, on a human scale, one of great sacrifice, hard work, perseverance, suffering, and survival. The native Californians' story, as a part of the history of the Camino Real, is about a people who struggled to preserve a way of life. Their story is represented in the patrimony of the Camino Real de California, which ought to be authenticated, preserved, and protected for future generations to enjoy.

The Spanish frontiersmen who ventured into California in 1769 were keenly aware that they were not the region's first settlers. They came, however, with a purpose that was broader than merely settling the area. They were part of a worldwide defense plan for the Spanish empire. They introduced a new system of governance and a new economy based on ranching, farming, and trade, combined with a new technology that allowed them to build on the land. On a cultural level, they introduced new language, religion, lore, music, foodstuffs, and other amenities.

Governance of the land required a political, legal, and organizational infrastructure that emanated from the king of Spain, who delegated executive power from a viceroy down to the governor and an *alcalde mayor*, a chief municipal administrator, who worked with a *cabildo*, the town council, of a given area. The cabildo, made up of elected and appointed officials, made decisions for each province and town. Property rights, such as those that governed land grants, as well as contractual and judicial procedures, were established through the Laws of the Indies. These first settlers' lives were not easy, for they suffered deprivation of the comforts of life, medicine, and security. The establishment of California, basically as a backwater area, depended on their sacrifice for the first decades of existence.

One aspect of their culture allowed them to plan for the future, for they could, through the written word, record and secure the corporate memory of their endeavors and, through architectural sketches, plan and construct the vertical world they would develop. In 1769, Spanish officials from Baja California Sur to Alta California envisioned a corridor of the Camino Real de California supported by an infrastructure comprising ports, presidios, missions, towns, and ranchos. Over time, the road's early pathways, forged from Indian trails, expanded into corridors for horse, mule, and wagon traffic that eventually supported modern-day motorized vehicles as a series of local, state, and regional roads and interstate highways.

In time, Spanish ports and towns became large cities with growing populations as the Camino Real faded into the romanticism of the past. In modern times its pathways were overrun by paved streets, roadways, buildings, parkways, concreted arroyos, and every other imaginable land use pattern.

Buried beneath today's California urban/rural infrastructures is the Camino Real de California, along with its native and Spanish colonial past. Education is a part of the remedy to salvage its patronage and promote the effort and commitment to preserve and protect the state's early history and heritage for future generations as a part of our national story. Authentication of its braided trajectories and corridors that served forts, ports, missions, ranches, and towns, as well as the settlements of First Peoples, is at the root of the preservation and conservation of this "royal road." Modern Californians are at a crossroads and can still rescue the Camino Real de California and its rich heritage from the further ravages of time, for it is a part of our national story that is shared with Spain, Mexico, and regional tribes in California.

APPENDIX A

❊ ❊ ❊ ❊ ❊

Identification of Presidios and Royal Presidio Ranchos

It goes without saying that the primary function of the presidio was defense of all establishments within the Spanish claim to California and the Pacific Northwest.[1] Spanish officials established four strategically placed coastal forts (presidios) along the California coast at the main ports of entry as the primary line of defense. The Camino Real de California tied the presidios by land, and the ports, as a part of the Camino Real corridor, formed a corresponding maritime corridor that connected to the land route.

The missions were also an important priority to defend the interior against possible Indian attacks, which over a long period of time did occur, either in terms of rebellions by mission Indians and attacks by local tribes or Utes. Warring Utes eventually attacked coastal and inland settlements between San Diego and San José, aside from later nineteenth-century establishments at Las Placitas, Agua Mansa, and Rancho Jurupa in the San Bernardino and Riverside area. They were settled by New Mexicans involved with trade from Santa Fe to Los Angeles via Utah. At the invitation of Spanish officials in California, the first two places were established by New Mexican traders from Abiquiu, long known for their prowess in war and peace, to defend against Ute attacks on coastal towns, ranchos, and missions.

Long before the establishment of inland settlements, however, the presidios were the forerunners of early coastal towns in California. By 1773, land was granted to presidio soldiers so that they could establish settlements outside of the forts. That year, Captain Fernando Rivera y Moncada was authorized to distribute land among his soldiers who wished to remain in California as settlers.[2] Despite the struggle to defend it internally from 1769 to 1845, Spanish/

Mexican California would fall from exterior forces in the form of an invasion by the United States in 1846.

As with all establishments in the New World, the Laws of the Indies also applied to military installations. All lands held in common were required to be near potable water, wooded areas, and pasturage. Common lands required water for irrigation of farmlands, grasslands for livestock grazing, and wood for everyday usage as well as construction of corrals, housing, and other building needs. Such requirements also applied to presidios.

A significant and often overlooked aspect of the Camino Real de California is its tie to presidial ranches and farms. These were properties of the king and, therefore, roads leading to them were a part of the Camino Real de California network. In 1777, for example, the Presidio de San Diego established a ranch to support its occupants, the "Rancho Real de San Diego." The ranch was established with ninety-four cows, forty-five calves, and ten bulls. Earlier, in 1774, during that critical time when food was still being rationed, Captain Rivera y Moncada had prohibited the sale and trade of any livestock, hoping to protect the dwindling herds. Soldiers at the Presidio de San Diego also established gardens of wheat, lentils, and vegetables that eventually developed into small irrigated farms. The presidial ranches and farms never produced enough foodstuffs to maintain the soldiers and their families. Ultimately, the people depended on trade with neighboring ranchos and missions. Still, the soldiers who had been the original laborers hired local natives whom they paid in kind with the products of their labor.[3] Along with the advantages of developing small garden farms and ranches for subsistence was the downside that these became targets for raids by marauding warriors.[4] Before long, other presidial ranches were established at Monterey, San Francisco,[5] and Santa Barbara. Overall, the Camino Real de California tied together presidios, missions, ports, towns, and ranchos within Alta California. Together, the presidios and their ranches are part of the corridor of the Camino Real de California.

Presidio Real de San Diego, 1769

The Presidio de San Diego dates to 1769 and was the first fort established in Alta California. Its Rancho del Rey, south of San Diego, became the Rancho de la Nación under Mexico. In 1845, it was granted to John Forster.

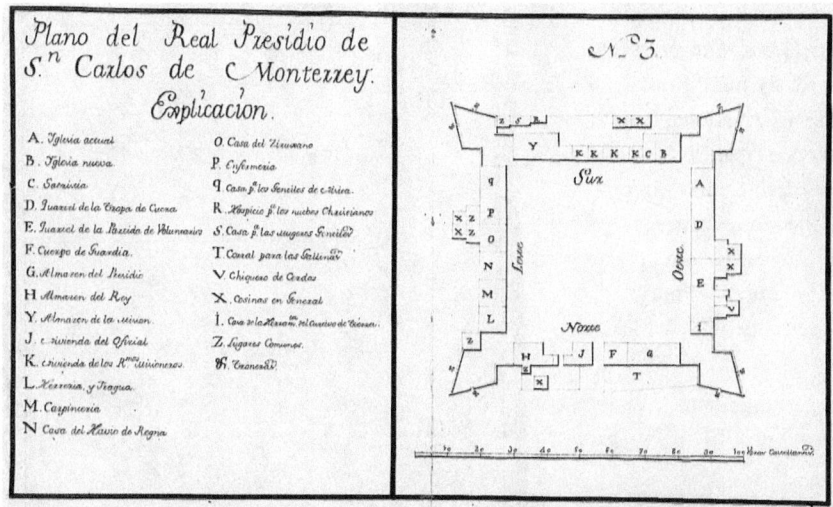

FIGURE 2   *Plano del Real Presidio de San Carlos de Monterey*, 1770. National Park Service–Spanish Colonial Research Center Map Collection, Center for Southwest Research, Zimmerman Library, University of New Mexico.

Presidio Real de San Carlos de Monterrey, 1770

The presidio at Monterrey was established in June 1770 to protect the missions being established in the area. It was located twenty-five leagues from San Antonio de Padua and fifteen leagues and beyond to the north. The royal fort of San Carlos de Monterey guarded the frontier in that region. It was located "two musket shots" from the Port of Monterrey. Its latitude was taken in 1770 at 36 degrees, 44 minutes.[6] Rancho del Rey San Pedro, the presidial ranch, which later became the Rancho Nacional, granted in 1839 to Vicente Cantua, was located in the vicinity of present-day Salinas.

Presidio Real de San Francisco, 1776

The Rancho del Rey became the Rancho de Buri Buri, granted in 1835. The Rancho de Buri Buri was located between San Francisco to the north and San Mateo to the south and west from San Francisco Bay to the mountains bordering Pacifica., California

FIGURE 3 *Plano del Presidio de San Francisco*, 1776. By José Joaquín Moraga. National Park Service–Spanish Colonial Research Center Map Collection, Center for Southwest Research, Zimmerman Library, University of New Mexico.

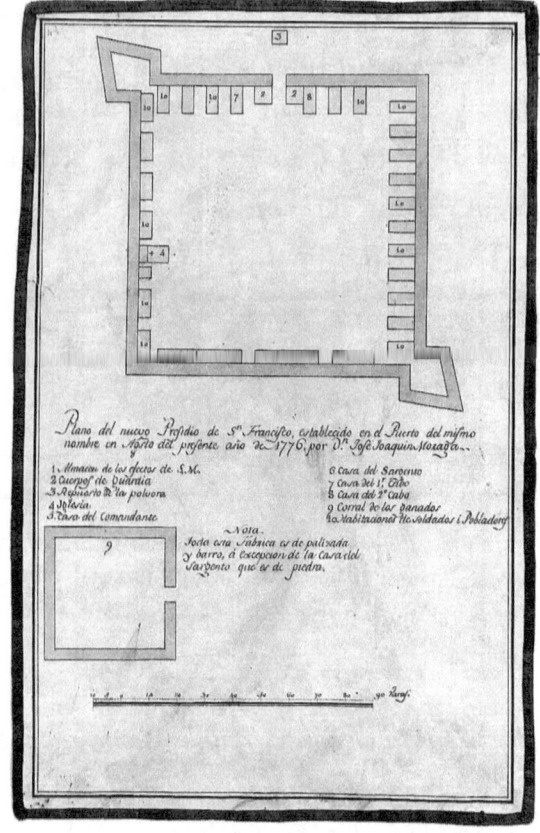

Presidio Real de Santa Bárbara, 1782

The establishment of the Santa Bárbara Presidio strategically cut the distance of travel between the Presidio of San Diego and the Presidio of Monterey. The location was strictly geographical, for the open bay, like that at Monterey, was hardly suitable for the protection of anchored ships. Santa Barbara, however, offered a corridor of travel into the interior between the ocean and the mountains. As open as Santa Barbara was by sea, so too was it open to the interior land, which made it vulnerable to attacks by sea by foreign ships and by land by warring tribes. The Rancho del Rey, the presidial ranch, became the Rancho San Julian in 1837 as a grant to José de la Guerra. It is west of Santa Barbara near Lompoc.

APPENDIX B

✵ ✵ ✵ ✵ ✵

The Missions of Alta California

Part I: The Missions of Alta California

The most popular mission route in California is coastal highway 1-101, which follows the corridor of the Camino Real de California. Although twenty of the twenty-one missions in Alta California were constructed during the Spanish Colonial period, the last one, San Francisco Solano de Sonoma, was completed during the Mexican Territorial period (1821–1848). The builders used available materials such as wood and adobe blocks, which survived earthquakes and long periods of neglect. The modern-day visitor to these sites experiences their historical integrity, despite the restoration and reconstruction measures undertaken to preserve them.

The founding of the first five missions in California determined the route of the Camino Real de las Misiones, another name for the Camino Real de California. These missions grew out of the many proposals for sites made by Father Juan Crespí during the two expeditions led by Governor Portolá in 1768–1770 and those led by Pedro Fages in 1770–1773. Succeeding expeditions by Father Junípero Serra and other Franciscans led to the actual establishment of the twenty-one missions in Alta California.

The early years of these first five missions were typical of the beginnings of other missions. Contrary to general beliefs, their success in converting entire Indian populations in their regions was nominal at best, as indicated in the minor progress demonstrated in their status reports. Still, they are monuments to the early beginnings of modern California and the establishment of the Camino Real de California, which formed the modern transportation corridor along today's California's coastal region. A 1773 report written by Father

Francisco Palou, summarized below, presented a status of the first five missions and their early progress.

SAN DIEGO DE ALCALÁ

The missionaries who founded the Mission San Diego de Alcalá (founded on July 16, 1769) located the site at 32 degrees 42 minutes north latitude alongside a hill that was "two musket shots from the beach." To the north of the site was a wide canyon through which ran a river with torrents of water during rainy periods. Along its banks were many trees and nearby were at least twenty native settlements. The mission was not far from the port of San Diego. When Governor Portolá left to explore the northern coastline in 1769, all of the remaining soldiers at San Diego were left unprotected. During that time, the Indians attacked them but were repulsed, leaving behind four dead warriors and many wounded. One Spanish servant was killed in the melee and three other expedition members wounded, one of them a priest. Many of the native people abandoned their settlements. Thus, the missionary effort at San Diego did not begin as planned. In time, the natives who had not fled were approached by the missionaries. Very few responded to the appeal in those early years, but soon enough, the Franciscans had catechized and baptized about eighty-three adults and children, buried seven baptized natives who had died, and performed weddings for twelve baptized couples. In 1773, the mission had seventy-five neophytes in training to be Christians. In time, the first mission structures and a church were constructed and farms with sheep herds set up nearby. Established at the far southern end of Alta California, Mission San Diego de Alcalá was the first mission on the Camino Real de California, which led to the far northern missions near Carmel, Monterey, and San Francisco Bay.[1]

SAN GABRIEL ARCÁNGEL

Established on September 8, 1771, Mission San Gabriel Arcángel was constructed at 34 degrees 10 minutes north latitude. The mission was about forty-four leagues north of San Diego on the Camino Real. Near the site, the Río San Gabriel (earlier called Río de los Temblores by Portolá's men) ran its mighty course to the sea. The area surrounding the mission had many amenities, for there was plenty of farmland as well as running water from several arroyos, many trees, and grasslands. Unlike those in San Diego, the natives in the Los Angeles area were friendly. However, the early mission founding was stymied by an incident in which a warrior fired an arrow at a soldier, and he returned fire. Many of the natives fled the area. The mission process in the early years was, consequently, slow. By the time of Palou's report, the missionaries had baptized seventy-three adults and children and buried two deceased baptized natives. No marriages were recorded in that early period. In 1773, the mission had seventy-one neophytes.

In time, a wooden church was constructed with a roof covered by reeds; the refectory, the offices, and the barracks for the soldiers were similarly constructed. The housing for the mission Indians consisted of ten houses for five families, inclusive of six unmarried young men. The farm fields included corn, beans, and other seeded plants. Several other Indian settlements were located nearby.[2]

SAN LUIS OBISPO DE TOLOSA

About seventy leagues north beyond San Gabriel, Mission San Luis Obispo de Tolosa was founded on September 1, 1772. The mission was located near the native settlement of La Asumpta near the Santa Bárbara Channel. The latitude taken at the time showed the site to be at 35 degrees 28 minutes north latitude.[3] Father Crespí had twice noted Asumpta as a good place to found a mission. He first saw the settlement, at the southern end of the Santa Bárbara Channel, on August 15, 1769. Just north of Ventura, at Whistle Point (which the soldiers named Pitas), the expedition came to a ranchería that they named Santa Cunegundis del Pueblo de la Asumpta. Nearly five months later, they returned to the settlement about which Crespí wrote that La Asumpta was the best of the settlements of the Santa Bárbara Channel.[4] Three years later, the Franciscans returned to establish the mission on a hill, below which ran a stream of water. The land was good for farming. In its early years, San Louis Obispo had baptized twelve adults and children, had no marriages contracted, and buried one Christian Indian. By 1773, it reported only eleven neophytes.[5]

About half a league from the mission site was the Cañada de los Osos and native settlements scattered to all four points of the compass. The beach was deep enough for anchorage by supply ships. A wooded area, with pasturage and fine farming land, along with flowing water, met the requirements for the new mission. The *padres* planted the first fields, along with the Baja California Indians who had come north with them. The wooden chapel made of poles and the priests' residences were among the first structures there. The soldier escorts set up their own quarters close to a corral with forty-one head of cattle, four mares, one stallion, two mules, and five hogs.[6]

SAN ANTONIO DE PADUA

Founded July 14, 1771, Mission San Antonio de Padua, located twenty-three leagues from Mission San Luis Obispo de Tolosa, developed quickly. By November, the mission had baptized 158 adults and children; eight of the baptized children had since died. The missionary had, between July and November, performed fifteen weddings, three of which were marriages between native women and Soldados de Cuera.[7] The mission was situated at 36 degrees, 30 minutes north latitude in the Sierra de Santa Lucía near a canyon called Cañada de los Robles. Within its first years, the mission was moved to another spot in the same canyon because the river dried up. Near the new site was the Arroyo de San Miguel, which had a continuous stream of water. There they built the church of adobes, with a roof covered with reeds. The priests' residence was similarly constructed, along with offices and houses with wattle walls and reed roofs covered with dirt. The three Soldados de Cuera lived in the mission compound with their wives. Nearby was an Indian settlement with houses made of poles and reeds. Forests in the area provided pine nuts and small game such as rabbits and squirrels. The mission farm housed thirty-eight hogs, four mares, one stallion, and two mules. The mission also had farmlands as well as a shed for carpentry purposes.

Palou reported that the missionaries took inspiration for their work from a letter written by María de Ágreda, who, in the 1620s, gifted with bilocation, had appeared in New Mexico to the Jumanos, who had asked for a missionary to attend to their religious needs. Of the number of neophytes at Mission San Antonio de Padua in 1773, 158 had been baptized, eighteen married within the church, and eight had died and been given Christian burials. The neophytes at that date numbered 150.[8]

MISSION SAN CARLOS DE MONTERREY

On his expedition in 1770, Pedro Fages performed an act of sovereignty formally establishing Monterey as a presidio.[9] On June 3 of that year, about a league from the Presidio of San Carlos de Monterrey, the priests founded the mission of the same name. Given the wooded area, the church was made partly of adobe and partly of pine and cypress wood, with dirt-covered reed roofs that leaked every time it rained.[10] The residences and offices were similarly made of wood. Inside, the rooms were separated by poles. Within the compound, near the soldiers' barracks, was housing for mission Indians.

In its early years, the missionary baptized 175 adults and children, eleven of whom had died and been buried at the time Palou drew up his report. Additionally, three Indian women married soldiers from the Compañía Franca de Voluntarious de Cataluña (Catalonian Volunteers) and another woman married one of the mission's Indian servants. In 1773, there were 154 neophytes in the mission compound.

Although the mission had good farmlands and water nearby, they depended on supply ships for foodstuffs. The ships, however, arrived infrequently, and it seemed that the mission, with seasonal crops, was constantly seeking foods from the hill country around it. The mission owned forty-eight head of cattle, twenty-eight hogs, four mares, one stallion, sixteen mules, and six oxen.[11]

The Missions of Alta California

MISSION	YEAR CONSTRUCTED	LOCATION
1. San Diego de Alcalá	1769	San Diego
2. San Carlos Borromeo de Carmelo	1770	Carmel
3. San Antonio de Padua	1771	Jolón
4. San Gabriel Arcángel	1771	San Gabriel
5. San Luis Obispo de Tolosa	1772	San Luis Obispo
6. San Francisco de Asís (Mission Dolores)	1776	San Francisco
7. San Juan Capistrano	1776	San Juan Capistrano
8. Santa Clara de Asís	1777	Santa Clara
9. San Buenaventura	1782	Ventura
10. Santa Bárbara	1786	Santa Bárbara
11. La Purísima Concepción	1787	Lompoc
12. Nuestra Señora de la Soledad	1791	Soledad
13. Santa Cruz	1791	Santa Cruz
14. San Fernando Rey de España	1797	Los Angeles
15. San José de Guadalupe	1797	Fremont
16. San Juan Bautista	1797	San Juan Bautista
17. San Miguel Arcángel	1797	San Miguel
18. San Luis Rey de Francia	1798	Oceanside
19. Santa Inés	1804	Solvang
20. San Rafael Arcángel	1817	San Rafael
21. San Francisco Solano de Sonoma	1823	Sonoma

Part II: Status of Missions of Alta California in 1813, Noting Distances, Latitudes, Baptisms, Marriages, and Deaths [12]

Estado delas Misiones dela alta California, dispuesto sobre los informes de sus Misioneros, en fin de Diciembre de 1813-/Desde su fundacion.

Nombres delas Misiones, y sus distancias succesivas Epocas de su fundacion. Sus Alturas-Polo, N. Existentes- de Bautismos- Casamientos- Difuntos-

Sⁿ Diego __ Dista dela ultima dela antigua California 23. leguas . . . 16. de Julio de 1769 , , , 32°, .48' 4.083. 1.098. 2.315. 1.537.

Sⁿ Luis Rey de Francia __ Dista dela anterior 13 ½. leguas . . . 13. de Junio de 1798 . . . 33. .03. 2.284. 513. 642. 1.815.

Sⁿ Juan Capistrano __ Dista dela anterior 12 ½ leguas . . . 1°. de Noviembre de 1776 . . . 33. .26. 3.438. 882. 1.970. 1.249.

Sⁿ Gabriel __ Dista dela anterior 18. leguas . . . 8. de Septiembre de 1771 . . . 34. .10. 5.474. 1.313. 3.417. 1678.

Sⁿ Fernando __ Dista dela anterior 9. leguas . . . 8. de Septiembre de 1797. . . 34. .16. 2.087. 586 1.038. 1.043.

Sⁿ Buenaventura __ Dista dela anterior 22. leguas . . . 31. de Marzo de 1782 . . . 34. .36. 2.958. 755. 1.761. 1.169.

Sta Bárbara __ Dista dela anterior 8/ leguas . . . 4. de Diciembre de 1786 . . . 34. .40. 4.058. 1.069. 2.353. 1.269.

Sta Ynés, V. y M __ Dista dela anterior 12. leguas . . . 17. de Septiembre de 1804 . . . 34. .52. 663. 175. 379. 607.

Purisima Concepción __ Dista dela anterior 8. leguas . . . 8. de Diciembre de 1787 . . . 35. .00. 2.682. 750 1.515. 1.010

Sⁿ Luis Obispo __ Dista dela anterior 18. leguas . . . 1. de Septiembre de 1772 . . . 35. .36. 2.375. 665. 1.578. 663.

Sⁿ Miguel __ Dista dela anterior 13. leguas . . . 25. de Julio de 1797. . . 35. .48. 1.763. 496. 771. 1.048.

Sⁿ Antonio de Padua __ Dista dela anterior 13. leguas . . . 14. de Julio de 1771 . . . 36. .30. 3.731. 935. 2.494. 1.074.

Nra Sra dela Soledad __ Dista dela anterior 11. leguas . . . 9. de Octubre de 1791 . . . 36. .38. 1.494. 429. 1.009. 547.

Sⁿ Carlos __ Dista dela anterior 15. leguas . . . 3. de Junio de 1770 . . . 36. .44 2.904. 812. 2.074. 448.

Sⁿ Juan Bautista __ Dista dela anterior 12. leguas . . . 24. de Junio de 1797 . . . 36. .58 2.028. 517. 1.231. 633.

Sta Cruz __ Dista dela anterior, por la Costa fuera del Camino de Sta Clara, 13 legˢ. . . . 28 de Agosto de 1791 . . . 37. .00 1.661. 562. 1.216. 398.

Sta Clara __ Dista dela anterior, atravesando la Sierra, 11. leguas . . . 18. de Enero de 1777 . . . 37. .20. 6.169. 1.660. 4.545. 1.347.

Sⁿ José __ Distadela anterior, al N. fuera del Camino de Sⁿ. Francisco, 7. Leguas . . . 11. de Junio de 1797 . . . 37. .30. 2.690. 814. 1.527. 1.151

Sⁿ Francisco __ Dista dela anterior 20. leguas, y de Sta Clara 15 . . . 9. de Octubre de 1776 . . . 37. .00. 4.786. 1.528. 3.427. 1.205.

Totales . . . 57.328 15.559 35.262. 19.891

Se regulan 210. leguas desde Sⁿ. Diego hasta Sⁿ. Francisco, de cuya direccion se desvian las Misiones de Sta Cruz, y Sⁿ. José, en sus anotadas distancias.

APPENDIX C

✻ ✻ ✻ ✻ ✻

The Missions of Baja California and the Early Camino Real de California

THE 1769 PLAN regarding Baja California included the founding of a string of missions between Velicatá and San Diego. Other missions were established in Baja California Sur and were a part of the Camino Real de las Misiones in that area. Father Francisco Palou wrote that ten priests would be assigned to establish these missions. Velicatá was surrounded by thirteen settlements and would require two priests for each.[1]

During the Spanish Colonial period, the coast of present-day Baja California Sur and Baja California would be aligned with a number of missions that would stretch from La Paz and Loreto to Velicatá and from there along the Pacific coastline to a point south of San Diego. They would mark the southern part of the Camino Real de California from Velicatá to Rosarito Bay. The first, Mission Nuestra Señora de Loreto, was founded in 1697 by the Jesuits and became known as "the mother of all missions" in Baja California. While nine of the ten missions described below were founded by missionaries of the Dominican order, San Fernando Rey de España de Velicatá was founded by Franciscan father Junípero Serra.

The Missions of Baja California

MISSION	YEAR CONSTRUCTED	LOCATION
1. Nuestra Señora de Loreto	1697	Loreto
2. San Fernando Rey de España de Velicatá	1769	Velicatá
3. Nuestra Señora del Santisimo Rosario de Viñacado	1774	El Rosario
4. Santo Domingo de la Frontera	1775	Colonia Vicente Guerrero
5. San Vicente Ferrer	1780	
6. San Miguel Arcángel de la Frontera	1787	Ensenada
7. Santo Tomás de Aquino	1791	
8. San Pedro Mártir de Verona	1794	
9. Santa Catarina Virgen y Mártir	1797	Ensenada
10. San Miguel de la Nueva (El Descanso)	1817	Rosarito
11. Nuestra Señora de Guadalupe del Norte	1834	Guadalupe

APPENDIX D

✦ ✦ ✦ ✦ ✦

"The King's Highway as Serra Knew It"

FATHER GEIGER AND CALIFORNIA'S CAMINO REAL DE LAS MISIONES

ACKNOWLEDGING THAT "The original Camino Real, of course, was the route taken by Portolá in 1769," Father Maynard Geiger added, "but this road of twists and turns, ascents and descents, did not remain fixed." Indeed, with the establishment of early California's infrastructure of presidios, ports, missions, towns, and ranches, a braided corridor evolved known as the Camino Real de California. Of the corridor, Father Geiger noted in 1959, "I have lived along California's Camino Real since 1913, have traveled over it countless times, with particularly studious intent since 1937. Serra's trail from San Francisco to San Diego can be traced with almost mathematical precision. Even without the descriptive documents, the mountainous nature of the land limits travel routes to a great extent. The intervening valleys, passes, and grades strongly suggest the proper way to go."[1] Father Geiger's account of Serra's route follows:

Geiger's Notations on Father Junípero Serra's North-to-South Route of Alta California's Camino Real de las Misiones

FROM MISSION SAN CARLOS BORROMEO TO MISSION SAN ANTONIO

1. The route from San Carlos Borromeo along the Camino Real to Mission San Antonio as noted by Father Serra, ran through some of the earliest farmlands in the area.

2. Río Road passes through bottom lands once cultivated by Serra and his missionary brothers to State Highway 1, a mile from the mission site.

3. Monterey is located five miles distant on this highway. The route runs over high hills and through dense forests of pine trees.

4. Remnants of an older dirt road wind in and out among the hills, at times crossing the modern boulevard. In Serra's day ride by horse or mule took over an hour.

5. Monterey Bay is visible from the hills on their northern side as it wends to the north and northwest.

6. The highway enters Monterey at the old presidio church of San Carlos.

7. At that point, the trail turns right onto Fremont Street, which follows the estuary. In Geiger's day, there was a park; and, the United States Postgraduate Naval School stood where the old Del Monte Hotel once thrived. The route goes from Fremont Street to the Salinas Highway.

8. The Salinas Highway follows the Camino Real for fifteen miles, through a narrow canyon, which, in Geiger's account still carries the name Cañada de Rey.

9. The canyon runs easterly-northeasterly, as it connects the coast with the interior valley.

10. Approaching the Salinas Valley, the road follows Toro Creek.

11. Serra's route approximated River Road, west of Salinas, and ran close to the Sierra de Salinas to a point west of King City.

12. Near King City, the Camino Real entered a broad canyon, and not far from there the Jolon grade begins. Once known as Kent Canyon, today it is known as Quinado Canyon.

13. Near the top of the steep Jolon grade is Hunter-Liggett Military Reservation.

14. The road led directly to Jolon Post Office. There a road to the northwest led to San Antonio Mission, five miles away.

15. Here, Geiger surmised that "the regular road . . . is today a paved road to the right after entering Hunter-Liggett; it becomes the Upper Milpitas Road which approaches the mission from the east" (p. 311).

FROM MISSION SAN CARLOS BORROMEO TO MISSION SAN ANTONIO

1. Geiger noted, "Far in the background is Junípero Serra Peak, the highest (5,844 feet) of the Santa Lucía Mountains" (p. 312).

2. Today a military highway runs southeast through Jolon and Lockwood to near Summit.

3. The road continues to Highway 101 and the Salinas River above Bradley.

4. Just before Summit, the Camino Real veered right and crossed the San Antonio River to Pleyto. A stagecoach station once stood there.

5. Between that point and Paso Robles, the Camino Real went approximately through ranches in the hill country and took secondary roads off the "beaten path of travel" (p. 312).

6. At Paso Robles, the Camino Real converged with Highway 101, the Southern Pacific Railroad, and the Salinas River. The Salinas River narrows in that area.

7. Both the railroad and highway followed Serra's route from that point to San Luis Obispo running south and southeast through Templeton, Atascadero, and Santa Margarita.

8. At Santa Margarita, the steep Cuesta Grade begins and descends into the Valley of San Luis Obispo.

9. The railroad line runs along the side of a mountain ridge west of the canyon, and the highway runs along the side of the mountain ridge east of it.

10. Located in the center of the city, Mission San Luis Obispo marks a point midway between San Francisco and Los Angeles.

FROM SAN LUIS OBISPO TO SANTA BARBARA

1. This portion of the Camino Real was considered extremely dangerous "not only because of the terrain but also because of the number of Indians of volatile character" (p. 313).

2. The distance from San Luis Obispo to Santa Barbara is 119 miles by rail.

3. The railroad and the road go through the San Luis Valley to Edna.

4. From that point they go southeast "through Pine Canyon, the Narrow Canyon of the Goitered Chief of the chronicles" (p. 313). Crespí called the place San Ladislao. The soldiers called the Chief El Buchón, a name that also attached to the place.

5. The route runs to the sea south of Pismo Beach.

6. Highway 101 leaves the Serra Trail east of Pismo Beach for sixty-one miles, as this is the shorter route through the mountain and hills.

7. Serra's route is better seen by traveling from Pismo to Gaviota by rail. Geiger noted, "There is no road complete along the entire length and some of the existing roads belong either to the military or to private ranches" (p. 313). Geiger believed that the railroad, like the Camino Real, followed close to the coast.

8. The terrain south of Pismo begins with great sand banks extending inland as far as Surf to the west of Lompoc (p. 313).

9. The rocky points of Arguello, Arlight, and Concepción that lead somewhat eastward to Santa Barbara were from the earliest times landmarks along the Camino Real.

10. At Gaviota Pass, Highway 101 again meets the Camino Real and parallels the railroad to Santa Barbara.

11. From Gaviota to Santa Barbara the terrain is of uneven land, sand dunes, hills with abundant ground cover, and rough arroyos.

12. Moving southward along the Camino Real are two visible and notable topographical features: on the left, the Santa Inés Mountains, which rise nearly four thousand feet above sea level, and on the right, the Pacific Ocean.

13. After Gaviota and nearing Ellwood, the coastal plain narrows and is crisscrossed by many small arroyos and canyons.

14. The coastal plain widens sixteen miles east of Santa Barbara toward the Rincón Mountains.

15. The Camino Real runs toward Santa Barbara and Montecito.

16. Mission Santa Bárbara is located 250 feet above sea level and is two and a half miles from the sea. There is also a maritime route between Monterey and Santa Barbara.

FROM SANTA BARBARA TO LOS ANGELES

1. From the Rincón Mountains to the south, the Camino Real ran between the northern foothills and Bird Refuge, a freshwater lake. Montecito (Little Woods) is within sight of the Camino Real. The modern road east of Montecito goes over Ortega Hill, while the railroad skirts the route close to the sea. La Serena and Carpintería Valley are a part of the Camino Real markers in the area.

2. At the Rincón, the valley and mountains follow the sea as far as Ventura and lead to Rincón Point, Punta Gorda, and Pitas Point.

3. Ventura, shortened from San Buenaventura, follows the coastal plain for three miles. The mission church stands on Main Street at the foot of the hills, five city blocks from the sea.

4. From there, the Camino Real goes to Los Angeles and, from there, to San Diego.

5. From Ventura to Camarillo, the Camino Real passes over a broad plain, nearly twenty miles long and about ten miles wide.

6. The Santa Clara River runs from the mountains in the north through the plain. Travelers noted that the Camino Real ran through the area.

7. The Santa Clara Valley is surrounded by Sulphur Mountain and South Mountain on the north and the Santa Monica Mountains on the east.

8. Santa Clara Mission near Newhall influenced the name of the valley and river.

9. The Conejo Grade, several miles from Camarillo near Newbury Park, Thousand Oaks, Agoura, and Calabasas and Woodland Hills, lines parts of the Camino Real in the San Fernando Valley.

10. Woodland Hills is the westernmost town along the Camino Real in the San Fernando Valley.

11. A sixteen-mile stretch of Highway 101, on the section known as Ventura Boulevard, runs from west to east through Woodland Hills, Tarzana, Encino, Sherman Oaks, and Studio City and may align with portions of the Camino Real as it developed in time. Geiger explains, "This highway leads directly into Hollywood by way of Cahuenga Pass and while this road was used as an alternate in pre-American days as part of the Camino Real and later as a stagecoach road, it is not certain it was so used in Serra's time" (p. 318).

12. Other potential sites follow the Los Angeles River near Griffith Park Mountain through Burbank and Glendale, then a trajectory along San Fernando Boulevard into East Los Angeles.

13. Where San Fernando Boulevard ends in East LA, Mission Road crosses toward Alhambra and San Gabriel and its historic mission.

14. From there, the Camino Real ran southeast past the original mission site near San Gabriel through the Old Paso de San Bartolo to Whittier Boulevard at Pico.

FROM LOS ANGELES TO SAN DIEGO

1. The Camino Real would have continued east of Whittier to La Habra and south through Fullerton, Anaheim, and Santa Ana.

2. Along the corridor of Highway 101, the Camino Real continued through Tustin and Irvine.

3. Between Irvine and El Toro, I-101 enters a narrow canyon between the Santa Ana Mountains and the San Joaquín Hills.

4. Just east of Mission San Juan Capistrano, a street has been named Camino Real.

5. The modern highway from San Juan Capistrano follows the coastline to San Diego.

6. Geiger notes, "The railroad does not follow the Camino Real between Los Angeles and Fullerton but from there to Las Flores Ranch in San Diego County it runs close to the highway which corresponds to it. The modern highway out of San Juan follows the ocean nearly to San Diego. However, the old Camino Real ascended the heights of Doheney or Capistrano Beach where the road ran over the elevated coastal plateau forming palisades along a considerable stretch of the beach" (p. 319).

7. The old Camino Real met the coastal highway near Pioche Landing.

8. From there it continues along the beach for four miles and turns inland past San Clemente.

9. The modern highway passes San Onofre and Las Flores.

10. From Las Flores to near San Diego, the old Camino Real left the routes of the modern highway and railroad.

11. The Camino Real passed through Camp Pendleton, through the railroad underpass, and east and southeast through the Valley of San Luis Rey.

12. From Santa Margarita to near San Diego, wide rivers and lagoons stretch inland for several miles, forcing the Camino Real to go inland, keeping the eastern ends of the lagoons close by to facilitate travel.

13. The interior road in Geiger's time was largely paved.

14. From San Luis Rey to Rose Canyon, the Camino Real want past present-day Olivehain. After Sorrento, it crossed the railroad line and turned southwest for several miles, where it joined the main highway at Camp Mathews. Ten miles beyond Rose Canyon, it reached Old Town San Diego and proceeded to Presidio Hill.

15. San Diego is still the originating point of the historic Camino Real at the southern end of Alta California as it was in 1769.

APPENDIX E

✤ ✤ ✤ ✤ ✤

Selected and Edited List of Land Grants in California, 1784–1848, Potentially Related to the Camino Real de California

Part I: Selected and Edited List of Spanish Period Land Grants in Alta California 1784–1821 Related to the Location of the Camino Real de California[1]

The Laws of the Indies required that when a settlement had its full complement of settlers, usually about one thousand people, a governing body had to be established, inclusive of an *alcalde mayor* and a *cabildo*, a town council, made up of appointed and elected officials. By the sixteenth century the long tradition of the cabildo had been firmly established at Santo Domingo, present-day Dominican Republic, as well as in Cuba, Puerto Rico, Mexico City, San Agustín in Florida, and San Juan de los Caballeros in New Mexico. By the eighteenth century, the requirement had established town councils with mayors from San Antonio, Texas, to Monterey, California. By the end of the Spanish Colonial period, many of the California ranchos (land grants) had become townships with the appropriate institutions for governance. After winning its independence from Spain, Mexico continued the practice of establishing land grants, which similarly became towns. Aside from the missions, the ranchos and settlements aligned with the route of, or at least a wide corridor that had developed along the old Camino Real.

SELECTED AND EDITED LIST OF LAND GRANTS

GRANT	DATE	GRANTOR	GRANTEE	LOCATION	COUNTY
Los Nietos	1784	Pedro Fages	Manuel Nieto	Long Beach, Downey, Whittier	Los Angeles
San Pedro	1784	Pedro Fages	Juan José Dominguez	San Pedro	Los Angeles
San Rafael	1784	Pedro Fages	José María Verdugo	Glendale	Los Angeles
Nuestra Señora del Refugio	1794	Diego de Borica	José Francisco Ortega	Refugio State Beach	Santa Bárbara
Buena Vista	1795	Diego de Borica	José María Soberanes and Joaquín Castro	Monterey	Monterey
Los Feliz	1795	Diego de Borica	José Vicente Feliz	Los Feliz	Los Angeles
Las Pulgas	1795	Diego de Borica	José Dario Argüello and Luis Antonio Argüello	San Mateo, Belmont, San Carlos, Menlo Park	San Mateo
Simi	1795	Diego de Borica	Patricio, Miguel, and Francisco Javier Pico	Simi Valley, Moorpark	Ventura
El Conejo	1802	Ygnacio Rodríguez and José Polanco		Newbury Park, Thousand Oaks, Lake Sherwood, Westlake Village, Oak Park	Ventura
Las Virgenes	1802	José Joaquín de Arrillaga	Miguel Ortega	Agoura Hills	Los Angeles
Las Animas	1803	Feliz Berenguer	José Mariano Castro	Gilroy	Santa Clara
Topanga Malibu Sequit	1804	José Joaquín de Arrillaga	José Bartolomé Tapia	Malibu	Los Angeles
Los Palos Verdes	1809		José Dolores Sepúlveda	Palos Verdes	Los Angeles
San Ysidro	1809	José Joaquín de Arrillaga	Ygnacio Ortega	Gilroy	Santa Clara
San Antonio	1810		Antonio María Lugo	Bell, South Gate	Los Angeles
Santiago de Santa Ana	1810	José Joaquín de Arrillaga	José Antonio Yorba and Juan Pablo Peralta	Santa Ana, Irvine	Orange
San Antonio	1820	Pablo Vicente de Solá	Luís María Peralta	Alameda, Berkeley, Oakland, San Leandro	Alameda
Rincon de los Bueyes*	1821	Pablo Vicente de Solá	Bernardo Higuera and Cornelio López	Culver City, Baldwin Hills	Los Angeles
Sausal Redondo*	1821		Antonio Ygnacio Avila	Solá	Los Angeles
Los Tularcitos*	1821	Pablo Vicente de	José Loreto Higuera	Richmond, San Pablo	Santa Clara
Vega del Río del Pájaro	1821	Pablo Vicente de Solá	Antonio María Castro	Manhattan Beach, Lawndale	Monterey

*These grants were approved during the Spanish Colonial period, but overlap into the Mexican Territorial period.

Part II: Selected and Edited List of Early Mexican Territorial Period Land Grants, 1821–1834, Potentially Related to the Late-Period Corridor of the Camino Real de California

Ranchos in the District of San Diego in Alta California, 1821–1834

NAME OF RANCHO	YEAR GRANTED	GRANTEE	APPROXIMATE LOCATION
Santa María de Peñasquitos	1823	Francisco María Ruiz	
San Antonio Abad	1828	Francisco María Alvarado	
Janal	1829	José Antonio Estudillo*	Chula Vista, San Diego County
Otay	1829	Magdalena Estudillo	Chula Vista, San Diego County
Temescal	1829	José Antonio Estudillo	
Jamul	1831	Pío Pico	Jamul, San Diego County
San Dieguito	1831	Familia Silva	Rancho de Santa Fe, San Diego
Melyo	1833	Santiago E. Arguello	
Cueros de Venado	1834	Juan María Marrón	
Tecate	1834	Juan Bandini	Tecate, Tecate County
Valle de San José	1834	Silvestre de la Portilla	San Diego, San Diego County

Ranchos in the District of Los Angeles in Alta California, 1821–1834

NAME OF RANCHO	YEAR GRANTED	GRANTEE	APPROXIMATE LOCATION
Rincón de los Bueyes*	1821	Bernardo Higuera	Culver City, Los Angeles County
Guaspita	1822	Antonio Ignacio Avila	
Salinas	1822	Antonio Ignacio Avila	
Palos Verdes or Palos Colorados	1827	José Sepúlveda	Palos Verdes, Los Angeles County
San Vicente y Santa Mónica	1828	Francisco Sepúlveda	Santa Mónica, Los Angeles County
Huerta de Cuati	1830	Victoria Reid	San Marino, Los Angeles County
Rosa de Castillo	1831	Juan Ballesteros	
Santa Gertrudis	1833	Josefa Cota de Nieto	
Alamitos	1834	Juan José Nieto	Los Alamitos/Seal Beach, Orange County
Bolsas	1834	Catarina Ruiz Nieto's widow	Huntington Beach, Orange County

NAME OF RANCHO	YEAR GRANTED	GRANTEE	APPROXIMATE LOCATION
Cañada de Santa Ana	1834	Bernardo Yorba	Yorba Linda, Orange County
Cerritos	1834	Manuela Nieto	Cerritos, Long Beach, Orange County
Coyotes	1834	Juan José Nieto	Cerritos, Stanta, Buena Park, Orange County

Ranchos of the District of Santa Bárbara in Alta California, 1821–1834

NAME OF RANCHO	YEAR GRANTED	GRANTEE	APPROXIMATE LOCATION
Pirú	1821	J. de la Guerra y Noriega	San Fernando Valley and Misión de San Fernando, Los Angeles County
Sauzal Redondo	1822	Antonio Ignacio Avila	Manhattan Beach/Lawndale, Los Angeles County
Ciénegas	1823	Januario (Francisco) Avila	Los Angeles, Los Angeles County
Brea	1824	José Antonio Rocha	Hollywood/West Hollywood, Los Angeles County
Sespe or San Cayetano	1833	Carlos Antonio Carrillo	Fillmore, Bardsdale/Pirú, Ventura County
Sisquoc	1833	María Antonio Caballero	Santa Bárbara County
Concepción	1834	Cosme Vanegas	Point Concepción, Santa Bárbara County
Las Pozas	1834	José Carrillo	Camarillo, Somis, Ventura County

Ranchos in the District of Monterey in Alta California, 1821–1834

NAME OF RANCHO	YEAR GRANTED	GRANTEE	APPROXIMATE LOCATION
Familia Sagrada or Bolsa de Potrero	1822	José Joaquín de la Torre	Castroville, Monterey County and Moro Cojo
Llano de Buena Vista	1822	Santiago and José Mariano Estrada	Spreckels, Monterey County
Alisal	1823	Feliciano Soberanes	Salinas, Monterey County
Sauzal	1823	Agustín Soberanes	Salinas, Monterey County
Bolsa del San Cayetano	1824	Ignacio Vicente Ferrar Vallejo	Watsonville, Monterey County
Bolsa del Moro Cojo	1825	Simeón Castro	Castroville, Monterey County
Escarpines, Escorpinas, or Escarpiones	1828	Salvador Espinosa	Monterey, Monterey County

NAME OF RANCHO	YEAR GRANTED	GRANTEE	APPROXIMATE LOCATION
Bolsa de San Miguel or Nueva Bolsa	1829	Francisco Soto	
Pescadero or San Antonio	1829	Joaquín Solís and José Antonio Botiller	Pescadero, San Mateo County
Nativiad	1830	Manuel Butrón and Nicolás Alviso	Salinas, Monterey County
Aptos	1833	Rafael Castro	Seacliff, Santa Cruz County
Guadalupe y Lanitos de los Correos	1833	Juan Malarín	Chualar, Monterey County
Laguna de las Calabazas	1833	Felipe Hérnandez	
Laguna Seca or Cañadita	1833	Catalina Manzaneli de Munras	Monterey County
Punta de Pinos	1833	José M. Armenta and José Abrego	Punta de Pinos, Monterey County
Rincón de las Salinas	1833	Cristina Delgado	Hunter's Point, San Francisco County
San Andrés	1833	Joaquín Castro	
Saucito	1833	Graciano Manjares	Del Rey Oaks, Monterey County
Sayante or Zayanate	1833	Joaquín Buelna	Zayante, Santa Cruz County
Shoquel or Soquel and Palo de Yesca	1833	Martina Castro and Francisco Pérez Pacheco	Soquel, Santa Cruz County
Alisal or Patrocino	1834	William E. Hartnell	Salinas, Monterey County
Arroyo del Rodeo	1834	Francisco Rodríguez	Live Oak, Monterey County
Carneros	1834	David Little John	Elkhorn, Monterey County
Encinal and Buena Esperanza	1834	David Spence	Spence, Monterey County
San Francisco de las Llagas	1834	Carlos Castro	San Martin, Santa Clara County
Sur	1834	Juan Bautista Alvarado	Molera State Park, Molera State Park, Monterey County
Tularcitos	1834	Rafael Gómez	Monterey

Ranchos in the District of San Francisco in Alta California, 1821–1834

NAME OF RANCHO	YEAR GRANTED	GRANTEE	APPROXIMATE LOCATION
Los Tularcitos	1821	José Higuera	Milpitas, Santa Clara County
Llano del Abrevadero	1822	José Higuera	
San Pablo, or Cochiyunes	1823	Francisco María Castro	Richmond/San Pablo, Contra Costa County

SELECTED AND EDITED LIST OF LAND GRANTS

NAME OF RANCHO	YEAR GRANTED	GRANTEE	APPROXIMATE LOCATION
Pulgas	1824	Luis Antonio Arguello	San Mateo/Belmont/ San Carlos/Menlo Park, San Mateo County
Buri Buri	1827	José Sánchez	San Bruno, San Mateo County
Laguna de los Bolones	1828	William Willis	
San Ignacio	1828		
Pinole	1829	Ignacio Martínez	Martinez/Pinole, Contra Costa County
Salsipuedes	182?	Francisco de Harro	Watsonville, Santa Cruz County
Santa Rosa	1831	Rafael Gómez	
Cañada del Corte de Madera	1833	Domingo Peralta	San Mateo County
San Ramón	1833	Rafael Soto de Pacheco	Alamo/Danville, Contra Costa County
San Ramón or Las Juntas	1833	Bartolo Pacheco Martinez/Pacheco/ Pleasant	Mariano Castro Hill, Contra Costa County
Yerba Buena or Socayre	1833	Antonio Chaboya	Evergreen, Santa Clara County
Acalanes	1834	Candelario Valencia	Lafayette/Moraga, Contra Costa County
Agua Caliente	1834	Fulgencio Higuera	Fremont, Alameda County
Arroyo de las Nueces	1834	Juan Sánchez Pacheco	Walnut Creek, Contra Costa County
Laguna Seca	1834	Juan Alvires	Coyote, Santa Clara County
Milpitas	1834	Nicolás Berreysa	
(Misión) Dolores	1834	José Cornelio Bernal	
Monte del Diablo	1834	Salvio Pacheco	Concord, Contra Costa County
Pescadero	1834	Antonio María Pico	Pebble Beach, Monterey County
San Luis Gonzaga	1834	José Ramon Estrada	Santa Clara County
San Ramón	1834	José María Amador	Danville, Contra Costa County
Santa Teresa	1834	Joaquín Bernal	San José, Santa Clara County

Adapted from Martha Ortega Soto, *Una Frontera Olvidada del Noroeste de México, 1769–1846* (Itzapalapa: Universidad Autónoma Metropolitana Unidad, 2001) Cuadros 28–32: "Ranchos del Distrito," 269–77. While Ortega Soto offers more information regarding, for example, notes and size of grants, for purposes of this study, which is concerned with the location of the ranchos in relation to the corridor of the Camino Real de California, those items have been deleted.

Part III: Selected and Edited List of Later Mexican Territorial Period Land Grants in California, 1835–1848, Potentially related to the Late-Period Corridor of the Camino Real de California

GRANT	DATE	GRANTOR	GRANTEE	LOCATION	COUNTY
Aguajito	1835	José Figueroa	Gregorio Tapia	Monterey	Monterey
Los Aromitas y Agua Caliente	1835	José Castro	Juan Miguel Anzar	Aromas	San Benito
Buri Buri	1835	José Castro	José Antonio Sánchez	San Bruno	San Mateo
Cañada de la Carpentería	1835	José Castro	Joaquín Soto		Monterey
Chamisal	1835	José Castro	Felipe Vásquez		Monterey
Juristac	1835	José Castro	Antonio and Faustino Germán	Sargent	Santa Clara
Laguna de la Merced	1835	José Castro	José Antonio Galindo	Daly City	San Mateo
Llano de Tesquisquita	1835	José Castro	José María Sánchez		San Benito
Los Meganos	1835	José Castro	José Noriega	Brentwood	Contra Costa
Milpitas	1835	José Castro	José María Alviso	Milpitas	Santa Clara
Noche Buena	1835	José Castro	Juan Antonio Muñoz	Seaside	Monterey
Ojo del Agua de la Coche	1835	José Figueroa	Juan M. Hernández	Morgan Hill	Santa Clara
Pala	1835	José Castro	José Higuera	San José	Santa Clara
Paso de Bartolo	1835	José Figueroa	Juan Crispín Pérez	Whittier, Pico Rivera	Los Angeles
El Rincon	1835	José Figueroa	Teodoro Arellanes	La Conchita	Ventura
San Francisquito	1835	José Castro	Catalina Manzaneli de Munras		Monterey
San Vicente	1835	José Castro	Esteban Munras	Soledad	Monterey
El Toro	1835	José Castro	José Ramón Estrada		Monterey
Los Vergeles	1835	José Castro	José Joaquín Gómez		Monterey
Corral de Tierra	1836	Nicolás Gutiérrez	Guadalupe Figueroa		Monterey
Guadalasca	1836	Mariano Chico	Ysabel Yorba	Camarillo, Point Mugu	Ventura
Pescadero	1836	Nicolás Gutiérrez	Fabian Barreto	Pebble Beach	Monterey
Rincon de la Puente del Monte	1836	Nicolás Gutiérrez	Teodoro Gonzalez	Gonzales	Monterey
Las Salinas	1836	Nicolás Gutiérrez	Gabriel Espinoza	Marina	Monterey
San Joaquin	1836	Nicolás Gutiérrez	Cruz Cervantes		San Benito
Valle de San José	1836	Nicolás Gutiérrez	Silvestre de la Portilla		San Diego

SELECTED AND EDITED LIST OF LAND GRANTS 183

GRANT	DATE	GRANTOR	GRANTEE	LOCATION	COUNTY
Bolsa de Chamisal	1837	Juan Alvarado	Francisco Quijado		San Luis Obispo
Bolsa de las Escorpinas	1837	Juan Alvarado	Salvador Espinoza		Monterey
Bolsa del Pájaro	1837	Juan Alvarado	Sebastián Rodríguez	Watsonville	Santa Cruz
Calleguas	1837	Juan Alvarado	José Pedro Ruiz	Camarillo	Ventura
Las Cruces	1837	Juan Alvarado	Miguel Cordero		Santa Bárbara
Los Gatos or Santa Rita	1837	Juan Alvarado	José Trinidad Espinoza	Santa Rita	Monterey
Jesús María	1837	Juan Alvarado	Lucas Antonio Olivera and José A. Olivera	Vandenberg Air Force Base	Santa Bárbara
Lompoc	1837	Juan Alvarado	José Antonio Carrillo	Lompoc	Santa Bárbara
La Natividad	1837	Juan Alvarado	Manuel Butron and Nicolás Alviso	Salinas	Monterey
Nipomo	1837	Juan Alvarado	William Dana	Nipomo	San Luis Obispo
Ojai	1837	Juan Alvarado	Fernando Tico	Ojai	Ventura
Punta de la Concepcion	1837	Juan Alvarado	Anastasio José Carrillo	Point Conception	Santa Bárbara
El Río de Santa Clara o la Colonia	1837	Juan Alvarado	Valentine Cota et al.	Port Hueneme, Oxnard	Ventura
San Francisquito	1837	Juan Alvarado	Antonio Buelna	Palo Alto	Santa Clara
San José	1837	Juan Alvarado	Ygnacio Palomares and Ricardo Vejar	Pomona, San Dimas, Covina	Los Angeles
San Juan Cajón de Santa Ana	1837	Juan Alvarado	Juan Pacífico Ontiveros	Anaheim, Fullerton, Placentia	Orange
San Julian	1837	Juan Alvarado	José de la Guerra y Noriega	Lompoc	Santa Bárbara
Santa Ana	1837	Juan Alvarado	Crisogomo Ayala and Cosme Vanegas	Oak View	Ventura
Santa Clara del Norte	1837	Juan Alvarado	Juan M. Sánchez	El Rio	Ventura
Santa Manuela	1837	Juan Alvarado	Francis Branch	Arroyo Grande	San Luis Obispo
Suey	1837	Juan Alvarado	Ramona Carrillo Pacheco Wilson		San Luis Obispo
Tepusquet	1837	Juan Alvarado	Tomas Olivera		Santa Bárbara
Tinaquaic	1837	Juan Alvarado	Benjamín Foxen	Santa Maria	Santa Bárbara

184 APPENDIX E

GRANT	DATE	GRANTOR	GRANTEE	LOCATION	COUNTY
Butano	1838	Juan Alvarado	Ramona Sánchez		San Mateo
Cañada de Verde y Arroyo de la Purisima	1838	Juan Alvarado	José María Alviso		San Mateo
Carbonera	1838	Juan Alvarado	José Guillermo Bocle	Santa Cruz	Santa Cruz
Huerta de Cuati	1838	Juan Alvarado	Victoria Reid	San Marino	Los Angeles
Milpitas	1838	Juan Alvarado	Ygnacio Pastor	Fort Hunter Liggett, Jolon	Monterey
Rincon de Los Esteros	1838	Juan Alvarado	Ignacio Alviso	Milpitas, San José	Santa Clara
Rodeo de las Aguas	1838	Juan Alvarado	María Rita Valdez de Villa	Beverly Hills	Los Angeles
Saucelito	1838	Juan Alvarado	William A. Richardson	Sausalito	Marin
La Zaca	1838	Juan Alvarado	Antonio		Santa Bárbara
Agua Caliente	1839	Juan Alvarado	Fulgencio Higuera	Fremont	Alameda
Los Alamos	1839	Juan Alvarado	José Antonio de la Guerra	Los Alamos	Santa Bárbara
La Ballona	1839	Juan Alvarado	Machado and Talamantes families	Culver City, Venice	Los Angeles
Boca de Santa Mónica	1839	Juan Alvarado	Francisco Márquez and Ysidro Reyes	Santa Mónica	Los Angeles
Cañada de la Segunda	1839	José Castro	Lazaro Soto	Carmel Valley	Monterey
Cañada de Pala	1839	Juan Alvarado	José de Jesús Bernal		Santa Clara
Cañada de San Felipe y Las Animas	1839	Manuel Jimeno	Thomas Bowen		Santa Clara
Chualar	1839	Manuel Jimeno	Juan Malarin	Chualar	Monterey
Corral de Tierra	1839	Manuel Jimeno	Francisco Guerrero y Palomares	Princeton	San Mateo
Corral de Tierra	1839	Manuel Jimeno	Tiburcio Vásquez		San Mateo
La Habra	1839	Juan Alvarado	Mariano Roldan	La Habra	Orange
Los Laureles	1839	Juan Alvarado	José M. Boronda and Vicente Blas Martínez	Carmel Valley Village	Monterey
Los Medanos	1839	Juan Alvarado	José Antonio Mesa and José Miguel Garcia	Pittsburg	Contra Costa
Nacional	1839	Juan Alvarado	Vicente Cantua	Salinas	Monterey
Paraje de Sánchez	1839	Juan Alvarado	Francisco Lugo		Monterey
Posa de los Ositos	1839	Juan Alvarado	Carlos Cayetano Espinoza	Greenfield	Monterey
Las Positas	1839	Juan Alvarado	Robert Livermore and José Noriega	Livermore	Alameda

SELECTED AND EDITED LIST OF LAND GRANTS 185

GRANT	DATE	GRANTOR	GRANTEE	LOCATION	COUNTY
Potrero de San Carlos	1839	Juan Alvarado	Fructuoso del Real		Monterey
Refugio	1839	Juan Alvarado	María Candida, Jacinta, and María de los Angeles Castro	Santa Cruz	Santa Cruz
Rincon de las Salinas y Potrero Viejo	1839	Manuel Jimeno	Cornelio Bernal	Hunters Point	San Francisco
Rinconada de Los Gatos	1839	Juan Alvarado	José María Hernández and Sebastián Fabian Peralta	Los Gatos, Monte Sereno	Santa Clara
San Antonio	1839	Juan Alvarado	Juan Prado Mesa	Los Altos	Santa Clara
San Francisco	1839	Juan Alvarado	Antonio del Valle	Camulos, Piru, Santa Clarita	Ventura
San Gregorio	1839	Juan Alvarado	Antonio Buelna	San Gregorio	San Mateo
San José y Sur Chiquito	1839	Juan Alvarado	Marcelino Escobar		Monterey
San Justo	1839	Juan Alvarado	José Castro	Hollister	San Benito
San Pedro	1839	Juan Alvarado	Francisco Sánchez	Pacífica	San Mateo
San Vicente y Santa Mónica	1839	Juan Alvarado	Francisco Sepúlveda	Santa Mónica	Los Angeles
Santa Ana y Quien Sabe	1839	Juan Alvarado	Francisco Negrete		San Benito
Santa Cruz Island	1839	Juan Alvarado	Andrés Castillero	Santa Cruz Island	Santa Bárbara
Santa Rita	1839	Juan Alvarado	José Pacheco	Pleasanton	Alameda
Santa Rosa	1839	Manuel Jimeno	Francisco Cota	Buellton	Santa Bárbara
Valle de San José	1839	Juan Alvarado	Antonio María Pico	Sunol	Alameda
Zanjones	1839	Manuel Jimeno	Gabriel de la Torre		Monterey
Arroyo de la Laguna	1840	Juan Alvarado	Gil Sánchez	Davenport	Santa Cruz
Arroyo Seco	1840	Juan Alvarado	Teodocio Yorba	Ione	Amador
Arroyo Seco	1840	Juan Alvarado	Joaquín de la Torre	Greenfield	Monterey
Bolsa de San Felipe	1840	Juan Alvarado	Francisco P. Pacheco		San Benito
Cañada de Raymundo	1840	Juan Alvarado	John Coppinger	Woodside	San Mateo
Casmalia	1840	Juan Alvarado	Antonio Olivera		Santa Bárbara
Guadalupe	1840	Juan Alvarado	Diego Olivera and Teodoro Arellanes	Guadalupe	Santa Bárbara

186 APPENDIX E

GRANT	DATE	GRANTOR	GRANTEE	LOCATION	COUNTY
Jamacha	1840	Juan Alvarado	Apolinara Lorenzana	Spring Valley	San Diego
Los Nogales	1840	Juan Alvarado	José de la Luz Linares	Diamond Bar	Los Angeles
Piedra Blanca	1840	Juan Alvarado	José de Jesús Pico	San Simeon	San Luis Obispo
Pismo	1840	Manuel Jimeno	José Ortega	Arroyo Grande, Pismo Beach	San Luis Obispo
Punta de Quentin	1840	Juan Alvarado	John B. R. Cooper	San Quentin	Marin
La Purisima Concepcion	1840	Juan Alvarado	José Gorgonio	Los Altos Hills	Santa Clara
Rincon de Sanjon	1840	Juan Alvarado	José Eusebio Boronda	Salinas	Monterey
San Bernardo	1840	Juan Alvarado	Vicente Canet	Morro Bay	San Luis Obispo
San José	1840	Juan Alvarado	Ygnacio Pacheco	Ignacio	Marin
Tolenas	1840	Juan Alvarado	José Armijo	Fairfield	Solano
Tujunga	1840	Juan Alvarado	Francisco and Pedro López	Tujunga	Los Angeles
Vallecitos de San Marcos	1840	Juan Alvarado	José María Alvarado	San Marcos	San Diego
Azusa de Dalton	1841	Juan Alvarado	Luis Arenas	Azusa	Los Angeles
Azusa de Duarte	1841	Juan Alvarado	Andrés Duarte	Duarte	Los Angeles
Cañada de Guadalupe la Visitación y Rodeo Viejo	1841	Juan Alvarado	Jacob P. Leese	Brisbane	San Mateo
Cañada del Corral	1841	Manuel Jimeno	José Dolores Ortega	Gaviota	Santa Bárbara
Cañada Larga o Verde	1841	Juan Alvarado	Joaquina Alvarado	Ventura	Ventura
Corral de Piedra	1841	Juan Alvarado	José Villavicencia	Edna	San Luis Obispo
El Sobrante	1841	Juan Alvarado	Juan José Castro and Victor Castro	El Sobrante	Contra Costa
La Bolsa Chica	1841	Juan Alvarado	Joaquín Ruiz	Huntington Beach	Orange
Laguna de los Palos Colorados	1841	Juan Alvarado	Joaquín Moraga, Juan Bernal	Lafayette	Contra Costa
Los Coches	1841	Juan Alvarado	María Josefa Soberanes		Monterey
Miramontes	1841	Juan Alvarado	Candelario Miramontes	Half Moon Bay	San Mateo
Quito	1841	Juan Alvarado	José Zenon Fernandez and José Noriega	Cupertino, Saratoga	Santa Clara
Rincon de la Brea	1841	Juan Alvarado	Gil Ybarra	Brea	Los Angeles
Rincon de San Francisquito	1841	Juan Alvarado	José Peña	Palo Alto	Santa Clara

SELECTED AND EDITED LIST OF LAND GRANTS   187

GRANT	DATE	GRANTOR	GRANTEE	LOCATION	COUNTY
Rinconada del Arroyo de San Francisquito	1841	Juan Alvarado	María Mesa	Menlo Park	Santa Clara
San Bernabe	1841	Juan Alvarado	Petronelo Ríos	San Ardo	Monterey
San Bernardo	1841	Juan Alvarado	Mariano Soberanes and Juan Soberanes		Monterey
San Lorenzo	1841	Juan Alvarado	Guillermo Castro	Castro Valley, Hayward	Alameda
San Lorenzo	1841	Juan Alvarado	Feliciano Soberanes	King City	Monterey
San Luisito	1841	Juan Alvarado	Guadalupe Cantua	San Luis Obispo	San Luis Obispo
San Miguel	1841	Juan Alvarado	Raimundo Olivas, Felipe Lorenzana	Ventura	Ventura
San Miguelito de Trinidad	1841	Juan Alvarado	José Rafael Gonzales		Monterey
Sanjon de Santa Rita	1841	Juan Alvarado	Francisco Soberanes	Santa Rita Park	Merced
Santa Margarita	1841	Manuel Jimeno	Joaquín Estrada	Santa Margarita	San Luis Obispo
Santa Margarita y Las Flores	1841	Juan Alvarado	Pío Pico	Mission Viejo	Orange
Santa Rosa	1841	Juan Alvarado	Julian Estrada	Cambria	San Luis Obispo
Todos Santos y San Antonio	1841	Juan Alvarado	W. E. P. Hartnell		Santa Bárbara
Agua Hedionda	1842	Juan Alvarado	Juan María Marrón	Carlsbad	San Diego
Arroyo de la Alameda	1842	Juan Alvarado	José Jesus Vallejo	Niles	Alameda
Arroyo Grande	1842	Juan Alvarado	Zefarino Carlón		San Luis Obispo
Atascadero	1842	Juan Alvarado	Trifon Garcia	Atascadero	San Luis Obispo
Boca de la Cañada del Pinole	1842	Juan Alvarado	María Manuela Valencia	Martinez, Lafayette	Contra Costa
Cañada de los Alisos	1842	Juan Alvarado	José Serrano	Lake Forest (El Toro)	Orange
Cañada de los Capitancillos	1842	Juan Alvarado	Justo Larios	San José	Santa Clara
Cañada de los Osos y Pecho y Islay	1842	Juan Alvarado	Victor Linares	Montaña de Oro State Park	San Luis Obispo
Cañada del Hambre y Las Bolsas	1842	Juan Alvarado	Teodora Soto	Lafayette, Moraga	Contra Costa

GRANT	DATE	GRANTOR	GRANTEE	LOCATION	COUNTY
Los Capitancillos	1842	Juan Alvarado	Justo Larios	San José	Santa Clara
Los Carneros	1842	Juan Alvarado	María Antonia Linares		Monterey
Cienega de los Paicines	1842	Juan Alvarado	Angel Castro and José Rodríguez	Paicines	San Benito
Dos Pueblos	1842	Juan Alvarado	Nicolás A. Den	Goleta	Santa Bárbara
Las Encinitas	1842	Juan Alvarado	Andrés Ybarra	Encinitas	San Diego
Huerhuero	1842	Juan Alvarado	Mariano Bonilla	Creston	San Luis Obispo
Huerta de Romualdo	1842	Juan Alvarado	Romualdo	Cerro Romauldo	San Luis Obispo
Lomerias Muertas	1842	Juan Alvarado	José Castro		San Benito
Moro y Cayucos	1842	Juan Alvarado	Martin Olivera and Vicente Feliz	Cayucos	San Luis Obispo
Niguel	1842	Juan Alvarado	Juan Avila	Laguna Niguel, Laguna Beach	Orange
Los Ojitos	1842	Juan Alvarado	Mariano Soberanes	Jolon	Monterey
Pastoria de las Borregas	1842	Juan Alvarado	Francisco Estrada	Sunnyvale, Mountain View	Santa Clara
El Pinole	1842	Juan Alvarado	Ygnacio Martinez	Martinez, Pinole	Contra Costa
El Piojo	1842	Juan Alvarado	Joaquín Soto		Monterey
Potrero de San Luis Obispo	1842	Juan Alvarado	María Concepcion Boronda	San Luis Obispo	San Luis Obispo
La Puente	1842	Juan Alvarado	John A. Rowland	Baldwin Park, La Puente, Covina	Los Angeles
Punta del Año Nuevo	1842	Juan Alvarado	Simeon Castro		San Mateo
Rio de los Putos	1842	Juan Alvarado	William Wolfskill	Winters	Solano
San Benito	1842	Juan Alvarado	Francisco Garcia	San Ardo	Monterey
San Bernardo	1842	Juan Alvarado	José Francisco Snook	Rancho Bernardo	San Diego
San Geronimo	1842	Juan Alvarado	Rafael Villavicencio		San Luis Obispo
San Joaquín	1842	Juan Alvarado	José Andres Sepúlveda	Irvine, Newport Beach	Orange
San Leandro	1842	Juan Alvarado	José Joaquín Estudillo	San Leandro	Alameda
San Lorenzo	1842	Juan Alvarado	Francisco Rico		Monterey
San Lorenzo Baja	1842	Juan Alvarado	Francisco Soto	San Lorenzo	Alameda
San Lucas	1842	Juan Alvarado	Rafael Estrada	San Lucas	Monterey
San Miguelito	1842	Juan Alvarado	Miguel Ávila	Avila Beach	San Luis Obispo

SELECTED AND EDITED LIST OF LAND GRANTS   189

GRANT	DATE	GRANTOR	GRANTEE	LOCATION	COUNTY
San Simeon	1842	Juan Alvarado	José Ramón Estrada		San Luis Obispo
San Vicente	1842	Juan Alvarado	José de los Reyes Berreyesa	San José	Santa Clara
Suisun	1842	Juan Alvarado	Francisco Solano	Fairfield	Solano
Las Uvas	1842	Juan Alvarado	Lorenzo Pineda	Morgan Hill	Santa Clara
Agua Puerca y las Trancas	1843	Manuel Micheltorena	Ramon Rodríguez and Francisco Alviso	Swanton	Santa Cruz
Cahuenga	1843	Manuel Micheltorena	José Miguel Triunfo	Burbank, Toluca Lake	Los Angeles
La Cañada	1843	Manuel Micheltorena	Ygnacio Coronel	Eagle Rock, La Cañada Flintridge	Los Angeles
Cañada de los Coches	1843	Manuel Micheltorena	Apolinaria Lorenzana	Lakeside	San Diego
Cañada de los Pinos	1843	Manuel Micheltorena	Seminary of Santa Inez	Santa Ynez, Solvang	Santa Bárbara
La Cienega o Paso de la Tijera	1843	Manuel Micheltorena	Vicente Sánchez	Los Angeles	Los Angeles
Cienega del Gabilan	1843	Manuel Micheltorena	Antonio Chaves		Monterey
Cuyama	1843	Manuel Micheltorena	José María Rojo	Cuyama	Santa Bárbara
Del Río Estanislao	1843	Manuel Micheltorena	Francisco Rico and José Castro	Knights Ferry	Stanislaus
Huasna	1843	Manuel Micheltorena	Isaac J. Sparks	Huasna	San Luis Obispo
La Tajauta	1843	Manuel Micheltorena	Anastasio Avila	Watts, Willowbrook	Los Angeles
Laguna de Tache	1843	Manuel Micheltorena	Joseph Yves Limantour	Hanford	Fresno
Nojoqui	1843	Manuel Micheltorena	Raimundo Carrillo	Solvang	Santa Bárbara
Olompali	1843	Manuel Micheltorena	Camilo Ynitia	Novato, Petaluma	Marin
Pescadero	1843	Manuel Micheltorena	Valentin Higuera and Rafael Feliz	Grayson	Stanislaus
Las Positas y La Calera	1843	Manuel Micheltorena	Narciso Fabregat and Thomas M. Robbins	Hope Ranch	Santa Bárbara
Providencia	1843	Manuel Micheltorena	Vicente de la Ossa	Burbank	Los Angeles
Los Putos	1843	Manuel Micheltorena	Juan Vaca and Juan Peña	Vacaville	Solano

APPENDIX E

GRANT	DATE	GRANTOR	GRANTEE	LOCATION	COUNTY
Rincon del Diablo	1843	Manuel Micheltorena	Juan Alvarado	Escondido, Rincon del Diablo	San Diego
San José de Buenos Ayres	1843	Manuel Micheltorena	Maximo Alanis	Westwood	Los Angeles
San Luis Gonzaga	1843	Manuel Micheltorena	Juan Pacheco and José Mejia		Santa Clara
Santa Paula y Saticoy	1843	Manuel Micheltorena	Manuel Jimeno	Santa Paula, Saticoy	Ventura
Santa Rosa Island	1843	Manuel Micheltorena	José Antonio Carrillo and Carlos Antonio Carrillo	Santa Rosa Island	Santa Bárbara
Temescal	1843	Manuel Micheltorena	Francisco López and José Arellanes	Piru	Ventura
Valle de Pamo	1843	Manuel Micheltorena	José Joaquín Ortega and Edward Stokes	Ramona	San Diego
Aguaje de la Centinela	1844	Manuel Micheltorena	Ygnacio Machado	Westchester	Los Angeles
Bolsa del Potrero y Moro Cojo	1844	Manuel Micheltorena	Joaquín de la Torre	Castroville	Monterey
Campo de los Franceses	1844	Manuel Micheltorena	William Gulnac	Stockton, French Camp	San Joaquin
Cañada de los Nogales	1844	Manuel Micheltorena	José María Aguilar	Mt. Washington, Highland Park	Los Angeles
Cañada de los Vaqueros	1844	Manuel Micheltorena	Francisco Alviso, Antonio Higuera, and Manuel Miranda		Contra Costa
Cañada de Salsipuedes	1844	Manuel Micheltorena	Pedro Cordero		Santa Bárbara
Cholame	1844	Manuel Micheltorena	Mauricio Gonzales		San Luis Obispo
Los Coches	1844	Manuel Micheltorena	Roberto Sunol	San José	Santa Clara
Los Corralitos	1844	Manuel Micheltorena	José Amesti	Corralitos	Santa Cruz
Corte de Madera	1844	Manuel Micheltorena	Maximo Martinez	Ladera	Santa Clara
Del Puerto	1844	Manuel Micheltorena	Mariano and Pedro Hernández	Patterson	Stanislaus
Feliz	1844	Manuel Micheltorena	Domingo Feliz	Millbrae	San Mateo

SELECTED AND EDITED LIST OF LAND GRANTS   *191*

GRANT	DATE	GRANTOR	GRANTEE	LOCATION	COUNTY
Las Juntas	1844	Manuel Micheltorena	William Welch	Martinez, Pacheco, Pleasant Hill	Contra Costa
Los Laureles	1844	Manuel Micheltorena	José Agricio		Monterey
Lomas de la Purificacion	1844	Manuel Micheltorena	Agustín Janssens		Santa Bárbara
Las Mariposas	1844	Manuel Micheltorena	Juan Alvarado	Mariposa	Mariposa
La Merced	1844	Manuel Micheltorena	Casilda Soto de Lobo	Montebello, Monterey Park	Los Angeles
Panoche de San Juan y Los Carrisolitos	1844	Manuel Micheltorena	Julian Ursua		Merced
Paso de Robles	1844	Manuel Micheltorena	Pedro Narváez	Paso Robles	San Luis Obispo
Pauma	1844	Manuel Micheltorena	José Antonio Serrano		San Diego
Posolmi	1844	Manuel Micheltorena	Lope Yñigo	Mountain View, Sunnyvale	Santa Clara
Potrero de los Cerritos	1844	Manuel Micheltorena	Tomas Pacheco and Agustín Alviso	Union City	Alameda
Potrero de Santa Clara	1844	Manuel Micheltorena	James Alexander Forbes	San José	Santa Clara
Punta de Laguna	1844	Manuel Micheltorena	Luis Arelanes and E M Ortega	Los Alamos	Santa Bárbara
Rancho Orestimba y Las Garzas	1844	Manuel Micheltorena	Sebastián Nunez	Newman	Stanislaus
Real de los Aguilas	1844	Manuel Micheltorena	Francisco Arias and Saturnino Carriaga		San Benito
San José del Valle	1844	Manuel Micheltorena	Juan José Warner	Warner Springs	San Diego
San Juan Bautista	1844	Manuel Micheltorena	José Narvaez	Willow Glen	Santa Clara
Sanjon de los Moquelumnes	1844	Manuel Micheltorena	Anastasio and María Chaboya	Galt	San Joaquin
Santa Ysabel	1844	Manuel Micheltorena	José Joaquín Ortega and Edward Stokes	Julian	San Diego
Santa Ysabel	1844	Manuel Micheltorena	Francisco Arce		San Luis Obispo
Tres Ojos de Agua	1844	Manuel Micheltorena	Nicolás Dodero	Santa Cruz	Santa Cruz

192 APPENDIX E

GRANT	DATE	GRANTOR	GRANTEE	LOCATION	COUNTY
Los Ulpinos	1844	Manuel Micheltorena	John Bidwell		Solano
Asuncion	1845	Pío Pico	Pedro Estrada and Francisco Urbano Estrada	Atascadero	San Luis Obispo
Buena Vista	1845	Pío Pico	Felipe	Vista	San Diego
El Cajon	1845	Pío Pico	María Estudillo	El Cajon	San Diego
El Chorro	1845	Pío Pico	John Wilson and James Scott	San Luis Obispo	San Luis Obispo
Corral de Quati	1845	Pío Pico	Agustín Davila	Los Olivos	Santa Bárbara
Cuca	1845	Pío Pico	María Juana de Los Angeles		San Diego
Cuyamaca	1845	Pío Pico	Agustín Olvera		San Diego
de la Nación	1845	Pío Pico	John (Don Juan) Forster	National City	San Diego
Los Encinos	1845	Pío Pico	Ramon, Francisco and Roque	Encino	Los Angeles
El Escorpión	1845	Pío Pico	Odon Eusebia, Urbano, and Manual	West Hills	Los Angeles
Ex-Mission la Purisima	1845	Pío Pico	Jonathan Temple	Los Berros	Santa Bárbara
Ex-Mission Soledad	1845	Pío Pico	Feliciano Soberanes		Monterey
Guajome	1845	Pío Pico	Andres and José Manuel	Vista	San Diego
Guejito y Cañada de Paloma	1845	Pío Pico	José María Orozco	Escondido	San Diego
La Laguna	1845	Pío Pico	Octaviano Gutiérrez	Santa Ynez	Santa Bárbara
Misión Vieja	1845	Pío Pico	John (Don Juan) Forster	Mission Viejo, San Juan Capistrano	Orange
Mission Vieja de la Purisma	1845	Pío Pico	Joaquín Carrillo and José Antonio Carrillo	Lompoc	Santa Bárbara
Pleyto	1845	Pío Pico	José Antonio Chaves	Pleyto	Monterey
Potrero de Felipe Lugo	1845	Pío Pico	Teodoro Romero and Jorge Morillo	South El Monte	Los Angeles
Potrero Grande	1845	Pío Pico	Manuel Antonio	Rosemead	Los Angeles
Potrero los Pinos	1845	Pío Pico	John (Don Juan) Forster	Cleveland National Forest	Orange
San Carlos de Jonata	1845	Pío Pico	Joaquín Carrillo and José María Covarrubias		Santa Bárbara

SELECTED AND EDITED LIST OF LAND GRANTS 193

GRANT	DATE	GRANTOR	GRANTEE	LOCATION	COUNTY
San Dieguito	1845	Pío Pico	Juan María Osuna	Rancho Santa Fe	San Diego
San Francisquito	1845	Pío Pico	Henry Dalton	Temple City	Los Angeles
San Miguel	1845	Pío Pico	José de Jesús Noé	San Francisco	San Francisco
Santa Anita	1845	Pío Pico	Hugo Reid	Arcadia	Los Angeles
Santa Rita	1845	Pío Pico	José Ramón Malo		Santa Bárbara
Sisquoc	1845	Pío Pico	María Domínguez de Caballero		Santa Bárbara
Tequepis	1845	Pío Pico	Joaquín Villa		Santa Bárbara
Ulistac	1845	Pío Pico	Marcelo, Pío and Cristóval	Agnew	Santa Clara
Boca de la Playa	1846	Pío Pico	Emigdio Vejar	San Clemente, Dana Point	Orange
Cañada de San Miguelito	1846	Pío Pico	Ramon Rodríguez	Ventura	Ventura
Cañada de San Vicente y Mesa del Padre Barona	1846	Pío Pico	Juan Bautisa López	Ramona	San Diego
Cañada del Rincon en el Río San Lorenzo	1846	Pío Pico	Pedro Sainsevain	Henry Cowell Redwoods State Park	Santa Cruz
Cuyama	1846	Pío Pico	Cesario Lataillade	Cuyama	Santa Bárbara
Ex-Mission San Buenaventura	1846	Pío Pico	José de Arnaz	Ventura	Ventura
Ex-Mission San Diego	1846	Pío Pico	Santiago Argüello	San Diego	San Diego
Ex-Mission San Fernando	1846	Pío Pico	Eulogio de Celis	San Fernando Valley	Los Angeles
Ex-Mission San José	1846	Pío Pico	Andrés Pico and Juan B. Alvarado	Fremont	Alameda
La Goleta	1846	Pío Pico	Daniel A. Hill	Goleta	Santa Bárbara
Los Huecos	1846	Pío Pico	Luis Arenas and John A. Rowland		Santa Clara
Lomas de Santiago	1846	Pío Pico	Teodosio Yorba	Irvine	Orange
Monserate	1846	Pío Pico	Ysidro Alvarado	Fallbrook	San Diego
San Diego Island	1846	Pío Pico	Pedro C. Carrillo	Coronado	San Diego
San Lorenzo	1846	Pío Pico	Rafael Sánchez		San Benito

GRANT	DATE	GRANTOR	GRANTEE	LOCATION	COUNTY
San Marcos	1846	Pío Pico	Nicolás A. Den and Richard S. Den		Santa Bárbara
San Mateo	1846	Pío Pico	Cayetano Arenas	Hillsborough	San Mateo
San Vicente	1846	Pío Pico	Blas A. Escamilla	Davenport	Santa Cruz
Santa Catalina Island	1846	Pío Pico	Thomas M. Robbins	Santa Catalina Island	Los Angeles
Thompson	1846	Pío Pico	Alpheus Basil Thompson	Oakdale	Stanislaus
Trabuco	1846	Pío Pico	John (Don Juan) Forster	Trabuco Canyon, Coto de Caza	Orange
Valle de San Felipe	1846	Pío Pico	Felipe Castillo		San Diego

Edited from "List of Ranchos of California," Wikipedia, the Free Encyclopedia, http://en.wikipedia.org/w/index.php? title=List_of_Ranchos_of_California&oldid=609629107. This is based largely on Burgess McK. Shumway, *California Ranchos: Patented Private Land Grants Listed by County* (San Bernardino, CA: Borgo Press, 1988). While the website offers more information regarding, for example, notes and size of grants, for purposes of this study, which is concerned with the location of the ranchos in relation to the corridor of the Camino Real de California, those items have been deleted.

APPENDIX F

✣ ✣ ✣ ✣ ✣

Examples of Maritime Lanes Used to Alta California

Examples of Sixteenth-Century Spanish Ships on the California Coast, 1542–1602

NAME	POINT OF ORIGIN	POINT OF ARRIVAL	DATE
Victoria, San Miguel, San Salvador	Navidad	The entire California coast; the southern Oregon coast	1542
San Agustín	Manila	Philippines; Cape Mendocino, Point Reyes, California coast	1595
San Diego, Tres Reyes, San Tomás	Acapulco	Acapulco, California coast	1602

Examples of Spanish Ships Using Maritime Lanes to Alta California, 1774–1820[1]

NAME	POINT OF ORIGIN	POINT OF ARRIVAL	DATE
Santiago	San Blas	California ports, Juan de Fuca, Queen Charlotte Island	1774
Sonora	San Blas	California ports, Juan de Fuca, Trinidad Bay (Alaska)	1774
Favorita	San Blas	San Francisco Bay, California ports, Alaska	1779
Princessa	San Blas	San Francisco Bay	1779
Santiago	San Blas	Monterey, San Francisco	1779
San Carlos	San Blas	California ports, Kodiak	
Princesa	San Blas	Monterey	1782
San Carlos	San Blas	Santa Bárbara, San Diego	1783

APPENDIX F

NAME	POINT OF ORIGIN	POINT OF ARRIVAL	DATE
Princesa	San Blas	California ports, Kodiak, Unalaska, Juan de Fuca	1788
Santa Ifigenia	San Blas	California ports, Nootka	1788
Unalaska		Juan de Fuca	1788
Aranzazu	San Blas	California ports, Juan de Fuca, Nootka Sound	1790
Concepción	San Blas	California ports, Juan de Fuca,	1790
Princesa, Real	San Blas	California ports, Juan de Fuca, Nootka Sound	1790
San Carlos	San Blas	California ports, Juan de Fuca, Nootka Sound	1790
San Carlos	San Blas	California ports, Juan de Fuca, Nootka Sound, Friendly Cove (Port Angeles). Puget Sound (Admiralty Inlet)	1791
Santa Justa (aka *Descubierta*)	South America/ San Blas	California ports, Nootka	1791
Santa Rufina (aka *Atrevida*)	South America/ San Blas	California ports, Nootka	1791
Santa Saturnina	San Blas	California ports, Juan de Fuca, Mt. St. Elias	1791
Activa	San Blas	California ports, Juan de Fuca, Alaska	1792
Mexicana	San Blas	California ports, Juan de Fuca, Alaska	1792
Princesa	San Blas	California ports, Juan de Fuca, Nootka Sound, Neah Bay	1792
Santa Gertrudes	San Blas/Nootka	Monterey	1792
Activo	San Blas	Monterey, Santa Bárbara	1803
Princesa	San Blas	Monterey, Santa Bárbara, San Diego	1803
Activo	San Blas	Monterey, San Diego	1804
Princesa	San Blas	Monterey, San Diego	1804
Activo	San Blas	Monterey	1805
Princesa	San Blas	Monterey	1805

EXAMPLES OF MARITIME LANES USED TO ALTA CALIFORNIA

NAME	POINT OF ORIGIN	POINT OF ARRIVAL	DATE
Activo	San Blas	Monterey, San Diego	1807
Princesa	San Blas		1807
Concepción	San Blas	Monterrey, San Diego	1808
Princesa	San Blas	San Diego	1808
*San Carlo*s	San Blas	Monterey, San Francisco	1808
Princesa	San Blas	Monterey, San Diego	1809
*San Carlo*s	San Blas	Monterey, San Diego	1809
Activo	San Blas	Monterey	1810
Mosca	Manila		1810
Princesa	San Blas	Monterey, San Dieigo	1810
Flora	Lima	Santa Bárbara	1813
Tagle	Lima	Santa Bárbara	1813
Tagle	Lima	San Luis Obispo	1814
San Carlos		Monterey	1816
Cazadora	Panama	Monterey, San Diego, San Pedro	1817
Hermosa Mexicana	Lima	Monterey	1817
San Antonio	Lima	Monterey	1817
Cazadora	Panama		1818
Hermosa Mexicana	Lima		1818
Nueva Reina de los Angeles			1818
San Carlos			1818
San Ruperto	Manila	Monterey	1819
Dos Hermanos	Mazatlán		1820
Europa	Callao		1820
San Francisco de Paula			1820
San Francisco Javier	San Blas		1820
Señoriana	San Blas		1820

APPENDIX G

✺ ✺ ✺ ✺ ✺

The Camino Real de las Californias

THE LAND ROUTE FROM BAJA CALIFORNIA TO SAN DIEGO IN 1769

The land route of the Camino Real de las Californias, as it is sometimes called, was established in 1769 as a part of the effort to supply and reinforce the maritime expeditions sent to San Diego. The early accounts of the land expeditions led by Governor Gaspar de Portolá and Captain Fernando Rivera y Moncada, who led the advance contingent of Portolá's command, present accounts of the overland trek from the east coast of Baja California Sur on the Gulf of California inland to Velicatá and over mountainous terrain to the west coast, heading north to San Diego Bay.[1]

Place-Names Associated with the Land Route within Baja California (1769) Beginning at Mission San Fernando de Velicatá in the Baja California Peninsula

After organizing the expedition on the Gulf of California at La Paz and at Mission Loreto, the group moved inland. From Velicatá, the first point of departure where the two expeditionary commands mustered, Portolá moved them northwesterly along the Arroyo Seco, the second point traversed by the expedition.

1. Arroyo Seco (near Mission San Fernando de Velicatá near the town of Ramona and Rancho Arenoso, north latitude 30° 02' and longitude 115° 16')
2. Arroyo de San Juan de Dios (north latitude 30° 06' and longitude 115° 16')
3. Arroyo de los Mártires (north latitude 30° 08' and longitude 115° 23')
4. Arroyo de las Palmas

5. Alamillo de la Tinaja (near San Antonio: north latitude 30° 12' and longitude 115° 21')

6. Arroyo de los Álamos

7. La Cieneguilla (near El Rosario: north latitude 30° 28' and longitude 115° 18')

8. San Ricardo

9. Cañada de San Isidoro (near San Isidro de Ochoa: north latitude 30° 41' and longitude 115° 32')

10. Arroyo de San Isidoro

11. San Dionisio (near San Antonio de los Meza: north latitude 31° 49' and longitude 115° 42')

12. Arroyo de San León

13. San Telmo (near San Telmo y Rancho Zepeda: north latitude 30° 58' and 116° 06 y longitude 116° 12')

14. San Rafael Arcángel (north of Colnett: north latitude 31° 04' and longitude 116° 12' or Rancho Johnson: north latitude 31° 06' and longitude 116° 16')

15. Cañada San Toribio (near El Salado: north latitude 31° 19' and longitude 116° 12')

16. Santa Isabel reina de Hungría (north of Verdugo de San Vicente: north latitude 31° 19' and longitude 116° 14')

17. Cañada de los Alisos Secos (near Rancho de los Alisos: north latitude 31° 32' and longitude 116° 21') Crespí, "Diario" (296–97) notes that they were at Arroyo Seco de los Alisos on April 20, 1769 and at Santa Isabel Reina de Hungría on April 19.

18. San Francisco Solano (near Puerto de Santo Tomás: north latitude 31° 34' and longitude 116° 37')

19. Valle de la Ciénega de San Jorge (near Punta Banda and Ejido Uruapán: north latitude 31° 38' and longitude 116° 26')

20. Los Mártires/Arroyo de los Santos Mártures San Cleto y Marcelino (near Chapultepec) and Punta Banda

21. Bajijal de los Santos Apóstoles (near Ensenada and Meneadero: north latitude 31° 41' and longitude 116° 37'. Father Crespí's readings near the Arroyo de San Carlos and the Playa del Estero: north latitude 31° 45' and longitude 116° 36')

22. La Santísima Cruz de las Pozas (near Ensenada: north latitude 31° 52' and 116° 37')

23. Las Pozas de Santa Mónica (near El Sauzal: north latitude 31° 54' and longitude 116° 41')

24. San Estanislao (near Mission San Miguel)

25. [Mesa del Paraje de] San Juan Bautista (near Mission San Miguel: north latitude 32° 07' and longitude 116° 52')

26. Pozas del Valle de San Antonio (north of Descanso: north latitude 32° 12' and longitude 116° 54')

27. Vallecito de San Pío (near Rosarito: north latitude 32° 19' and longitude 117° 02')

28. Pocita de la Ranchería de los Santos Mártires (near La Joya)

29. Ranchería y Arroyo de Sancti Spiritus (near Tijuana: north latitude 32° 31' and longitude 117° 07')

30. Puerto de San Diego (Present-day San Diego, California)

APPENDIX H

✣ ✣ ✣ ✣ ✣

Summary of Fray Juan de Crespí's Diary Entry Locations by Date, and Notations by H. E. Bolton

July 14. (1769) The start of the Portolá expedition, to "ranchería de los ojitos de agua de la rinconada de San Diego." Bolton believed the ranchería was "near the northeast point of" False Bay. Campsite at "Los Ojos del Valle de San Diego" was likely near Ladrillo, California. Bolton called the campsite "Pools of the Valley of San Diego."

July 15. That day they passed through a small valley they named "el valle de Santa Isabel, reina de Portugal." They named the *real*, or campsite, San Jácome de la Marca. Possibly Soledad Valley, near Sorrento. Note: San Jácome de la Marca was at or near Dieguito Canyon and Valley, east of Del Mar.

July 16. At San Alejo, Crespí noted that they named the place "la cañada del Triunfo de la Santíssima Cruz" Nearby, they found a small waterhole that they named "el ojito de agua de la cañadita de los Encinos." Moving on, they stopped the *real* at "la lomita de la cañada de San Alejo" (present-day Batequitos Lagoon). The camp was near an Indian settlement. At that point, Crespí wrote "I observed our latitude and it proved to be thirty-three degrees, exactly." Another possibility has it at San Marcos Creek, east of Batiquitos Lagoon, which the explorers called San Alejo. Bolton notes that Valle del Triunfo de la Santíssima Cruz was at San Elijo Lagoon.

Note: For the next six days, July 16 to 22, the expedition marched north through the Soledad Valley, San Dieguito Canyon (near Del Mar), Buena Vista Creek (near Carlsbad), the future site of San Luis Rey Mission, Las Pulgas Canyon, and Cristianitos Canyon (north of San Onofre). At a place they called "beato Simón de Lípnica," they entered a valley close to the beach but out of sight of the sea. Passing through the area, it seemed to them that perhaps there could be a saline flat nearby.

July 17. They traveled north through the valley called San Simón Lípnica at Agua Hedionda Creek. Finally, they camped at Santa Sinforonsa at Buena Vista Creek near Carlsbad.

July 18. At the San Luis Rey River (Notably: SRL 239). Although he named the place San Juan Capistrano, several years later a mission was established near there called Mission San Luis Rey. They noted the possibility of saltpeter in the area, for Crespí wrote that "*aunque algo parece que pinta en salitroso en algunas partes.*"

July 19. Spent a second day at San Luis Rey River. That day, Crespí located the site at 33 degrees and 6 minutes.

July 20. Camped along the Santa Margarita River near Home Ranch and Las Flores Rancho.

July 21. At Las Pulgas Canyon. Probing northward, they came to a place they called Santa María Magdalena, present-day San Juan Capistrano. They called it Valle de Santa Praxedis de los Rosales. They were not far from the Santa Margarita Range.

July 22. At Cristianitos Canyon (north of San Onofre). Notably: SRL 562. There, they baptized two deathly ill children, María Magdalena and Margarita.

July 23. In the Valle de Santa María Magdalena, near or at the present site of San Juan Capistrano Mission. At San Juan Canyon (Notably: SRL 200).

July 24. Stopped at a place they called Señor San Francisco Solano. Their march had taken them to the foothills of the Santa Ana Valley, near El Toro, The place was probably Aliso Creek, near the town of El Toro.

July 25. Crespí noted that they were at the arroyo y cañada de San Francisco Solano. (Notably, they were probably a day or two at Aliso Creek, near the town of El Toro.) Crespí noted the latitude at 33 degrees 18 minutes.

July 26. They camped at a spot with two waterholes they named "los dos ojitos de agua de San Pantaleón." (Notably, the place could be Tomato Spring along the edge of the Santiago Hills near Tuston.)

July 27. They were probably in the vicinity of the Santiago Hills east of Tuston. There they found water in a small creek they had named Señor Santiago Apóstol, present-day Santiago. They observed the latitude at 33 degrees and 36 minutes. (Notably: they were at Santiago Creek, northeast of Orange.)

July 28. They were the first Europeans to record a California quake and the three aftershocks that followed it. Crespí noted that it was named the place Dulcísimo Nombre de Jesús de los Temblores, but the soldiers simply called it the "Río Santa Ana," by which the Santa Ana River is known today. They were likely at the Santa Ana River near Olive, east of Anaheim.

July 29. They reached a place they called Ranchería de la pocita y valle de Santa Marta, north of present-day Fullerton. Likely they were at or near La Brea Canyon, north of Fullerton.

July 30. They had reached the area of La Habra near Puente Hills. Crespí wrote that the arroyo was muddy and, fearing getting stuck in it, the soldiers constructed a bridge over it. That day, Crespí observed the latitude to be at 33 degrees and 24 minutes. They called the valley San Miguel Arcángel, today's San Gabriel River Valley. Shortly, they set up camp near present-day Bassett. Thus, they were at or near Bassett, on the San Gabriel River.

July 31. They had covered forty-two and a half leagues from San Diego to El Monte, south of present-day Mission San Gabriel. They camped for the night and reported a strong earthquake. Likely, they were north of the Whittier Narrows. Bolton opined that they were at Lexington Wash, near El Monte. Their camp was south of present-day Mission San Gabriel.

August 1. That day they were three leagues from the San Gabriel River, north of Puente Hills and the Whittier Narrows. It appears that the Whittier Narrows were discovered in January 1770, on the return trip. Of that occasion, Crespí, on January 18, wrote that as they headed south, they passed through a gap in the valley of San Miguel and managed to march six leagues. They had traveled a long distance to the southeast on the edge of a stream in the gap, forded the river by the same name as the valley, and traveled southeast to the river they had earlier named El Río de los Temblores, which they forded. They also noted that the Río de los Temblores was carrying more water than the Río Porciúcula. That night they camped in the valley of San Miguel, where they had stopped outbound on the night of July 30, 1769. Their latitude was observed by Costansó, whose readings were always higher than those taken by Crespí, to be 34 degrees, 30 minutes. Crespí's reading was 34 degrees and 10 minutes.

August 2. They reached the Los Angeles River and named the valley and the river Nuestra Señora de los Angeles de la Porciúncula. Likely, they were near the Los Angeles River, at North Broadway (Notably, SRL 655, in Elysian Park).

August 3. They reached the Alisos de San Estévan at Ballena Creek west of La Cienega. Nearby they noted springs of pitch, or tar pits. Bolton surmised that they were at La Brea. Notably at La Cienega Park, on La Cienega Blvd. between Olympic Blvd. and Gregory Way. (SRL 665).

August 4. The expedition had crossed present day La Cienega and were headed in the direction of Santa Monica and Sepúlveda Canyon. (Notably they were near or on the campus of University High School, West Los Angeles [SRL 522].) Not far from there, they hunted for antelope and wild goat in today's Greater Los Angeles area and noted the tar pits, which readily gave its modern toponym the La Brea Tar Pits. Another place-name near there was the "Antelope Springs or literally, Springs of El Berrendo," probably present-day Serra Springs (California Historical Landmark 522). North of El Berrendo, the explorers marched along a beach with steep mountains that did not allow easy passage. There, they turned northwest and saw a pass in the mountains. Bolton believed they had been moving along the beach west of Santa Monica and, therefore, concluded that the pass was Sepúlveda Canyon.

August 5. That day, they camped in a place they called Santa Catalina de Bononia de los Encinos, near present-day Encino, in the San Fernando Valley. Their camp was just northwest of present-day Mission San Gabriel. Crespí took the latitude at 34 degrees and 37 minutes. They were in the Valle de Santa Catalina, or Valle de los Encinos.

August 6. They spent a second day in the Valle de los Encinos. Today the area is marked by Los Encinos State Historical Park in Encino (SRL 689).

August 7. The expedition went through Valle y poza de Santa Catarina de Bononia. Having departed late that day, at about 3:00 p.m., they headed north and stopped in a canyon for the night at the foot of a mountain. It is likely that they were northwest of the present-day site of Mission San Fernando (SRL 157).

August 8. They passed through a canyon they had entered at the end of the previous day. Excellent farming soil. That day they reached the mountain where they ascended a high pass. Bolton surmised that the expedition crossed over San Fernando Pass near Newhall. The expedition followed the canyon throughout the day. Along the way, Natives from nearby settlements came out to meet them and led them to their ranchería. They came to other rancherías and traded for food along the way. They named one of them the pueblo Santa Rosa de Viterbo. Bolton noted another Indian settlement, which the soldiers called Ranchería del Corral because the settlement was nothing more than an enclosure for protection. Bolton wrote that it was on the Santa Clara River near present-day Castac in Los Angeles County. All that day, they had followed the valley along an arroyo in which they said began the long canyon they had called La Cañada de Santa Clara.

August 9. They stayed there recuperating and sent out scouts. That day, Crespí observed the latitude to be at 34 degrees 47 minutes, near the pueblo they named Santa Rosa de Viterbo. They were at or near Castaic Junction.

August 10. The expedition continued through the La Cañada de Santa Clara heading west-northwest before turning west-southwest through the twisting canyon. The scouts told them that they had another day in the canyon. They traveled three hours for three leagues. They stopped to camp near present-day Camulos Rancho at Piru, California. Their camp was probably two miles east of Piru (Notably: SRL 624, Warring Park, Piru).

August 11. They were still in the long canyon that day, which they called La cañada de la Señora de Santa Clara. Probably near Sespe Creek, just west of Fillmore.

August 12. That day they reached a place near the canyon they called Ranchería de San Pedro Moliano del Pueblo de Santa Clara. Bolton noted that the settlement was near present-day Fillmore.

August 13. Still plagued by tremors north of Fillmore, they followed the canyon bearing southwest. After one league of marching, they were near the end of the winding canyon. After two leagues, they arrived at the abra, or narrow pass made by the mountain. They stopped at a place they called Ranchería de los Santos Mártires San Hipólito y Casiano, Bolton noted that they were near Santa Paula (Notably: SRL 727). Perhaps at or near Saticoy.

August 14. That day, they broke camp to look for the landmark they called "la punta de la Concepción." Traveling along a long curve on the land, they could see a high mountain point along the coast which they thought could be the "Point Concepción." They also noted that the land curved and formed a cove in the shape of a half moon. Near Asunción de María Santísima de los Cielos, they observed the latitude to be at 34 degrees 36 minutes. Possibly they were at or near Ventura (Notably: SRL 310, Mission San Buenaventura).

August 15. That day they crossed the river and went westward. They came to another ranchería, where they stopped to camp. Crespí credited the soldiers as having named present-day Pitas (Whistle), today's Pita Point north of Ventura. They named the village Santa Cunegundis del pueblo de la Asumpta. They were at or near Pitas Point.

August 16. Heading west, they arrived at a ranchería, which they named Santa Clara de Montefalco. The soldiers called it the town of El Bailarín. They observed the latitude at 34 degrees and 40 minutes. Possibly, at or near Rincón Point on Rincón Creek.

August 17. Continuing west, they crossed over hills and came down a steep incline to the beach. They saw a point and a bay. Nearby they came to a large settlement with thirty-eight houses, round with thatched roofs, which they named Carpintería. At or in the vicinity of present-day Carpintería.

August 18. Moving in a westerly direction, they arrived at a place near a large lagoon that they called Laguna de la Concepción, present-day Santa Barbara. Bolton states that the lagoon was to the east of the modern city. From there, they could see the long, low point they thought to be "la punta de la Concepción." Nearby was another Indian settlement that they called the ranchería de San Joaquín de la Laguna de la Punta de la Concepción.

August 19. Unsure that they had reached Point Concepción, they came upon another settlement and named the place Santa Margarita de Cortona.

August 20. Still, traveling in a westerly direction, they saw a bay with an island. Beyond them were four other prosperous towns. The soldiers named the towns collectively as Mescaltitlán, today's Mescal Island. This was in or in the direction of the West side of Santa Barbara, possibly at or near Arroyo Burro or possibly to the south of Goleta. Crespí observed the latitude to be at 34 degrees, 43 minutes.

August 21. Miles away, they reached a place they called San Luís Obispo, Crespí observed the latitude to be at 34 degrees and 45 minutes. They were at or near Dos Pueblos Canyon, at Naples.

August 22. They spent the next day resting at Dos Pueblos Canyon, at Naples.

August 23. After traveling over high hills, ravines, and gullies along an arroyo, they came to Tajiguas Creek. The nearby Indian settlement was named San Guido de Cortona.

August 24. Traveling westward they arrived at a place they named La Gaviota, still so named today. Crespí observed the latitude to be at 34 degrees, 47 minutes.

August 25. Traveling close to the seashore, they came to an Indian village they named San Serafino, the Pope. Bolton surmised that they were near El Bullito Creek or possibly at Cañada de la Brea.

August 26. Moving west, the expedition reached the Ranchería del Cojo. Bolton remarks that "the valley is still called Cañada del Cojo."

August 27. Traveling westward they arrived at "the low, bare point of land which is conjectured to be Point Concepción." Bolton writes that they were Espada Creek.

August 28. Still near Point Concepción, they came to a place they called Los Pedernales, today's Rocky Point.

August 29. Beyond Point Concepción, they could see Point Arguello. They were near an arroyo at Cañada Honda. The camped just south of Surf, California.

August 30. That day, they reached a river they called Santa Rosa, present-day Santa Inéz River, There Crespí observed the latitude to be 34 degrees and 55 minutes. They were probably near Ocean Beach County Park.

August 31. They reached a lake they named San Ramón Nonato near present-day San Antonio Creek.

September 1. Traveling directly north they reached a large valley with a lake. They named it Laguna Grande de San Daniel. Bolton wrote it was Guadalupe Lake. Crespí noted the latitude at 35 degrees and 13 minutes.

September 2. Moving northwest, the reached a place near a lake they called Oso Flaco (lean or skinny bear). Bolton noted Oso Flaco Lake still bears the same name.

September 3. Spent the day at Oso Flaco Lake.

September 4. The expedition moved along the beach toward the northwest, then east across some sand dunes until they reached a lagoon. Then they marched northwest and headed north into the mountains. They came to a village they named the place and the chief El Buchón. They were in Price Canyon, north of Pismo.

September 5. They traveled northwest to a narrow valley they named Cañada de Santa Elena or Cañada de Angosta. Bolton noted it was San Luis Canyon, or possibly Gragg Canyon.

September 6. A second day was spent resting there.

September 7. Moving forward, they reached Chorro Creek. From there they continued until they reached a place they called Los Osos. Bolton notes that it is still referred to as Cañada de los Osos west of San Luis Obispo.

September 8. Traveling through the valley/canyon of Los Osos, they came to an arroyo at the end of which, they looked toward the north and saw a large rock jutting out from the sea, which they called El Morro, near Morro Creek. Bolton noted that it was "Morro Creek. The bay where they stopped is now called Morro Bay, and the rock in front of their camp is now called Morro Rock." Thus, they were at or near Morro Bay State Park (Morro Rock, SRL 821).

September 9. By this date, they had traveled northwest to a "broad valley with an estuary fed by an arroyo." They named it the Estuary of Santa Serafina. It was, according to Bolton, Ellysly's Creek, just east of Point Estero. Nearby to the north it is joined by Villa Creek.

September 10. That day they headed northward through the valley. Bolton noted, "They ascended Ellysly's Creek, went over Dawson Grade, and camped on Santa Rosa Creek, near Cambria."

September 11. Traveling northwest, they arrived at "Little Pico Creek, which enters San Simeon Bay straight east of San Simeon Point."

September 12. That day they arrived at a place they called Arroyo de San Vicente. Crespí noted the latitude was 36 degrees and 10 minutes. Bolton surmised that they ascended "Arroyo Laguna to Arroyo de la Cruz."

September 13. Marching northwesterly, the expedition arrived at a place they named Santa Humiliana. Bolton figured it was "Near Ragged Point, on San Carpoforo Creek." Here the coast becomes impassable. They called their campsite Pié de la Sierra de Santa Lucía, foot of the Santa Lucía Mountains.

September 14. The next day was spent at the foot of the Santa Lucía Mountains at or near San Carpoforo Creek, near Ragged Point.

September 15. A third day was spent at or near San Carpoforo Creek, near Ragged Point.

September 16. Moving into a narrow valley that entered the mountain, they reached a point, which Bolton noted as the upper San Carpoforo Creek that formed a junction with Chris Flood Creek.

September 17. Wending their way north, they arrived at a place they called La Hoya de la Sierra de Santa Lucía, noted by Bolton to be Wagner Creek.

September 18. They spent the day at Wagner Creek, Santa Lucía Mountains.

September 19. They spent a third day at Wagner Creek, Santa Lucía Mountains.

September 20. The day was spent zig-zagging through hills, woods, sand dunes, swamps for five hours. They camped at a place they called Los Piñones. Bolton reckoned that they were near Los Burros Creek, west of the Nacimiento River.

September 21. Camped near the Nacimiento River. The expedition rested throughout the day.

September 22. Near Los Burros Creek, west of the Nacimiento River.

September 23. Day three at Los Burros Creek, west of the Nacimento River. Scouts reported having seen a river which they thought to be the Río del Carmelo, but Bolton believed it to be the Salinas River.

September 24. They reached a stream of water. Bolton concluded it was the San Antonio River near Jolón.

September 25. They marched all day to a place they named The Wounds of our Seraphic Father San Francisco, which Bolton figured was in the Upper Jolón Valley.

September 26. Traveling northeastward through the mountain, they camped at a place they called Río de San Elizario. Bolton figured they had "descended Kent Canyon, reaching the Salinas near King City."

September 27. Followed the valley and the river in a northwesterly direction. That day they reached a place Bolton remarked that "Below King City and above Metz, the Salinas River runs close to the eastern range. This passage in Crespí is in itself proof that Portolá reached the river near King City." They named their camp Real del Alamo. Bolton wrote that the "Camp on the 27 (*Real del Alamo*) was near Metz."

September 28. Wending their way for hours, they found several Indian paths along the Salinas River, southwest of Camphora. Bolton reckoned that their camp, Real Blanco, was near Camphora.

September 29. Moving through the mountainous terrain, they camped at a place they called Real de los Cazadores, which Bolton explains was near Chular.

September 30. They continued through the same valley to a campsite near Old Hill Town. They were now surely out of the Santa Lucía Mountains and headed toward the sea in search of Monterey Bay, which had eluded them.

October 1. Following the Salinas River (according to Bolton), they reached the beach and camped near Blanco.

October 2. Day two camped at the Salinas River, near Blanco. Soldiers explored area in search of elusive Monterey Bay. Crespí reads latitude at 36 degrees 53 minutes.

October 3. Day three camped at the Salinas River, near Blanco. Exploring soldiers found an arroyo than went from mountains to the shore. Bolton surmised: Carmel Bay and River.

October 4. Day four camped at the Salinas River, near Blanco. Meeting held to move northward.

October 5. Day five camped at the Salinas River, near Blanco. Sergeant Ortega and men searched for Monterey Bay toward Point Año Nuevo.

October 6. Day six camped at the Salinas River, near Blanco. Scouts reported having reached the area of the Pájaro River near Watsonville.

October 7. Breaking camp, they moved north-northwest from Salinas River until they reached a place they called Laguna de las Grullas. Bolton wrote that they were "near Del Monte Junction. The laguna was perhaps Espinosa Lake."

October 8. The expedition reached and named the Río Pájaro near Watsonville. Pájaro River still so called today. Bolton writes "The route from this point to Soquel Creek (El Rosario), reached on October 16th, is difficult to trace with minute precision, but the explorers evidently ascended Corralitos Creek and swung round some distance to the north, for they crossed Soquel Creek a league from the coast. Their route was close to the present highway from Watsonville to Soquel."

October 9. Day two camped at the Río Pájaro. Scouts sent out to explore the area.

October 10. Traveling northwest, the expedition reached a redwood forest and camped near a lagoon which Bolton identified as "College Lake or Pinto Lake, evidently." To College Lake, north of Watsonville.

October 11. Day two spent recovering at camp near College Lake, north of Watsonville.

October 12. Day three still at camp near College Lake, Crespí observed the latitude at 37 degrees, 35 minutes.

October 13. Day four, those ailing from scurvy still recovering.

October 14. Day five, still at camp at College Lake. Scouts returned to camp and reported no information on location of Monterey Bay as they did not find anything resembling the harbor they sought.

October 15. Traveling slowly toward the northwest, they arrived at an arroyo that Bolton believed to be Corralitos Creek. That day they camped at a place they named Santa Teresa, which Bolton deduced to be Pleasant Valley.

October 16. Still headed northwest, they reached a place they named El Rosario del Beato Serafín de Asculi, Bolton's Soquel Creek, probably near Porter Gulch.

October 17. Traveling north-northwest, they reached the San Lorenzo River, probably near Santa Cruz.

October 18. That day they marched along the coast in a west-northwest direction over high hills near the sea. They came to an arroyo they named Santa Cruz and proceeded beyond the redwood forest to an estuary they named Arroyo de San Lucas, which Bolton said is Coja Creek.

October 19. Following the coast along where it turns to the northwest, they came to a small beach near some pines on a hill. They named the place San Pedro de Alcántara. The soldiers called it El Alto del Jamón. Bolton figured it was Scott Creek.

October 20. They headed northward, then northwest after a league until they came to a place they named San Luís Beltrán. Bolton supposed it to be Waddell Creek.

October 21. Day two at camp near Waddell Creek. Scouts sent out to reconnoiter the area.

October 22. Day three at Camp near Waddell Creek. Drenching rain and ailing men detained the expedition from moving forward.

October 23. Having recovered, the ailing men called the camp La Salud. From there they followed the beach northward and climbed a mesa until they came to an Indian settlement and beyond there to an arroyo where they camped. Bolton supposed it to be Gazos Creek. Also see, to the south of Gazos Creek, Whitehouse Creek (SRL 23).

October 24. They left Gazos Creek and, moving northerly within sight of the sea, reached a lagoon after crossing two arroyos which Bolton surmised as follows: "The two arroyos crossed were Arroyo de los Frijoles and Pescadero Creek. The lake mentioned is still at Arroyo de los Frijoles halfway between Bolsas Point and Pescadero Point." Crespí named the lake San Pedro Regalado. Moving on they came to a settlement of bearded Indians and camped near an arroyo that they called Father Santo Domingo. Bolton supposed the camp to be "at San Gregorio Creek, near the coast." See San Gregorio (SRL 26).

October 25. Remained at San Gregorio Creek.

October 26. Day three was spent recovering at San Gregorio Creek.

October 27. Moving north, over high hills, the expedition, reached an Indian settlement at a place they named Arroyo de San Ibón, which Bolton wrote is "Now called Purísima Creek." See Purisima Creek (SRL 22).

October 28. They traveled near the beach over low mesas past Indian settlements to a place with many wild geese, which they named Los Ansares, today, as Bolton surmised, "Pilarcitos Creek, just north of the town of Half Moon Bay (or possibly Frenchman creek). The point of land is Pillar Point." See Pilarcitos Creek (SRL 21).

October 29. Spent the day recovering at Pilarcitos Creek.

October 30. Moving along the beach, they crossed some arroyos, one of which Bolton noted was San Vicente Creek, near present-day Martini Creek (SRL 25).

They camped near a point called Ángel Custodio or Punta de las Almejas del Ángel de la Guarda for the large number of mussels there. Bolton noted that it is present-day San Pedro Point.

October 31. They spent the day at Punta de las Almejas. See San Pedro Creek (SRL 24).

November 1. A second day was spent at Punta de las Almejas. Crespí observed the latitude at 37 degrees and 49 minutes.

November 2. Still at Punta de las Almejas on the third day. Hunters were sent out. They reported seeing a large arm to the sea, a wide opening, which precluded that they could reach Point Reyes by land if they followed that route.

November 3. Scouts return to camp and erroneously supposed that they were at Monterey Bay. Later it was decided that this was not the case. They did, however, think that they had reached present-day Drake's Bay, which they knew from Manila Galleon mariners' accounts as the Bahía de San Francisco. The Natives had told them that two days hence was a port with a Spanish ship. Part of the expedition's next objectives was to find them.

November 4. To that end, the expedition departed Punta de las Almejas. Following the beach northward they entered the mountains headed northeast. From the summit, they could now see the great estuary and the arm of the sea which extended four to five leagues. Moving away from the bay, they went south and southwest. They stopped at a place Bolton described as being "on the west slope of Sweeny Ridge, west of San Andreas Lake." See Discovery site on Sweeney Ridge (SRL 394). It is believed that the expedition's campsite is today covered by San Andreas Lake (SRL27 along Skyline Blvd).

November 5. Traveling southerly along the edge of the estuary, they kept the mountains and the redwood and oak forests to their right. They crossed an arroyo and stopped near a lake. Bolton identified that they were "Near the southern end of Crystal Springs Lake." See Crystal Springs Reservoir (SRL 94).

November 6. Traveling along the same trajectory, they arrived, as Crespí wrote, at "an arroyo whose waters descend from the mountains and run precipitously to this estuary." Bolton surmised it to be "San Francisquito Creek, near Palo Alto. Costansó tells us that they turned east (from Searaville Lake) before making camp, and halted near the bay." See San Francisquito Creek in Menlo Park (SRL 2).

November 7. They spent the day at rest, while scouts went out to continue seeking signs of the bay with a ship that Indians had told them about.

November 8. Still at San Francisquito Creek, Crespí observed the latitude to be 37 degrees and 46 minutes.

November 9. Spent the day at camp at San Francisquito Creek waiting for the scouts to return.

November 10. That night the scouts returned, disappointed that the reports that they found no signs of a bay with a ship in it.

November 11. Having seen the coast, all the signs of the harbor of San Francisco as described by the pilot Cabrera Bueno, Portolá, after a vote by his officers, decided to head back to San Francisco. They believed that Monterey Bay had eluded them. Bolton wrote that they camped at Woodside. See Woodside (SRL 92).

November 12. Heading north-northwest and north, they followed the valley of San Francisco. Bolton wrote that they stopped at San Andreas Lake, or possibly at Pilarcitos Lake.

November 13. Backtracking on the trail they had used to enter the area, they continued southward. Bolton wrote that they were at San Pedro Creek.

November 14. Heading south, they reached a campsite near Las Almejas. Bolton wrote that they were at San Vicente Creek. Also possibly near Martini Creek.

November 15. The expedition remained there to rest. Bolton figured they were near Half Moon Bay.

November 16. The expedition continued moving southward to the vicinity of Los Ansares. Crespí wrote that they camped at a place they called the "Holy Apostles San Simón and San Judas on the plain of Los Ansares." Probably near Pilarcitos Creek where Bolton had placed them on October 28, 1769.

November 17. Moving south they halted on the banks of a deep arroyo. Bolton placed them at Tunitas Creek. See Tunitas Creek (SRL 375).

November 18. They reached the Valley of San Ibón, where they had been on October 27. Bolton reckoned they were at or near Pescadero Creek. Also see possibly the confluence of Pescadero Creek at Butano Creek.

November 19. They halted at a steep rock in sight of Point Año Nuevo. Bolton wrote that they camped at Año Nuevo Creek.

November 20. That day, they reached San Pedro de Alcántara, alias El Alto del Jamón in the area where they had been on October 19. Bolton wrote that they were at Scott Creek. Also see possibly south of Scott Creek near Molino Creek.

November 21. They stopped at the Arroyo de las Puentes de San Lucas near where they had been on October 18. Bolton wrote that they were at Coja Creek. Also see area between Laguna Creek and Majors Creek.

November 22. They crossed the San Lorenzo River and camped at El Rosario de San Serafino, near where they had been on October 16. Bolton surmised that they were at Soquel Creek. Possibly near Porter Gulch.

November 23. They reached a place they called Los Avellanos de Nuestra Señora del Pilar, where they had been between October 10 and 14. Bolton wrote that they were in the Corralitos Valley.

November 24. They followed the trail where they had been on October 9, along the Río Pájaro. Bolton wrote that they were at Elk Slough.

November 25. They rested at their camp while scouts went to explore along the coast.

November 26. They reached the Río Santa Delfina, where they had camped on October 1 to 6. Bolton wrote that they were on the Salinas River southeastward of Blanco.

November 27. Departing their camp at Santa Delfina, they went upriver and stopped within site of the Punta de los Pinos. Bolton wrote that "they crossed the Salinas and went to camp on the site of Monterey."

November 28. Following the beach, they entered a large pine forest and halted at a medium-sized bay. Bolton: they "halted beyond the Carmel River, near Point Lobos, where they remained in camp until December 10. It was from this camp that the exploration of Santa Lucía Range was made, and it was here that the council was held on December 7." See possibly San José Creek where it flows into Carmel Bay. San José Creek, where it flows into Carmel Bay.

November 29. They spent the day at rest.

November 30. Another day was spent resting while scouts explored the area.

December 1. Another day was spent resting while scouts explored the area.

December 2. Another day was spent resting while scouts explored the area.

December 3. Another day was spent resting while scouts explored the area.

December 4. Another day was spent resting while scouts explored the area.

December 5. Another day was spent resting while scouts explored the area.

December 6. Another day was spent resting while scouts explored the area.

December 7. Another day was spent resting while scouts explored the area.

December 8. Another day was spent resting while scouts explored the area.

December 9. Another day was spent resting while scouts explored the area.

December 10. Following Crespí's diary, Bolton wrote that the expedition broke camp at Carmel Bay within sight of Punta de los Pinos, left a cross and a message, and headed south toward Monterey.

December 11. Crespí wrote "We started in the morning over a plain toward the northeast as far as the river, which we forded, and camped . . . in the same place where we had been on September 30." Bolton wrote that they were "near Blanco." On September 30, they had been along the Salinas River, near Old Hill Town.

December 12. They camped at Los Cazadores where they had been on September 29. Bolton wrote that they were "near Chualar."

December 13. They stopped at a place called El Real Blanco and hunted. Bolton wrote that they were "near Camphora." On September 28, they had been along the Salinas River, southwest of Camphora.

December 14. They passed their old camp at Real del Alamo. Bolton wrote that they were "above Metz." On September 27, they had been along the Salinas River, near Metz.

December 15. Crespí wrote that they had reached the valley of San Elceareo and camped in the same place where they had been on September 26. Bolton wrote that it was near King City.

December 16. They reached an Indian settlement they named Palo Caido. Bolton noted that they were "in the Jolón Valley."

December 17. Traveling in a southwest direction, they stopped at a river they called Las Truchas de San Elceareo, near where they had been from September 21–23. Bolton wrote that the river was "the Nacimiento River."

December 18. They camped at Los Piñones where they had been on September 20. Bolton wrote that they were "near Los Burros Creek."

December 19. After two leagues through difficult terrain, they stopped at a "hollow in Sierra de Santa Lucía" where we had been on the 20th of September. Bolton surmised that they were "in the Hollow at the forks of Campoforo Creek." Bolton noted that earlier, September 17–19, they had been at or near Wagner Creek.

December 20. That day, they rested at the same place: at or near Wagner Creek.

December 21. They came out of the Sierra de Santa Lucía, and reached an Indian settlement near, as Bolton wrote "Arroyo del Oso."

December 22. They spent the day camped near Arroyo del Oso as the cloudy weather appeared threatening.

December 23. Despite threatening weather, they departed the Arroyo del Oso area and reached a place they called El Laurel. Bolton noted that they were "Near San Simeon Bay." They were probably near Little Pico Creek.

December 24. Christmas Eve Day found them as Bolton wrote "At Santa Rosa Creek." On September 10, they had been at Santa Rosa Creek, probably east of Cambria.

December 25. On Christmas Day they reached Santa Serafina. Bolton surmised that they were "East of Ellysby's Creek, at the north end of Estero Bay." They had been there on September 9.

December 26. Moving forward they stopped near their old camp where they had been on September 7, in the Valley of San Adrián or Los Osos. Bolton wrote that they were "at Chorro Creek."

December 27. Marching in a drenching rainfall, they reached a site Bolton described as being "near the site of San Luís Obispo." Likely they were southeast of San Luis Obispo toward Edna.

December 28. Muddy conditions stalled the expedition at that place.

December 29. They reached El Buchón that day. Bolton noted that they were "in San Luís Canyon." On September 4, they were in that area of Price Canyon north of Pismo.

December 30. Leaving El Buchón, they arrived at a lake near a sand dune. Bolton identified it as at Oso Flaco Lake. They had been there on September 2 and 3.

December 31. Three leagues away, they arrived at another lake. Bolton identified it as "Guadalupe Lake," where they had been on September 1. Crespí noted that on that day they were at the lake was called "Holy Martyrs Saint Daniel and his Companions."

January 1. (New Year's Day, 1770). Crespí wrote that they arrived at the Lake of San Ramón Nonato, where they had been on August 31. Bolton noted that they were at or near San Antonio Creek.

January 2. They reached a large river known as the Río San Bernardo, also as the Río Santa Rosa. Crespí wrote that they were in La Cañada Seca. Bolton noted that they were near Surf.

January 3. They arrived at San Juan Bautista de los Pedernales. From their camp, they could see Point Concepción at the most western point of the Santa Bárbara Channel. Bolton wrote that they were at Pedernales Point.

January 4. Crespí wrote that they passed La Espada and continued to Santa Teresa ruled by Chief Cojo. They left the valley of El Oso. Bolton wrote that they were at the "Cañada del Cojo," where they had been on August 26, 1769.

January 5. They reached San Serefino, the Pope, near where they had been on August 25, 1769. Bolton surmised that they were at the Arroyo del Bullito.

January 6. Still headed southward, they arrived at San Luís Rey, and camped at the same place where they had been on August 24. Bolton noted that they were at La Gaviota.

January 7. Traveling over rough terrain, they reached San Guido de Cortona, where they had been on August 23. Bolton wrote that they were along Tajiguas Creek.

January 8. They stopped at place called San Luís Obispo, where they had been from August 21–22. Bolton wrote that they were at Dos Pueblos Creek near Naples.

January 9. Stopped at La Isla, where they had been on August 20. Bolton noted that they were at or near the lagoon at Mescal Island, not far from Goleta.

January 10. Departing La Isla, they bypassed their previous campsites until they got to Carpintería. Bolton acknowledged that they camped at Carpintería, where they had been on August 17.

January 11. Crespí mentioned that they had spent the day at Asumpta and bypassed El Bailarín. Bolton wrote that they were at or near Ventura, where they had been on August 14.

January 12. Crossing through the Valley of Santa Clara in a southwesterly direction, they entered the Sierra de la Conversión and crossed the San Hipólito River. They were near their old camp of August 13 as they veered southeast and stopped near an Indian settlement. Bolton commented that they were in the Santa Clara Valley near Camarillo.

January 13. They marched to a campsite in a small valley they named El Triunfo del Dulcísimo Nombre de Jesús. Bolton wrote that they were in the Potrero Valley.

January 14. Moving beyond the valley, they reached an Indian settlement they named El Triunfo del Nombre de Dios. Bolton wrote that "Russell Valley (Triunfo Canyon) opens into the valley from the south. The guides had misled them into the Santa Monica Mountains)." They returned to the settlement and asked for more reliable guides before moving on to present-day Russell Valley.

January 15. They crossed into the Valley of Santa Catarina de Bononia and reached Los Robles, where they had camped on August 7. Bolton wrote that they went "through Calabazas Pass into San Fernando Valley (camp was near Encino)." Also Los Encinos State Historical Park.

January 16. Traveled southeasterly through a pass leading to a plain called Los Alisos. Bolton commented that "Portolá left San Fernando Valley by Cahuenga Pass, and camped near its mouth north of Hollywood." Possibly near the Hollywood Freeway and Franklin Avenue. Bolton noted that "From there the northward route was retraced to San Diego, but as the homeward marches were so long, several of the old camps were passed without stopping."

January 17. That day they reached the Porciúncula River. Bolton wrote that Portolá "camped at the San Gabriel River near Bassett." Earlier on July 30, the expedition had been along the San Gabriel River, near Bassett.

January 18. Traveling through the Valley of San Miguel, they went southeast along a stream and forded the river they had named El Río de Jesús de los Temblores. Bolton observed that "instead of recrossing Puente Hills through La Habra, he followed the San Gabriel till near Whittier, then struck southeastward to his old camp on the Santa Ana near olive" [where they had camped on July 28].

January 19. They stopped at the springs of San Pantaleón near where they had been on July 26. (Notably: the place could be along the edge of the Santiago Hills near Tuston.)

January 20. To San Juan Canyon, where they had been on July 23.

January 21. They entered the Valley of Santa María Magdalena. Bolton wrote that the "camp was apparently on San Onofre Creek."

January 22. Traveling past the Valley of Santa Margarita without stopping, they reached the Valley of San Juan Capistrano and followed the road over sloping hills. On July 18–19, they had passed through the area and reached the Río San Luís Rey.

January 23. They marched all day, passing Santa Sinforosa and San Alejo en route to their camp at San Jácome de la Marca. On July 15, 1769, they had camped at San Dieguito Creek and Valley.

January 24. Finally, they returned to San Diego.

NOTES

❊ ❊ ❊ ❊ ❊

Preface

1. Nathan Masters, "How El Camino Real, California's 'Royal Road,' Was Invented," *Lost LA*, January 4, 2013. See https://www.kcet.org/show/lost la/how-el-camino-real-californias-royal-road-was-invented. Masters posits, among other points, that "the stories told today about the footpath diverge from its actual history" and that the actual route was not fixed: it changed over time. Masters also discusses the importance of the water route between Baja California Sur and Alta California.

2. In 2016, representatives of the California Missions Foundation, the Instituto Nacional de Antropología e Historia (INAH–Centro Baja California, Mexico), CAREM (Tecate, Mexico), and the Santa Barbara Trust for Historic Preservation met in Tecate to discuss moving forward with a binational proposal to UNESCO.

3. I define the historical process as an occurrence, a state, or a phenomenon that has to do with the evolution of an idea or concept that ties to an event or a series of events. The historical process is a function of the interactions of the affairs of humankind with time, events, the sequence and continuities of events, causes, and effects, and the change or changes that develop as a consequence. The historical process may provide directionality. In summary, the historical process is evident in the questions "who are we?," "where do we come from?," and "where are we going?." In the historical dialectic, the historical process is best defined as an unanswerable paradox that can never be completed because it is in a perpetual state of becoming.

4. See http://www.cahighways.org/elcamino.html.

5. See, for example, "Que los descubridores descrivan su viage, leyendo cada día lo escrito, y firmando alguno de los principales," in *Recopilación de leyes de los reynos de las Indias. Mandadas imprimir, y publicar por la Magestad Católica del Rey Don Carlos II* (Madrid: Julian de Paredes, 1681), Ley vii, Libro IV, Titulo I; see also "Que los descubridores pongan nombres a las provincias, montes, rios, puertos y pueblos," Ley viii, Libro IV, Titulo I.

Chapter One

1. The *Recopilación de leyes de los reynos de Indias* was a compilation of legislation, decrees, ordinances, policies, etc., promulgated by the Spanish king to govern Spain's

far-flung empire, from north Africa and the Americas to the Philippines. The main compilors were Antonio de León Pinelo and Juan de Solórzano Pereira. King Carlos II approved the *Recopilación* on May 18, 1680. Other versions followed, such as the *Novísima Recopilación de 1805*. In 1789, a specific compilation of the laws known as the *Plan de Pitic* was used for settlement purposes. In California, it was consulted in the founding of the Villa de Branciforte (1797) near Santa Cruz. See Joseph P. Sánchez, "El Plan de Pitic de 1789 y las nuevas poblaciones proyectadas en las Provincias Internas de la Nueva España," *Colonial Latin American Historical Review (CLAHR)* 2 no. 4 (1993): 449–67.

2. For a comprehensive history of the Camino Real de Tierra Adentro, see Joseph P. Sánchez and Bruce A. Erickson, *From Mexico City to Santa Fe: A Historical Guide to the Camino Real de Tierra Adentro* (Los Ranchos, NM: Río Grande Books, 2011).

3. For a comprehensive history of the Camino Real de los Tejas, see Joseph P. Sánchez and Bruce Erickson, comp. and ed., *From Saltillo, Mexico, to San Antonio and East Texas: An Historical Guide to El Camino Real de los Tejas during the Spanish Colonial Period* (Los Ranchos, NM: Río Grande Books, 2016).

4. The *Recopilación de Leyes de los Reynos de Indias*, for example, established Spain's legal traditions and governance of the Americas as well as the state's expectations of those performing the king's business. It is divided into nine books bound in four volumes. Its index is summarized as follows: Libro Primero. De la Santa Fé Catolica; Libro Segundo. De las Leyes, Provisiones, Cédulas, y Ordenanzas Reales; Libro Tercero. De el Dominio, y jurisdicción Real de las Indias; Libro Cuarto. De los Descubrimientos; Libro Quinto. De los Terminos, Division, y Agregacion de las Governaciones; Libro Sexto. De los Indios; Libro Séptimo. De los Pesquisidores, y jueces de Comision; Libro Octavo. De las Contadurias de Cuentas, y sus Ministros; Libro Nono. De la Real Audiencia, y Casa de Contratacion, que reside en Sevilla; Erratas. Fé de Erratas.

5. See Ramón Carande, *Carlos V y sus Banqueros* (Barcelona: Edición Crítica, 1990). Carande explores the rise of the modern Spanish state in terms of antecedents regarding obligations, needs, and prerogatives of the crown dating to the Low Middle Ages that extended not only to Spanish enterprises in Europe but to the Americas, as well. See particularly pp. 31–45, 166–75, and 235–39.

6. Carande, *Carlos V y sus Banqueros*.

7. Juan Nepomuceno Rodríguez de San Miguel, *Pandectas hispano-mexicanas* (Universidad Naciónal Autónoma de Mèxico, 1980 [1852]).

8. See Julius Klein, *La Mesta: Estudio de la Historia Económica Española, 1273–1836* (Madrid: Alianza Editorial, 1985). See also David Ringrose, *Los transportes y el estancamiento económico de España* (Madrid: Tecnos, 1985), 129–43; Andrés Diez Navarro, ed. *Quaderno de leyes y privilegios del Honrado Conçejo de la Mesta* (Madrid: 1731).

9. Viceroy Branciforte to the King, February 28, 1798, Veracruz, AGI, Estado 27, No. 35.

10. William H. Dusenberry, *The Mexican Mesta* (Urbana: University of Illinois Press, 1963), 168.

11. "Autos sobre la abertura de Camino desde Yucatan hasta Guatemala," AGI, Patronato 237, ramo 3.

Chapter Two

1. "Partio Juan Rodriguez del Puerto de Navidad para descubrir la costa de la Nueva España, 1542," AGI, Patronato 87, No. 2, Ramo 4.r.

2. "Partio Juan Rodriguez del Puerto de Navidad."

3. "Partio Juan Rodriguez del Puerto de Navidad." Cabrillo's role in the conquest of Mexico is noted in the interrogatory "Si saven q[u]e en la dicha conquista y toma de La d[ic]ha çiu[da]d/y Laguna el dicho Juan rrodrigues sirvio muy bien A/su mag[esta]d do paso grandes Travajos y peligros y salio herido/Al tienpo que tomaron La dicha çiu[da]d de mexico/y Laguna della digan lo que saben." (The original Spanish orthography has been maintained in all quotations from archival documents.) The most authoritative biography about Cabrillo is Harry Kelsey, *Juan Rodríguez Cabrillo* (San Marino, CA: Huntington Library, 1986). Kelsey surmised correctly that Cabrillo was a Spaniard, not Portuguese. In her unpublished manuscript, "A Tale of Two Identities," Iris Engstrand writes (p. 2): "Wendy Kramer, a researcher from Toronto, Canada, uncovered absolute proof of Cabrillo's birth in Palma del Rio, province of Cordoba, Spain. Interestingly, early in the 20th century, Cabrillo's Spanish origins had been largely accepted as fact. For example, The founding documents of the Cabrillo National Monument show that he was honored in 1913 as the first European explorer to enter San Diego Bay (named San Miguel by Cabrillo). The document had him correctly identified as Spanish as did the Balboa Park Committee of 1913 when the Order of Panama established Cabrillo Day at the Park." A contemporary of Cabrillo testified that he was "a native of Palma de Miçergillo": see "Relación de la probança hecha por parte de Gabriel de Cabrera sobre el oro que traya a su magestad de Guatimala," AGI, Justicia 706, in Wendy Kramer, "Juan Rodríguez Cabrillo, Citizen of Guatemala and Native of Palma del Rio: New Sources from the Sixteenth Century," *The Journal of San Diego History* 62 no. 3/4 (2016): 217–48.

4. "Partio Juan Rodriguez del Puerto de Navidad." Cabrillo's role in the early planning of the expedition is noted in the statement "Por mas serVir a Su mag[esta]d fue/al descubrimiento de la china Con Cargo de almirante/yendo por Jeneral don p[edr]o de alVarado aViendo prim[er]o/ASistido Con su persona a la fabrica de los naVios que Se/hiZieron en el puerto de Ystapa y anidiendo SerViZios/a SerViZios hizo y fabrico Un nabio a Su costa y le pertecho/."

5. "Partio Juan Rodriguez del Puerto de Navidad." Regarding Alvardo's plan to go to China, one witness, Francisco Sanches, testified, "Que El d[ic]ho Jeneral despues de

aVer pasificado las d[ic]has pro/VinZias de guat[emal]a y las demas Por mas serVir a Su mag[esta]d fue/al descubrimiento de la china."

6. That Cabrillo was trying to find a large strait of water across North America is the popularly narrated notion. However, the Strait of Anian would have left him off somewhere on the Atlantic coastline away from his goal of the Philippines. Indeed, the search for the Strait of Anian was always in the minds of Spanish officials, who feared their European rivals would find it first and threaten Spanish claims and possessions. Still, the plan to follow a supposed westward curve on the coast toward Asia prevailed. While many theories existed regarding the geography of North America, in *The Island of California: A History of the Myth* (Lincoln: University of Nebraska Press, 1991), Dora Beale Polk analyzes the theories inclusive of the Estrecho de Anian, the Strait of California, or "the big water" that cut across North America eastward to the Atlantic Ocean. "The records are slender," writes Polk, "but there are several hints that Cabrillo was seeking the mouth of a great river" (p. 160). Doubtless, given the thinking of the times, he considered such ideas seriously. See also "Partio Juan Rodriguez del Puerto de Navidad": "Que aviendo Conquistado Y Pazificado las d[ic]has provinZias a/EL dicho Juan rrodriguez cabrillo fue a haçer/EL dicho descubrimiento Por mandado DeL visorrey de la/ Nueba españa don antonio de mendoça EL qual Le dio/Titulo y comision para ello y Le nonbro Por capitan/general del dicho descubrimiento Por aber fallesçido eL/d[ic]ho adelantado don pedro de alvarado."

7. Henry R. Wagner, *Spanish Voyages to the Northwest Coast of America in the Sixteenth Century* (San Francisco: California Historical Society, 1929), 72.

8. Harry Kelsey, *Juan Rodríguez Cabrillo*, 123.

9. Kelsey, *Cabrillo*, 131–33.

10. Kelsey, *Cabrillo*, 143.

11. Kelsey, *Cabrillo*, 144, 150.

12. Kelsey, *Cabrillo*, 145–55.

13. Kelsey, *Cabrillo*, 145–55.

14. Monterey Bay was so named in 1602 by Sebastián Vizcaíno in honor of the viceroy of New Spain, the Conde de Monterey.

15. Álvaro del Portillo and José Maria Diez de Sollano, *Descubrimientos y exploraciones en las costas de California* (Madrid: Escuela de Estudios Hispano-Americanos de Sevilla, 1947), 156.

16. Some historians ascribe the discovery and naming of Cabo Mendocino to Fray Andrés de Urdaneta in 1565, or possibly Alonso de Arrellano, who crossed the ocean ahead of Urdaneta that year.

17. Portillo and Sollano, *Descubrimientos y exploraciones*, 156. The authors write, "Se aproximaba ya a los 40 grados cuando encontró un gran cabo, al que en honor del Virrey, que le enviaba llamó Mendocino; y una gran Ensenada que apellido de los Pinos.

En enero de 1543 llegó al cabo de Fortuna (a 40 grados). Arrastrando después por los vientos y sufreindo horribles frios, ascendió el día 10 de marzo de ese año hasta los 44 grados. Este fué el limite de la expedicion." Parentheses in original.

18. Throughout the Spanish Colonial period, the viceroy of New Spain had jurisdiction over the Caribbean, New Spain, the area of present-day Central America, and the Philippines.

19. Portillo and Sollano, *Descubrimientos y exploraciones*, 243.

20. Kelsey, *Cabrillo*, 159–61, passim. Portillo and Sollano, *Descubrimientos y exploraciones*, 243.

21. Piloto Francisco Manuel, "Derrotero del Padre Urdaneta," British Museum, London; copy in Spanish Colonial Research Center Collection, Center for Southwest Research, Zimmerman Library, University of New Mexico.

22. For an account of the Arrellano expedition, see Alonso de Arrellano, "Relación mui singular y circunstanciada hecha por Dn. Alonso de Arellano, capitán del Patax San Lucas del Armada del General Miguel López de Legazpi, que salió del Puerto de Navidad para el descubrimiento de las Islas del Poniente en 19 de Noviembre de 1564, siendo Piloto de él Lope Martín, vecino de Ayamonte," in *Coleción de Documentos Inéditos, relativos al descubrimiento conquista y organización de las antiguas posesiones españolas de ultramar*, Second Series, Vol. 2: *Islas Filipinas* (Madrid: Sucesores de Rivadeneyra, 1886).

23. See Joseph P. Sánchez, trans. and ed., "From the Philippines to the California Coast in 1595: The Last Voyage of *San Agustín* under Sebastián Rodriguez Cermeño," *Colonial Latin American Historical Review* 10 no. 2 (2002): 223–52.

24. Sebastián Rodriguez Cermeño, commenting on the aftermath of the loss of the *San Agustín*, described having found a fish "so large that with it we, seventy persons in number, sustained ourselves more than eight days." Later, in his 1596 testimony, he states that while on the California coast he had "nearly eighty people" ("cerca de ochenta personas") to find food for after the loss of the *San Agustín*. There were at least four slaves and seven "yndios grumetes," who, if not counted among the original seventy, would bring the number to eighty-one. "Log and Account of the Discovery Made by Sebastián Rodríguez Cermeño, by Order of His Majesty, from the Philippines to Cedros Island," Autos hechos por Sebastián Rodríguez Cermeño, AGI, Mexico 23. Rodríguez Cermeño did not give a count of casualties, but it is known that at least two people drowned when the *San Agustín* went down, thus decreasing the count—if eighty-one is correct—to seventy-nine people. Official correspondence regarding the loss of two personnel reads: "a barefooted friar and another person of those on hoard had been drowned": "Paragraph of a letter from the royal officers at Acapulco to the viceroy of New Spain, dated Acapulco, 1st February 1596," in Donald C. Cutter, ed., *The California Coast: A Bilingual Edition of Documents from the Sutro Collection* (1891; reprint, Norman: University of Oklahoma Press, 1969), 32. In footnote 3, p. 32, Cutter

comments that one of the victims was "Probably an Augustinian friar. The spiritual care of all things connected with the Philippines had been assigned to the Augustinians." See also Sánchez, "From the Philippines to the California Coast in 1595."

25. Sánchez, "From the Philippines to the California Coast in 1595," 237–38.

26. Cape Mendocino along the northern California coast was discovered in 1542 by Captain Ruy López de Villalobos at 41½° north latitude. It was named after Viceroy Antonio de Mendoza. See, "Father Antonio de la Ascension's Account of the Voyage of Sebastián Vizcaíno," in *Spanish Voyages to the Northwest Coast of America in the Sixteenth Century*, edited by Henry Raup Wagner (San Francisco: California Historical Society, 1929), 252.

27. Cutter, *The California Coast*, 33 fn. 2, comments, "The *viroco* was a pre-fabricated vessel brought from the Philippines aboard the *San Agustín* to be assembled on the California coast and subsequently employed in surveying the shallow waters anticipated along the coast. It was given the name *San Buenaventura*."

28. Juan Gutierres, a witness, testified that Rodríguez Cermeño had twelve men with him. Autos hechos por Sebastián Rodríguez Cermeño.

29. Juan del Río presented the most detail on the incident, stating that when "llegado donde Estava el humo hallaron que avia cantidad de yndios Poblados que serian entre hombres y mugeres y muchachos que algunos dellos tenian sus arcos y flechas y Estando con estos Ilegaron alli Otros Veinte yndios estavan Poblados e[n] la playa cerca donde se hazia la Lancha estava El Trio al q[ue] Se ausentaron Porque les fueron a quitar cierta madera que avian tornado de la que salio del navio y se pusieron con sus arcos y flechas en arena defendiendose del d[ic]ho capitan y don Garcia de Paredes Y el piloto Juan de Morgana que avian ydo a ello y quitarles la madera y acudiendo de parte a nuestra ayuda Ins yndios flecharon a los espanoles uno de ellos dio un flechazo en el pecho a un espanol que le hirio E se fueron huiendo." Autos hechos por Sebastián Rodriguez Cermeño.

30. Sánchez, "From the Philippines to the California Coast in 1595," 244 fn. 68.

31. Sánchez, "From the Philippines to the California Coast in 1595," 245–247.

32. Sánchez, "From the Philippines to the California Coast in 1595," 247.

33. "Derrotero cierto y verdadero para navegar desde el Cavo Mendocino que es desde altura de 42 grados, hasta el Puerto de Acapulco por la costa de la Mar del Sur; hecho quando se hizo el descubrimiento desde el dicho Cabo Mendocino al del Señor Conde de Monte-Rey Birrey de la Nueva España el año de 1602, siendo General Sevastian Bizcayno de la Armada que fue a hacer el dicho descubrimiento. Hecho por el Padre Fray Antonio de la Ascension, Religioso Descalzo de Nuestra Señora del Carmen, que fue por segundo cosmógrafo del dicho descuvrimiento," in *Californiana*, vol. 1: *Documentos para la Historia de la Demarcación Comercial de California, 1583–1632*, edited by W. Michael Mathes, 430–51 (Madrid: José Porrua Turanzas, 1965). For references to the place-names mentioned above, see pages 431–36. See also "Primer parecer de Fray

Antonio de la Ascención sobre expediciones de descubrimiento y colonización en California, 20 de Mayo de 1629, Sevilla," AGI, Patronato 30. As cosmographer and cartographer, Ascensión's maps and place-names replaced most of those made by Cabrillo and Ferrelo six decades prior.

34. See "Derrotero. . . hecho por el Padre Fray Antonio de la Ascension," 430–51. See also "Relación que Sebastián Vizcaíno a cuyo cargo fue la jornada de las Californias desde el Puerto de Acapulco hasta paraje de veinte y nueve grados de la Ensenada de las Californias a la parte de noroeste que es desde donde se volvio," AGI, Guadalajara 133; "Instrucción dada a Sebastián Vizcaíno para el viaje de 1602," Sevilla, AGI, Guadalajara 133; and "Actas de las Juntas celebradas por los capitanes, pilotos y cosmógrafos, durante la segunda navegación de Sebastián Vizcaíno a California (1602)," AGI, Mexico 372.

Chapter Three

1. See, for example, "Compendio Histórico de las navegaciones practicadas por oficiales y pilotos, en Buques de la Real Armada, sobre las costas septentrionales de las Californias, con el objeto de descubrir, y determinar la extensión, y posición de sus distritos, e yslas adycentes, ordenado por un oficial de la Marina Real Española, Año de 1799," Museo Naval, Madrid, Ms. 575 bis.

2. In 1539, Hernán Cortez attempted to settle a place on the east coast of Baja California Sur that he called Villa de la Santa Cruz, a port that would later be known by the enduring name "La Paz." Given the hostilities of the local tribes, Cortez abandoned his enterprise, but even so, La Paz became an important stopping place. See, for example, Nicolás Cardona, *Descriptions of Many Northern and Southern Lands and Seas in the Indies, Specifically of the Discovery of the Kingdom of California (1632)*, edited by Michael W. Mathes (Los Angeles: Dawson's Book Shop, 1974).

3. J. Ignácio Rubio Mañé, *Introducción al Estudio de los Virreyes de Nueva España, 1535–1746* (Mexico, D.F.: Universidad Naciónal Autónoma de México Instituto de Historia), vol. 1: 256.

4. See Arthur Aiton, "Spanish Colonial Reorganization under the Family Compact," *Hispanic American Historical Review* 12 (August 1932): 269–80.

5. For a history of this military unit, see Joseph P. Sánchez, *Spanish Bluecoats: The Catalonian Volunteers in Northwestern New Spain, 1767–1810* (Albuquerque: University of New Mexico Press, 1990).

6. Gálvez to Marqués de Croix, December 16, 1768, AGI, Guadalajara 416.

7. Compendio Histórico de las navegaciones practicadas."

8. Hubert Howe Bancroft, *History of California* (San Francisco: A.I. Bancroft, 1884), vol. 1: 120.

9. Don Miguel Costansó, "Diario histórico de los viages de mar, y tierra hechos al norte de la California de orden del Excelentíssimo Marqués de Croix, Verrey, Governa-

dor, y Capitan General de la Nueva España y por dirección del Illustríssimo Señor D. Joseph de Gálvez, del consejo y cámara de S.M. En el Supremo de Indias de Ejército, Visitador General de este Reyno," October 14, 1770, Museo Naval, Madrid, Ms. 334.

10. Costansó, "Diario histórico de los viages de mar."

11. Vicente Vila, "Diario de Navegación del Paquebot de S.M. Nombrado el San Carlos, Alias el Toyson, su comandante Don Vicente Villa . . . 1769," Museo Naval, Madrid, Ms. 575.

12. "Instrucciones que ha de observea el teniente de infantería (January 5, 1769)," AGI, Guadalajara, file 416.

13. "Instrucciones que ha de observar el teniente de infanteria."

14. Costansó, "Diario histórico de los viages de mar."

15. In 1605, Hernando de los Rios Coronal, sailing from the Philippines, ran up the coast from Cabo Mendocino to Acapulco. While exploring the Baja California coastline for harbors, he discovered the Isla de Guadalupe, sketched it, and took its latitudinal reading at 29 degrees, 20 minutes N, 118 degrees, 50 minutes W. John Newscome Crossley, *Hernando de los Rios Coronel and the Spanish Philippines in the Golden Age* (Farnham, UK: Ashgate, 2011), 68.

16. David Burckhalter and Mina Sedgwick, *Baja California Missions: In the Footsteps of the Padres* (Tucson: University of Arizona Press, 2013), 21.

17. Since the sixteenth century, when Spanish explorers first heard about California, the myth evolved that it was an island. French cartographers continued to show it as such well into the eighteenth century. While the east coast of Baja California had been explored, the *contracosta*—that is, the west coast—would prove that it was, in fact, a peninsula. Despite the fact that Juan Rodríguez Cabrillo and his men had gone north up the coast beyond Cape Mendocino in the early 1540s, the stories persisted. In the 1680s, the Jesuit Eusebio Francisco Kino believed he had put the stories to rest when he proclaimed, "California no es isla, sino peninsula." Indeed, native tribes in the region informed Kino of that fact. Kino's successors, Father Fernando Consag in 1747, and the last known Jesuit in the area, Father Wenceslao Linck, who explored the interior of Baja California in 1766, similarly attested to Kino's dictum. Still, the insular theory persisted. The first Spaniards to walk the length of the Baja California coast to San Diego, then north to San Francisco Bay, led by Governor Gaspar de Portolá and Captain Fernando Rivera y Moncada in 1767, quietly and finally put the myth to rest.

18. Harry W. Crosby, *Antigua California: Mission and Colony on the Peninsular Frontier, 1697–1768* (Albuquerque: University of New Mexico Press, 1994), 350.

19. Richard A. Minnich and Ernest Franco Vizcaíno, *Land of Chamise and Pines: Historical Accounts and Current Status of Northern Baja California's Vegetation* (Berkeley: University of California Press, 1998). See "Appendix B. Place-Names of Camps and Intervening Landscape Features Refered to in Text," 145–46. Latitude North 29 degrees 58 minutes. Longitude West 115 degrees 14 minutes.

20. Juan Crespí, "Diario y Descripción de los dilatados caminos, que a mayor gloria de Dios, y servicio del Rey nuestro señor, que Dios guarde, hicieron los Reverendos Padres Predicadores Apostólicos del Colegio de San Fernando de México, del orden de nuestro seráfico Padre San Francisco, recién entregados de las misiones de la California, hacia el norte de aquella peninsula, desde la misión de Los Ángeles, hasta los famosos puertos de San Diego, Monterrey, y San Francisco [1769 y 1770]," in Francisco Palou, *Recopilación de Noticias de la Antigua y de la Nueva California (1767–1783)*, translated and edited by José Luis Soto Pérez, vol. 1 (Mexico, D.F.: Editorial Porrúa, 1998), 276. See 265–317 for entire diary.

21. Crespí, "Diario," 277.
22. Crespí, "Diario," 278. A league is about 2.6 miles.
23. Crespí, "Diario," 278.
24. Crespí, "Diario," 278.
25. Crespí, "Diario," 279.
26. Minnich and Vizcaíno, *Land*, 145. Latitude North 30 degrees, 09 minutes. Longitude West 115 degrees 15 minutes.
27. Crespí, "Diario," 279.
28. Minnich and Vizcaíno, *Land*, 145. Latitude 30 degrees 10 minutes, Longitude 115 degrees 23 minutes.
29. Crespí, "Diario," 279.
30. Crespí, "Diario," 280.
31. Minnich and Vizcaíno, *Land*, 145. Latitude North 30 degrees, 16 minutes. Longitude West 115 degrees 27 minutes.
32. Crespí, "Diario," 280–81.
33. Minnich and Vizcaíno, *Land*, 145. Latitude North 30 degrees, 22 minutes. Longitude West 115 degrees 27 minutes.
34. Crespí, "Diario," 283
35. Minnich and Vizcaíno, *Land*, 145. Latitude North 30 degrees, 32 minutes. Longitude West 115 degrees 24 minutes.
36. Crespí, "Diario," 278.
37. Crespí, "Diario," 283
38. Minnich and Vizcaíno, *Land*, 145. Latitude North 30 degrees, 09 minutes. Longitude West 115 degrees 15 minutes.
39. Crespí, "Diario," 283.
40. Crespí, "Diario," 283.
41. Crespí, "Diario," 284.
42. Minnich and Vizcaíno, *Land*, 146. Latitude North 30 degrees, 37 minutes. Longitude West 115 degrees 26 minutes. Also see entry for La Rinconada at Latitude N 30 degrees 35 minutes; Longitude W 115 degrees 25 minutes.
43. Crespí, "Diario," 285.

44. Crespí, "Diario," 285.

45. Crespí, "Diario," 285.

46. Minnich and Vizcaíno, *Land*, 146. Latitude North 30 degrees, 41 minutes. Longitude West 115 degrees 27 minutes.

47. Crespí, "Diario," 286.

48. Minnich and Vizcaíno, *Land*, 146. Latitude North 30 degrees, 46 minutes. Longitude West 115 degrees 33 minutes.

49. Crespí, "Diario," 287.

50. Crespí, "Diario," 287.

51. Minnich and Vizcaíno, *Land*, 146. Latitude North 30 degrees, 48 minutes. Longitude West 115 degrees 38 minutes.

52. The "large wolves" may have been a different species. Nevertheless, wolves, especially gray wolves (*Canis lupus*), roamed throughout California into the twentieth century; they were extirpated during the 1920s.

53. Crespí, "Diario," 288.

54. Minnich and Vizcaíno, *Land*, 146. Latitude North 30 degrees, 49 minutes. Longitude West 115 degrees 42 minutes.

55. Crespí, "Diario," 289–90.

56. Crespí, "Diario," 290.

57. Crespí, "Diario," 290.

58. Minnich and Vizcaíno, *Land*, 146. Latitude North 30 degrees, 52 minutes. Longitude West 115 degrees 42 minutes.

59. Crespí, "Diario," 291.

60. Crespí, "Diario," 291.

61. Minnich and Vizcaíno, *Land*, 146. Latitude North 30 degrees, 58 minutes. Longitude West 116 degrees 04 minutes.

62. Crespí, "Diario," 292–93.

63. Crespí, "Diario," 293–94.

64. Minnich and Vizcaíno, *Land*, 146. Latitude North 31 degrees, 05 minutes. Longitude West 116 degrees 05 minutes.

65. Crespí, "Diario," 294–95.

66. Crespí, "Diario," 295–96.

67. Minnich and Vizcaíno, *Land*, 146. Latitude North 31 degrees, 12 minutes. Longitude West 116 degrees 10 minutes.

68. Minnich and Vizcaíno, *Land*, 146. Latitude North 31 degrees, 20 minutes. Longitude West 116 degrees 16 minutes.

69. Minnich and Vizcaíno, *Land*, 146. Latitude North 31 degrees, 24 minutes. Longitude West 116 degrees 21 minutes.

70. Crespí, "Diario," 296–97.

71. Crespí, "Diario," 297.

72. Minnich and Vizcaíno, *Land*, 146. Latitude North 31 degrees, 26 minutes. Longitude West 116 degrees 24 minutes.

73. Crespí, "Diario," 298.

74. Minnich and Vizcaíno, *Land*, 146. Latitude North 31 degrees, 31 minutes. Longitude West 116 degrees 25 minutes.

75. Crespí, "Diario," 298.

76. Crespí, "Diario," 298.

77. Minnich and Vizcaíno, *Land*, 146. Latitude North 31 degrees, 33 minutes. Longitude West 116 degrees 25 minutes.

78. Crespí, "Diario," 299.

79. Crespí, "Diario," 299.

80. Crespí, "Diario," 299.

81. Minnich and Vizcaíno, *Land*, 146. Latitude North 31 degrees, 37 minutes. Longitude West 116 degrees 26 minutes.

82. Crespí, "Diario," 300.

83. Minnich and Vizcaíno, *Land*, 146. Latitude North 31 degrees, 33 minutes. Longitude West 116 degrees 25 minutes.

84. Crespí, "Diario," Crespí, Diario in Soto Pérez, *Recopilación de Noticias de la Antigua y de la Nueva California*, p. 301.

85. Minnich and Vizcaíno, *Land*, 146. Latitude North 31 degrees, 42 minutes. Longitude West 116 degrees 27 minutes.

86. Crespí, "Diario," 301

87. Crespí, "Diario," 301.

88. Crespí, "Diario," 302.

89. Minnich and Vizcaíno, *Land*, 146. Latitude North 31 degrees, 46 minutes. Longitude West 116 degrees 35 minutes.

90. Crespí, "Diario," 302.

91. Crespí, "Diario," 302–3.

92. Minnich and Vizcaíno, *Land*, 146. Latitude North 31 degrees, 52 minutes. Longitude West 116 degrees 37 minutes.

93. Crespí, "Diario," 303.

94. Crespí, "Diario," 303.

95. Crespí, "Diario," 304.

96. Minnich and Vizcaíno, *Land*, 147. Latitude North 31 degrees, 54 minutes. Longitude West 116 degrees 42 minutes.

97. Crespí, "Diario," 304.

98. See *Californiana*, vol. 2: *Documentos para la historia de la explotación comercial de California, 1611–1679*, edited by W. Michael Mathes (Madrid: José Porrua Turanzas, 1965) and review by Maynard Geiger, *Southern California Quarterly* 54, no. 1 (Spring 1972): 84–86.

99. Crespí, "Diario," 304.

100. Crespí, "Diario," 304.

101. Minnich and Vizcaíno, *Land*, 147. Latitude North 31 degrees, 56 minutes. Longitude West 116 degrees 40 minutes.

102. Minnich and Vizcaíno, *Land*, 147. Latitude North 32 degrees, 00 minutes. Longitude West 116 degrees 40 minutes.

103. Minnich and Vizcaíno, *Land*, 146. Latitude North 31 degrees, 33 minutes. Longitude West 116 degrees 25 minutes.

104. Crespí, "Diario," 306.

105. Crespí, "Diario," Crespí, Diario in Soto Pérez, *Recopilación de Noticias de la Antigua y de la Nueva California*, p. 306.

106. Minnich and Vizcaíno, *Land*, 147. Latitude North 32 degrees, 01 minutes. Longitude West 116 degrees 46 minutes. Also see entry for La Misión de San Miguel at Latitude North 32 degrees, 05 minutes, Longitude West 116 degrees 52 minutes.

107. Crespí, "Diario," 307–8.

108. Crespí, "Diario," 308.

109. Crespí, "Diario," 309.

110. Crespí, "Diario," 309–10.

111. Crespí, "Diario," 310.

112. Crespí, "Diario," 311–12.

113. Crespí, "Diario," 312.

114. Crespí, "Diario," 312.

115. Minnich and Vizcaíno, *Land*, 146. Latitude North 31 degrees, 33 minutes. Longitude West 116 degrees 25 minutes.

116. Minnich and Vizcaíno, *Land*, 146. Latitude North 31 degrees, 33 minutes. Longitude West 116 degrees 25 minutes.

117. Crespí, "Diario," 314.

118. Minnich and Vizcaíno, *Land*, 147. Latitude North 32 degrees, 31 minutes. Longitude West 117 degrees 03 minutes.

119. Crespí, "Diario," 314–15.

120. Crespí to Palou, San Diego, June 9, 1769, in Herbert Eugene Bolton, *Fray Juan Crespí, Missionary Explorer on the Pacific Coast 1769–1774* (New York: AMS Press, 1971), 2.

121. Serra to Andrés, San Diego, July 3, 1769, in Lino Gómez Canedo, *De México a la Alta California: Una gran epopeya missional* (México: Jus, 1969), 77.

122. Donald Andrew Nuttall, "Pedro Fages and the Advance of the Northern Frontier of New Spain, 1767–1782," (PhD Diss., University of Southern California, 1964), p. 52.

123. Francisco Palou, *Palóu's Life of Fray Junípero Serra*, translated and edited by Maynard Geiger (Washington, DC: Academy of American Franciscan History, 1955), 74. Of the Catalonian Volunteers, Palou noted that "many had died."

124. José de Gálvez to Marqués de Croix, Cabo San Lucas, February 16, 1769; see

also Estado, "Memorias e Inventario de los que ha, llevado el paquetbot de S. M. San Joseph, alias el Descubridor a los Puertos de San Diego, y Monterey. . . Hecho de orden del governador interino Don Juan Gutiérrez Ensenada de Loreto, June 5, 1769," both in AGI, Guadalajara 416.

125. Portolá to Marqués de Croix, Monterrey, June 15, 1770, Archivo General de la Nación, Mexico City (AGN), Californias 76. The *San Joseph* left San Blas in May 1769 and was never heard from again.

Chapter Four

1. Crespí reported that seven Catalan Volunteers marched with Fages: Bolton, *Crespí*, 120; Costansó, "Diario histórico de los viages de mar" mentions only six Catalonian Volunteers; Portolá noted eight in his group: Portolá to Marqués de Croix, San Diego, July 4, 1769, AGN, Californias 76. Portolá probably agreed with Crespí if one counts Fages as the eighth Catalonian Volunteer.

2. Later, Crespí noted that the expedition had dogs with them. He reported an incident where a bear had killed some of their dogs. Crespí, "Diario," 445.

3. Crespí's Diario in Palou, *Recopilación de Noticias*, vol. 1, 369.

4. Crespí, "Diario," 369.

5. A league measures approximately 2.6 miles as the crow flies. They had marched nearly seven miles before sunset. For a narrative of the expedition, see Sánchez, *Spanish Bluecoats*, 44–56.

6. In his study, Bolton noted that the campsite at "Los Ojos del Valle de San Diego" was likely near Ladrillo, California. Bolton, *Crespí*, 123.

7. Crespí, "Diario," 370.

8. Crespí, "Diario," 369–70.

9. Crespí, "Diario," 370.

10. Crespí, "Diario," 371.

11. Crespí, "Diario," 372. Bolton, *Crespí*, 128.

12. Bolton, *Crespí*, 123–35 passim.

13. Crespí, "Diario," 373. Crespí: "nos pareció debe de tener salina."

14. Bolton, *Crespí*, 131. Crespí, "Diario," 375.

15. Crespí, "Diario," 376–77. See note in margin of page 376.

16. Bolton, *Crespí*, 135.

17. Crespí, "Diario," 381

18. Bolton, *Crespí*, 137. Bolton concluded that the place and the one after it near Cristianitos Canyon where two dying children were baptized were "commemorated in the name of Santa Margarita y Las Flores Rancho."

19. Bolton, *Crespí*, 136.

20. Crespí, "Diario," 382.

NOTES TO PAGES 56–58

21. Crespí, "Diario," 383
22. Crespí, "Diario," 382
23. Bolton, *Crespí*, 138.
24. Crespí, "Diario," 383.
25. Miguel Costansó, "Diario Histórico de los Viages de Mar y Tierra hechos al norte de la California," in *Noticias y documentos acerca de las Californias, 1764–1795* (Madrid: José Porrua Turanzas, 1959), 106–7.
26. Jan Timbrook. "Chia and the Chumash: A Reconsideration of Sage Seeds in Southern California," *Journal of California and Great Basin Anthropology* 8, no. 1: 50–64. See also http://www.healwithfood.org/nutrition-facts/chia-seeds-value.php#ixzz 4Vf6CXR5I:

Yes, chia seeds are an extremely good source of antioxidants. According to a research paper by Dolores Alvardado from the University of the Valley of Guatemala, chia seeds have an antioxidant rating of over 1900, expressed as Vitamin C Equivalent Antioxidant Capacity (milligrams of vitamin C per 100 grams). With this antioxidant rating, chia seeds beat many common food sources of antioxidants including blackberries, grapes, pineapple, mango, noni fruit and carambola. Nutrients and phytochemicals that contribute to the antioxidant capacity of chia seeds include flavonoids (such as quercetin, myricetin, kaempferol), phenolic acids (such as caffeic acid), lignin (don't confuse this with lignan which is a phytoestrogen found in flaxseed), and vitamins C and E.

27. Timbrook, "Chia and the Chumash."
28. Crespí, "Diario," 383. See the August 6, 1769 entry for more on the bearded men from the east.
29. Joseph P. Sánchez, "The Baffling Case of New Mexican Traders along the California Coast prior to 1769: New Light on Early Trail Blazers of the Old Spanish Trail." *New Mexico Historical Review* 92, no. 3 (2017): 381–99. See also Joseph P. Sánchez, *Explorers, Traders and Slavers: Forging the Old Spanish Trail, 1678–1850* (Salt Lake City: University of Utah Press, 1997). The study deals with Hispanic New Mexicans who went northwest from Santa Fe into southern Colorado and as far west as the Great Salt Lake and the Great Basin to trade with Ute tribes by the middle seventeenth and throughout the eighteenth century. In 1806 members of the Moraga-Muñoz expedition were told by several tribes that they had been visited by New Mexican traders near the Tulares along the San Joaquín River valley near Fresno. See Herbert Ingram Priestley, *Franciscan Explorations in California*, edited by Lillian Estelle Fisher (Glendale, CA: Arthur H. Clark Company, 1946), 89–93. See also "The Gabriel Moraga Expedition of 1806: The Diary of Fray Pedro Muñoz," edited by Robert Glass Cleland and Haydée Noya, *Huntington Library Quarterly* 9 no. 3 (1946): 223–48.
30. Crespí, "Diario," 383–84.
31. Crespí, "Diario," 385.

32. Bolton, *Crespí*, 140. Crespí, "Diario," 385.
33. Bolton, *Crespí*, 142. See Bolton's note at bottom of page.
34. Crespí, "Diario," 386. Bolton, *Crespí*, 142.
35. Bolton, *Crespí*, 142. See Bolton's note at bottom of page.
36. Bolton, *Crespí*, 143 states fifty-two natives. Crespí, "Diario," 386 writes "cincuenta y cuatro gentiles."
37. Crespí, "Diario," 387.
38. Crespí, "Diario," 387.
39. Bolton, *Crespí*, 143. See Bolton's note at bottom of page. Crespí, "Diario," 388.
40. Crespí, "Diario," 389. See note at bottom of page.
41. Bolton, *Crespí*, 144.
42. Bolton, *Crespí*, 144.
43. Bolton, *Crespí*, 145. Crespí, "Diario," 389–390.
44. Bolton, *Crespí*, 146.
45. Crespí, "Diario," 391.
46. Bolton, *Crespí*, 147. Bolton wrote that their "Camp was probably near Downey Avenue." See footnote symbol. Crespí, "Diario," 393.
47. Crespí, "Diario," 392.
48. Bolton, *Crespí*, 149.
49. Bolton, *Crespí*, 149.
50. Bolton, *Crespí*, 149. Crespí, "Diario," 394.
51. Bolton, *Crespí*, 152. Crespí, "Diario," 394.
52. Crespí, "Diario," 395.
53. Bolton, *Crespí*, 150.
54. Bolton, *Crespí*, 151.
55. Bolton, *Crespí*, 151.
56. Bolton, *Crespí*, 150. See note symbols at bottom of page.
57. Crespí, "Diario," 398. Bolton, *Crespí*, 151.
58. Crespí, "Diario," 398. Bolton, *Crespí*, 151. Bolton's translation varies but little. He writes that the Indians told Crespí that "bearded people, clothed and armed as they saw the soldiers, had come into their country motioning that they had come from the east. One of them said he had been to their countries and had seen their towns formed of large houses, and that each family occupied its own."
59. See Sánchez, *Explorers, Traders and Slavers*. See also Joseph P. Sánchez, "Spanish Colonial Map Makers and the Search for Aztlán, Teguayo, Copala, Sierra Azul and the Siete Cuevas," in *Aztlan: Essays on the Chicano Homeland*, edited by Rudolfo A. Anaya, Francisco A. Lomelí, and Enrique Lamadrid (Albuquerque: University of New Mexico Press, 2016).
60. Costansó, "Diario Historico de los Viages de Mar," in *Noticias y Documentos*, 387.
61. Crespí, "Diario," 399.

62. Bolton, *Crespí*, 152. See Bolton's note at the bottom of the page where he surmises that the expedition camped within the "San Fernando Valley northwest of Mission San Fernando." Crespí, "Diario," 399. See entry for August 7, 1769.

63. Crespí, "Diario," 399.

64. Bolton, *Crespí*, 152. Bolton wrote that they went "over San Fernando Pass to Newhall." See his note at the bottom of the page.

65. Bolton, *Crespí*, 153 See Bolton's note at bottom of the page.

66. Crespí, "Diario," 400.

67. Crespí, "Diario," 401.

68. Crespí, "Diario," 402.

69. Bolton, *Crespí*, 155.

70. Bolton, *Crespí*, 155. See Bolton's note at bottom of the page.

71. Crespí, "Diario," 404.

72. Crespí, "Diario," 403.

73. Bolton, *Crespí*, 157.

74. Crespí, "Diario," 404.

75. Crespí, "Diario," 405.

76. Bolton, *Crespí*, 157. See Bolton's note at bottom of page.

77. Bolton, *Crespí*, 157.

78. Crespí, "Diario," 405.

79. Crespí, "Diario," 404.

80. Bolton, *Crespí*, 158. See Bolton's note at bottom of the page.

81. Crespí, "Diario," 405.

82. Crespí, "Diario," 406.

83. Crespí, "Diario," 406.

84. Crespí, "Diario," 408.

85. Crespí, "Diario," 406–7.

86. Crespí, "Diario," 408.

87. Crespí, "Diario," 408.

88. Bolton, *Crespí*, 160. Crespí, "Diario," 408.

89. Bolton, *Crespí*, 160.

90. Costansó, "Diario histórico de los viages de mar."

91. Crespí, "Diario," 408.

92. Bolton, *Crespí*, 161. Crespí, "Diario," 409. See Soto Pérez's note at bottom of page.

93. Crespí, "Diario," 409.

94. Crespí, "Diario," 409.

95. Crespí, "Diario," 409.

96. Bolton, *Crespí*, 162 and 266. See Bolton's note at bottom of page. Crespí returned there on January 11, 1770.

97. Crespí, "Diario," 410.

98. Crespí, "Diario," 410.
99. Crespí, "Diario," 411. Bolton wrote (*Crespí*, 164) that "the present-day town of Carpintería is near the same site."
100. Crespí, "Diario," 411.
101. Crespí, "Diario," 411. Bolton, *Crespí*, 164.
102. Bolton, *Crespí*, 165. See Bolton's notes at bottom of page ("Now Santa Bárbara. The lagoon lies east of the city").
103. Crespí, "Diario," 412.
104. Bolton, *Crespí*, 165.
105. Crespí, "Diario," 412.
106. Bolton, *Crespí*, 165. Crespí, "Diario," 412.
107. Crespí, "Diario," 413.
108. Crespí, "Diario," 413.
109. Crespí, "Diario," 413.
110. Bolton, *Crespí*, 166 and 168. See Bolton's note at bottom of page 166.
111. Bolton, *Crespí*, 166–7.
112. Bolton, *Crespí*, 166 and 168. See Bolton's note at bottom of page 166.
113. Bolton, *Crespí*, 168. Crespí, "Diario," 414–15. Crespí, "Diario Retrovuelta," in Palou, *Recopilación de Noticias*, vol. 1, 491.
114. Bolton, *Crespí*, 167–69. Crespí, "Diario," 415.
115. Crespí, "Diario," 413–14.
116. Crespí, "Diario," 413–14.
117. Crespí, "Diario," 414.
118. Crespí, "Diario," 415–16.
119. Bolton, *Crespí*, 170. Crespí, "Diario," 414.
120. Crespí, "Diario," 416.
121. Crespí, "Diario," 417.
122. Bolton, *Crespí*, 170. Crespí, "Diario," 417.
123. Crespí, "Diario," 417.
124. Crespí, "Diario," 417. Crespí wrote, "se conjetura ser esta punta la de la Concepción, y no la pasada."
125. Crespí, "Diario," 418.
126. Crespí, "Diario," 418.
127. Bolton, *Crespí*, 171. Crespí, "Diario," 418.
128. Crespí, "Diario," 418.
129. Crespí, "Diario," 419.
130. Bolton, *Crespí*, 172. See Bolton's note at bottom of page. Crespí, "Diario," 418.
131. Bolton, *Crespí*, 172.
132. Crespí, "Diario," 419.
133. Crespí, "Diario," 419.

134. Crespí, "Diario," 420.

135. Bolton, *Crespí*, 173. Bolton concluded that they were near El Bullito Creek (or possibly at Cañada de la Brea).

136. Costansó, "Diario histórico de los viages de mar"; "Diary of the Portolá Expedition."

137. Crespí, "Diario," 420.

138. Crespí, "Diario," 421.

139. Bolton, *Crespí*, 174

140. "Partio Juan Rodriguez del Puerto de Navidad."

141. Crespí, "Diario," 420. See note at bottom of page. Crespí writes about the "macho rojo."

142. Crespí, "Diario," 421.

143. Crespí, "Diario," 421.

144. Crespí, "Diario," 421.

145. Crespí, "Diario," 422. See note at bottom of page. See also Joseph P. Sánchez, "New Light on Francisco Javier Ochoa, 'La Espada' and California's Heritage," *Nuestras Raices Journal* 29 no. 2 (Summer 2017): 43–46.

146. Crespí, "Diario," 421–22. See note at bottom of page. Bolton, *Crespí*, 175–76. See Bolton's note at bottom of page.

147. Crespí, "Diario," 422.

148. Crespí, "Diario," 422.

149. Bolton, *Crespí*, 176–77. See Bolton's note at bottom of page.

150. Bolton, *Crespí*, 176.

151. Crespí, "Diario," 422.

152. Bolton, *Crespí*, 176.

153. Bolton, *Crespí*, 177. See Bolton's note at bottom of page.

154. Bolton, *Crespí*, 177.

155. Crespí, "Diario," 423.

156. Bolton, *Crespí*, 177. See Bolton's note at bottom of page.

157. Bolton, *Crespí*, 178. Crespí, "Diario," 423.

158. Crespí, "Diario," 424.

159. Bolton, *Crespí*, 178.

160. Crespí, "Diario," 424.

161. Bolton, *Crespí*, 179.

162. Crespí, "Diario," 424.

163. Bolton, *Crespí*, 179.

164. Crespí, "Diario," 425.

165. Bolton, *Crespí*, 179.

166. Crespí, "Diario," 425. Bolton, *Crespí*, 179.

167. Bolton, *Crespí*, 179. See Bolton's note at bottom of page.

Chapter Five

1. See appendix H.
2. Crespí, "Diario," 427.
3. Crespí, "Diario," 427.
4. Bolton, *Crespí*, 180.
5. Crespí, "Diario," 427.
6. Crespí, "Diario," 428.
7. Crespí, "Diario," 427.
8. Crespí, "Diario," 427.
9. Bolton, *Crespí*, 181. Crespí, "Diario," 427.
10. Crespí, "Diario," 428.
11. Bolton, *Crespí*, 181–82. Crespí, "Diario," 429.
12. Crespí, "Diario," 429.
13. Crespí, "Diario," 429.
14. Bolton, *Crespí*, 182, See Bolton's note at bottom of page.
15. Bolton, *Crespí*, 182.
16. Crespí, "Diario," 429.
17. Bolton, *Crespí*, 183. Bolton wrote that they were at Price Canyon, north of Pismo. See his note at bottom of page.
18. Bolton, *Crespí*, 183.
19. Bolton, *Crespí*, 183–84.
20. Crespí, "Diario," 430.
21. Bolton, *Crespí*, 184. See Bolton's note at bottom of page. Crespí, "Diario," 430.
22. Crespí, "Diario," 430.
23. Crespí, "Diario," 431.
24. Crespí, "Diario," 431.
25. Bolton, *Crespí*, 184. See Bolton's note at bottom of page.
26. Crespí, "Diario," 431.
27. Bolton, *Crespí*, 184. See Bolton's note at bottom of page.
28. Bolton, *Crespí*, p. 184–85. Crespí, "Diario," 432.
29. Crespí, "Diario," 433.
30. Bolton, *Crespí*, 186.
31. Bolton, *Crespí*, 186. Crespí, "Diario," 433.
32. Bolton, *Crespí*, 186.
33. Crespí, "Diario," 434.
34. Bolton noted that they were at "Ellysly's Creek, just east of Point Estero. A short distance north it is joined by Villa Creek." See footnote symbols on p. 187.
35. Crespí, "Diario," 434. Bolton, *Crespí*, 187.
36. Crespí, "Diario," 434.

37. Crespí, "Diario," 434.

38. Costansó, "Diario histórico de los viages de mar"; "Diary of the Portolá Expedition."

39. Bolton wrote, "They ascended Ellysly's Creek, went over Dawson Grade, and camped on Santa Rosa Creek, near Cambria." See footnote symbol, p. 187.

40. Bolton, *Crespí*, 188. Crespí, "Diario," 435.

41. Bolton, *Crespí*, 188.

42. Bolton, *Crespí*, 188. See Bolton's note at bottom of page. As in countless other sites within the Santa Lucía Mountains traversed by the expedition, archaeologists have plied their art and trade in unraveling the past. See, for example, D. M. Abrams, "Little Pico Creek: Beach Salinan, Barnacles and Burials." Master of Arts Thesis, University of California, Davis, 1968; Philip Hines, "The Prehistory of San Simeon Creek: 5800 B. P. to Missionization," MS on file at the Department of Parks and Recreation, Sacramento, 1986; and Terry L. Jones and Georgie Waugh, *Central California Coastal Prehistory: A View from Little Pico Creek* (Los Angeles: Institute of Archaeology, UCLA), 1995.

43. Crespí, "Diario," 435.

44. Crespí, "Diario," 436.

45. Crespí, "Diario," 436.

46. Bolton, *Crespí*, 188. See Bolton's symbol-marked footnote.

47. Bolton, *Crespí*, 189.

48. Crespí, "Diario," 436.

49. Crespí, "Diario," 436–37. Bolton, *Crespí*, 189.

50. Crespí, "Diario," 437. Bolton, *Crespí*, 189.

51. Bolton, *Crespí*, 189–90. See Bolton's note at the bottom of the page.

52. Crespí, "Diario," 437.

53. Crespí, "Diario," 437 and 438.

54. Bolton, *Crespí*, 190.

55. Crespí, "Diario," 437–38. Bolton, *Crespí*, 190.

56. Crespí, "Diario," 438.

57. Bolton, *Crespí*, 190. See Bolton's note at the bottom of the page.

58. Bolton, *Crespí*, 190.

59. Crespí, "Diario," 438.

60. Crespí, "Diario," 438.

61. Crespí, "Diario," 438.

62. Bolton, *Crespí*, 191.

63. Bolton, *Crespí*, 191. Crespí, "Diario," 438.

64. Bolton, *Crespí*, 191–92.

65. Bolton, *Crespí*, 192. Bolton believed it was Wagner's Creek. Crespí, "Diario," 440.

66. Bolton, *Crespí*, 192.

67. Crespí, "Diario," 439. Crespí writes that they stayed there for two and a half days. There is no entry in this version for September 18 or 19.

68. Bolton, *Crespí*, 192–94 passim. See also Bolton's footnote symbols at bottom of page.

69. Bolton, *Crespí*, 192.

70. Bolton, *Crespí*, 195. See also Bolton's footnote symbols at bottom of page. Bolton wrote that they were "Near Los Burros Creek, west of the Nacimiento River." Crespí, "Diario," 440.

71. Crespí, "Diario," 440.

72. Crespí, "Diario," 440.

73. Crespí, "Diario," 440.

74. Crespí, "Diario," 441.

75. Crespí, "Diario," 441.

76. Bolton, *Crespí*, 195. See also Bolton's footnote symbols at bottom of page.

77. Crespí, "Diario," 441.

78. Crespí, "Diario," 442.

79. Bolton, Crespí, 196.

80. Crespí, "Diario," 442.

81. Bolton, *Crespí*, 195.

82. Bolton, *Crespí*, 197 noted that they were on the Upper Jolón Valley.

83. Bolton, *Crespí*, 196. Also see Bolton's footnote symbols at bottom of page.

84. Crespí, "Diario," 442.

85. Crespí, "Diario," 443.

86. Crespí, "Diario," 443.

87. Bolton, *Crespí*, 197–98 stated that they had descended Kent Canyon, reaching the Salinas near King City. See Bolton's note at bottom of page. Crespí, "Diario," 433–44.

88. Crespí, "Diario," 443.

89. In his note, Bolton, *Crespí*, 198, writes that "Below King City and above Metz the Salinas River runs close to the eastern range. This passage in Crespí is in itself proof that Portolá reached the River near King City."

90. Crespí, "Diario," 445.

91. Crespí, "Diario," 445.

92. Bolton, *Crespí*, 199. See Bolton's note at bottom of page.

93. Crespí, "Diario," 445.

94. Crespí, "Diario," 445.

95. Bolton, *Crespí*, 200. See Bolton's note at bottom of page.

96. Crespí, "Diario," 445.

97. Crespí, "Diario," 447.

98. Bolton, *Crespí*, 201. Bolton wrote that their camp was "below Old Hill Town."

99. Crespí, "Diario," 446.

100. Bolton, *Crespí*, 201. See note at bottom of page.

101. Crespí, "Diario," 447.

102. It seemed that over and over, they repeated that the river emptied "into the estuary that enters the sea through the valley . . . and that the coast forms an immense bay; and that to the south is seen a ridge, which terminates in a point in the sea, and is covered with trees that look like pines." Bolton, *Crespí*, 201.

103. Bolton, *Crespí*, 202.

104. Bolton, *Crespí*, 236. Bolton translated this passage from Joseph González Cabrera Bueno, *Navegación Espéculativa y Prática* (Manila, 1734), 303.

105. Bolton, *Crespí*, 202.

106. Costansó, "Diario histórico de los viages de mar"; "Diary of the Portolá Expedition."

107. Crespí, "Diario," 449.

108. Bolton, *Crespí*, 203. See note by Bolton at bottom of page.

109. Crespí, "Diario," 449.

110. Crespí, "Diario," 451.

111. Crespí, "Diario," 449.

112. Bolton, *Crespí*, 204. Crespí, "Diario," 450. Another version of Costansó's reading of the latitude was "36 degrees 43 minutes." See Soto Pérez's note at bottom of p. 450. Depending on where one stands when taking a reading of latitude, Crespí and Costansó were close to the actual latitude of Monterey Bay, which the Spaniards believed to be between Point Año Nuevo and Point Pinos. At the north end of Monterey Bay is the City of Santa Cruz, California, which is at 36.9741° N. Latitude. To its northwest is Point Año Nuevo, which is at 37.1130031° N. Latitude. At the south end of Monterey Bay is Point Pinos, at 36.6334° N. Latitude. The City of Monterey is at 36 degrees 36 minutes. Thus, between Santa Cruz and Point Pinos, Monterey Bay lies between 36 degrees 53 minutes North and 36.878192° North Latitude. Keeping in mind that Portolá and his men were looking for Monterey Bay between Point Pinos and Point Año Nuevo. Cabrera Bueno took a reading of the sun at 37 degrees North Latitude, probably as his ship passed along the north end of Monterey Bay, closer to or to the south of Point Año Nuevo, which as stated above is at 37.1130031° N. Cabrera Bueno wrote, "From this Point [Año Nuevo] the coast runs more to the east, making a large bay until it comes out from a point of low land, very heavily forested to the very sea, to which was given the name of Punta de los Pinos, and [Point Año Nuevo] is in 37° of latitude." Bolton, *Crespí*, 236, translated from Cabrera Bueno, *Navegación Espéculativa y Prática*, 303.

113. Bolton, *Crespí*, 204.

114. Bolton, *Crespí*, 204 noted that Fages and his men were at "Carmel Bay and River."

115. Crespí, "Diario," 450.

116. Bancroft, *History of California*, vol. 1: 253–54 n11.

117. Crespí, "Diario," 450. Bolton, *Crespí*, 205.
118. Crespí, "Diario," 450.
119. Bolton, *Crespí*, 205–6.
120. Bolton, *Crespí*, 205–6.
121. Crespí, "Diario," 450.
122. Crespí, "Diario," 450. See Soto Pérez's note at bottom of page.
123. Crespí, "Diario," 450.
124. Crespí, "Diario," 451.
125. Crespí, "Diario," 451.
126. Bolton, *Crespí*, 207. See Bolton's note at bottom of page.
127. Bolton, *Crespí*, 207. See Bolton's note at bottom of page. Bolton said they were near Watsonville.
128. Bolton, *Crespí*, 207–8.
129. Bolton, *Crespí*, 208.
130. Crespí, "Diario," 451.
131. Bolton, *Crespí*, 209. See Bolton's note at bottom of page.
132. Crespí, "Diario," 452.
133. Bolton, *Crespí*, 210–11. See Bolton's note at bottom of page. Crespí, "Diario," 452.
134. Crespí, "Diario," 452.
135. Crespí, "Diario," 452.
136. Crespí, "Diario," 453.
137. Bolton, *Crespí*, 211.
138. Crespí, "Diario," 453. See note at bottom of page.
139. Bolton, *Crespí*, 211. See Bolton's note at bottom of page.
140. Bolton, *Crespí*, 212. Crespí, "Diario," 453.
141. Crespí, "Diario," 453.
142. Crespí, "Diario," 452.
143. Crespí, "Diario," 453.
144. Bolton, *Crespí*, 213. Crespí, "Diario," 454.
145. Crespí, "Diario," 454, 459.
146. Bolton, *Crespí*, 213.
147. Crespí, "Diario," 454.
148. Bolton, *Crespí*, 213. See Bolton's note at bottom of page.
149. Bolton, *Crespí*, 214. See Bolton's note at the bottom of page. Crespí, "Diario," 455.
150. Bolton, *Crespí*, 215. See Bolton's note at the bottom of page. Crespí, "Diario," 455.
151. Crespí, "Diario," 456.
152. Bolton, *Crespí*, 216. See Bolton's note at the bottom of page.
153. Bolton, *Crespí*, 216. Crespí, "Diario," 456.
154. Crespí, "Diario," 456.
155. Crespí, "Diario," 456.

156. Bolton, *Crespí*, 217.
157. Crespí, "Diario," 456.
158. Bolton, *Crespí*, 217.
159. Bolton, *Crespí*, 217. See Bolton's note at the bottom of page.
160. Crespí, "Diario," 456.
161. Bolton, *Crespí*, 217.
162. Crespí, "Diario," 457.
163. Crespí, "Diario," 457.
164. Bolton, *Crespí*, 218. See Bolton's note at bottom of page.
165. Crespí, "Diario," 457.
166. Bolton, *Crespí*, 218.
167. Bolton, *Crespí*, 218. Crespí, "Diario," 457.
168. Costansó, "Diario histórico de los viages de mar"; "Diary of the Portolá Expedition."
169. Bolton, *Crespí*, 218.
170. Bolton, *Crespí*, 219.
171. Bolton, *Crespí*, 220.
172. Crespí, "Diario," 458.
173. Bolton, *Crespí*, 220. See Bolton's note at bottom of page.
174. Crespí, "Diario," 458.
175. Crespí, "Diario," 458.
176. Bolton, *Crespí*, 220. See Bolton's note at bottom of page. He writes that the arroyos crossed were Arroyo de los Frijoles and Pescadero Creek. The lake mentioned is still at Arroyo de los Frijoles, halfway between Bolsas Point and Pescadero Point.
177. Bolton, *Crespí*, 220.
178. Crespí, "Diario," 458.
179. Bolton, *Crespí*, 221.
180. Bolton, *Crespí*, 221. See Bolton's note at bottom of page. Crespí, "Diario," 459.
181. Crespí, "Diario," 459.
182. Bolton, *Crespí*, 220.
183. Costansó, "Diario Historico de los Viages de Mar," in *Noticias y Documentos*, 113.
184. Crespí, "Diario," 459.
185. Crespí, "Diario," 459.
186. Bolton, *Crespí*, 222–23.
187. Bolton, *Crespí*, 223. The Farallon Islands or Farallones are a group of islands and sea stacks off the coast of San Francisco. They are about twenty-five to thirty miles out to sea and about twenty miles south of Point Reyes.
188. Bolton, *Crespí*, 223–24. See Bolton's note at bottom of page.
189. Crespí, "Diario," 460.
190. Crespí, "Diario," 460.

191. Bolton, *Crespí*, 224.
192. Bolton, *Crespí*, 224.
193. Bolton, *Crespí*, 225.
194. Crespí, "Diario," 460.
195. Bolton, *Crespí*, 225.
196. Bolton, *Crespí*, 226. Crespí, "Diario," 460.
197. Crespí, "Diario," 460.
198. Bolton, *Crespí*, 226. Crespí, "Diario," 460.
199. Crespí, "Diario," 460.
200. Crespí, "Diario," 461.
201. Crespí, "Diario," 461.
202. Crespí, "Diario," 461. Bolton, *Crespí*, 226–27.
203. Crespí, "Diario," 461.
204. Bolton, *Crespí*, 226. Crespí, "Diario," 461.
205. Crespí, "Diario," 461.
206. Bolton, *Crespí*, 227.
207. Bolton, *Crespí*, 228. See Bolton's note at bottom of the page. He writes, "The Gulf of the Farallones, with Drake's Bay at the northern extremity. The camp was on the San Pedro Creek, near San Pedro station."
208. Bolton, *Crespí*, 228.
209. Bolton, *Crespí*, 228.
210. Bolton, *Crespí*, 228.
211. Crespí, "Diario," 463.
212. Bolton, *Crespí*, 229–30.
213. Bolton, *Crespí*, 230.
214. Crespí, "Diario," 463.
215. Bolton, *Crespí*, 229.
216. Crespí, "Diario," 463.
217. Bolton, *Crespí*, 231.
218. Crespí, "Diario," 463.
219. Bolton, *Crespí*, 231.
220. Bolton, *Crespí*, 230.
221. Bolton, *Crespí*, 231. Crespí, "Diario," 463.
222. Crespí, "Diario," 464.
223. Bolton, *Crespí*, 231.
224. Bolton, *Crespí*, 231, Bolton wrote that they were on "the west slope of Sweeny Ridge, west of San Andreas Lake." See his note at the bottom of the page. Crespí, "Diario," 463–64.
225. Crespí, "Diario," 464.
226. Bolton, *Crespí*, 232. Bolton wrote that they were "Near the southern end of

Crystal Springs Lake." See his note at the bottom of the page. Crespí, "Diario," 464.

227. Crespí, "Diario," 464. Madroños are often defined as strawberry trees. Bolton, *Crespí*, 232.

228. Crespí, "Diario," 464.

229. Crespí, "Diario," 464.

230. Crespí, "Diario," 465.

231. Crespí, "Diario," 465.

232. Crespí, "Diario," 465. Bolton, *Crespí*, 233. Bolton wrote that they had reached "San Francisuito Creek, near Palo Alto. Costansó tells us that they turned east (from Searsville Lake) before making camp, and halted near the bay."

233. Crespí, "Diario," 465. Bolton, *Crespí*, 233–34.

234. Bolton, *Crespí*, 234. Bolton's copy indicates that the latitude was taken on November 8. Crespí, "Diario," 465 says that it was taken on November 9.

235. "Diario del Viage que hace por tierra D. Gaspar de Portolá, a los puertos de San Diego y Monterrey de las Californias," in *Noticias y documentos acerca de las Californias, 1764–1795* (Madrid: José Porrua Turanzas, 1959), 69. Original document in Biblioteca Nacional de Madrid, MS 19.266.

236. Bolton, *Crespí*, 234.

237. Bolton, *Crespí*, 234–35. Crespí, "Diario," 466.

238. Crespí, "Diario," 466.

239. See Sánchez, *Spanish Bluecoats*, 55–56. Bolton, *Crespí*, 231, 234, and 235. Bolton concluded, "This was San Pablo Bay. The explorers, under Sergeant José Francisco de Ortega, went far enough north to be able to see this bay from a distance."

240. Bolton, *Crespí*, 235.

241. Crespí, "Diario," 466.

242. Costansó, "Diario histórico de los viages de mar"; "Diary of the Portolá Expedition."

243. Crespí, "Diario," 466.

244. William Lytle Schurz, "The Manila Galleon and California," *Southwestern Historical Quarterly* 21 no. 2 (October 1917): 110.

245. Bolton, *Crespí*, 196.

Chapter Six

1. See appendix H.

2. Bolton, *Crespí*, 237. Bolton's note on p. 243 notes that their camp was actually near Woodside. Crespí, "Diario Retrovuelta," 467.

3. Crespí, "Diario Retrovuelta," 468.

4. Crespí, "Diario Retrovuelta," 468.

5. Bolton, *Crespí*, 237. Crespí, "Diario Retrovuelta," 468.

6. Crespí, "Diario Retrovuelta," 468.
7. Bolton, *Crespí*, 237.
8. Bolton, *Crespí*, 237.
9. Bolton, *Crespí*, 237. Crespí, "Diario Retrovuelta," 468–69.
10. Bolton, Crespí, 237.
11. Crespí, "Diario Retrovuelta," 468–69.
12. Bolton, *Crespí*, 238. Crespí, "Diario Retrovuelta," 469.
13. Crespí, "Diario Retrovuelta," 469.
14. Crespí, "Diario Retrovuelta," 469.
15. Crespí, "Diario Retrovuelta," 470.
16. Crespí, "Diario Retrovuelta," 470.
17. Bolton, *Crespí*, 249. Crespí, "Diario Retrovuelta," 470.
18. Crespí, "Diario Retrovuelta," 470.
19. Bolton, *Crespí*, 239 and 217. Crespí, "Diario Retrovuelta," 470.
20. Crespí, "Diario Retrovuelta," 472.
21. Bolton, *Crespí*, 214. Crespí, "Diario Retrovuelta," 471.
22. Crespí, "Diario Retrovuelta," 471.
23. Crespí, "Diario Retrovuelta," 472.
24. Crespí, "Diario Retrovuelta," 472.
25. Bolton, *Crespí*, 208.
26. Bolton, *Crespí*, 240.
27. Crespí, "Diario Retrovuelta," 472.
28. Crespí, "Diario Retrovuelta," 473.
29. Crespí, "Diario Retrovuelta," 473.
30. Crespí, "Diario Retrovuelta," 473.
31. Bolton, *Crespí*, 241.
32. Bolton, *Crespí*, 241.
33. Crespí, "Diario Retrovuelta," 473.
34. Crespí, "Diario Retrovuelta," 474–75.
35. Crespí, "Diario Retrovuelta," 475.
36. Bolton, *Crespí*, 242.
37. Costansó, "Diario histórico de los viages de mar"; "Diary of the Portolá Expedition."
38. Bolton, *Crespí*, 243.
39. Crespí, "Diario Retrovuelta," 475.
40. Crespí, "Diario Retrovuelta," 477–78.
41. Bolton, *Crespí*, 244.
42. Bolton, *Crespí*, 244. Crespí, "Diario Retrovuelta," 477.
43. Bolton, *Crespí*, 244–45.
44. Bolton, *Crespí*, 245.

45. Costansó, "Diario histórico de los viages de mar"; "Diary of the Portolá Expedition."

46. Neither Costanso, Crespí, nor Cabrera Bueno was that far off the mark. Monterey sits at 36.8007° N., 121.9473° W.

47. Costansó, "Diario histórico de los viages de mar"; "Diary of the Portolá Expedition."

48. Costansó, "Diario histórico de los viages de mar"; "Diary of the Portolá Expedition."

49. Fages and Crespí returned in May 1770. They found one of the crosses they had left behind and determined that they had, indeed, found Monterey Bay. In December 1769, they simply did not believe that the open bay was Monterey. Of the event in 1770, Crespí wrote (Bolton, *Crespí*, 51–52):

> Satisfied with having seen the cross, we returned to the beach and went down to it. There we began to see thousands of sea lions which looked like a pavement. About a hundred yards from land we saw two whales together, the sea being very quiet as though calmed with oil, or like a very quiet lake. At the same time, we noticed that the very large bay which begins at Point of Pines was enclosed by the land, the two points coming together and forming a large O. Seeing this, all three of us broke forth in the same breath, saying that this doubtless was the harbor of Monte rey [*sic*] which according to the histories is northeast of the Point of Pines.

50. Crespí, "Diario Retrovuelta," 478.
51. Bolton, *Crespí*, 245–48.
52. Bolton, *Crespí*, 249. Crespí, "Diario Retrovuelta," 478.
53. Bolton, *Crespí*, 249–51.
54. Bolton, *Crespí*, 252.
55. Bolton, *Crespí*, 251.
56. Bolton, *Crespí*, 252. Crespí, "Diario Retrovuelta," 477–78.
57. Crespí, "Diario Retrovuelta," 479.
58. Crespí, "Diario Retrovuelta," 479.
59. Bolton, *Crespí*, 253. Crespí, "Diario Retrovuelta," 479.
60. Bolton, *Crespí*, 253. Crespí, "Diario Retrovuelta," 479.
61. Bolton, *Crespí*, 253.
62. Crespí, "Diario Retrovuelta," 480.
63. Crespí, "Diario Retrovuelta," 480. Bolton, *Crespí*, 253.
64. Bolton, *Crespí*, 253.
65. Bolton, *Crespí*, 254. Crespí, "Diario Retrovuelta," 480.
66. Bolton, *Crespí*, 254. Crespí, "Diario Retrovuelta," 481.
67. Crespí, "Diario Retrovuelta," 481.

68. Crespí, "Diario Retrovuelta," 481. Bolton, *Crespí*, 354.
69. Crespí, "Diario Retrovuelta," 481.
70. Bolton, *Crespí*, 254.
71. Crespí, "Diario Retrovuelta," 481.
72. Bolton, *Crespí*, 255.
73. Crespí, "Diario Retrovuelta," 482.
74. Bolton, *Crespí*, 256.
75. Bolton, *Crespí*, 257.
76. Bolton, *Crespí*, 257.
77. Crespí, "Diario Retrovuelta," 482.
78. Bolton, *Crespí*, 258. Crespí, "Diario Retrovuelta," 483.
79. Bolton, *Crespí*, 258. Crespí, "Diario Retrovuelta," 483.
80. Crespí, "Diario Retrovuelta," 482. Bolton, *Crespí*, 258–59.
81. Bolton, *Crespí*, 259.
82. Crespí, "Diario Retrovuelta," 483–84.
83. Crespí, "Diario Retrovuelta," 484.
84. Bolton, *Crespí*, 260.
85. Bolton, *Crespí*, 184.
86. Crespí, "Diario Retrovuelta," 484.
87. Bolton, *Crespí*, 260–61.
88. Crespí, "Diario Retrovuelta," 484–85. Bolton, *Crespí*, 260–61.
89. Bolton, *Crespí*, 261.
90. Crespí, "Diario Retrovuelta," 485.
91. Crespí, "Diario Retrovuelta," 485.
92. Bolton, *Crespí*, 263. Crespí, "Diario Retrovuelta," 486.
93. Bolton, *Crespí*, 262.
94. Crespí, "Diario Retrovuelta," 487.
95. Crespí, "Diario Retrovuelta," 487.
96. Bolton, *Crespí*, 263. Crespí, "Diario Retrovuelta," 487.
97. Crespí, "Diario Retrovuelta," 424. Crespí calls it the "gran paraje los Santos Mártires San [*sic*] Berardo y sus compañeros," which on August 30 was at 34 degrees and 55 minutes.
98. Bolton, *Crespí*, 264. Crespí, "Diario Retrovuelta," 487–88.
99. Crespí, "Diario Retrovuelta," 488.
100. Crespí, "Diario Retrovuelta," 488.
101. Crespí, "Diario Retrovuelta," 488.
102. Crespí, "Diario Retrovuelta," 488.
103. Bolton, *Crespí*, 264.
104. Costansó, "Diario histórico de los viages de mar"; "Diary of the Portolá Expedition." By "Verardo," he may have meant "Bernardo" or "Berardo."

105. Crespí, "Diario Retrovuelta," 488.
106. Bolton, *Crespí*, 264.
107. Crespí, "Diario Retrovuelta," 489.
108. Bolton, *Crespí*, 264–65.
109. Crespí, "Diario Retrovuelta," 489.
110. Costansó, "Diario histórico de los viages de mar"; "Diary of the Portolá Expedition."
111. Crespí, "Diario Retrovuelta," 490.
112. Crespí, "Diario Retrovuelta," 490.
113. Crespí, "Diario Retrovuelta," 490.
114. Costansó, "Diario histórico de los viages de mar"; "Diary of the Portolá Expedition."
115. Costansó, "Diario histórico de los viages de mar"; "Diary of the Portolá Expedition."
116. Costansó, "Diario histórico de los viages de mar"; "Diary of the Portolá Expedition."
117. Costansó, "Diario histórico de los viages de mar"; "Diary of the Portolá Expedition."
118. Crespí, "Diario Retrovuelta," 491.
119. Crespí, "Diario Retrovuelta," 491. See also Bolton, *Crespí*, 168. Crespí, "Diario," 414–15.
120. Bolton, *Crespí*, 265–66.
121. Crespí, "Diario Retrovuelta," 491.
122. Crespí, "Diario Retrovuelta," 492.
123. Bolton, *Crespí*, 266.
124. Crespí, "Diario Retrovuelta," 492.
125. Crespí, "Diario Retrovuelta," 493.
126. Costansó, "Diario histórico de los viages de mar"; "Diary of the Portolá Expedition."
127. Bolton, *Crespí*, 266.
128. Bolton, *Crespí*, 266–67. Crespí, "Diario Retrovuelta," 493.
129. Crespí, "Diario Retrovuelta," 494.
130. Crespí, "Diario Retrovuelta," 494.
131. Crespí, "Diario Retrovuelta," 494.
132. Bolton, *Crespí*, 268.
133. Crespí, "Diario Retrovuelta," 495.
134. Crespí, "Diario Retrovuelta," 495.
135. Bolton, *Crespí*, 268.
136. Bolton, *Crespí*, 269.
137. Crespí, "Diario Retrovuelta," 495.

138. Bolton, *Crespí*, 270. Crespí, "Diario Retrovuelta," 495–96.
139. Crespí, "Diario Retrovuelta," 496.
140. Crespí, "Diario Retrovuelta," 497.
141. Bolton, *Crespí*, 270–71. Crespí, "Diario Retrovuelta," 497.
142. Bolton, *Crespí*, 271. Crespí, "Diario Retrovuelta," 497.
143. Crespí, "Diario Retrovuelta," 497.
144. Crespí, "Diario Retrovuelta," 498.
145. Bolton, *Crespí*, 271. See Bolton's note at bottom of page.
146. Crespí, "Diario Retrovuelta," 498. Bolton, *Crespí*, 271.
147. Bolton, *Crespí*, 272.
148. Bolton, *Crespí*, 271–72. Crespí, "Diario Retrovuelta," 498.
149. Crespí, "Diario Retrovuelta," 499. In another passage (Bolton, *Crespí*, 47), Crespí estimated 210 winding leagues or 542 miles through the Santa Lucía Mountains, which approximates the estimated 502 driving miles between San Diego and San Francisco on a modern highway.
150. Bolton, *Crespí*, 272–73.
151. Crespí, "Diario Retrovuelta," 499.
152. Crespí, "Diario Retrovuelta," 500.
153. Emma Helen Blair, translator, "Expedition Which Was Made by Don Pedro Fages, Lieutenant of the Catalonian Volunteers, with Six Soldiers and a Muleteer," in *California under Spain and Mexico, 1535–1847*, edited by Irving Berdine Richman (New York: Houghton Mifflin, 1911), 517–18.
154. Blair, "Expedition," 518.
155. "Informe a S. M. en que el Colegio de San Fernando de México, da cuenta de los nuevos descubrimientos hechos en California desde 1769 hasta el presente de 1776 y de las Misiones que a su cargo se han fundado," signed by Fray Esteban Antonio de Arenaza, Fray Juan Ramos Lora, and Fray Domingo de Bengoechea, Colegio de San Fernando de México, February 26, 1776, AGI, Guadalajara 515.
156. Pedro Fages, signed statement, June 11, 1770, AGN, Californias 76.
157. "Diario que hizo desde la Mision y Rel Presido del Señor Don Carlos del Puerto de Monte-Rey en busca del Puerto de San Francisco, y se compusó el cuerpo de esta Expedición del Reverendo Padre Fray Juan Chrespy, Capitán Don Pedro Fages, Catorze soldados y un Yndio Christiano Paje del Reverendo Padre," signed by Pedro Fages, Real Presidio de San Carlos de Monterey, November 27, 1773, AGN, Californias 66.
158. Bolton, *Crespí*, 287n.
159. "Diario que hizo desde la Mision."
160. "Diario que hizo desde la Mision." See Bolton, *Crespí*, 293n.
161. Bolton, *Crespí*, 293n.
162. Bolton, *Crespí*, 295.
163. Bolton, *Crespí*, 295n.

164. "Relación hecho y firmado por Pedro Fages sobre los establecimientos en California, desde el de San Diego de Alcalá hasta el Puerto de San Francisco, México, November 3, 1775"; and Don Pedro Fages incluyendo relación y testimonio de los asuntos de la California Septentrional, Mexico, March 25, 1776," both in AGI Guadalajara 515. See also Pedro Fages, *A Historical, Political and Natural Description of California by Pedro Fages, Soldier of Spain*, edited by Herbert I. Priestley (Berkeley: University of California Press, 1937).

165. "Diario que hizo desde la Mision."

166. Bolton, *Crespí*, 295n.

167. Sánchez, *Spanish Bluecoats*, 56–57.

Chapter Seven

1. For a complete history of the Anza expedition, see Pedro Font, *With Anza to California 1775–1776: The Journal of Pedro Font, O.F.M.*, translated and edited by Alan K. Brown (Norman, OK: Arthur H. Clark Co., 2011).

2. While mission Indian populations were always a lesser percentage of the larger tribal entity, in California and the Greater Southwest entire native populations were never converted by Spanish missionaries. In the end, missionization by Spanish and Anglo-American missionaries resulted in natives' adopting a symbiotic religious style to this day. The concept of a Native American homeland survived not only Spanish, English, Portuguese, and French colonization of the Americas, but also the most destructive phase of California's history: the Gold Rush period under the United States, in which Native American tribes were finally dispossessed of their lands and nearly exterminated.

3. Herbert Eugene Bolton, *Bolton and the Spanish Borderlands*, edited by John Francis Bannon (Norman: University of Oklahoma Press, 1964), 201–2.

4. Angie Debo, *Geronimo: The Man, His Time and Place* (Norman: University of Oklahoma Press, 1989), 420.

5. Antonio María Osio, *The History of Alta California: A Memoir of Mexican California*, translated by Rose Marie Beebe and Robert M. Senkewicz (Madison: University of Wisconsin Press, 1996), 66–67.

6. For a transcribed copy of the Plan de Pitic, see Sánchez, "El Plan de Pitic de 1789." As regards the funds raised through rents of *propios*, the document states (p. 460): "Divididas assi las Suertes de las mas utiles e inmediatas al Pueblo que lo gozen el beneficio del riego se señalaran y amojonaran ocho que quedaren aplicadas para fondo de propios cuyo productos se adminsitraran por el Mayordomo que nombrare el Ayuntamiento con obligación de dar quentas anualmente que se examinaran y aprovaran oyendo previamente sobre ellas al Procurador, Sindico or Personero del Comun . . ."

7. Iris H. W. Engstrand, "A Note on the Plan of Pitic," *Colonial Latin American Historical Review* 3 no. 1 (1994): 78. For a brief view of the historical precedent of the Plan

de Pitic, see Jane C. Sánchez, "The Plan of Pitic: Galindo Navarro's Letter to Teodoro de Croix, Comandante General de las Provincias Internas," *Colonial Latin American Historical Review* 3 no. 1 (1994): 79–89. Sánchez writes (p. 79): "The correspondence . . . discusses the need for formation of the Plan of Pitic for an area in which the laws of the Recopilación de Indias de 1680 could not be applied in toto. The correspondence also contains many suggestions about what should be included in the plan, most of which were implemented. Like many legal papers of the period, it draws an accurate picture of the legal values of the colonial culture."

8. *Treaty of Guadalupe Hidalgo: Findings and Possible Options Regarding Longstanding Community Land Grant Claims in New Mexico*, GAO-04-60 (Washington, DC: General Accounting Office, June 2004), 71.

9. "Regulations for the Colonization of the Territories, November 21st, 1828," in Matthew G. Reynolds, *Spanish and Mexican Land Laws: New Spain and Mexico* (St. Louis: Buxton & Skinner Stationery Co., 1895), 141–42.

Epilogue

1. For a definition of "historical processes," see footnote 3 above.

2. See Section 1 of the National Historic Preservation Act, Pub. L. No. 89–665, as amended by Pub. L. No. 96–515.

3. Section I of the National Historic Preservation Act reads as follows:
(b) The Congress finds and declares that—1. the spirit and direction of the Nation are founded upon and reflected in its historic heritage; 2. the historical and cultural foundations of the Nation should be preserved as a living part of our community life and development in order to give a sense of orientation to the American people; 3. historic properties significant to the Nation's heritage are being lost or substantially altered, often inadvertently, with increasing frequency; 4. the preservation of this irreplaceable heritage is in the public interest so that its vital legacy of cultural, educational, aesthetic, inspirational, economic, and energy benefits will be maintained and enriched for future generations of Americans; 5. in the face of ever-increasing extensions of urban centers, highways, and residential, commercial, and industrial developments, the present governmental and nongovernmental historic preservation programs and activities are inadequate to insure future generations a genuine opportunity to appreciate and enjoy the rich heritage of our Nation; 6. the increased knowledge of our historic resources, the establishment of better means of identifying and administering them, and the encouragement of their preservation will improve the planning and execution of Federal and federally assisted projects and will assist economic growth and development; and 7. although the

major burdens of historic preservation have been borne and major efforts initiated by private agencies and individuals, and both should continue to play a vital role, it is nevertheless necessary and appropriate for the Federal Government to accelerate its historic preservation programs and activities, to give maximum encouragement to agencies and individuals undertaking preservation by private means, and to assist State and local governments and the National Trust for Historic Preservation in the United States to expand and accelerate their historic preservation programs and activities.

Appendix A

1. See Sánchez, *Spanish Bluecoats*.
2. Martha Ortega Soto, *Una Frontera Olvidada del Noroeste de México, 1769–1846* (Itzapalapa: Universidad Autónoma Metropolitana Unidad, Mexico City D.F., 2001), 61.
3. Ortega Soto, *Una Frontera Olvidada*, 65.
4. Ortega Soto, *Una Frontera Olvidada*, 64–65.
5. Ortega Soto, *Una Frontera Olvidada*, 64.
6. "Estado de las Cinco Primeras Misiones," in Palou, *Recopilación de Noticias*, vol. 2, 808.

Appendix B

1. "Estado de las Cinco Primeras Misiones," 800–1.
2. "Estado de las Cinco Primeras Misiones," 802–4.
3. "Estado de las Cinco Primeras Misiones," 804–5.
4. Crespí, *Diario Retrovuelta*, 493.
5. "Estado de las Cinco Primeras Misiones," 815.
6. "Estado de las Cinco Primeras Misiones," 805–6.
7. "Estado de las Cinco Primeras Misiones," 806–7.
8. "Estado de las Cinco Primeras Misiones," 808.
9. "Informe a S. M. en que el Colegio de San Fernando de México."
10. "Estado de las Cinco Primeras Misiones," 808–9.
11. "Estado de las Cinco Primeras Misiones," 810.
12. Transcription of the original document. Real Academia de Historia, Copy in Spanish Colonial Research Center Collection, Zimmerman Library, University of New Mexico. Note on document: Es Copia del Estado que adquirió en la alta California el Piloto dela Fragata Fagle d^n. Mariano Clavillés, en su viage á aquellos Puertos en 1814, y-/que me entregó á su regreso á esta Capital. Academia R^l. de Nautica Lima 7. de Marzo de 1816 = Andres Baleato-/Es Copia- Baleato {Rúbrica}.

Appendix C

1. Fr. Francisco Palou to Fr. Rafael Verger, Loreto, February 12, 1772, in *Cartas desde la Península de California (1768–1773)*, translated and edited by José Luis Soto Pérez (Mexico, D.F.: Porrúa,1994), 231.

Appendix D

1. Maynard Geiger, *The Life and Times of Fray Junípero Serra, O.F.M., or The Man Who Never Turned Back (1713–1784)* (Washington, DC: Academy of American Franciscan History, 1959), vol. 1, 309–10.

Appendix E

1. Selected and edited from "List of Ranchos of California," Wikipedia, the Free Encyclopedia, http://en.wikipedia.org/w/index.php? title=List_of_Ranchos_of_California&oldid=609629107. While the website offers more information regarding, for example, notes and size of grants, for purposes of this study, which is concerned with the location of the ranchos in relation to the corridor of the Camino Real de California, those items have been deleted.

Appendix F

1. Sánchez, *Spanish Bluecoats*, 71–88. See also Warren L. Cook, *Flood Tide of Empires: Spain and the Pacific Northwest 1543–1819* (New Haven, CT: Yale University Press, 1973), 119, 330, 356, 357. The edited list of Spanish ships is adapted from Martha Ortega Soto, *Una Frontera Olvidada*, "Cuadro 25 Buques españoles en Alta California, 1801–1820," 220–21. While Ortega Soto offers more information concerning trade and shipping, this study is concerned with the maritime lanes in relation to the corridor of the Camino Real de California.

The maritime lanes opened by Manila Galleon mariners came into prominent use with the establishment of California. By the early nineteenth century, foreign vessels consistently sailed into California's ports. Antonio María Osio penned his memoirs in 1851, in which he mentions various ships that visited California, some of which returned there several times during his lifetime. The ships he cites in *The History of Alta California* are the *Albatross, Altivo, Angelina, Aquiles, Argentina, Asia, Brookline, California, Catalina, Clarion, Clementine, Columbia, Constante, Constanza, Cyane, Danube, Don Quixote, Fidelidad, Halcón, Isabella, Joven Guipuzcoana, Juno, La Flora, Las Ánimas, Loriot, María, Mercury, Morelos, Natalia, Nieves, O'Cain, Pocahontas, Portsmouth, Prueba, San Carlos, Santa Rosa, Savannah, Sultana, 25th of May, United States, Urbana*, and *Volunteer*.

Appendix G

1. The main sources for this route are the diaries kept by the participants, among them the *Diario Ejecutado por tierra desde el paraje de Vilacatá a este puerto de San Diego, 1769 por José Cañizares*. Cañizares was a *pilotín*, a maritime navigator, who was assigned to serve on the land expedition and keep a diary with latitudinal/longitudinal readings taken along the winding route of the Camino Real de Baja California. Approximate latitudinal and longitudinal readings of places along the route based on his diaries were published in María Luisa Rodríguez-Sala, *Exploraciones en Baja y Alta California, 1769–1775: escenarios y personajes* (Mexico, D.F.: Universidad Nacional Autónoma de México, 2002), 44–60. The place-names in this appendix are based on Cañizares' diary and partially on Crespí, "Diario," 265–317.

BIBLIOGRAPHY

❊ ❊ ❊ ❊ ❊

Documents

ARCHIVO GENERAL DE INDIAS (AGI), SEVILLE

Actas de las Juntas celebradas por los capitanes, pilotos y cosmógrafos, durante la segunda navegación de Sebastián Vizcaíno a California. 1602–03. Mexico 372.

Autos hechos por Sebastián Rodríguez Cermeño. 1596. Mexico 23.

Autos sobre la abertura de Camino desde Yucatan hasta Guatemala. 1793. Patronato 237, ramo 3.

Don Pedro Fages incluyendo relación y testimonio de los asuntos de la California Septentrional, Mexico, March 25, 1776. Guadalajara 515.

Estado, Memorias e Inventario de los que ha, llevado el paquetbot de S. M. San Joseph, alias el Descubridor a los Puertos de San Diego, y Monterrey . . . Hecho de orden del governador interino Don Juan Gutiérrez Ensenada de Loreto, June 5, 1769. Guadalajara 416.

José de Gálvez to Marqués de Croix, Cabo San Lucas, February 16, 1769, Guadalajara 416.

José de Gálvez to Marqués de Croix, December 16, 1768. Guadalajara 416.

"Informe a S. M. en que el Colegio de San Fernando de México, da cuenta de los nuevos descubrimientos hechos en California desde 1769 hasta el presente de 1776 y de las Misiones que a su cargo se han fundado," signed by Fray Esteban Antonio de Arenaza, Fray Juan Ramos Lora and Fray Domingo de Bengoechea, Colegio de San Fernando de México, February 26, 1776. Guadalajara 515

Instrucción dada a Sebastián Vizcaíno para el viaje de 1602. Guadalajara 133.

Instrucciones que ha de observea el Teniente de Ynfanteria Don Pedro Fages como comandante de la Partida de veinte y cinco Hombres. N.d. (January 5, 1769). Guadalajara 416.

Partio Juan Rodríguez del Puerto de Navidad para descubrir la costa de la Nueva España. 1542. Patronato 87, No. 2, Ramo 4. r.

Pedro Fages, Relación hecho y firmado por Pedro Fages sobre los establecimientos en California, desde el de San Diego de Alcalá hasta el Puerto de San Francisco, México, November 3, 1775. Guadalajara 515.

Primer parecer de Fray Antonio de la Ascención sobre expediciones de descubrimiento y colonización en California. 20 de Mayo de 1629. Patronato 30.

Relación que Sebastián Vizcaíno a cuyo cargo fue la jornada de las Californias desde el Puerto de Acapulco hasta paraje de veinte y nueve grados de la Ensenada de las Californias a la parte de noroeste que es desde donde se volvio. Guadalajara 133.

Viceroy Branciforte to the King. February 28, 1798. Veracruz, Estado 27, no. 35.

ARCHIVO GENERAL DE LA NACIÓN (AGN), MEXICO CITY

Fages, Pedro. Diario que hizo desde la Mision y Rel Presido del Señor Don Carlos del Puerto de Monte-Rey en busca del Puerto de San Francisco, y se compusó el cuerpo de esta Expedición del Reverendo Padre Fray Juan Chrespy, Capitán Don Pedro Fages, Catorze soldados y un Yndio Christiano Paje del Reverendo Padre, signed by Pedro Fages, Real Presidio de San Carlos de Monterey, November 27, 1773. Californias 66.

Fages, Pedro. Signed statement, June 11, 1770. Californias 76.

Portolá, Gaspar de, to Marqués de Croix, Monterrey, July 4, 1769. Californias 76.

Portolá, Gaspar de, to Marqués de Croix, Monterrey, June 15, 1770. Californias 76.

BIBLIOTECA NACIONAL, MADRID

"Diario del Viage que hace por tierra D. Gaspar de Portolá, a los puertos de San Diego y Monterrey de las Californias." Mss. 19.266.

BRITISH MUSEUM, LONDON

(Piloto) Francisco Manuel, "Derrotero del Padre Urdaneta." Copy in Spanish Colonial Research Center Collection, Center for Southwest Research, Zimmerman Library, University of New Mexico.

MUSEO NAVAL, MADRID

"Compendio Histórico de las navegaciones practicadas por oficiales y pilotos, en Buques de la Real Armada, sobre las costas septentrionales de las Californias, con el objeto de descubrir, y determinar la extensión, y posición de sus distritos e yslas adyacentes, ordenado por un oficial de la Marina Real Española, Año de 1799." Ms. 575 bis.

Costansó, Don Miguel. "Diario Histórico de los viages de mar, y tierra hechos al norte de la California de orden del Excelentíssimo Marqués de Croix, Verrey, Governador, y Capitan General de la Nueva España y por dirección del Illustríssimo Señor D. Joseph de Gálvez, del consejo, y cámara de S. M. En el Supremo de Indias de Ejército, Visitador General de este Reyno (De la Impresa del Superior Gobierno)." October 14, 1770. Ms. 334.

Vila, Vicente. "Diario de Navegación del Paquebot de S. M. Nombrado el San Carlos, Alias el Toyson, su comandante Don Vicente Villa . . . 1769." Ms. 575.

Books, Articles, and Printed Primary Sources

Abrams, D. M. "Little Pico Creek: Beach Salinan, Barnacles and Burials." MA thesis, University of California, Davis, 1968.

Aiton, Arthur. "Spanish Colonial Reorganization under the Family Compact." *Hispanic American Historical Review* 12 (August 1932): 269–80.

Arrellano, Alonso de. "Relación mui singular y circunstanciada hecha por Dn. Alonso de Arellano, capitán del Patax San Lucas del Armada del General Miguel López de Legazpi, que salió del Puerto de Navidad para el descubrimiento de las Islas del Poniente en 19 de Noviembre de 1564, siendo Piloto de él Lope Martín, vecino de Ayamonte." In *Colección de Documentos Inéditos, relativos al descubrimiento conquista y organización de las antiguas posesiones españolas de ultramar*. Second Series, Vol. 2: *Islas Filipinas*, no. 37, 1–76. Madrid: Sucesores de Rivadeneyra, 1886.

Bancroft, Hubert Howe. *History of California*. 7 vols. San Francisco: A. I. Bancroft and Company, 1884–1890.

Blair, Emma Helen, trans. "Expedition Which Was Made by Don Pedro Fages, Lieutenant of the Catalonian Volunteers, with Six Soldiers and a Muleteer." In *California under Spain and Mexico, 1535–1847*, edited by Irving Berdine Richman, 517–18. New York: Houghton Mifflin, 1911.

Bolton, Herbert Eugene. *Bolton and the Spanish Borderlands*, edited by John Francis Bannon. Norman: University of Oklahoma Press, 1964.

———. *Fray Juan Crespí, Missionary Explorer on the Pacific Coast 1769–1774*. New York: AMS Press, 1971.

Burckhalter, David, and Mina Sedgwick. *Baja California Missions: In the Footsteps of the Padres*. Tucson: University of Arizona Press, 2013.

Carande, Ramón. *Carlos V y sus Banqueros*. Barcelona: Edición Crítica, 1990.

Cardona, Nicolás. *Descriptions of Many Northern and Southern Lands and Seas in the Indies, Specifically of the Discovery of the Kingdom of California*, translated and edited by W. Michael Mathes. Los Angeles: Dawson's Book Shop, 1974 [1632].

Cook, Warren L. *Flood Tide of Empires: Spain and the Pacific Northwest 1543–1819*. New Haven, CT: Yale University Press, 1973.

Coronado, José Maria. *Biblioteca de Legislación Ultramarina en forma de diccionario*. Madrid: Imprenta de J. Martín Algería, 1846.

Costansó, Miguel. "Diario Histórico de los Viages de Mar y Tierra hechos al Norte de la California." In *Noticias y documentos acerca de las Californias, 1764–1795*, 79–123. Madrid: José Porrua Turanzas, 1959.

Costansó, Miguel. "Diary of the Portolá Expedition, 1769–70." http://www.scvhistory.com/pico/costanso-diary.htm.

Crespí, Fray Juan. "Diario y Descripción de los dilatados caminos, que a mayor gloria de Dios, y servicio del Rey nuestro señor, que Dios guarde, hicieron los Reverendos Padres Predicadores Apostólicos del Colegio de San Fernando de México, del orden de nuestro seráfico Padre San Francisco, recién entregados de las misiones de la California, hacia el norte de aquella peninsula, desde la misión de Los Ángeles, hasta los famosos puertos de San Diego, Monterrey, y San Francisco [1769 y 1770] . . . Descríbelo el Padre Predicador Fray Juan Crespí." In Fray Francisco Palou, O.F.M., *Recopilación de Noticias de la Antigua y de la Nueva California (1767–1783)*, 265–500, edited by José Luis Soto Pérez. Mexico, D.F.: Editorial Porrúa, 1998.

Crosby, Harry W. *Antigua California: Mission and Colony on the Peninsular Frontier, 1697–1768*. Albuquerque: University of New Mexico Press, 1994.

Crossley, John Newsome. *Hernando de los Rios Coronel and the Spanish Philippines in the Golden Age*. Farnham, UK: Ashgate, 2011.

Cutter, Donald C., ed. *The California Coast: A Bilingual Edition of Documents from the Sutro Collection*. First published in 1891 by Historical Society of Southern California. Norman: University of Oklahoma Press, 1969.

Debo, Angie. *Geronimo: The Man, His Time and Place*. Norman: University of Oklahoma Press, 1989.

"Diario del Viage que hace por tierra D. Gaspar de Portolá, a los puertos de San Diego y Monterrey en las Californias." In *Noticias y Documentos Acerca de las Californias, 1764–1795*, 49–76. Madrid: José Porrua Turazas, 1959. See also copy at the Museo Naval, Madrid, Mss. 19.266.

Díez Navarro, Andrés, ed. *Quaderno de leyes y privilegios del Honrado Conçejo de la Mesta*. Madrid: 1731.

Dusenberry, William H. *The Mexican Mesta*. Urbana: University of Illinois Press, 1963.

Engstrand, Iris H. W. "A Note on the Plan of Pitic." *Colonial Latin American Historical Review* 3 no. 1 (1994): 73–78.

Fages, Pedro. *A Historical, Political and Natural Description of California by Pedro Fages, Soldier of Spain*, edited by Herbert I. Priestley. Berkeley: University of California Press, 1937.

Font, Pedro. *With Anza to California 1775–1776: The Journal of Pedro Font, O.F.M.*, translated and edited by Alan K. Brown. Norman, OK: Arthur H. Clark Co., 2011.

"The Gabriel Moraga Expedition of 1806: The Diary of Fray Pedro Muñoz." Edited by Robert Glass Cleland and Haydée Noya. *Huntington Library Quarterly* 9 no. 3 (1946): 223–48.

Geiger, Maynard. *The Life and Times of Fray Junípero Serra, O.F.M., or The Man Who Never Turned Back (1713–1784)*. 2 vols. Washington, DC: Academy of American Franciscan History, 1959.

Gómez Canedo, Lino. *De México a la Alta California: Una gran epopeya missional*. México: Editorial Jus, 1969.

Hines, Philip, "The Prehistory of San Simeon Creek: 5800 B.P. to Missionization." MS on file at the Department of Parks and Recreation, Sacramento. 1986.
Jones, Terry L., and Georgie Waugh. *Central California Coastal Prehistory: A View from Little Pico Creek.* Los Angeles: Institute of Archaeology, UCLA, 1995.
Kelsey, Harry. *Juan Rodríguez Cabrillo.* San Marino, CA: Huntington Library, 1986.
Klein, Julius. *La Mesta: Estudio de la Historia Económica Española, 1273–1836.* Madrid: Alianza Editorial, 1985.
Masters, Nathan. "How El Camino Real, California's 'Royal Road,' Was Invented." *Lost LA*, January 4, 2013. https://www.kcet.org/shows/lost-la/how-el-camino-real-californias-royal-road-was-invented.
Mathes, W. Michael, ed. *Californiana.* 4 vols. Madrid: José Porrua Turanzas, 1965.
Minnich, Richard A., and Ernest Franco Vizcaíno. *Land of Chamise and Pines: Historical Accounts and Current Status of Northern Baja California's Vegetation.* Berkeley: University of California Press, 1998.
Nuttall, Donald Andrew. "Pedro Fages and the Advance of the Northern Frontier of New Spain, 1767–1782." PhD diss., University of Southern California, 1964.
Ortega Soto, Martha. *Una Frontera Olvidada del Noroeste de México, 1769–1846.* Itzapalapa: Universidad Autónoma Metropolitana Unidad, Mexico City D.F., 2001.
Osio, Antonio María. *The History of Alta California: A Memoir of Mexican California*, translated by Rose Marie Beebe and Robert M. Senkewicz. Madison: University of Wisconsin Press, 1996.
Palou, Francisco. *Cartas desde la Península de California (1768–1773)*, translated and edited by José Luis Soto Pérez. Mexico, D.F.: Editorial Porrúa, 1994.
———. *Palóu's Life of Fray Junípero Serra*, translated and edited by Maynard Geiger. Washington, DC: Academy of American Franciscan History, 1955.
———. *Recopilación de Noticias de la Antigua y de la Nueva California (1767–1783)*, translated and edited by José Luis Soto Pérez. Two vols. México, D.F.: Editorial Porrúa, 1998.
Polk, Dora Beale. *The Island of California: A History of the Myth.* Lincoln: University of Nebraska Press, 1991.
Portillo, Álvaro del, and José Maria Diez de Sollano. *Descubrimientos y exploraciones en las costas de California.* Madrid: Escuela de Estudios Hispano-Americanos de Sevilla, 1947.
Priestley, Herbert Ingram. *Franciscan Explorations in California*, edited by Lillian Estelle Fisher. Glendale, CA: Arthur H. Clark Company, 1946.
Recopilación de leyes de los reynos de las Indias. Mandadas Imprimir, y Publicar por la Magestad Católica del Rey Don Carlos II. Madrid: Por Julian de Paredes, 1681.
Repertorio de la nueva recopilación de las leyes del reino hecho por el licenciado Diego de Atiença. Alcalá de Henares: Andrés de Angulo, 1571.

Reynolds, Matthew G. *Spanish and Mexican Land Laws: New Spain and Mexico.* St. Louis: Buxton & Skinner Stationery Co., 1895.

Richman, Irving Berdine. *California under Spain and Mexico, 1535–1847.* New York: Houghton Mifflin, 1911.

Ringrose, David, *Los transportes y el estancamiento económico de España.* Madrid: Edición Tecnos, 1972.

Rodríguez de San Miguel, Juan Nepomuceno. *Pandectas hispano-mexicanas.* Mexico: Universidad Nacionál Autónoma de Mèxico, 1980 [1852].

Rodríguez-Sala, María Luisa. *Exploraciones en Baja y Alta California, 1769–1775: escenarios y personajes* (Mexico, D.F.: Universidad Nacional Autónoma de Mèxico, 2002).

Rubio Mañé, J. Ignacio, *Introducción al estudio de los virreyes de Nueva España, 1535–1746.* 4 vols. Mexico, D.F.: Universidad Nacionál Autónoma de México Instituto de Historia, 1955–1963.

Sánchez, Jane C. "The Plan of Pitic: Galindo Navarro's Letter to Teodoro de Croix, Comandante General de las Provincias Internas." *Colonial Latin American Historical Review* 3 no. 1 (1994): 79–89.

Sánchez, Joseph P. "The Baffling Case of New Mexican Traders along the California Coast prior to 1769: New Light on Early Trail Blazers of the Old Spanish Trail." *New Mexico Historical Review* 92, no. 3 (2017): 381–99.

———. *Explorers, Traders and Slavers: Forging the Old Spanish Trail, 1678–1850.* Salt Lake City: University of Utah Press, 1997.

———, trans. and ed. "From the Philippines to the California Coast in 1595: The Last Voyage of *San Agustín* under Sebastián Rodríguez Cermeño." *Colonial Latin American Historical Review* 10, no. 2 (2002): 223–52.

———. "New Light on Francisco Javier Ochoa, 'La Espada' and California's Heritage." *Nuestras Raices Journal* 29, no. 2 (2017): 43–46.

———, trans. and ed. "El Plan de Pitic de 1789 y las nuevas poblaciones proyectadas en las provincias internas de la Nueva España." *Colonial Latin American Historical Review* 2, no. 4 (1993): 449–67.

———. *Spanish Bluecoats: The Catalonian Volunteers in Northwestern New Spain, 1767–1810.* Albuquerque: University of New Mexico Press, 1990.

———. "Spanish Colonial Mapmakers and the Search for Aztlán, Teguayo, Copala, Sierra Azul and the Siete Cuevas." In *Aztlán: Essays on the Chicano Homeland*, edited by Rudolfo A. Anaya, Francisco A. Lomelí, and Enrique Lamadrid, 77–96. Albuquerque: University of New Mexico Press, 2016.

Sánchez, Joseph P., and Bruce A. Erickson. *From Mexico City to Santa Fe: A Historical Guide to the Camino Real de Tierra Adentro.* Los Ranchos, NM: Río Grande Books, 2011.

———, comp. and ed. *From Saltillo, Mexico, to San Antonio and East Texas: An Historical*

Guide to El Camino Real de los Tejas during the Spanish Colonial Period. Los Ranchos, NM: Río Grande Books, 2016.

Schurz, William Lytle. "The Manila Galleon and California." *Southwestern Historical Quarterly* 21, no. 2 (1917): 106–26.

Suárez Argüello, Clara. *Trabajo y Sociedad en la Historia de México,* Siglos XVI–VIII. México: Colección Miguel Othón de Mendizábal, 1992.

Timbrook, Jan. "Chía and the Chumash: A Reconsideration of Sage Seeds in Southern California." *Journal of California and Great Basin Anthropology* 8, no. 1 (1986): 50–64.

Wagner, Henry R. *Spanish Voyages to the Northwest Coast of America in the Sixteenth Century.* San Francisco: California Historical Society, 1929.

Wikipedia. "List of Ranchos of California." http://en.wikipedia.org/w/index.php?title =List_of_Ranchos_of_California&oldid=609629107.

INDEX

Page numbers in *italic text* indicate illustrations.

❈ ❈ ❈ ❈ ❈

Acevedo, José de, 9
Age of Faith, 142
Ágreda, María de, 164
Agua Grande, 41
Aguilar, Martín de, 26
Alamillo de la Tinaja, 35, 199
Alaska, *xiii*, *195–96*
alcalde mayor (chief municipal administrator), 2, 9, 154, 176
Alexander VI (pope), 10
Alta California, xiv, 155; Alta California route across, 107; braided corridor, 3–4; Camino Real de California route on, 3, 198–200; land grants, 176, *177*; land route, 107; Los Angeles ranchos, *178–79*; maritime lanes, *195–97*; mission latitude and status, 166–67; missions, 142, 161–65, *165*; Monterey ranchos, *179–80*; San Diego ranchos, *178*; San Francisco ranchos, *180–81*; Santa Barbara ranchos, *179*; Spanish ships routes, *195–97*
Alvarado, Dolores, 234n26
Alvarado, Pedro de, 15–16
Anacapa Island, 18
Anaheim, California, 58, 174, 183
Año Nuevo, 25–26, 87, 90, 95, 111, 114, 117–18, 210
Año Nuevo Creek, 215
Antigua, California, 31
Anza, Juan Bautista de, 141–42

Arrellano, Alonso de, 22
Arroyo de la Cruz, 80
Arroyo de las Palmas, 34
Arroyo de las Puentes de San Lucas, 111
Arroyo de los Frijoles, 212, 244n176
Arroyo de los Mártires, 34
Arroyo del Oso, 217
Arroyo del Pinal de San Benvenuto, 79
Arroyo de San Anselmo, 42
Arroyo de San León, 38
Arroyo de San Nicolás, 79
Arroyo de San Ricardo, 36
Arroyo de San Vicente, 208
Arroyo Grande de San Vicente, 80
Arroyo Grande y Hondo de la Sierra de Santa Lucía, 81
Arroyo San Juan de Dios, 33–34
Arroyo San Juan de Dukla, 122
Arroyo Seco de los Alisos, 41
Arroyo y Cañada de las Llagas de Nuestro Señor Padre San Francisco, 84
Arroyo y Estero de la Cañada de la Señora Santa Serafina, 78
Arroyo y La Ranchería de Sancti Spiritus, 70
Ascención, Antonio de la, 25–26
Assembly Bill 1707, xiv
Assembly Bill 1769, xiv
Asumpta de María Santíssima en los Cielos, 130–31
Asunción de Nuestra Señora, 64

266 INDEX

Austin, Moses, 150
Austin, Stephen, 150

Badiola (mulatto man), 121
Bahía de los Fumos, 18
Bahía de San Diego. *See* San Diego Bay
Bahía de San Francisco. *See* Drake's Bay
bailador, 40
Baja California, xii, xvi, 3–4, 18, 25–38, 106, 155, 163, 168
Baja California Sur, xii, xiv, 3–4, 227n2
Bajial de los Santos Apóstoles, 45
Bajial sin Agua, 44
Barranca de la Olla, 94
Basocs, Antonio de, 7
Batequitos Lagoon, 55, 201
bear population, 22, 33, 42, 58, 66, 76–78, 94, 123, 125
Beato Simón de Lípnica, 55
Black Current, 23
Blanco, California, 88
Bodega Bay, 23
Bolton, Herbert E., 60, 62–64, 75–79, 80–88, 90–93, 202–10, 220
Book of Prophecies (Columbus), 143
Boquilla de Santa Rosa, 47
Bourbon reforms, 28–29
burial ritual, of native tribes, 130
Burros Creek, 83

Cabaña Real (1734–1807), 8
cabildos (town councils), 2, 154, 176
Cabo Blanco, 20
Cabo del Engaño, 18
Cabo Mendocino. *See* Cape Mendocino
Cabrera Bueno, Joseph González: Naval Career, author of *Navegación Especulativa y Practica (1734)*, 46
Cabrillo-Ferrelo expedition (1539–1542), 27–28

Cabrillo, Juan Rodríguez, xv, 223n3; California coast explored by, 15, 21; China destination of, 21; as hacendado, 16; injury and death of, 19–20; Philippines route sought by, 16, *17*; Point Concepción and, 18, 20; San Pedro Bay sailed to by, 18; Strait of Anian sought by, 224n6
Cámara de Indias, 10
Camino de la Plata (Silver Road), 7
camino real, xiv; ancient indigenous pathways of, 4–5, 107; braided corridors of, 5; concept of, 1–2; local use of, 10–11; privileges in, 7; travelers on, 8–9
Camino Real de los Tejas National Historic Trail, xvii
Camino Real de Tierra Adentro, xvii, 2–4, 7–9
Camino Real de Tierra Afuera, 2
Camulos Rancho, 63
Cañada Angosta, 77
Cañada del Cojo, 71
Cañada de los Osos, 77–78, 163
Cañada de los Robles, 164
Cañada de San Isidoro, 199
Cañada de San Ladislao, 123
Cañada de Santa Clara, 64, 205
Cañada los Álamos, 35
Cañada y Arroyo de las Llagas de Nuestro Señor Padre San Francisco, 84
Cañada y Estero de el Arroyo de la Señora Santa Serafina, 78
Cañizares, José, 33, 44, 256n1
Cañón Arce, 46
Cañón el Chocolate, 42
Cañón la Grulla, Uruápan, 43
Cañón San Antonio, 37
Cañón San Carlos, 45
Cañón San Francisquito, 44

Cantua, Vicente, 159
Cape Mendocino, 12–13, 20–21, 23–24, 27–28, 46, 106, 195, 224n16, 226n26
Cape of Good Hope, 14
Carlos II (king of Spain), 221n1
Carlsbad, California, 55–56, 187, 201–2
Carpintería, 66, 120, 173, 182, 206, 237
Carquinez Strait, 104, 138–39
Carrillo, Guillermo, 36, 38, 40
Cartagena, Romualdo, 144–45
Casa Grande, 111
Catalonian Volunteers, 29–30, 51, 54, 60, 115, 137, 165
cemeteries, 68
Cermeño, Sebastián Rodríguez. *See* Rodríguez Cermeño, Sebastián
chia seeds, 57–58, 234n26
China, 21, 27–28
Chorro Creek, 77
Cochimí settlement, 32
College Lake, 211
Colonization Act of 1824. *See* land grants
Concepción, Francisco de la, 24
Consag, Fernando, 228
Coronado, Francisco Vázquez de, 20
Coronal, Hernando de los Rios, 228n15
Corralitos Creek, 93
Cortéz, Hernán, 15–16, 227n2
Costansó, Miguel (engineer and diarist of Portolá Expedition), 30–31
Cosumes tribe, 148
Crespí, Juan (diarist of Portolá expedition), xv–xvi, 54
Croix, Marqués de, 11

dancer. See *bailador*
de la Cosa, Juan, 142
de la Guerra, José, 160
Del Monte Junction, 91
Drake, Francis, 28

Drake's Bay, 23–25, 99, 213
Durán, Narciso, 148

earthquakes. *See* Temblores
El Bailarín, 66
El Baile de las Indias, 73
El Buchón chief, 76, 123, 124, 172, 208, 218
El Cantil, 79
El Laurel, 122, 217
El Loco (native guide), 70, 123–27
Ellysly's Creek, 208, 239n34, 240n39
El Osito, 79, 122, 184
El Rosario del Beato Serafín de Asculi, 112, 169, 199, 210–11, 215
El Rosarito, 50
El Salado, 41
El Salto, 35
Encino, California, 60
Ensenada, California, 45
Eximiae Devotionis, 10

Fages, Pedro, xv, 15, 29–31, 51, 104, 136–40, 161, 164, 177
Farallones, 101, 106, 109, 118, 244n187
Figueroa, José, 149
Fillmore, CA, 63, 179, 205
Las Flores, 175, 187, 202
Forster, John, 158
forts. *See* presidios
Fuca, Juan de, 28
Fuero Juzgo, laws of, 3
Fullerton, California, 59, 174–75, 183, 293

Gálvez, José de, 29, 31, 84, 106
García de Mendoza, Antonio, 32
Gaviota Pass, 173
Gazos Creek, 96, 212
Geiger, Maynard, 170–75

Gerónimo, 37, 146
Gila River Trail, 150
Golden Gate Bridge, 137
Gold Rush, 148, 252n2
Gomes, Alonso, 24
Grande Arroyo y Cañada de las Llagas de Nuestro Señor Padre San Francisco, 84
Great Central Valley, 5, 139
Guadalupe Lake, 75, 218

Isla de Guadalupe, 228n15

Jesuits, 61, 168; expulsion, 33
Juan Bautista de Anza Historical Trail, 141
Julius II (pope), 10

King City, 124, 171, 187, 209, 213, 216, 241n89
Kino, Eusebio Francisco, 228

La Brea Tar Pits, 60, 204
La Cienega, 60, 204
La Cieneguilla, 35–36, 199
Laguna de la Concepción, 206
Laguna de las Grullas, 91, 210
Laguna Grande de San Daniel, 207
La Habra, 59, 134, 174, 184, 203, 220
La Isla (Towns of the Island), 129–30, 219
land grants: in Alta California, 176, *177*; California ranchos established by, 149; Camino Real de California late-period, *182–94*; Colonization Act of 1824, 150; contracts in, 5–6; Mexican Territorial period with, *178–81*; square leagues per, 150; towns created by, 6, 10; West Coast ranchos and, 150–51
La Salud, 96

Laws of the Indies, xv, 2–4, 6, 8, 15–16, 142, 149, 154, 158, 176, 222, 257n7
leather-jacket soldiers. See *soldados de cuera*
León, Alonso de, 9
León Pinelo, Antonio de, 221n1
Leyes de Indias. See Laws of the Indies
Linck, Wenceslao, 32, 34–35
Line of Demarcation, 14
López de Villalobos, Ruy, 14–15
Los Álamos, 119
Los Angeles, xii, 6, 18, 25, 57–60, 140–41, 157, 165, 172–79, 182–89, 190–97, 204–5
Los Angeles River, 59, 132–33, 140, 174, 204, 219. See also Porciúncula River
Los Ansares, 97, 111, 214
Los Cuatro Coronados islands, 50
Los Dos Ojitos de Agua de San Pantaleón, 58
Los Piñones, 217
Los Robles, 120, 132, 164, 219
Los Santos Mártires San Daniel y Sus Compañeros, 75, 124

Magellan, Ferdinand, 13–15
Manila Galleon routes, xii, xiv, 13, 19–23, 28, 46, 74, 106, 136, 213
María, José, 135
Martin, Lope, 22
Martini Creek, 212
Mathes, W. Michael, xii
Matyropi, 40
Mendoza, Antonio de, 16, 20
Mesa de Paraje de San Juan Bautista, 47
Mexican National Congress, 149–50
Mexican Territorial period (1821–1848), 148–49, 161, *178–94*
missions: of Alta California, 142, 161–65, *165*; Alta California status of, 166–

67; of Baja California, 33, 168, *169*; California coast establishing, 140–41; California establishing, 142–45; conversion plans for, 145; Dolores, 142, 149; as imperial institutions, 147; Monte Alverne, 82; Native Americans rebellions over, 147–48; New Mexico, 144; Nuestra Señora de Loreto, 168; population decline of, 148–49; San Antonio, xvii, 170–72; San Antonio de Padua, 164; San Buenaventura, 64, 149; San Carlos de Monterrey, 164–65; San Diego de Alcalá, 162; San Fernando de Velicatá, 33, 198; San Fernando Rey de España de Velicatá, 168; San Gabriel, 59–60, 139, 141, 203; San Gabriel Arcángel, 162–63; San José, 148; San Juan Capistrano, 56, 149, 174–75; San Luis Obispo, 172; San Luis Obispo de Tolosa, 163; San Luis Rey, 56; San Miguel, 47; Santa Bárbara, 173; Serra establishing San Diego, 142; in Spanish Colonial period, 145–46; structural purpose of, 144

Monte Alverne mission, 82

Monterey, ranchos in, *179–80*

Monterey Bay, 19–20; Cabrera Bueno and location of, 87, 90, 113, 116–17; Costansó and location of, 116–17; Crespí commenting on location of, 115–16, 248n49; latitude reading, 89, 242n112; no signs of, 104; Portolá confirmation of, 136; Portolá expedition and elusive, 87–88, 98–99, 105, 136, 214; Portolá expeditionary force goal of, 74–75, 105; Portolá's expedition to, 54–73, 98–99; unraveling mystery of, 105–6; Vizcaíno and location of, 116; Vizcaíno naming, 224n14

Monterey presidio. *See* Presidio de San Carlos de Monterey

Moraga, José Joaquín, *160*

Moraga-Muñoz expedition, 234n29

Morro Creek, 208

National Historic Preservation Act, 152, 253n3

Native Americans, xiii; of Alta California, 148; California and reduction of, 153; California coast influenced by, 152; along *camino real*, 154; Christianity and culture of, 33–34, 37, 148; indigenous pathways of, 4–5, 107; mission rebellions of, 147–48; Portolá noticing children of, 13; trails of, 4; US history of, 153–54; wars of extermination against, 153–54

native settlements, 102; in Baja California, 31; Crespí describing culture of, 67–68, 96, 130; Portolá expedition encountering, 45, 54–55, 66, 85; Ranchería de los Reyes, 132; Rivera y Moncada encountering, 46–47; Rodríguez Cermeño and, 24–25; of San Luis Obispo, 129; Serra encountering, 42–43

native tribes: ancient pathways to, xiii–xiv; bearded people stated by, 235n58; El Buchón chief of, 124; burial ritual of, 130; Cosumes, 148; Crespí and informants of, 61; expedition not seeing any, 93–94; extensive, 69; Fages and peaceful intent of, 31; Fages trading goods with, 126, 131; Gálvez expedition and stealing by, 49–50; El Loco guide from, 70, 125–27; Manila Galleon debris found by, 117; Ortega trading goods with, 91; pine nuts traded by, 83; Portolá expedition and

native tribes (*continued*)
fishing, 65–66; Portolá expedition guided by, 96–97; Portolá expedition not seeing, 93–94; Portolá expedition passage blocked by, 104; Portolá expedition trading goods with, 58–60, 64, 80, 103, 121, 130, 132; ports with ships explained by, 102; by Río de las Truchas, 84–85; Rio del Carmelo and, 90; San Diego attack of, 135; Spaniards trading gifts with, 35; Spanish expeditions encountering, 20–21; subterranean houses of, 63; Utes, 58, 61, 157
Nativitas B. Mariae, 123
New Mexicans, 234n29; Crespí and, 58; traders, 58–59, 61–62
Northwest Passage, 28
Nuestra Señora de Loreto, 168
Nuestra Señora del Pilar, 112
Nuestro Padre Santo Domingo, 111
Núñez de Balboa, Vasco, 14

Ochoa, Corporal (Francisco Javier), 72
Old Spanish Trail, 150
Oregon-California Trail, 150
Ortega, José Francisco de, 42, 76, 90–93, 99, 101–4, 177
Osio, Antonio María, 147–48, 255n1
Oso Flaco Lake, 76

Padua, Antonio de, 164
Pájaro River, 92
Palou, Francisco, 162, 168
Paraje de San Isidoro, 37
Paraje las Pozas de Santa Mónica, 46. *See also* El Sauzal
La Paz, xii, xiv, 3–4, 22, 28–32, 52, 168, 198, 227n2
Pedernales Point, 218
Pérez, Juan, 29–31

Philippines, 12–18, 21–28, 32, 195
Piccolo, Francisco María, 32
Pilarcitos Creek, 97–98, 212
Pimería Alta, 144
Pismo Beach, 172–73
Plan de Pitic, 149, 252nn6–7
Plano del Puerto de San Francisco, 110
Plano de San Diego, *30*
Pleasant Valley, 93, 212
Point Año Nuevo, 25–26, 87–88, 90, 95, 111, 114, 117–18, 198, 210, 215
Point Arguello, 72, 207
Point Concepción, xvi, 18, 20, 24–26, 64–72, 100, 106, 118, 126–29, 165, 173–79, 183, 205–7, 218
Point of the Pines. *See* Punta de los Pinos
Point Reyes, 19, 22–28, 88, 99, 100–106, 118, 136–39, 195, 213
Polk, Dora Beale, 224n6
Porciúncula River. *See* Los Angeles River
Portolá, Gaspar de, xv, 141; camino real pathway, 136; illness of, 98; king's business of, 11, 54; land route of, 198–200; Monterey Bay expedition of, 54–73, 98–99, 136; officer meeting called by, 104–5; pack animal concerns of, 39; San Diego return ordered by, 105; scouting party reports to, 89; Spanish expeditions under, 153–54; wooden cross erected by, 118
Pozas del Valle de San Antonino, 49
Prat, Pedro, 30
Presidio de San Carlos de Monterrey (1770), 137, 159, *164–65*
Presidio de San Diego (1769), 158–59
Presidio Real de San Francisco (1776), 159, *160*
Presidio Real de Santa Bárbara (1782), 160

Presidio Santa Bárbara, 160
presidios (forts), 140–41, 157–58
Pueblo Santa Rosa de Viterbo, 62
Las Pulgas, 97
Las Pulgas Canyon, 56, 202
Punta de la Concepción. *See* Point Concepción
Punta del Año Nuevo. *See* Point Año Nuevo
Punta de los Ángeles Custodios, 109–11
Punta de los Pinos, 19, 87–88, 91, 105, 111, 113, 115, 117–19, 215–16
Punta de los Reyes. *See* Point Reyes

quelites (herbs), 37

Ranchería de la Espada, 72
Ranchería del Corral, 62
Ranchería de los Reyes, 132
Ranchería de los Santos Mártires San Hipólito y Casiano, 63
Ranchería de San Ladislao, 123
Ranchería de Santa Ana, 71, 127
Ranchería de San Zeferino Mártir, 70
Rancherías de Santa Teresa, 71
Ranchería y Arroyo de Sancti Spiritus, 50
Rancho de Buri Buri (1835), 159
Rancho de la Nación, 158
Rancho del Rey, 158–60
ranchos: in Los Angeles, *178–79*; in Monterey, *179–80*; in San Diego, 158, *178*; in San Francisco, *180–81*; in Santa Barbara, *179*
Real Blanco, 86, 119, 210, 216
Real de Chocolate, 120
Real del Alamo, 85–86, 210
Real de las Víboras, 76
Real de los Cazadores, 86, 210, 216
Real Patronato, 9–10

regalía (privileges from the king), 6–10
repairs money, of roads, 6–7
El Riachuelo del Beato Serafín de Asculdón, 93–94
Rincón de las Almejas, 105
Rincón Mountains, 173
Rincón Point, 173, 206
Río de la Señora Santa Delfina, 105, 119
Río de las Truchas, 84–85
Río del Carmelo, xvi, 25, 75–78, 81–87, 90–92, 113, 115, 119, 141, 209
Río de los Temblores. *See* Temblores
Río de San Dionisio, 37
Rio de San Francisco, 142
Río San Elzeario, 84, 119–20
Río Santa Delfina, 215
Río Santa Rosa, 73, 218
Rivera y Moncada, Fernando, xv; expeditionary forces led by, 29–52; land distributed by, 157–58; land expedition led by, 32; land route of, 198–200; native settlement encounter of, 46–47; pack animal concerns of, 39; Punta de los Pinos explored by, 88; scouts exploring of, 81, 83–84, 104, 113–14
Robles del Puerto de San Francisco, 138
Rodríguez Cermeño, Sebastián, 22–28, 225n24
Roosevelt, Theodore, 146
Royal Patronage of the Indies (Patronato Real de las Indias), 143

Sacra Congregatio de Proganda Fide, 10
Sacred Expedition, 140–41
Salinas River, 84–85, 114, 210, 215–16
San Adriano, 123
San Agustín (ship), 22–24, 26, 225n24
San Andreas Lake, 213
San Ángel, 39

San Antonio (ship), 29–31, 49, 51, 137
San Antonio Creek, 73
San Antonio de Padua (1771), 164
San Antonio mission, xvii, 170–72
San Antonio River, 84
San Apolinario, 134
San Bartolomé, 69–70
San Bernardino river, 125
San Buenaventura Mission, 64, 149. *See also* Ventura, California
San Carlos Borromeo, 170–72
San Carlos (ship), 29–30, 49, 51–52, 102
San Clemente, California, 175, 193
San Clemente Islands, 4, 25, 56, 134
San Diego Bay, iv, 18, 20, 25, 28–29, 32–33, 49, 53–54, 108, 136, 141, 198
San Diego de Alcalá (1769), 51, 162
San Diego: Los Angeles to, 174–75; native tribes attack, 135; Plano de, *30*; port of, 108; Portolá expedition arriving at, 134–35; Presidio de, 158–59; Rancho Real de, 158; ranchos in, *178*; *San Carlos* reaching, 30; Serra establishing missions in, 142
San Fernando de Velicatá mission, 33, 198
San Fernando Rey de España de Velicatá, 168
San Fernando Valley, 59–60, 62, 134, 174, 179
San Francisco Bay, 12, 15, 23–25, 42–43, 74, 101–33, 141–42, 158, 170; name reserved of, 84; Presidio Real de, 159, *160*; ranchos in, *180–81*; Robles del Puerto de, 138
San Francisco de Asís (Mission Dolores), 142, 149
San Francisco Solano, 42–43, 142
San Francisuito Creek, 246n232
San Gabriel Arcángel (1771), 162–63
San Gabriel mission, 59–60, 139, 141, 203

San Gabriel River Valley, 59, 219–20
San Gregorio Creek, 97
San Guido de Cortona, 69, 207, 218
San Higinio, 131
San Isidoro, 37
San Jácome de la Marca, 55, 134, 220
San Joaquín, 130, 139
San José, 36, 137, 157
San José mission, 148
San Joseph (packet boat), 52, 102
San Juan Bautista de los Pedernales, 126
San Juan Capistrano, 55–56, 134, 174–75, 202, 220
San Juan Capistrano mission, 56, 149, 174–75
San Juan de Dukla arroyo, 122
San Juan de los Caballeros, 8
San Judas, feast day of, 98
San Lorenzo Creek, 138
San Lucas (ship), 22
San Luis Canyon, 77
San Luis Obispo de Tolosa (1772), 163, 172–73, 206, 217–18; Fages en route to, 139; mission, 172; native settlement of, 129
San Luis Rey, 123, 128–29
San Luis Rey de Francia, 70, 127
San Luis Rey de la Canal, 123
San Luis Rey mission, 56
San Luis Rey River, 202
San Miguel Arcángel, 59, 203
San Miguel de Horcasitas, 141
San Miguel Island, 20
San Miguel mission, 47
San Miguel (ship), 18
San Miguel valley, 133
San Onofre, 56, 175
San Onofre Creek, 134
San Pablo Bay, 104, 138–39, 246n239
San Pedro Bay, 18

San Pedro de Alcántara, 111
San Pedro Mártir, 132
San Pedro Point, 99, 213
San Pedro Regalado, 96
San Rafael, 40–41
San Raimundo Nonato, 125
San Salvador (ship), 18
San Serafino, 207, 218
Santa Ana River, 58, 112, 203
Santa Bárbara, 66, 70, 74, 172–73, *179*
Santa Bárbara Channel, 69, 71–72, 118, 123–28, 130, 134, 163, 218
Santa Bárbara islands, 128, 131
Santa Bárbara mission, 165, 173
Santa Bárbara Presidio, 160
Santa Bárbara ranchos, 179
Santa Barbara Trust for Historic Preservation, xii
Santa Catalina, 19
Santa Catalina de Bononia de los Encinos, 60–61
Santa Clara de Montefalco, 66
Santa Clara River, 205
Santa Clara valley, 131
Santa Cruz, 41, 94
Santa Cunegundis del Pueblo de la Asumpta, 65, 163
Santa Delfina, 91, 112–13, 119, 215, 217
Santa Humiliana de la Playa, 81, 122
Santa Inés Mountains, 173
Santa Inés River, 73
Santa Lucía, 121
Santa Lucía de Salerno, 121
Santa Lucía Mountains, 20, 74, 106, 115, 251n149
Santa Margarita, 134, 172, 175, 187, 202–6, 220
Santa Margarita de Cortona, 67–68
Santa Margarita y Las Flores Rancho, 233n18

Santa María Magdalena, 133–34
Santa Monica, California, 18, 60, 204
Santa Monica Mountains, 174, 176, 219
Santa Paula, 63
Santa Rosa, 125
Santa Rosa de Viterbo, 62, 205
Santa Serafina, 78, 122–23, 208, 217
San Telmo (Principio del Llano de), 39–40
Santiago Hills, 203
Santo Domingo, 2
San Toribio, 41
Santos Mártires, 50
San Vicente, 41
San Zeferino Papa, 128
El Sauzal. *See* Paraje las Pozas de Santa Mónica
Schurz, William Lytle, 106
Scott Creek, 95
Sebastián Elcano, Juan, 14–15
Señor San Francisco Solano, 56–58
Serra, Junípero, 11, 32–33, 36, 42, 50, 135; expeditions led by, 161; Geiger's account of route by, 170–75; native settlements encountered by, 42–43; San Diego missions established by, 142; San Fernando Rey de España de Velicatá founded by, 168
Serrão, Francisco, 14
Serra Springs, 204
Sierra de la Conversión, 131–32
Sierra de Santa Lucía, 81–84, 88, 113, 117–18, 122
Silver Road. *See* Camino de la Plata
soldados de cuera (leather-jacket soldiers), 33, 42, 47, 54, 137, 164
Solórzano Pereira, Juan de, 221n1
Sonora War, 29
Soquel Creek, 94, 210–11, 215
Soto, Hernando de, 20

Strait of Anian, 28, 224n6
Strait of Juan de Fuca, 28
Strait of Magellan, 14

Temblores, 29, 58–61, 133, 161–62, 203, 220
Texas, 150
Tijuana, 42, 50
Timbrook, Jan, 57
Timpanogos, 61
Treaties: of Guadalupe Hidalgo (1848), 150; of Tordesillas (1494), 14; of Zaragosa (1539), 15
Tribunal del Consulado, 7, 10
El Triunfo de Dulcísimo Nombre de Jesús, 132
Las Truchas de San Elceareo, 120
Tunitas Creek, 214

Universalis Ecclesiae Regimini, 10
Urdaneta y Ceraín, Andrés de, 21–22
US-Mexico War of 1846, 150
Ute tribes, 58, 61, 157

Valladares, Manuel, 38
Vallecito de San Pío, 49
Valle de los Encinos, 204
El Valle de San Estanislao, 46–47
Valle de San Juan Bautista, 48
Valle Guadalupe, 46
Valle Santa María Magdalena, 133
Valle Santo Tomás, 42
Valle y Ciénega de San Jorge, 43
Valley of San Ibón, 214
Valle y Poza de Santa Catarina de Bononia, 62, 204
Vargas, Diego de, 9
Velasco, Don Luis de, 21, 23
Ventura, California, 64–65, 163, 219; San Buenaventura became Venture, 173
Verde Island Passage, Philippines, 22
La Victoria (ship), 18
Vila, Vicente, 29
Vizcaíno, Sebastián, xv, 135; expedition of, 25; follow-up expedition of, 26; Mexico's northern coast and, 28; Monterey Bay location from, 116; Monterey Bay named by, 224n14; place-names mapped by, 25–26

Waddell Creek, 95, 212
Wagner, Henry R., 16

yerba tabardillo (medicinal plant), 39
Yorba, Antonio, 30, 177, 179

www.ingramcontent.com/pod-product-compliance
Lightning Source LLC
Chambersburg PA
CBHW021340230426
43666CB00006B/350